State Building and Democracy in Southern Africa

Botswana, Zimbabwe, and South Africa

STATE BUILDING AND DEMOCRACY IN SOUTHERN AFRICA

Botswana, Zimbabwe, and South Africa

Pierre du Toit

UNITED STATES INSTITUTE OF PEACE PRESS
Washington, D.C.

United States Institute of Peace
1550 M Street, N.W.
Washington, D.C. 20005

First published 1995

Printed in the United States of America

The paper used in this publication meets the minimum requirements of American National Standard for Information Sciences—Permanence of Paper for Printed Library Materials, ANSI Z39.48-1984.

The following publishers have generously given permission for the use of copyrighted material (full publication details are given in each instance alongside the material): The Royal African Society, London; Ashgate Publishing Limited, Aldershot, England; the Ford Foundation, New York; the Journal of Legal Pluralism, Groningen, Netherlands; the International Union of Local Authorities, The Hague; Oxford University Press, Oxford; Lynne Rienner Publishers, Inc., Boulder, Colorado; Sage Publications, Inc., Thousand Oaks, California. The cover drawing illustrates the north gate of Great Zimbabwe (from Gertrude Caton-Thompson, *Zimbabwe Culture*).

Library of Congress Cataloging-in-Publication Data
Du Toit, P. van der P. (Pierre)
    State building and democracy in Southern Africa : Botswana, Zimbabwe, and South Africa / Pierre du Toit.
       p. cm.
    Includes bibliographical references and index.
    ISBN 1-878379-50-X (hard). — ISBN 1-878379-46-1 (pbk.)
    1. Botswana—Politics and government—1966– 2. Democracy—Botswana. 3. Zimbabwe—Politics and government—1980– 4. Democracy—Zimbabwe. 5. South Africa—Politics and government—1978–1989. 6. South Africa—Politics and government—1989–1994. 7. Democracy—South Africa. I. Title.
JQ2760.A91D8 1995
320.96883—dc20
                                 95-22653
                                     CIP

❋ CONTENTS ❋

❖ FOREWORD ❖

Something remarkable seems to have happened in South Africa: democracy. After decades of minority rule, racial division, and violence, South Africans agreed to work together politically within the framework of a constitutional democracy, an agreement that culminated in the April 1994 elections that ended apartheid. Where once the political system dictated discrimination, it now respects difference; where once racial inequality was mandated, now political equality has institutional support.

Less widely noted in the West—but no less remarkable—the past decade has witnessed the cessation of divisive conflict and the beginnings of democracy in several other countries of southern Africa. In Namibia and Mozambique bloody struggle has been replaced by elections and postwar reconstruction. Even in Angola, where earlier peace accords broke down, the warring factions finally may be ready to work together in peace. Southern Africa, a region of the continent that until recently was wracked by violence, is now transforming itself into an area of stability, raising prospects for an economic takeoff.

But what are the prospects for these hopeful developments taking root and enduring?

Answering that question is a central objective of this book. Pierre du Toit, himself a South African and a frequent contributor to the debate on his country's democratic transition, takes a long, hard look at the prospects for democratic sustainability in South

Africa and neighboring Botswana and Zimbabwe. These three countries share many similarities, yet have very different political track records. His analysis of Botswana, which gained independence peacefully three decades ago, is both enlightening and encouraging: enlightening not least because few people, even among African scholars, are familiar with Botswana's impressive economic and political development since the end of colonial rule; encouraging because Botswana is arguably the most successful democracy in continental Africa.

Du Toit's assessment of Zimbabwe, though equally illuminating, is a good deal less heartening. Tracing the country's history from the 19th century through to the 1990s, he finds that the legacy of British colonial rule and of the civil war that led to the demise of the undemocratic Rhodesian regime is a Zimbabwean state where, despite constitutional safeguards, democracy is underdeveloped.

As he explores the contrasting experiences of these three countries—assessing the influence of each nation's precolonial and colonial heritage, ethnic composition, and economic and environmental circumstances—du Toit finds that democratic outcomes depend on the degree to which democratic institutions are imbedded in a wider network of state and social institutions. Where a state is both strong and autonomous, and where a civil society is strong, democracy can survive and grow. Where those conditions are absent, democracy is unlikely to endure.

The implications of this conclusion are evident throughout southern Africa and far beyond, confirming or questioning assumptions about democratization in many areas of contemporary policymaking and academic endeavor—areas in which the United States Institute of Peace has long worked to promote research, awareness, and discussion. Pierre du Toit, a former Jennings Randolph Peace Fellow at the Institute, has written a book that promises to stimulate debate on topics ranging from the nature of divided societies to the preconditions for democratic success, from the causes of ethnic conflict to its management and resolution, from the promotion of democracy and stability throughout the world to the prospects for political freedom and peace in Africa in particular.

Recognizing the importance of these topics for the U.S. policymaking and scholarly communities, and for many Americans in other walks of life, the United States Institute of Peace has developed an extensive track record of research support and dissemination of policy-relevant and academically insightful scholarship. To take the example of Africa, over just the past two years the Institute has published John L. Hirsch and Robert B. Oakley's reflections on peacekeeping in Somalia, *Somalia and Operation Restore Hope;* UN special representative Mohamed Sahnoun's analysis of earlier international intervention in the same country, *Somalia: The Missed Opportunities;* David Smock's edited volume on foreign intervention throughout Africa, *Making War and Waging Peace;* and a workshop-inspired Special Report, *Dealing with War Crimes and Genocide in Rwanda.*

On the subject of ending violent conflict in southern Africa, the Institute has published Cameron Hume's firsthand account of mediation in Mozambique, *Ending Mozambique's War,* and Peter Gastrow's analysis of South Africa's National Peace Accord, *Bargaining for Peace.* The Institute's Grant Program has also supported conflict resolution training by nongovernmental organizations through grants to organizations in Somalia and South Africa.

In the tradition of this Institute effort, *State Building and Democracy in Southern Africa* represents our continuing commitment to providing readers with the tools needed to better understand and debate the prospects for peace and democracy in Africa and elsewhere around the world where political reformers struggle for nonviolent change and open politics.

Richard H. Solomon, President
United States Institute of Peace

❧ PREFACE ❧

Africa's contribution to the global "third wave" of democratization has thus far been distinctly modest.[1] Events in Africa during the early 1990s do little to suggest that this situation is about to change. Some African countries appear to hover on the edge of anarchy, and seem to be quite remote from any democratic threshold. The spectacular and catastrophic explosions of domestic violence in Somalia in 1991 and in Rwanda in 1994 reveal the collapse of the very institution required to overcome anarchy and impose order—the state. Less dramatic but equally significant is the slow implosion of state institutions in Zaire, so vividly demonstrated by the forests retaking the national road network, which in 1959 still extended over 140,000 kilometers, but which covered only 20,000 kilometers by the early 1970s.[2] Such profound breakdowns in the African state pose the question of whether Africa can be expected to produce any truly significant contribution to the global wave of democratization.

This book takes up this question by examining the requirements for order as well as those for democracy, and by exploring the link between them. The conceptual focus is on the relationship among state strength, societal strength, and democratic viability. The empirical focus is a comparative study of Botswana, Zimbabwe, and South Africa, all of which continue to face the African challenges to order and democracy presented by conditions of scarcity, communal conflict, and environmental constraints. All three states have responded to these challenges differently, with major implications for their democratic viability. Botswana has succeeded in establishing what is generally considered to be continental Africa's most successful democracy. Zimbabwe has been less successful, emerging from white minority rule and civil war into a semidemocratic state with questionable political and economic liberty. South Africa, the closest comparable case to Zimbabwe, has likewise gone through white minority rule and violent insurrection into a process of democratic transition. Should this transition from the infamous system of apartheid into liberal democracy be sustained, then Africa may well produce what could become one of *the* landmark cases in the third wave of global democratization. A central ambition of this study is to examine what South Africans can learn from the other two African cases about how to secure their own process of transition.

This study differs from other analyses of African politics in its selection of cases and its analytical focus on the role of state strength and societal strength in creating the conditions within which democracy can be sustained. The study examines two related propositions: that democratic institutions are embedded in the wide-ranging institutional network of state and societal institutions; and that the institutions that make up this network must be robust and resilient if effective democracy is to be achieved. The study therefore joins the broad academic debate on the preconditions for democracy. It also addresses the policy debate on how to manage and facilitate transitions to democracy in such a way as to secure stable outcomes. The conclusion reached is that a particular kind of strong autonomous state is a necessary, but still insufficient condition for sustaining democracy. This finding does not challenge the established consensus on the necessary preconditions for democracy, but it does argue for the inclusion of state strength and autonomy on the list of recognized preconditions. Likewise, it adds to the existing body of policy advice on effecting successful democratic transitions by suggesting that policymakers must not only aim for the establishment of a democratic regime but also work to create and maintain a strong and autonomous state in the process of transition.

While academic analysts, policymakers, and practitioners may find value in these conclusions, the results of this study are presented as a book, not as a manual. There is no checklist of do's and don'ts. The study gladly pays cognitive respect to the hands-on judgment of policymakers, who confront policy issues of a singular complexity that no author can hope to anticipate. The insights and recommendations that follow from this study are thus presented at one or more steps removed from such immediate policy detail. Practitioners are invited to make these general findings their own, and to convert them into policy actions appropriate to the specific problems with which they are required to deal.

ACKNOWLEDGMENTS

This project was undertaken with the support of the United States Institute of Peace, which awarded the author a Peace Fellowship for 1992–93 from the Jennings Randolph Program for International Peace. The views expressed in this book are, however, those of the author alone, and do not necessarily reflect the views of the United States Institute of Peace.

At the Institute, the entire research support system of the Jennings Randolph program contributed to an environment congenial to the completion of the project; even so, special mention must be made of the research assistance provided by Mike Nojeim and the all-round support of Joe Klaits, director of the Jennings Randolph program. Nigel Quinney and Daniel R. Snodderly, director of the Institute's Publications and Marketing department, did the major work of converting the manuscript into book form. The text itself was scrutinized by many readers, but special mention must go to Jannie Gagiano; Norma Kriger, who provided incisive assessments of various chapters; and to Professors Roger Southall and Robert M. Price, who read the entire manuscript. The valued friendship of Tim Sisk and Sarah Peasley greatly contributed to the ease with which we were able to establish ourselves in Washington, D.C., for the duration of the fellowship. Finally, our family's stay in the United States in 1993 was immeasurably enriched by those larger-than-life Americans Ellen Philip and Cal Donly, Phil and Elaine Waggener, and Colonel Donald and Jennifer McCarthy.

❖ INTRODUCTION ❖

Africa's Future: Democratic Stability or Impending Anarchy?

Peace, prosperity, and democratic stability are valued but rare commodities in Africa. In parts of West Africa these goods appear to be utterly unobtainable. For example, Robert D. Kaplan finds Sierra Leone devoid of almost every condition conducive to such outcomes: The official government effectively controls only the capital city (and then only by day), the interior is a contested terrain in which four armies vie for ascendancy, and the official borders of the state are cartographical fictions. People, goods, and money traverse these boundaries with impunity, beyond any control by the state. In the cities, social and economic decay is destroying the fabric of communities as rapidly as new migrants arrive from the ecologically devastated countryside.

For Kaplan, Sierra Leone is a microcosm of the kind of anarchy he predicts will envelop all of West Africa and much of the underdeveloped world: "the withering away of central governments, the rise of tribal and regional domains, the unchecked spread of disease, and the growing pervasiveness of war." At the core of this coming anarchy Kaplan is describing lies the decay and collapse of the political institution of the modern state: "West Africa is reverting to the Africa of the Victorian Atlas. It consists now of a series of coastal trading posts, such as Freetown and Conakry, and an interior that,

1

owing to violence, volatility and disease, is again becoming, as Graham Greene once observed, 'blank' and 'unexplored.'"[1]

This vivid doomsday scenario holds grave implications for the democratic prospects of the African continent. Democratic practices are embedded in the institutions of the modern state. Where states decay and dissolve, democracies are also likely to falter. The likelihood of a livable, democratically stable future for virtually any African state in a continent beset by problems of this order seems remote. To examine this question seriously may lay one open to charges of wishful thinking. Yet the aim of this study is to take up this very issue and consider the problems of securing democratic stability in African states. The focus is precisely the same one identified by Kaplan: to explore the link between the durability of democratic practices and the resilience of the state structures within which these practices are conducted.

This study's broad focus on Africa is narrowed down to a comparison of Botswana, Zimbabwe, and South Africa. The most important consideration behind that selection is the policy problem of democratic transition in South Africa. For most of this century South Africa epitomized the deplorable features of state-driven racial discrimination and exploitation through the infamous policies of apartheid. For decades it was considered the least likely case for successful democratization, but since early 1990 the country has entered into an extraordinarily complex process of transition toward democracy. Few, if any, directly comparable examples of successful transition are available to South Africans to guide them through this unfamiliar landscape. Yet this study asks whether South Africa can learn from other *African* countries about successful democratization. This question is somewhat unusual, given the dismal political, social, and economic track record of most of the continent's independent states. Against this backdrop one might expect that if there is anything to be learned, it is what to avoid. This study does indeed look for what to avoid, but it also looks for examples of actions that are worth emulating.

Botswana is arguably the most successful democracy in continental Africa. It has exhibited continuous democratic stability since independence in 1965, coupled to remarkable economic progress. Clearly there must be something positive to draw from this case. Zimbabwe, markedly less democratic but still, in comparative African terms, a success story, is generally considered the example most comparable with South Africa. It has also proceeded further along the route on which South Africans set out in 1990. A revolt against white minority rule led to a violent civil war between 1972 and 1980 that culminated in constitutional negotiations and the inauguration of democracy in independent Zimbabwe in 1980. Since then, both the democratic quality of political life and the economic prosperity of the country have declined in the face of adverse circumstances. From this qualified success South Africans may be able to learn what should be avoided as well as what can be applied to their own situation.

The concept of democracy is therefore central to the study. The prevailing tendency among many political scientists is to define democracy in procedural terms. An authoritative definition is Samuel P. Huntington's: "The central procedure of democracy is the selection of leaders through competitive elections by the people they govern."[2] Scholars engaged in the study of divided societies tend to add a further criterion: not only should voters be free to express their choice of rulers, but the expression of choice should result in parties alternating as rulers and as opposition. Democratic institutions should not only allow this alternating to occur but also encourage the process. The case for this extended definition of democracy is strongly argued by Donald L. Horowitz.[3] This concern is understandable: in divided societies floating voters tend to be rare, and electoral majorities and minorities are likely to coalesce in more or less permanent units, thus perpetuating the positions of those in power and those deprived of power. Neither Botswana nor Zimbabwe can boast elections in which a ruling party has been defeated. Yet neither can be written off as completely undemocratic.

The approach adopted in this study goes beyond Huntington's minimal definition but stops short of insisting on the criteria set by Horowitz. The procedural criterion set by Huntington is used in conjunction with the criterion of citizenship of equal value. This is a very flexible yardstick. Citizenship provides the basis for making claims against the state. In democracies, states are obliged to submit to certain kinds of claims, namely, those that demand equity in the provision of public goods. Public goods can range from physical to symbolic commodities; included is the entire range of civic rights and obligations that characterize democracies. With this yardstick one can also judge the extent to which the perennial losers in elections in both Botswana and Zimbabwe have a quality of life that is meaningful and democratic. Useful insights may also be gained as to how to secure and enhance democracy for both the electoral winners and the electoral losers in South Africa after apartheid.

Four considerations behind the selection of cases for study also should be pointed out. First, the unit chosen for analysis is a state, not a society, community, group, or region. The interaction between states and other such social units is analyzed, but with the state as the primary focus. Second, the theoretical perspective developed in this study to assess problems confronting the selected African states draws on the literature on so-called divided societies and, it is hoped, contributes to the theory of that body of work. The selected African states therefore have to conform to the definitional attributes of divided societies. Two of the cases, Zimbabwe and South Africa, are generally accepted as such, while the third case, Botswana, is more often considered an exceptional example of an African state that is basically undivided. It is argued later that despite notable differences between Botswana and the other two cases, all three are functionally equivalent units of analysis and that Botswana should be considered a potential or incipient divided society.

A third consideration is the requirement that Richard Rose calls "bounded variability" and Arend Lijphart calls the "comparable cases" yardstick.[4] That is, the cases selected for comparison should be "similar in a large number of important characteristics (variables) which one wants to treat as constants, but dissimilar as far as those variables are concerned which one wants to relate to each other." The advantage of such a selection lies in the fact that "while the total number of variables cannot be reduced, by using comparable cases in which many variables are constant, one can reduce considerably the number of operative variables and study their relationships under controlled conditions without the problem of running out of cases."[5] With only three cases under examination this requirement becomes crucial.

Botswana, South Africa, and Zimbabwe share a number of sociopolitical as well as economic features. The populations of all three countries were profoundly influenced by the Mfecane, a social, political, and military transformation that affected many societies throughout Southern Africa during the first half of the 19th century. All three cases experienced colonial rule, and all three had Britain as the metropolitan power. All three had important white minorities in their populations and still do. Cultural pluralism, extending well beyond the white-black distinction, is a prominent feature of each case. The forces of modernization, as measured in the phenomena of urbanization, industrialization, and technologically sophisticated networks of communication, are operative in each of the three cases. All three fit in the same categories within the global political economy: in the ranks of the South rather than the North, or, if you prefer, as part of the Third World instead of the First. All three have young populations; almost half of Botswana's population was under the age of 15 by the end of 1991, and almost 45 percent of Zimbabwe's. South Africa and Botswana are close in relative standards of living; Botswana leads with gross domestic product (GDP) per head at U.S.$2,585 versus U.S.$2,474 for South Africa. Zimbabwe lags at U.S.$617 per head. As for life expectancy, the three countries are remarkably close at 63 years for South Africa and 61 years for the other two.[6]

Broadly similar attributes notwithstanding, there are a number of important differences. British colonial rule in South Africa was achieved through methods of conquest that differed greatly from the methods used to gain control over what became Southern Rhodesia. Both these cases again stand apart from the way Bechuanaland (now Botswana) became a British possession. The direct political impact of white minority domination in what became Zimbabwe and in South Africa has no equivalent in the colonial history of modern Botswana. These minorities differed in size (both relative and absolute), ethnic composition, historical memory, and political as well as economic power. The overall extent of cultural pluralism in South Africa also exceeds that of Zimbabwe and of Botswana. While all three states are experiencing rapid modernization, South Africa has a far bigger industrial base, is more urbanized, and has a larger population than the other two. South Africa covers an area roughly twice the size of Texas, with a population of around 40 million in the early 1990s. Zimbabwe, about the size of Montana, has a population of about 10 million people. Botswana, a territory almost the size of Texas, has a population of just over 1.3 million, making it the country with the third lowest population density after Mongolia and Australia. The economic performance of Botswana has outstripped that of the other two. It produced an average annual increase in real GDP of 14.2 percent for the years 1965–80, second highest in the world after Oman. From 1980 to 1991, growth rates remained high at an annual rate of 9.3 percent, third highest in the world after South Korea and China. In crucial aspects of government performance Botswana also outstripped its two neighbors. It recorded the highest services growth rate in the world for the decade 1980–90, with an average annual increase of 11.9 percent.[7] It follows that each case can therefore also be placed into a distinct slot within the broad categories South and Third World.

These finer distinctions make it possible to meet the fourth criterion for selecting comparable cases, that is, "to maximize the variance of the independent variables."[8] The primary independent variables used in this study consist of forces that shape the extent and patterns of social control among the populations of the cases. The three cases illustrate the impact of different kinds of British colonial imposition on the patterns of social control that existed in the colonies. They also illustrate the differential impact of white minorities on the networks of social control within sectors of society as well as the state. A comparative perspective can be achieved on how these two factors, plus cultural pluralism and modernization, have contributed to forming class and/or ethnic solidarities. The impact of these ethnic solidarities on patterns of societal and state social control can also be assessed. The different kinds and quality of leaders produced by these forces in each of these populations, and the impact of leadership on networks of social control located both in and beyond the state, can be evaluated. Finally, the power relations that are produced by asymmetrical relations of interdependence between adversaries within states, between states within the regional economy, and between states in the global economy can be analyzed.

These forces are the primary independent variables whose impact on and shaping of societally and state-based patterns of social control are examined in this study. Social control is exercised by a given agency when it "involves the successful subordination of people's own inclinations of social behavior or behavior sought by other social organizations in favor of the behavior prescribed by (its own) rules."[9] These patterns of social control in turn are examined as crucial determinants of the processes of state building and democratization.

Comparative analysis is the parallel analysis of events within selected units, such as states, which are presumed to have occurred because of internally generated causal factors: "What happens in each country is considered as independent of what happens elsewhere."[10] International relations explores the causal effects of interactions between states in an international system. The interdependence of states challenges the validity of a method of analysis that permits the search for causality to extend only to politically defined boundaries. "For comparative analysis," writes Richard Rose, "the critical question is the extent to which the idea of states operating independently in parallel is being eroded by changes in the international system."[11] Comparative study needs an analytical framework that can respond to the theoretical demands contained in this challenge.

The interdependence of Botswana, South Africa, and Zimbabwe follows from their geographical contiguity and shared colonial experience. An interlinked economic infrastructure, especially with regard to rail and road networks as well as shared markets for both commercial products and labor, grew as socioeconomic modernization proceeded in the colonies, and later the independent states, of southern Africa.[12] By the 1980s the regional economy had acquired some distinctive characteristics. The first was the dominant position of South Africa in the region. In 1988–89, while the GDP of Botswana stood at U.S.$4.88 billion and Zimbabwe's at U.S.$5.80 billion, South Africa's GDP was U.S.$87.50 billion— between 15 and 18 times greater than its neighbors'.[13] Within the region as a whole, South Africa accounted for 87 percent of electricity generated, 88 percent of steel produced, and 84 percent of cement produced. South Africa produced 75 percent of the region's exports and received 68 percent of its imports.[14] The second feature is what has been described as asymmetrical dependence. In 1984–85 South Africa was contributing 82 percent of the imports of Botswana while receiving only 6 percent of Botswana's exports.[15]

Zimbabwe was more favorably placed, with 18 percent of its imports coming from South Africa and 20 percent of exports going to South Africa. Both countries were also unfavorably engaged with South Africa with respect to rail and road links, ports, and access to petroleum products.[16]

These structural features are repeated in the global context. Although Africa accommodates 12 percent of the world's population, in 1988 it generated only 2.8 percent of the global GDP versus the 31 so-called core countries, which produced more than 80 percent of that GDP. Africa lagged far behind on other major indicators as well; per capita gross national product (GNP) in 1985 was U.S.$683 (versus the core country figure of U.S.$10,169); literacy was 45 percent (versus the core country figure of 99 percent and the global level of 69 percent); and the economic sector produced only 3.4 percent of the world's exports (versus the core country figure of more than 77 percent).[17]

This context of inequality and interdependence became the source of increasingly intense political conflicts after the decolonization of the region. From the conflicts grew a number of policy issues that affect the well-being of not only these three states but others in the region as well. Problems arise from the abundance of small arms in the subcontinent (one estimate places the number of Kalashnikov rifles in circulation in Mozambique by 1991 at 1.5 million); from civil war, which creates rebel bands and refugees with little regard for international boundaries and legal conventions; from population growth, drug trafficking, and AIDS; and from the environmental interdependence on water resources.[18] The extent to which this interdependence influences the dynamics of domestic politics in each of the three cases is addressed through the analytical framework adopted in this study.

The core proposition of this framework is that democratic stability requires a certain kind of state strength and a certain kind of societal strength. A strong state is needed in which the identity of citizenship is salient and in which the institutions and capabilities of the state remain autonomous and do not become the personal domain of any particular set of incumbents. A strong society in which the norms of civility prevail—that is, a civil society—is also required.[19] The impending anarchy Kaplan sees emerging in certain West African states stems directly from the pervasive conditions of state weakness and societal weakness within the region.

Sierra Leone exhibits the qualities of a weak state. No single jurisdiction applies: the population is effectively ruled by four armies, each carving out a territorial domain within what is supposed to be a single sovereign unit. The official rulers cannot even command their own enclaves with authority: by night, criminal gangs hold undisputed power in the capital city of Freetown. Each powerholder rules over a subject population on his own terms. "Informal" systems of justice enforce rules reflecting the interests of the powerholder. These conditions rule out one of the most basic requirements for democratic governance: that every individual be recognized as a citizen and that a single authority, the state, engage all citizens on an equal basis in the exercising of reciprocal rights, obligations, and duties.

Nor is the identity of citizenship itself of great value to the peoples of this West African region. The economic activity authorized and formalized by the laws of states are paralleled by informal economic networks, beyond state control and subject to arbitrary and discriminatory practices completely incompatible with those that citizens of democratic states claim in terms of their human rights. Claims for state protection, even if they could be formally registered, are unlikely to be effective. When the party against which such claims are presented—the state—is as fragmented as Sierra Leone, then it is unable to meet such obligations, even if the incumbents of the state wanted to.

Whether the incumbents even sense such an obligation is another matter. Kaplan cites a report on the Sierra Leone coup in which one of the leaders is said to have used the powers of the state as an instrument of revenge. He ordered the execution of his childhood benefactors to nullify previous experiences of personal humiliation. This action reflects an ethos and practice of state action in which the state is used as the personal property of the incumbents. It violates the norm of state autonomy and is again entirely hostile to the conditions required for nurturing democracies.

These West African examples also exhibit the features of weak societies, marked by civil disorder and the absence of institutions, rules, and practices of society conducive to democracy. Traditional values and ways of life either unravel or start producing socially disruptive effects. Kaplan notes that the extended family system, as currently practiced in the modern urban environment of West Africa, in effect undermines social stability through the inadvertent spreading of the human immunodeficiency virus (HIV). The mass population movements triggered by environmental catastrophes add to the turmoil that leads to social decay and normlessness. The end result is an environment of desperation where individuals have to survive and cope without recourse to public institutions, rules, and practices, or societal norms, values, and conventions. Under these conditions of state and societal weakness the idea of recognizing the moral dignity of a fellow citizen as the basis of civil conduct becomes a hugely risky strategy, for no shared identity or loyalty is there to buttress such mutual trust. Instead, the most trusted loyalties seem to be the most basic ones: family, clan, village, tribe, and ethnic group.

The basic thesis argued by Kaplan is that in the next few decades African states will decay further, and African societies will unravel even more. States are likely to succumb under the strains of environmentally generated conditions of scarcity, cultural and racial conflict, and unsustainable boundary demarcations. The end result is bound to be pervasive ungovernability, utterly incompatible with the requirements for stable democracy. This study examines three African states that have confronted in the past and continue to confront these conditions of conflict and scarcity. The findings of the study challenge the dismal prognosis of inescapable anarchy and show that African democratic stability is attainable provided that both state strength and societal strength are present.

The comparative analysis of the link between state building and democratic stability in three southern African countries begins with Botswana. (Readers unfamiliar with the theoretical literature and nomenclature relevant to state building may find it helpful to turn first to the appendix to this book, where key concepts and terms are discussed in detail.) The evolution of the modern state of Botswana has been shaped by precolonial as well as colonial experiences; these experiences and their impact on both society and the emergent modern economy are described and analyzed in chapter 1. The chapter presents an overview of the social, political, and economic contexts within which democratic politics, arguably the most successful in Africa, are conducted.

In chapter 2 an explanation for the remarkable (by African standards) democratic track record of Botswana is developed. It is argued that specific characteristics of the Botswana state contributed to its relative strength and autonomy. The strength of the state ensured that politics came to be conducted within the jurisdiction of the state, not beyond it. The kind of state autonomy that developed in Botswana made the state an adequate arena within which democratic politics could be conducted. This autonomy ensured that politics evolved into contests about who gets what (and when and how they get it) *within* the state, not contests about the character of the state itself. It is also argued that the way these state attributes evolved influenced the character of Botswana society in such a way that society was strengthened. This societal strength has buttressed democratic practices and contributed to the resilience of constitutional rules.

Colonial politics in Southern Rhodesia was shaped dramatically by the rebel state of Rhodesia. This state, characterized as an ethnic state, highly undemocratic and partisan, shaped society along racially imposed lines. The response escalated into a contest for hegemony in which the Rhodesian notions of statehood, peoplehood, and democracy were challenged in every sense. The resulting civil war weakened the Rhodesian state to the point of capitulation, also weakening society by eroding the social fabric of many communities. In chapter 3 the salient features of the Rhodesian state and society are described and are contrasted with those of Botswana, and the chapter concludes with an analysis of the impact of the contest for hegemony on the strength of both state and society.

In chapter 4 the dynamics of state-society interaction in independent Zimbabwe are described. An explanation is offered as to why Zimbabwe is markedly less democratic than Botswana. The explanation focuses on some of the weaknesses of the Zimbabwean state, which are traced to specific policy choices made by the state leaders in Zimbabwe since independence. The contrast with the policy choices of state leaders in Botswana, who confronted a similar set of constraints, is highlighted and explained. The core proposition emerging from this chapter is that state leaders in Zimbabwe have been guided by a different *ethos of state action* than has been the case in Botswana since independence.

The implications of these actions and policy choices for state strength, societal strength and cohesion, and democratic stability are shown.

The principles, practices, and policies of apartheid in South Africa are described in chapter 5 from a state-centered perspective. It is argued that the apartheid state, like its Rhodesian counterpart, was partisan and undemocratic and delivered public goods in a highly inequitable manner. The impact of apartheid on South African society through racially imposed social engineering is well known, but chapter 5 also shows how these policies weakened society in many ways. Less familiar are the sources of weaknesses in the apartheid state. Unlike Botswana, and like Rhodesia, South Africa was ultimately weakened by certain crucial features and was unable to confront effectively the hegemonic challenge of the 1980s.

The escalating confrontation between the apartheid state and its major challengers had by the late 1980s assumed the characteristics of a contest for hegemony. In chapter 6 the impact of this confrontation on society (a further weakening of its social fabric) and on the state (an overall erosion of state strength) is described. The mutually hurting stalemate that led to formal negotiations is analyzed, and the formal outcome of negotiations is assessed. The extent to which the new constitution is a step toward the construction of an autonomous state and therefore is a viable forum for democratic conflict resolution is also examined.

In the last chapter the comparative insights from the three cases are taken together to assess the question of democratic viability in the three. For Botswana the question is sustainability: How long can the current level of democratic success continue? For Zimbabwe the question is extendability: What factors can contribute to making the country more democratic? For South Africa the question is, What must to be done to sustain the new democratic constitution? All three questions produce similar, if not identical, answers. In Botswana the factors that erode the strength of state and society have to be curtailed. A number of such environmental, social, economic, and political factors are identified. A similar set of factors undermines the strengthening of both state and society in Zimbabwe. It is then argued that to secure democracy in South Africa, yet similar forces will have to be confronted.

In both Botswana and Zimbabwe the particular ethos of state action that guided public policymaking shaped the extent to which state leaders could measure up to these forces. The study closes with an examination of the learning process that the prospective leaders of the postapartheid South African state have undergone since 1990 and compares it with the formative experiences of the leaders of the two other states. This comparison yields the final perspective on the prospects for democratic stability in South Africa after apartheid.

PART I

BOTSWANA

The Strong State and Strong Society

❋ 1 ❋

CONSTRUCTING STATE
AND SOCIETY

In African terms, Botswana is easily recognized as an exceptional case of democratic success. Samuel Huntington, in his analysis of global trends in democratization (for example) notes that of all the African countries that became independent in the 1960s, "the only African country consistently to maintain democratic practices was Botswana." By contrast, events elsewhere on the continent bring him to the conclusion that "the decolonization of Africa led to the largest multiplication of independent authoritarian governments in history."[1]

Huntington's assessment of the democratic quality of Botswana's politics derives from a minimal definition of democracy centered on the procedural yardstick of regular, free, and fair elections. By this yardstick Botswana does well, having held competitive multi-party elections at regular intervals from 1965 through 1989. Other analysts, relying (explicitly or implicitly) on a more expansive yardstick for democratic success, have been less complimentary about the democratic quality of Botswana's politics. Noting that elections have yet to yield an alternation in ruling party, John D. Holm characterizes the overall political process within which these elections take place as a "paternalistic" democracy.[2] Louis A. Picard is equally unflattering in depicting the country as a "*de facto* one-party state."[3] Horowitz makes the charade of electoral politics explicit:

"Botswana's opposition is ascriptively limited. . . . Ascriptive minorities cannot become majorities, so elections are safe."[4]

The exact significance of electoral politics in Botswana thus continues to be disputed, as is the explanation for this enduring phenomenon of political contestation so rare on the African continent. The one obvious explanation on offer is that Botswana is virtually an ethnically homogeneous, therefore an undivided, society and therefore also more easily able to sustain democratic practices.[5] Ethnic homogeneity is often claimed for Botswana on the basis of the linguistic predominance of Setswana, which is spoken by nearly 98 percent of the population.[6] This claim rests on two errors. The first is to mistake cultural homogeneity (or heterogeneity) for ethnic singularity (or plurality). As is argued in the appendix, it is widely accepted that ethnic identities are constructed around cultural criteria, but which criteria assume predominance and in what form they do so tend to be functions of context and historical circumstance. Cultural plurality does not necessarily translate into ethnic diversity on a one-to-one basis. The second error is that the linguistic predominance of Setswana obscures the extent of cultural diversity in Botswana at the same time as it reflects the extent to which Tswana culture has achieved predominance: "What is remarkable in Botswana is how much, up till now, the legitimacy of Tswana-dom has been accepted and even supported by non-Tswana groups."[7] The major Tswana-speaking tribes—the Bakgatla, Bakwena, Bamalete, Bamangwato, Bangwaketse, Barolong, Batawana, and Batlokwa—share the country with the Tswapong (Pedi-speaking), Kalanga (Shona-speaking), Subiya (Tonga-speaking), Lete (Nguni-speaking), Europeans (English-, Afrikaans-, and German-speaking), as well as Khoisan, Xhosa, and Indian minorities. Given such cultural diversity, Parsons warns, the national legitimacy of Tswana culture may well be challenged in the future, as it has been in the past. What needs explanation, therefore, is why this range of cultural diversity from Tswana to non-Tswana has not yet surfaced in more assertive ethnic identities in Botswana.

Equally in need of explanation is why the tribal differences within the ranks of the Tswana culture have not assumed overwhelming significance as ethnic identities in Botswana politics. A comparison with Lesotho is apt. With 99 percent of the population speaking Sotho, Lesotho outranks even Botswana in terms of cultural homogeneity.[8] Furthermore, the dominant cultures of both countries share the same heritage. Linguistically, both derive from the Sotho group within the southern Bantu-speaking peoples, the Tswana being part of the west Sotho and the population of Lesotho being from the southern Sotho.[9] Yet politics in Lesotho has been dominated by lineage conflict between different chieftaincies, which has not been containable within multiparty electoral politics of the type that characterizes Botswana politics.[10] Electoral politics in Lesotho endured only until 1970 and was followed by a coup d'état and one-party rule until 1986, when the first of a series of military rulers took power. Viewed from that perspective, then, democratic stability in Botswana is not explained at all, neither by the presence of cultural homogeneity (which there is not), nor by reputed ethnic homogeneity (which itself, to the extent that it exists, needs explanation). Instead, the further question is asked, Why is politics in Botswana not more like politics in Lesotho? The presence of numerous cultures and tribal fault lines in the dominant Tswana culture should make Botswana a potential (or even incipient) multiethnic society and also a potentially divided society. What needs to be explained is why a multiethnic society has not yet emerged.

In this chapter is presented a description of the main features of the Botswana state and society that emerged from the precolonial, colonial, and independence eras. In this largely chronological descriptive account the key components for examining the presence or absence of a contest for hegemony—the strength of society and state—and for explaining the continuous practice of stable democratic politics in Botswana are described. These components are used in the next chapter in an explanatory analysis of the dynamics of state-society interaction.

THE PRECOLONIAL ERA

The Mfecane (also known as the Difaqane)[11] has been described as "one of the great formative events of African history," which "permanently modified the ethnic map of much of Bantu Africa and thereby played an important part in establishing the framework of political and cultural life in a number of modern African states."[12] It started as a social, political, and military revolution in Zululand in the early 1800s, which created the Zulu kingdom under Shaka Zulu. The resultant process of conquest, warfare, population flight, and social dislocation affected the peoples of the entire subcontinent from the Fish River in southern Africa to the southern shores of Lake Victoria. These events directly affected the demographic features of the populations of what eventually became the independent states of Botswana, South Africa, and Zimbabwe.

The Tswana tribes were most directly affected by the passage of two separate conquering groups, the Kololo under the leadership of Sebetwane, and the Ndebele of Mzilikazi.[13] The Kololo, molded together from a number of groups among the east Sotho who fled the Zulu armies of Shaka, and led by Sebetwane, moved north into the territory occupied by the various Tswana tribes. There they engaged in military confrontations with first the Barolong, then the Bahurutse, followed by the Batlokwa, the Bakwena, and the Bangwaketse. Clashes with the Bamangwato and the Batawana followed. The Kololo finally moved across the Zambezi into Barotseland, beyond the range of the Tswana tribes.[14] The Ndebele had a far more devastating impact on the Tswana tribes. The Bakwena, the Bakgatla, and the Bahurutse all suffered military defeat. The Bangwaketse, who had earlier successfully withstood the Kololo, were hit hardest and "were completely routed and driven into the Kalahari and their position as the dominant Tswana tribe was destroyed for ever"[15]—an outcome that eventually left the Bamangwato in the dominant position, a crucially important point in the later evolution of Botswana politics. After settling in Matabeleland, the Ndebele for a while extracted taxes from the Bamangwato, who acknowledged Ndebele supremacy.

The overall sociopolitical impact of this series of events lies in the fact that more densely constructed political units with greater levels of cohesion and organization became established throughout the region among the affected peoples. According to Omer-Cooper, "this change involves a principle which can be seen in any human society developing in the direction of greater political centralization and more active government. It can be paralleled in the transition from feudal to bureaucratic administration which marks the emergence of the modern European state."[16] This process of merging formerly disparate, spatially isolated, and clan-based populations into new, larger, and more tightly organized political units did not proceed uniformly throughout the region that became Botswana. The result is that some communities grew stronger as political units while others remained dispersed and relatively weak.[17] The stronger Tswana tribes managed to use their comparative advantage to dominate other weaker communities. The peoples who eventually were designated as the Basarwa, Bakgalagadi, and Bayei communities were drawn into a relationship of economic subordination characterized as serfdom.[18]

The institution of kingship (*bogosi*) was the pivot of the political structure and a focal point of political, religious, legal, economic, and symbolic authority and practice.[19] The king was functioning under constraints, however, the most important of which were located in the administrative system. An informal council of confidential and trusted advisers, the *bagakolodi*, provided the first check on arbitrary rule. In addition, the ruler was obliged to consult a wider, more representative formal body of advisers—the ward heads—and also the public assembly of all adult men, held in the great *kgotla* (pl. *lekgotla*) of the king. In these assemblies, which constituted the customary law and the customary courts of the Tswana chieftaincies, everyone was entitled to speak and frequently did so, even with the effect of overruling decisions reached in earlier consultations. This was not a common occurrence, however, and the *lekgotla* meetings generally served as a public forum where grievances were aired, public consent was sought and conferred, and consensus was molded on matters of public policy.

These sociopolitical systems were characterized by hierarchy and stratification, public participation and consultation, and limited consent within the given stratified social and political system. They not only survived the Mfecane but consolidated their positions east of the Limpopo River in the following decades leading up to the era of contact with white colonial settlers. Early contact was through the London Missionary Society, led by David Livingstone in 1844. Shortly afterward, commercial trade was established, as was labor migration to Cape Colony (now Northern Cape province of South Africa). Regional confrontation followed suit, and in 1852 the Bakwena capital of Dimawe was attacked from the Transvaal Republic. Interest in the region escalated with the discovery of gold in the Tati district in 1867. Tswana leaders, especially Khama III of the Bamangwato, fearing hostile intervention in their domain from

the Transvaal Republic in the east and from the German presence
in the west, sought protection under British influence. That protection was secured with an "informal protectorate relationship,"
which was consolidated by 1880 between the Tswana leaders and
the British government in Cape Town. This relationship was formalized with the declaration of a British protectorate over the
southern section of Tswana territory, known as British Bechuanaland, in 1884. This area became a crown colony in 1885, when the
northern section of Tswana country was declared a formal possession: Bechuanaland Protectorate. In 1889 a charter was drawn up,
providing for the eventual transfer of this protectorate to the
British South Africa Company (BSAC), then under the leadership
of Cecil John Rhodes. The southern section, British Bechuanaland, was made part of Cape Colony in 1895, but the transfer of
the northern section to the BSAC was revoked after the Jameson
Raid of 1895 and its political repercussions, which discredited
Rhodes with the British imperial authorities.[20] The boundaries of
Bechuanaland Protectorate were drawn so as to accommodate
almost fully the Tswana kingdoms of the Bangwaketse, the Bakwena, the Bamangwato, and the Batawana. The Barolong and the
Bakgatla kingdoms, however, were almost cut in half by the boundary line with Cape Colony.[21] The boundary lines also demarcated
the protectorate from the other areas under the control of the
BSAC, which were later to become Southern Rhodesia and, eventually, Zimbabwe.[22] The physical environment of the protectorate
comprising 220,000 square miles was then, as now, fairly hostile,
being mostly semiarid Kalahari sandveld. The annual rainfall
varies from 27 inches in the east to about 8 inches in the west and,
being irregular, subjects the entire country to recurring drought.[23]

THE COLONIAL ERA

Constitutional politics in Bechuanaland Protectorate in the 80
years of colonial rule from 1885 to 1966 was dominated by two
issues: the status of the territory itself and the relationship
between the indigenous political systems of the Tswana kingdoms
and those of the colonial power. The colonial status of the territory
was jeopardized by attempts at incorporation by both the Union of
South Africa and the colony of Southern Rhodesia. South Africa

abandoned these attempts only in 1961, when it became a republic and left the Commonwealth. Rhodesia persisted into the 1950s as a member of the then Federation of Rhodesia and Nyasaland.[24]

The order in council of 1885 by which Bechuanaland Protectorate was established did not specify any system of law and administration for the territory, reflecting the initial intention to allow the local leaders (from then on designated as chiefdoms instead of kingdoms by the colonial authorities) maximum freedom to continue governing on their own terms. An increase in European settlers prompted a rapid change, however. An order in council of 1890 gave the governor of British Bechuanaland the authority to exercise British jurisdiction over the territory. Another order in council (the Foreign Jurisdiction Act of 1890) followed in 1891, establishing a basic administrative framework. This order gave the high commissioner wide-ranging power, including the power to enact legislation by proclamation, subject to respecting "any native laws and customs by which the civil relations of any native chiefs, tribes or populations under Her Majesty's protection are now regulated, except so far as the same may be incompatible with the due exercise of her majesty's power and jurisdiction."[25] The General Administration Proclamation of 1891, which gave effect to the above order, as well as Proclamation No. 2 of 1896, established a system of courts and personnel modeled on the system of resident magistrates then operative in Cape Colony. The General Law Proclamation of 1909 stipulated that the Roman-Dutch law of Cape Colony was to become the common law of the territory.

That proclamation completed the establishment of a system of legal duality, which persists (in a varied form) in present-day Botswana. The customary law of the Tswana chiefdoms and the Roman-Dutch law of the colonial powers represented not only two legal systems but, in a wider sense, two distinct networks of social control as well. Each legal tradition was informed by a distinctive set of cultural values, norms, prescriptions, and symbolic endorsements. The way these two legal systems with their accompanying political and social systems evolved is a crucial factor in explaining the construction of a strong state and of a strong society in what emerged as modern Botswana.

The political and legal system of resident magistrates was imposed onto a grid of regional delimitations for each of the five major Tswana chiefdoms; land was set aside specifically for the Tswana people in so-called reserves. These boundaries, drawn in 1899, formed the basis of the districts of contemporary Botswana. A tax system (a 10-shilling hut tax to be collected by the chiefs) was implemented the same year. The initial pattern of administration that emerged has been called "parallel rule," in which the Roman-Dutch law was intended to apply to Europeans only: "In the European areas, the resident magistrate had the direct responsibility for the district's population, both European and African. In the reserves, the magistrate heard cases involving Europeans and heard serious cases and appeals from the chief's *kgotla*."[26] Parallel rule became further institutionalized with the introduction in 1920 of both an African council and a European council to advise the resident commissioner of the protectorate.

In theory the magistrates were supposed to leave the application of customary law entirely to the chiefs and the institution of the *kgotla*. In practice, magistrates increasingly intervened so as to draw the chiefs into their own administration and made them extensions thereof. In maintaining order and collecting the hut tax the colonial authorities tended to side with the chiefs against all opposition, directly affecting the fabric of the indigenous system of rule: "Colonial rule destroyed the traditional balance of power between the chiefs, their advisors, and the *kgotla*, and the chiefs became increasingly authoritarian."[27] Under colonial rule, therefore, the formerly independent Tswana kingdoms became extensions of the administrative body of British imperialism.

The emergent de facto system of dual but subordinate administration became formalized with the policy of indirect rule, enacted in the Native Administration Proclamation and the Native Tribunals Proclamation, both of 1934. The first proclamation brought the chiefly administration under direct government control, the chiefs themselves becoming subordinate officials, and provided for the nomination of councilors with whom chiefs had to meet and consult in the execution of their duties. The second proclamation formalized the application of the customary law in the *kgotla* court system. The validity of both these enactments was unsuccessfully challenged in the High Court by Chiefs Bathoen II and Tshekedi Khama. The establishment of tribal treasuries through the Native Treasuries Proclamation of 1938, to replace the tribal fund that was under the personal control of the chief, accelerated the process of supplanting personal rule with bureaucratic rule. Although the 1943 proclamations restored the legal status of the *lekgotla* assemblies (instead of transferring them to tribunals, as foreseen in the 1934 proclamations), they did not revoke those assemblies' subordinate status.

Indirect rule having proved unsatisfactory both as a system of administrative control (financial indiscipline appeared to be a prominent malady) and as a system of participation (officials and some of the chiefs had little enthusiasm for the reforms), the move was made to directly elected bodies with retention of the institution of chieftainship. The Local Councils Proclamation of 1957 required the establishment of elected tribal councils to assist the chief in administration. The shift to elective bodies was completed with the Local Government Act of 1965, through which nine district councils were established to replace the tribal councils. These elected bodies were to be the basic units of local government. At the local level the chiefs retained their judicial functions only. At the national level they gained representation in the House of Chiefs, a separate body of parliament.

In summarizing the cumulative impact of the colonial policy of indirect rule on the process of state building in preindependence Botswana, Louis Picard points to the pattern of bureaucratic initiative (by the colonial authorities) that shaped the evolution of political institutions at the local level and secured the supremacy of the modern Weberian institutions over the established Tswana kingdoms. Yet this very process inhibited the emergence of a domestic political process at the local level that could effectively occupy the political space within this modern set of institutions. The process of state building after independence could therefore be expected to proceed along similar lines: initiatives taken at the center would shape the further evolution of state and society at all other levels.[28]

The character of the political center of Botswana at independence was again influenced greatly by the colonial policies in establishing an indigenous public service. The colonial authorities' patterns of recruiting into the public service were shaped initially by budgetary parsimony and, after 1935, also by adherence to the values that informed British imperialism and indirect rule. The stated priority was to recruit administrative personnel from the "Oxbridge" ranks to ensure that the policies of indirect rule were implemented with the appropriate guidance and leadership. Whatever else this policy achieved, it established the public service as an elite entity, one with high status and influence as well as expertise. The recruitment and training of local Batswana for positions of leadership in the public service became a matter of policy focus only after the 1948 Fitzgerald Commission report. Even then, such concerns were tempered by the emphasis on the need for gradualism to ensure that professional standards were not jeopardized. Thus the first African assistant district officer was appointed only in 1951, and the second appointment came in 1959. By 1962 the upper levels of the civil service still held exceedingly few Africans. In the administrative and professional grades only 4 positions of the 155 were taken by Africans; in the technical grades, 15 of 260; and in the middle-level executive grade, 22 of 182.[29] At independence Botswana thus inherited a bureaucratic elite largely occupied by expatriates as "the most important, and perhaps the only significant domestic interest group in the country, and they influenced policy decisions far out of proportion to their numbers."[30] The groundwork was laid for the establishment of the "administrative state," a state dominated by administrative personnel and guided by their interests and priorities.

The society of preindependence Botswana was also shaped by colonial economic policies. Whether by design or default, the overall impact of these policies was to bequeath to the new rulers at independence an underdeveloped economy dependent on the South African economy and also on the global economy. British colonial policy was shaped by, among other factors, the continually uncertain status of the territory until 1961, the original intent behind the establishment of the protectorate in 1885, and the declining economic prospects of the region during the first half of the century. Taken together, these factors inhibited any substantial and concerted investment in the socioeconomic infrastructure of the protectorate.

Bechuanaland, like the other two High Commission Territories, Swaziland and Basotholand, was drawn into the economic ambit of the Union of South Africa through the use of the South African currency, a single customs union, and the linking of road, rail, and communications networks. This common market (especially the customs union) worked to the advantage of the South African economy and to the detriment of the others by attracting industry to the most developed part of the region. The hut tax imposed in 1899, to be paid in cash instead of in kind, compelled increasingly large numbers of Batswana to find employment in the cash economy, specifically in the South African mining sector. The emergence of a commercial Tswana trading community was inhibited by the discriminatory practices of colonial officials, who rejected African applications for trading licenses. Investment in the social and economic infrastructure remained very low, and the institutional infrastructure for implementing such investments also remained correspondingly weak.[31]

The result was that at independence in 1966, Botswana showed a distinctive profile of underdevelopment. In a country roughly the size of Texas (or of France and Belgium combined), only 25 kilometers of road were tarred.[32] The colonial authorities had invested in primary school facilities but virtually ignored secondary education. At independence the country had only eight secondary schools, of which only one, the Gaborone school, had been established as a government school. That school came into operation only in 1965, the year before independence.[33] Most of the population was still engaged in subsistence cattle farming, and GNP per capita stood at U.S.$14, the third lowest in the world at that time.[34] The emergence of Tswana commercial enterprise was hampered by the denial of trading licenses. By 1949 only 10 stores were owned and operated by Africans (in contrast to the 155 under European ownership). By 1959 the number of licensed African traders was up to 53, but the major sector of the retail trade was still being controlled by foreigners at independence.[35] Migrant labor to the Union of South Africa showed a steady increase during the first half of this century. In 1910, according to the official statistics of the Union, just over 2,000 men from the protectorate were involved; by 1935, more than 10,000[36] and by the 1960s, about 50,000.[37] The institutions for development also reflected the priorities of colonial policy. Until 1934 the Public Works Department of the protectorate consisted of one person—the government engineer—assisted by one clerk and one foreman. Until 1935 there was no department for agriculture. The cattle industry, the main economic enterprise of the country, was served by a veterinary department with a single veterinary doctor from 1905 to 1914, when a second position was created. In 1935 three additional posts were added, and with a number of stock inspectors and cattle guards the department remained essentially unchanged until the 1950s.[38]

The overall social conditions and quality of life of the population can be gauged in part from some of the social indicators reported in World Bank statistics. In 1965 the infant mortality rate was 112 (per 1,000 live births). Life expectancy at birth for females stood at 49 years; for men, 46. There was one medical doctor for every 27,450 people and one nurse for every 17,710. The net enrollment rate at primary schools stood at 65 percent, and at secondary schools, 3 percent.[39] It is hardly surprising that by 1960 Bechuanaland had produced only eight university students and that not one student graduated from secondary school that year.[40]

THE POSTINDEPENDENCE ERA

State and Regime

The process of state building in the postindependence era in Botswana was characterized by three interrelated trends. The first was the continued converting of the chiefs from political leaders into public servants. The second was the further consolidation of the system of legal dualism, in which the customary courts with their dual but subordinate status were institutionalized parallel to the judicial system based on Roman-Dutch law. The third was the establishment, at both the local and the national levels, of an extensive system of modern administrative institutions as well as representative political institutions.

The decline in the status, authority, and jurisdiction of the chiefs to a politically subordinate position followed immediately after independence. The Chieftainship Act of 1956 (put into effect on July 1, 1966, three months before independence) reserved chiefly representation at the national level in the House of Chiefs, a chamber separate from the legislative body in parliament with advisory functions only. The chiefs became salaried officers of the state, and the minister of local government and lands was authorized to determine the salary of each chief. The Local Government (District Councils) Act as well as the Local Government Tax Act removed from the chiefs the right to impose local taxation. The Matimela Act of 1968 transferred the responsibility of dealing with stray cattle from the chiefs to the newly established district councils. The Tribal Land Act, also passed in 1968, removed their right to allocate land and transferred this responsibility to institutions called land boards. The chiefs therefore became public servants: bound within the hierarchy of the public service bureaucracy, accountable ultimately to parliamentary executive authority; appointed by the parliamentary executive and liable to removal from office by the same authority, and receiving a remuneration package similar to that of other officials, including leave, allowances, retirement, a salary scale, medical coverage, and gratuities.[41]

The dual but subordinate status of customary law was retained in the legal system of Botswana after independence. The legal system comprises 15 "modern" courts, which apply Roman-Dutch common and statutory law in Botswana. These 15 courts consist of a number of magistrates courts, the High Court, and the Court of Appeal. An additional 210 "customary" courts deal with the civil and penal laws of the country. These courts are presided over by the chiefs and their representatives and headmen. Four categories of customary courts are recognized: (1) Warranted courts are empowered to enforce the penal code and are further subdivided into senior customary courts and junior customary courts. (2) The unwarranted, recognized customary courts are allowed to engage only in reconciliation and may not impose punitive rulings. (3) Informally recognized customary courts engage in the same practice. At the lowest level (4), unwarranted and unrecognized customary courts operate.[42] Figure 1.1 provides an outline of the courts in Botswana.

This legal system consolidated the judicial function of the institution of chieftaincy and retained the *lekgotla* as courts of law over and above their status as popular assemblies. The customary law and the *lekgotla* became formal extensions of the institutional reach of the modern state. The way that was done, and the way this institutional arrangement has evolved—so it will be argued later—is another crucial factor in explaining the link between state building and democratic stability in Botswana.

The new set of political and administrative institutions at the national level gave limited recognition to the political structures of

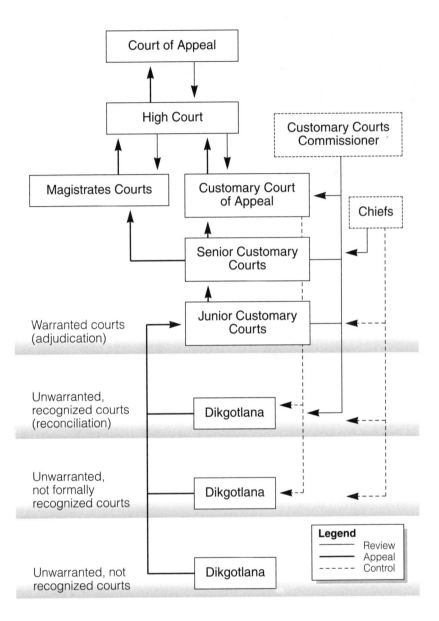

Figure 1.1 — Official and Unofficial Courts in Botswana

Source: Marlies Bouman, "A Note on Chiefly and National Policing in Botswana," *Journal of Legal Pluralism*, nos. 25–26 (1987): 275–300 at 278, 279, figure 1. Copyright © by *Journal of Legal Pluralism*. Used by permission of the Publisher.

ne Constitution of Botswana offi-
s, which thereby gain represen-
district boundaries of the state
tribal territories and therefore
.... to some extent both as administrative units and as representative units at the local level. These
boundaries were also taken into consideration with the drawing
up of electoral districts for national election.[43] However, few other
features of the modern structure of the state reflect Botswana's
political heritage.

The constitution describes Botswana as a unitary state and a
parliamentary republic. Legislative authority is vested in parliament, which consists of the National Assembly, the House of
Chiefs, and the president. Parliament acts in consultation with the
House of Chiefs on certain matters, such as constitutional change.
The National Assembly comprises a speaker, a nonvoting attorney
general, 32 elected members, and four members appointed by the
president. Since 1970 the president has been an ex officio member
of the National Assembly. The independent judiciary with its High
Court and Court of Appeal can enforce the code of human rights
specified in chapter 2 of the constitution and can also interpret
the constitution.

The executive authority is vested in the president, who heads a
cabinet appointed from the ruling party in the National Assembly.
The president is formally selected by the elected members of the
National Assembly and retains office until the assembly is dissolved or a vote of no confidence is passed against him or her,
subject to the maximum term of office of the assembly, which is
five years. Although parliament functions largely in the Westminster tradition, a number of variations apply to the executive. Rule
by cabinet is replaced by rule by the president. The cabinet advises
the president, who in turn is obliged only to consult with it, but it
is still required to accept collective responsibility for his actions.
The president also has the power to dissolve the National Assembly
and has extensive powers of appointment, extending not only to
cabinet ministers but also to the vice president, assistant ministers, and permanent secretaries. The president is commander in
chief of the armed forces. The assent of the president in the legislative process is essential for effective government. He may refuse

to sign any bill, and if he does, it has to be reintroduced in the assembly. Should it pass again, the president is compelled to sign it within three weeks or dissolve parliament. Furthermore, only on the recommendation of the president can the assembly pass legislation that increases taxation or expenditures or that affects the terms of government debt.[44]

The political subordination of the chiefs did not terminate their political representation. In the prelude to independence they strenuously negotiated for a position of guaranteed legislative authority in the independence constitution. At the first round of preparatory constitutional negotiations in Lobatse in August 1963 they argued for an upper chamber in a bicameral legislature to be reserved for them. The political representatives from the emergent political parties, especially the "new men" assembled under Sir Seretse Khama, were prepared to grant them only two options: two or three reserved seats in the elected assembly, or an entirely advisory body in which they all could gain representation. The latter option eventually prevailed and became institutionalized as the House of Chiefs.

The House of Chiefs consists of the incumbent chiefs of the eight constitutionally recognized Tswana tribes (Bakgatla, Bakwena, Bamalete, Bamangwato, Bangwaketse, Barolong, Batawana, and Batlokwa) as ex officio members. They elect four additional members, one each from the ranks of the subchiefs in Chobe, Francistown, Ghanzi and Kgalagadi districts. These four *elected members*, together with the ex officio members, then elect another three *specially elected members* from the citizenry, under the condition that they have not actively engaged in politics in the preceding five years and are fluent in written and spoken English.[45] It has been pointed out that this arrangement affirms the ascendancy of the Tswana at the expense of other minorities. The Bayei, Hambukushu, Basarwa, Babirwa, Bakalanga, Bakgalagadi, and Basubiya are denied similar constitutional recognition.[46]

Regional political institutions that evolved after independence mirrored the trends established during colonial rule. At the initiative of the political center, new institutions were established, taking functions away from tribal institutions and at the same time attempting to assert control over these new institutions from the center. The Local Government Act of 1965 provided for the creation of district councils (within the regional boundaries set in 1899).

That act was followed by the creation of district land boards and village development committees in 1968 and district development committees in 1970. The colonial institutions of district administrations and tribal administrations were retained, and so a crowded field of six institutions occupied the political and organizational space at the district level, contesting for influence. The resulting dynamic has been, quite predictably, that each district-level institution vies with the others for ascendancy, all of them trying to gain autonomy from the center, and the center trying to assert control instead of granting autonomy. In addition, within the center there was rivalry among the Office of the President, the Ministry of Local Government and Lands, and the Ministry of Finance and Development Planning for control over the district-level institutions. Figure 1.2 outlines this institutional arrangement. Within this institutional landscape the impact of party politics and electoral competition added another dimension of complexity.[47]

The underdeveloped public bureaucracy that was the legacy of colonial rule was rapidly transformed in the two and a half decades after independence. In 1964 the central government service comprised only 2,175 positions.[48] At independence there were only seven ministries in addition to the Office of the President, the Public Service Commission, the attorney general, and the National Development Bank. During the first decade of independence six new ministries were created, as well as four new departments within ministries. Seven parastatals (government-owned institutions that are required to operate on commercial principles) were also established. The result was a rapid increase in the employment of personnel in the central government sector: 3,609 in 1968–69; 5,153 in 1972; and 6,317 in 1975. The annual rate of expansion of this sector between 1964 and 1972 was 11 percent versus the 7 percent expansion in formal employment in other sectors of the economy.[49] Between 1979 and 1983, growth in this sector continued at an annual rate of 7 percent. The overall level of public sector employment also rose dramatically, to 13,550 in 1972 and to 33,903 in 1982, increasing at an annual rate of about 10 percent.[50]

A striking feature of this institutional expansion has been the extent to which the colonial pattern of expatriates holding crucial public service positions endured. In 1964, just two years before

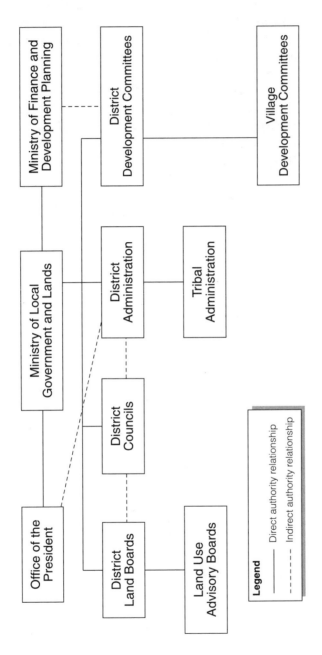

Figure 1.2 — District-Level Organization in Botswana

Source: Louis A. Picard, *The Politics of Development in Botswana: A Model for Success?* (Boulder, Colo.: Lynne Rienner, 1987), p. 179. Copyright © 1987 by Lynne Rienner Publishers, Inc. Used with permission of the Publisher.

independence, expatriates in the central government numbered 683 (31 percent). In the following years the number declined only slightly; by 1975 they still held 584 positions. Given the growth of this sector, however, the expatriate proportion decreased to 19 percent in 1968–69, to 13 percent in 1972, and to 9 percent in 1975.[51] This pattern is repeated in the public sector as a whole, where expatriates in 1972 numbered 1,149 (8.5 percent of the positions) and increased to 1,896 in 1980 but decreased in ratio to 6 percent of the public work force. The impact of this section of the public sector is a function not only of numbers but even more so of strategic placement. In 1964, expatriates held 61 percent of so-called group A (senior and middle-level staff) positions. By 1972 the percentage had decreased dramatically to 19 percent, but it rose again in 1982 to 23.5 percent. In the professional and technical categories expatriates' presence remained marked in 1983, at 51 percent and 29 percent, respectively.[52] It is argued in the next chapter that this expatriate sector of the public work force contributed a vital ingredient to the quality of statehood that evolved in postindependence Botswana. The expatriate sector added not only to the strength of the state but also to its autonomy.

Five distinctive traits soon emerged in the democratic politics that evolved in the postindependence state. First, at the national level, presidential politics dominated other aspects of the parliamentary process. Second, a distinctive form of regional government emerged. Although the institutional framework of the state allows for substantial decentralization of government to the district levels, what evolved was a process of deconcentration of government functions only, with centralized bureaucratic control being maintained over both the political and the administrative processes at district level. Third, electoral politics and party competition were dominated from the outset by one party, the Botswana Democratic Party. Fourth, a well-defined set of development priorities was identified early on by the incumbent political leadership and consistently pursued throughout the postindependence era. Fifth, a well-defined coalition of interests formed among the bureaucracy, the ruling party, and the commercial sectors of the society.

The 1966 constitution made it possible for an astute incumbent president to dominate in parliamentary politics as well as in national politics, and the first holder of this position succeeded in doing so comprehensively. Sir Seretse Khama used the authority of the position of president, buttressed by the electoral strength of his Botswana Democratic Party (BDP), to direct the state-building process in Botswana along a specific course.[53] His personal circumstances in Botswana politics were unique. Sir Seretse Khama, deposed chief of the Bamangwato, was educated at Oxford, married an Englishwoman, became the founder and leader of a profoundly modern institution (the BDP), and had interests in the commercial cattle industry. Being amenable to the colonial program for decolonization, he alone could muster support from the commercial cattle ranching interests, the educated Tswana elite, the traditionalists, and the colonial public service. It is argued in the next chapter that the way he used this position to build a broad coalition of interests *within* the state to pursue the construction of a specific *kind* of state has been another of the crucial factors in the strength of the state and the stability of democracy in Botswana.

The ostensible political autonomy of the local district councils, which came into operation as elected bodies in 1965, belies their actual role. Although these bodies were established as decentralized representative institutions, they rapidly evolved into extensions of the political and administrative center. The councils experienced recurring and persistent problems in recruiting capable personnel and maintaining administrative discipline. The solution was to make district administration an extension of the national public service. This occurred primarily through the working of the Unified Local Government Service, which was established in 1973 as a division of the Ministry of Local Government and Lands and effectively drew the district council work force into the jurisdiction of that ministry. This subordination, coupled to financial dependence on the central government, soon dissolved the autonomy of the district councils.[54]

Political parties and national elections have showed certain characteristics from early on. The first and most obvious was the dominance of the BDP, founded by Sir Seretse Khama. The BDP contested every election from the first preindependence election in 1965 and won every one by a large margin. It did so largely (but not exclusively) by consolidating and extending the wide coalition of interests that Sir Seretse appealed to from the start by virtue of his personal circumstances. The challenge to the BDP was initially taken up by the Botswana People's Party and later by the Botswana National Front. Neither of these parties has succeeded in loosening the hold of the BDP on the electorate, although the first-past-the-post, single-member-constituency–based electoral system has obscured the actual support of the Botswana National Front in some of the more recent elections.[55] This uninterrupted series of elections, unequalled in Africa, is claimed by Botswana politicians to measure up to the minimum requirements of being free and fair in terms of competitiveness and is the outstanding credential (along with the government's record of respecting human rights) in Botswana's claim to meeting the requirements of the minimalist procedural definition of liberal democracy.[56] The extent of adherence to these rules should the electorate choose to return a different party to power has yet to be tested.

A second characteristic of the evolving party system has been the lack of clear ideological differences in the positions taken by the different parties.[57] An initial impetus toward a radical populist form of socialism by the Botswana People's Party has not been sustained. By the early 1980s it was being characterized as "more a party of political opportunism than of socialist purity," and the BDP as "moderate and prudent."[58] The Botswana National Front, despite its clear formal position in favor of socialism, has emerged as a coalition of urban and traditional interests and has "not offered a concrete alternative vision of the future."[59] The significance of the electorate being offered no ideological choice has been the subject of some analysis; the primary conclusion is that the quality and depth of democracy in Botswana are diminished.[60] In the next chapter it is argued that this characteristic reveals more about the quality of statehood in Botswana than about the party system only.

A third characteristic of parties and elections has been the ease with which these modern institutions have supplanted the traditional institutions built around the chieftaincies as the appropriate institutions through which to express political choice and political loyalty. The issue of preference for modern political institutions versus traditional ones did not shape the party system and has not been the predominant line of cleavage in electoral politics.[61] Both the dominant parties in the current parliament, the Botswana Democratic Party and the Botswana National Front, have made ample use of support from traditional structures and of support from individuals associated with these institutions during the past 25 years.

Directly related to this is a fourth and equally important characteristic, namely that the challenges to the constitution (especially by the disaffected chiefs) were conducted within the rules set for party politics and elections. The most notable examples were the challenges by Chief Linchwe II of the Bakgatla (who supported the Botswana People's Party in the Mochudi electoral district in the 1965 and 1969 national elections) and Chief Bathoen II of the Bangwaketse, who resigned his position and joined the Botswana National Front to contest the 1969 national election.[62] It is argued in the next chapter that these events and choices made by the two chiefs represent decisive victories for the state and are indicative of the strength of the state that was being constructed.

A fifth feature of party politics in Botswana is that no clear-cut class-based division has emerged as a significant criterion for party choice. Although rapid economic growth since independence has been accompanied by growing inequalities in the living standards of the rich and the poor, the emergence of this increasingly more visible social cleavage has yet to be successfully exploited by any political party; no party has projected itself as representing the rural and urban poor, those who stand at the losing side of rapid capitalist industrial development. The inability of parties to use the obvious, visible social inequalities as a basis to confront the ruling BDP has yet to be explained satisfactorily. It is argued in the next chapter that the state-society framework being deployed in this study is able to combine some of the current explanations into a more comprehensive account of electoral behavior in Botswana.

What has been claimed with a large measure of confidence is the role played by ethnic factors in party choice, especially in the support base of the BDP. John D. Holm notes that the core support of the BDP lies with the Bamangwato and the Bakwena tribes. "In effect, within these two tribes," argues Holm, "a vote for the BDP is an affirmation of ethnic membership."[63] In more general terms, he concludes that with other ethnic preferences taken into account, more than three-quarters of the vote in Botswana elections can be explained by this factor.[64] If he is correct, then why has the

Botswana state not developed as an *ethnic* state? Following from that question, why has the Botswana society not fractured along these lines into a divided society? How did competitive electoral politics survive and prosper without deepening the ethnic cleavages that appear to be the only discernible social cleavage represented by the party system? In the next chapter it is argued that the role of the state as an autonomous actor in Botswana politics must be taken into account in considering these questions.

A sixth and final feature of electoral politics is the number of rules that shape elections. A number of analysts have pointed to the restrictive rules covering elections as well as the rules that shape participation in the modern representative institutions. What has yet to be shown is that these rules have a direct bearing on the type of regime and therefore on the character of the state. The impact of these rules on both state and regime and also on the quality of democratic politics in Botswana is elaborated on in the next chapter.

The development priorities of the postindependence leadership were formulated early on, under the presidency of Sir Seretse Khama, and have been upheld consistently by his successor, President Masire. This set of priorities has been described as an explicit commitment to rapid economic growth through rational policies that combine formal legal procedures with a utilitarian calculation of means with ends.[65] The bureaucratic dominance of the colonial administration in the preindependence era and the deliberate choices of Sir Seretse Khama in establishing an ideological rationale for political rule reinforced one another in the immediate postindependence period. The priorities of growth (before redistribution) and stability (before participation) became part of what Morrison has called the "general logic" of state building that guided the governing elite.[66] These technocratic priorities gave a consistent direction not only to day-to-day public policymaking but also to the process of state building and hence to the arena in which democratic party politics was being conducted.

Society and Economy

The construction of a modern state and the conduct of democratic politics in Botswana were achieved in a society undergoing rapid modernization. The scope and range of this process of modernization can be gauged from the rapid and large-scale changes in the population and economy of independent Botswana.

Census data reveal the population more than doubled from 1971 (574,094) to 1991 (1,325,000).[67] The annual population growth rate for 1990 stood at 3.4 percent.[68] This rapid growth rate corresponded with a shift in the distribution patterns of the population. A concentration of numbers along the eastern borders and a rapid move toward urban areas (mostly along the eastern side of the country) have become striking trends. By the mid-1980s nearly 80 percent of the population were located within the 80-mile eastern strip of the country.[69] During the 1970s Botswana was already registering the highest rate of urbanization of all sub-Saharan African countries.[70] This is reflected in the changing ratio between the urban and rural populations. The urban component of the population stood at 17.7 percent in 1981, rose to 24 percent by 1989, and was expected to increase to 25.3 percent by 1991.[71] The growth of the country's capital, Gaborone, epitomizes this trend. The new capital (established in 1966) was planned to house a population of 20,000 by 1990. In 1971 it had already grown to 18,700; in 1991 the population was 134,000. This growth, in some years as much as 24 percent, ranks among the highest in Africa.[72]

The economic development of Botswana since independence has been little less than spectacular. From 1965 to 1980, GDP rose by an annual rate of 13.9 percent; from 1980 to 1990, 11.3 percent.[73] In 1987 alone, GDP grew by a staggering 14.7 percent.[74] When the years 1965–85 are taken as a benchmark, Botswana achieved the highest growth rate in the world.[75] Much of this growth has been led by development in mining and related industry. The industrial sector grew at an annual rate of 24 percent between 1965 and 1980 and maintained an annual rate of growth of 13 percent for the next 10 years.[76] The result was a drastic change in the structure of the country's economy. The contribution of agriculture, which was 40 percent of GDP at independence, declined to 3 percent by 1988–89, while that of mining rose from 0 to 51 percent in the same period. Similar change occurred in the composition of the country's exports. Income from beef exports declined from 90 percent of export earnings in 1966 to 4.2 percent in 1990. The income from diamond exports rose from 0 to 77 percent in the same period, with mineral exports as a whole comprising 88 percent of export earnings for 1990. The diamond boom was created with the opening of the mine at Orapa in 1971, followed by the Letlhakane mine in 1977 and the mine at Jwaneng in 1982. Other crucial industrial developments were the establishment of the copper-nickel matte plant at Selebi-Pikwe in 1974, the coal mine at Moropule in 1986, and the soda ash plant at Sua Pan in 1991.[77]

One of the persistent structural features of the Botswana economy has been its inability to provide formal employment to the full complement of the domestic labor force. The postindependence economic boom did employ more people, but it did not eradicate the problems of unemployment. Although the rate of economic growth exceeded the rate of population growth during most of the independence era, enough jobs were not created in the formal sector to fully absorb the new entrants into the labor force. The size of the formal sector increased from 24,750 in 1968, to 62,000 by 1977, and to 168,200 by 1988, averaging an annual rate of growth of more than 10 percent in those last 10 years.[78] Still the rate of entry into the labor market was not matched.[79] The trend of declining opportunities for employment across international boundaries must be factored in as well, especially in South Africa. From a peak of nearly 70,000 in the mid-1970s, this category of employment decreased, partly as a result of deliberate policy measures by the South African government, to 18,800 by 1983.[80] In all, the economy has been unable to do away with large-scale unemployment, which stood at about 25 percent by mid-1989 and was expected to increase to 35 percent in 1991.[81]

Unemployment has exacerbated another of the prominent features of the Botswana economy: marked inequality. The origins of the economic inequalities in the country can be traced to the cattle economy, which existed in precolonial times. Within the Tswana chieftaincies, land was held by the chief for the tribe's use and allocated by him to specific individuals for their own private use. It was a communal system only in the sense that individuals did not acquire ownership of the land as a resalable commodity. Land remained a communal property, through the chief. Communal use through the pooling of resources and produce, in a way that would appeal to the socialist ideal, was not the general practice.[82] Land was held communally, cattle privately. Through the system of *mafisa*, cattle could also be loaned to less wealthy individuals.[83]

The system of individual ownership of cattle herds with equal access to grazing rights on communally owned lands yielded equitable results and was ecologically sustainable only as long as the frontier was moving. Once land became scarce, inequalities rapidly developed. Owners of large herds tended to have a better chance of surviving droughts and cattle diseases, both of which are perennial scourges of Botswana's cattle economy. This structural tendency to inequality was rapidly reinforced during colonial times by the effects of de facto ownership of boreholes and surrounding land, which again favored the wealthier cattle ranchers.[84] Colonial policies that took away the chiefs' authority for allocating land set the stage for the commercialization of grazing land soon after independence, most notably through measures such as the Tribal Grazing Land Policy, which favored the more prosperous cattle owners at the expense of those with small herds.[85] As a consequence, poverty as a function of a maldistribution of assets rather than of income rapidly emerged.[86]

Moreover, the impact of cattle ownership on other sectors of the economy has been cumulative, negatively affecting those without cattle: "They have lower arable production because of reduced access to draught power; suffer from absolute labour shortages because of the link between a male head of household and cattle ownership; suffer from greater poverty because cattle are an important source of income; have little access to rural credit because cattle or other fixed assets are required for security; are more vulnerable in times of drought because cattle and small stock represent a reserve of food and wealth; have not benefitted from agricultural extension which has been usually directed towards cattle owners."[87] Data on the productive yield of arable land in 1972 confirm this pattern. Twenty percent of the farmers produced 60 percent of the crops, and the less productive half of the farmers produced only 10 percent. This productive variance has been found to correlate strongly with cattle ownership. The overall distribution of household incomes in 1974–75 in the rural areas shows similar results. Only 12 percent of the income went to the poorest 40 percent of the households, while the most affluent 20 percent received 58 percent of the income. These data also correlate strongly with cattle ownership. The inequality of cattle ownership at various times in the history of independent Botswana has been reported by many analysts. The official rural income distribution survey of 1974–75, cited by many, shows that 45 percent of all rural households owned no cattle. Another 40 percent of these households owned 25 percent of the national herd, and the remaining 15 percent owned 75 percent. Within this last category the wealthiest third (that is, the top 5 percent) owned 50 percent of the cattle.[88] This distribution was even more skewed than that reported in the 1968–69 official agricultural survey, and it supports the contention that this inequality is increasing.[89]

The rapid development of a modern mining, industrial, manufacturing, and commercial sector in the largely urban areas of the country along capitalist lines had, by the mid-1980s, added a rural-urban dimension to the distribution of poverty in Botswana.[90] The overall dimensions of inequality in the economy have been expressed in various ways. Research that cites the 1985–86 official household income and expenditure survey reveals that the poorest 40 percent of households received 10.7 percent of the income and the top 20 percent, 61.5 percent of the income. This inequality of income distribution is expressed in a Gini coefficient of 0.556.[91] World Bank statistics confirm this distribution.[92] According to one analyst, this level of inequality is exceeded only by Brazil.[93]

Viewed from this angle, the question can again be put, Why and how did competitive electoral politics survive amid growing inequalities of the scale described above? Part of the answer, as is argued in the next chapter, lies in the way the state went about using the greatly increased revenues generated by this growth economy. That economic growth did affect the population at large favorably, despite the huge socioeconomic inequalities, can easily be seen from some social indicators. By 1989, infant mortality had declined to a rate of 39 per 1,000 live births (versus 112 in 1965). Life expectancy for women had risen to 69 (from 49 in 1965) and for men, to 65 (from 46). By 1984 there was one physician for every 6,900 persons (versus one for every 27,450 in 1965), and primary school enrollment had risen to 97 percent by 1988. Secondary school enrollment, which was only at 3 percent in 1965, had also gone up to 33 percent by 1988.[94] The role of the state in managing this process of socioeconomic change, and the way in which the relevant policy measures were formulated and implemented, contributed not only to these rapid changes in living conditions but, so it will be argued, to the strength of the state and to democratic stability as well.

The final crucial feature of the political economy that emerged in Botswana is the coalition of interests that has shaped the state-building process of the country since preindependence years. This coalition was forged through the initiative of Sir Seretse Khama and the so-called new men assembled by him in the BDP. At first the "new men" consisted of the Tswana elite in the BDP and crucial sectors of the colonial bureaucracy. Khama then extended the coalition to include the mostly white elite of the commercial cattle economy. After independence the new set of elected representatives and appointed officials who came to occupy the national- and district-level institutions were drawn in, and later, the upper levels of the rapidly expanding civil service as well. As capitalist industrial development took off, the private-sector industrial and commercial elites also moved closer to the coalition. The coalition, comprising those at the apex of the regime, state, and commercial economic sectors, was from the outset very small. The new men numbered no more than 100; during the mid-1950s the European freehold ranches numbered fewer than 250, of which only 30 ranchers were considered economically influential.[95] The independence constitution created a new political elite of no more than 250. The largest segment of this coalition was located in the public service, which by the early 1980s already numbered 18,000. The middle-class income positions in the public service of that time even outnumbered those in the private sector, which registered only about 6,000 such positions.[96] In terms of numbers, then, this coalition was from very early on dominated by public servants. It was in this coalition that the state builders were located and crucial decisions were made in shaping the state and society of Botswana. The interests, norms, and concerns shared by this coalition, the context within which they had to confront difficult choices, and the way they responded to incentives and threats, opportunities and constraints, have been crucial to the direction of state building and also to democratic politics in Botswana.

❊ 2 ❊

THE DYNAMICS OF
STATE-SOCIETY INTERACTION

The absence of any significant challenge to the hegemony of the state in Botswana; the failure of deep fault lines to develop within society along class, regional, or ethnic lines; the maintenance of social order amid rapid socioeconomic modernization; and the consistently successful conduct of democratic politics were described in the previous chapter. Of these features, all of which require explanation, the democratic success of Botswana is the most intriguing. On a checklist of the typical preconditions considered to be causes of democratic success, Botswana falls short on a number of notable items.[1]

Cultural homogeneity cannot account for this success, for the marked linguistic predominance of Setswana reflects a potentially explosive condition—cultural dominance. Ethnic homogeneity is absent, even within the Tswana cultural group, where tribal affiliation is the strongest predictor of electoral choice. The strikingly successful two and a half decades of economic development cannot serve as a single-variable explanation either. The economic growth ought instead to predict greater instability, for it was accompanied by many of the disruptive forces characteristic of rapid modernization: rapidly increasing population growth and urbanization; increasing socioeconomic inequality in the rural sector, between the rural and urban sectors, and in society overall; and the inability of the

45

formal sector of the economy to absorb the new entrants into the labor market. The single outstanding potentially favorable aspect of economic growth is the large amounts of revenue generated for the incumbent governments of the day. The modernization of Botswana society has not yet resulted in the formation of a large, autonomous, indigenous bourgeoisie as a distinctive force for democratization. The critical mass of middle-class occupations still lie inside the state, not outside it.

The external environment presents a set of mixed variables, some favorable to democratic development, others less so. The British colonial experience has been depicted as one of benign neglect. That neglect in the development of institutions, infrastructure, and services did not present an attractive foundation for democratic politics at independence, nor did the economic underdevelopment that tied Botswana into a dependent and vulnerable relationship with the southern African regional economy. One aspect of the colonial period that could be considered favorable is that very few of the traditional institutions of the Tswana kingdoms were destroyed.

The cultural context of these kingdoms also constitutes a mixed set of variables. Samuel Huntington puts it that "a political culture that values highly hierarchical relationships and extreme deference to authority presumably is less fertile ground for democracy than one that does not." The institution of chiefly rule is such a culture. More conducive to sustaining democratic practice, argues Huntington, would be a "willingness to tolerate diversity and conflict among groups and to recognize the legitimacy of compromise."[2] These features are also represented within Tswana culture, in the lekgotla assemblies with their emphasis on consent, consensus, participation, and consultation.

An adequate account of the establishment and persistence of democratic politics in Botswana, so it will be argued, is to be found in the way rulers have, through deliberate policy choices, confronted these unfavorable conditions and responded to the constraints imposed by these conditions.

In line with the views of Louis A. Picard it will be argued that Botswana exhibits the characteristics of a strong state. And, following John Steven Morrison, it will be argued that the democratic success of Botswana can be accounted for by the distinctive process of state building through which it emerged.[3] In addition, the further argument will be that this process also largely protected the strength of the society. From the resulting state-society interactions that emerged through this process, the conditions in which democracy could prosper were created.

The main themes of this chapter are as follows: First, a strong enough state was established in Botswana so that it could preclude political participation and contestation from emerging in arenas beyond the state. Effective state building foreclosed any contest for hegemony (such as secessionist policies or insurrection by disaffected chiefs such as Bathoen II and Linchwe II) from emerging immediately after independence. The only avenues open for them (and others) to express their dissent was through the party political channels, as specified by the constitution. Second, electoral politics within the constitutional framework is not about very high stakes. The stakes are lowered because the bureaucracy acts as an autonomous interest group, which wields considerable influence on policy outcomes, insulated even from parliament. The ruling party can at best, therefore, establish a working coalition with the bureaucrats. The party that wins the election cannot capture the state in any realistic sense. In electoral politics the state is not at stake. Third, the autonomous bureaucracy, in coalition with the ruling Botswana Democratic Party (BDP), has succeeded, through its technocratic priorities of growth and stability (at the expense of participation and equity), in establishing a solvent state that can deliver public goods (roads, schools, watering facilities, clinics, etc.) on a nontribal, nonregional basis, ensuring that the minimum requirements of jointness of supply and nonexcludability are met. Consequently, the state is seen as neutral, not as an ethnic body, and the legitimacy of the state, the regime, the constitution, and the parliamentary system is enhanced with the incumbent parties. Fourth, the strong society ensures maintenance of civil order and restraint, which inhibits social and political mobilization and lowers the range, intensity, and scale of demands on the political establishment. The democratic political system can therefore function within tolerable bounds of strain. The strong society also ensures that important rules of social control such as respect for open discussion are upheld. At the grassroots level, these norms help to nurture tolerance, which is crucially important to the continued practice of competitive party politics.

THE STRONG STATE

Weak states are prone to fail in asserting social control, or "getting people to behave differently from what they would otherwise do."[4] The most immediate requirement of state social control is enforcing the laws enacted by successive governments. Evidence of pervasive lawlessness in Botswana is hard to find.[5] The country is not notorious for its crime rate and is not considered a haven for lawbreakers, neither organized nor unorganized.

A second-order level of resistance to state social control is deliberate challenges to the state's legal authority. Organized civil disobedience and organized tax revolts indicate more than a lack of individual discipline; they signal a challenge to the state to exercise the authority it claims for itself. Neither of these phenomena is characteristic of Botswana politics.

A third type of transgression is the sort committed within the state by its own personnel; corruption of public servants or elected politicians or both is an obvious subcategory. A few notable examples stand out in the postindependence era of Botswana politics. Allegations of electoral fraud by the losing parties against the BDP have been a regular feature of many elections. In the late 1970s, even Dr. K. J. Masire, then vice president, was implicated in accusations of nepotism. An official inquiry into the matter was taken to cabinet, but no actions were taken. One evaluation of the incident concludes that "the fact that the government both examined the situation and debated it gives evidence of the extent to which violations of the law by high political officials are taken seriously."[6] When a 1992 presidential commission of inquiry into suspect land deals revealed illegal practices by the then vice president and the minister of agriculture, both resigned pending further legal action.[7]

Another subcategory of illegal actions by government officials would be the creation of power centers or triangles of accommodation (community-based protection rackets) within the public service bureaucracies. True, there is constant rivalry between civil service departments for influence in Botswana's policymaking process, but the purpose is to gain influence *within* the state, not *against* the state.[8] Potential triangles of accommodation could have coalesced around the chiefs, but, as will be argued shortly, such a coalescence has been effectively precluded. Other potential sites for the emergence of strongmen (individuals who control such illegal protection rackets) are the rapidly growing urban centers, especially the capital, Gaborone. Yet, no evidence of the emergence of such power structures can be found.[9] The last subcategory of illegal actions by the personnel of the state is dirty tricks by the security forces. The typical actions reported by Migdal, such as death squads, assassinations, illegal imprisonment, and deportation of political opponents, have been wholly absent from the political history of Botswana. Instead, it has an excellent record of upholding human rights.[10]

The fourth and last type of illegality that marks the weak state is the appearance and persistence of a parallel economy outside the formal control of the state. These economic enterprises typically try to evade domestic state controls such as taxation and licensing requirements; in importing and exporting, they try to circumvent the customs, excise, and passport requirements states typically use as control measures on their borders. Operations beyond the boundaries of legality, such as black marketeering, extortion, and embezzlement, define this economic sector. The many Batswana who have failed to find permanent employment in the formal sector of the economy have tried to survive in the rural, agricultural, subsistence economy of crops and cattle—a largely informal economy in the sense that the state does not maintain extensive legal surveillance of it. However, it is not a parallel economy in the sense that there is a concerted attempt to evade what control measures the state does use or that its viability derives from its very illegality.

Illegal conduct is the narrow gauge of state strength and weakness; the larger measure is the extent to which state hegemony has been asserted, challenged, and upheld. A remarkable feature of Botswana's political history has been that hegemonic challenges to the state have been precluded, despite the numerous opportunities various actors have had. Potential challengers were the dissident chiefs, who disputed the new political status they were being assigned in the colonial and immediate postindependence eras. Their dispute was fundamental and had constitutional substance. It could easily have escalated into contests over the nature of statehood, peoplehood, and the appropriate unit for democracy. The fact that it did not is a measure of the strength of the then emergent state.

The first significant challenge developed from the Native Administration Proclamation (which formalized the political subordination of the chiefs to their respective resident district commissioners) and the Native Tribunals Proclamation (which delimited the operating procedures for the customary courts), both of 1934. Chiefs Bathoen II and Tshekedi Khama challenged the validity of these proclamations in the High Court in 1935, raising two issues of principle. The first was whether the colonial authorities had the right to prescribe on matters already covered by customary law and tradition. The second issue, the far more fundamental one, was whether these proclamations were compatible with the rights of the Ngwato and Ngwaketse who signed the original treaties of protection as kingdoms, that is, as the equivalent of *sovereign peoples*. The chiefs put it that the appropriate political relationship was "between the roles of an ambassador (the district commissioner) and head of state (the chief)."[11] Such argumentation immediately invoked questions of peoplehood and statehood, with potential ramifications for international relations (between the metropolitan power and the protectorate) and also for domestic relations (among the Tswana chieftaincies as sovereign peoples, each entitled to claim and exercise the right to statehood). The High Court ruled against the chiefs, however, and asserted that ultimate authority rested with the colonial authority.

Tshekedi Khama's political career then became embroiled in the so-called Sir Seretse Affair, from which he emerged in 1956 stripped of any claims to chieftainship. In the next year the Local Councils Proclamation followed, which provided for tribal councils at district level to assist the chief. Tshekedi Khama then took up the position as first secretary of the Bamangwato tribal council. "From that point on Tshekedi was eager to strengthen the administrative and political capability of the tribal council, which he may have viewed as a base from which to assume territorial political office as constitutional developments occurred."[12] This was a decisive victory for the incipient state. Tshekedi Khama's death in 1959 notwithstanding, a crucial momentum in favor of new institutions had been generated. As Picard notes, "his change of position on the issue of councils ended effective resistance to local government reform and paved the way for more substantive reforms during the 1960s."[13]

Chief Bathoen II initially acquiesced and even supported the BDP in the 1965 elections; but soon after independence he grew more dissatisfied with the way BDP policies were treating the chiefs. Mounting tension between himself and the resident district commissioner was engineered into a confrontation that led to his resignation as chief of the Bangwaketse. Apparently it was hoped that he would then take early retirement from public life. Instead, he joined the Botswana National Front (BNF) and contested the 1969 elections, promptly winning the seat from the vice president, Dr. K. Masire of the BDP. The BNF also took the other two Ngwaketse seats and won the majority in the district council of Southern District. This turn of events has been widely interpreted as a defeat for the BDP, or at least a setback, which it surely was. What has been less appreciated is that it also signaled an important victory for the state. Like his ally, Tshekedi Khama, Bathoen II had in 1935 registered his opposition by implicitly disputing the state's interpretation of the nature of statehood and peoplehood and the appropriate unit for democracy; by 1969 he was registering opposition by contesting elections within the constitutional rules set by the state he had disputed so fundamentally in 1935. Opposition to the founding principles of the polity was converted into opposition within the rules of the game set by that polity.

At the other side of the spectrum stood Chief Linchwe II of the Bakgatla. With his apparent sympathies toward socialism, he was the only chief who did not support the BDP in the 1965 election. The immediate electoral opposition then was the Botswana People's Party (BPP), which in the early 1960s was offering a radical socialist program. Although remaining nominally neutral, he was reported to have given tacit support to the BPP candidate in Mochudi, who went on to win the seat. In 1968, a year before the next elections, the position of ambassador to the United States became vacant. It was offered to Linchwe, and he accepted, thus removing himself from domestic politics until the end of 1972.[14] Again the state was the winner, having outbid the BPP in offering the more attractive career avenue.

The last important early event with potential hegemonic implications was created by the opposition in North-East District. Most people in that district are of the Kalanga-speaking group, who are more closely related to the Ndebele of Zimbabwe than to any of the

Tswana tribes. In this district the practice of cultural domination is most obvious and explicit, for official policy dictates that the meetings of the district council be conducted in English or Setswana, not in Kalanga, the indigenous language spoken by most of the district's councilors.[15] This policy clearly broadcasts who owns the country, and any political entrepreneur intent on mobilizing an ethnic constituency could interpret this language policy as provocative and offensive. As might be expected, both the BPP and the BNF found strong support in the district, with the BPP capturing the majority of elected seats in the district council elections of 1966. A major opposition figure was Daniel Kwele, national president of the BNF, who spoke Kalanga and was from the district. Kwele was neutralized politically in 1969 when the government offered him the post of secretary of the North-East District Council. Kwele obliged by accepting the appointment, which he held until 1978. Co-optation by the state was taken even further when Kwele was appointed a special member of parliament and later became an assistant minister. (After being dropped from the cabinet, he resigned in 1983 to form his own party, showing the limits of co-optation.)[16]

These victories for the state, produced by effective co-optive measures and the ascendancy of the political party system, consolidated the strength of the state in the early years of independence. A measure of that strength is that none of these challenges developed into an attempt to balkanize the state or assert hegemonic agendas in party politics. The potential for balkanization through secessionist movements in those years was noted by a number of analysts. Separatist preferences were noted at times among the Kalanga speakers of North-East District and among the white settlers in the Tuli, Tati, Ghanzi, and Lobatse cattle-farming blocks.[17] The institutions that were at the disposal of potential secessionists must also be noted. The district boundaries, coinciding largely with the Tswana chieftaincies, were already in place by 1899. All subsequent local government institutions were built on these demarcations. The electoral districts also followed the tribal boundaries (see chapter 1), and the final layer of institutional reinforcement available to a would-be ethnoregional breakaway movement was the presence of a dual police force. In 1885 the Bechuanaland Border Police was formed, followed by the

Protectorate Police Force in 1895. The two forces were unified in the Bechuanaland Police Force in 1902, but a dual system was again set up with the Tribal Police Force after World War II. The explicit task of this force (renamed Local Police in 1972) was to assist the chief in executing his duties.[18]

Despite all these incentives for the secession-minded, no secession occurred. Tshekedi Khama and Chief Linchwe II, as well as Kalanga kingpin Daniel Kwele, were co-opted directly into the state, and the big commercial cattle farmers were later drawn subtly into a dependent relationship with the state and other commercial enterprises.[19] Even the group considered potentially the most recalcitrant, the economically backward Afrikaners in Ghanzi, were quick to accept the ascendancy of the new state: "They apply for citizenship, register as voters, and pin posters of Seretse Khama on their walls."[20]

The way in which challenges to the new Botswana state that were launched through party-political channels dissipated is another measure of the strength of the state. The BPP (formed in 1960) had its roots in the South African politics of that time. Shortly after the Sharpeville tragedy and the banning of the South African Pan Africanist Congress (PAC) and the African National Congress (ANC), some former members returned to Bechuanaland. Two of the founder-leaders of the BPP, P. G. Matante and M. Mpho, were members of the PAC and the ANC, respectively. Much of the initial ideological substance of the BPP policies was therefore carried over from the South African and wider African context. The BPP has been described as "the first political party to bring into the territory [the] 'radical' nationalism and national consciousness that was sweeping across the continent of Africa." The political views of the eventual sole leader of the BPP, Mr. Matante, were described as being, initially at least, "those of a militant pan-Africanist—beliefs which were based on the belief that Africa belongs to Africans alone and whites have no decisive role to play in the political arrangements that were taking place in Africa." The other major electoral opposition to the BDP has been the BNF, which was established in 1966. At the time, the rationale for forming the BNF was, according to one analyst, "to oppose the BDP which was seen as neocolonialist and reactionary by the founders of the BNF. They believed that a pro-socialist government was

essential for Botswana; hence the adoption of socialism as the ideology of the BNF."[21]

Chief Linchwe II leaned to the BPP, and Chief Bathoen II joined
the BNF. Had their political ambitions dovetailed with parties that
were consistently and strenuously pursuing Pan-Africanist or
socialist agendas, then disputes about the defining qualities of the
Botswana state and democracy would probably have become the
dominant cleavages in the electoral arena. Yet, contemporary party
politics in Botswana is marked by an absence of ideological differences (see chapter 1). The nature of statehood, peoplehood, and
democracy is not hotly contested. Parties do not differ radically on
policy. Instead, they argue on the instrumentalities of achieving
largely agreed-on objectives. The basic defining features of state
and society have been accepted and internalized within the parameters of daily political conduct. The embryonic ideological divide
that set up the BNF and the BPP against the BDP dissolved in favor
of the technocratic priorities of the BDP and the state.

The strong state the BDP succeeded in constructing has thus far
complied with a number of the criteria for an autonomous state
and has tended not to show the features typical of an ethnic state.
The autonomy of the state can be gauged from two sets of public
policy measures: the distribution of public goods (notably through
policies concerned with physical rural infrastructure, housing,
schools, health and welfare, and drought relief measures) and the
symbolic trappings of the state (e.g., language policy).

In distributing public goods an autonomous state meets two criteria, nonexcludability and jointness of supply. Because the BDP
rulers inherited a country whose most striking measure of underdevelopment was its absence of physical and social infrastructure,
their ability to provide public goods according to the two criteria
was tested in a context of pervasive scarcity and immense back-
logs. What is instructive about their approach to this policy problem is that they converted benign neglect into a strategic advantage
instead of succumbing to it as an insurmountable and perpetually
crippling inheritance.

The first major policy measure to address the backlog in rural
infrastructure was the Accelerated Rural Development Plan, which
was announced in 1973 and ran through the end of the 1975–76
financial year. The targeted sectors of expenditure were rural and

village roads, primary schools, village water supplies, rural health posts and clinics, and rural administrative buildings.[22] According to one report the plan was implemented with meticulous precision and delivered an equitable result: "All twenty-seven of the larger villages and 195 of the smaller ones benefitted. Each region obtained a share of construction approximately proportionate to its population."[23] The plan also yielded a favorable election result. In the 1974 elections the BDP regained the ground it had lost to opposition parties in 1969. It won back three seats in the National Assembly and raised its overall percentage of the vote from 69.6 percent to 77.7 percent. In the district council elections it captured 149 of the seats (versus 113 in 1969), an increase of 31.8 percent.[24]

Other government expenditures on infrastructure also increased. During the first six years after independence, for example, expenditure on the communications network remained at about 16 percent of the capital budget. Then it rose sharply, and by 1976–77 it stood at 40 percent.[25] The resulting change has been dramatic and highly visible. The infamously short 25-kilometer strip of tarred road in 1966 was extended to 2,000 kilometers by 1992. By 1987 there were 12,511 telephones installed, as opposed to the mere 2,096 in 1966.[26]

A similar pattern emerged in the area of urban development. Given its political priority of rural development, the government tried to provide urban services on a cost-covering basis instead of subsidizing urban dwellers. The three primary parastatals established in 1971 to administer urban development were the Botswana Housing Corporation, the Botswana Power Corporation, and the Water Utilities Corporation. These institutions managed to provide an urban infrastructure for the upper- and middle-income groups of the urban populations, but not for the poor.[27] A rapid policy evolution toward "self-help" site-and-service housing schemes by and for the urban poor followed. The policy was initiated with the 1977 Botswana Development Plan and then by the 1987 Self-Help Housing Agency and was deployed with a large measure of success, especially with the upgrading of the Old Naledi shantytown in Gaborone.[28]

The investment in education (which led to a doubling of primary school enrollments in the first decade of independence and a sevenfold increase in secondary school enrollments) and health care (by 1975, 80 percent of the population lived within 10 miles of a health facility of some kind) are further evidence of an equitable provision of infrastructure and services.

Arguably the most outstanding achievement in the provision of public goods, however, has been the program of drought relief, crucial to a country so vulnerable to fluctuating weather patterns.[29] The drought relief program launched by the state was contained in the 1985 National Food Strategy, the planning of which started in 1983. This plan provides for the Botswana Drought Early Warning System as well as the Post-Drought Recovery Program (PDRP). The impact of these programs has been remarkable. The feeding program has reached 90 percent of the rural families—nearly 600,000 people, or 60 percent of the total population. The cash-for-work schemes employed about 60,000 people and generated income equivalent to 35 percent of the estimated crop loss from drought. Free seed packages reached almost all of the country's 70,000 crop farmers, and subsidies covered up to 85 percent of their costs for plowing and planting.[30]

An evaluation of the significance of the drought relief program has emphasized the program's differential merits over the short and long terms. The PDRP, it concludes, "is likely to lead to a more equitable distribution of immediate incomes and public sector benefits among rural dwellers, but may do little to address the underlying inadequacies of access to productive assets faced by most small farmers, and, more generally, the fragile basis of rural production systems in the context of long term social and ecological change."[31] The policy therefore alleviates the problem without transforming it. When drought hits, the PDRP provides a safety net for the rural poor who fall; it does not prevent them from falling. The larger, long-term problem of inequality under conditions of ecological constraints and the implications it holds for the sustainability of democracy are addressed later in the chapter. What is important here is that the safety net is spread widely and equitably. The PDRP, like the Accelerated Rural Development Plan, has had an electoral benefit for the ruling BDP, enabling it to retain its dominance in the 1984 elections.[32]

A second measure of autonomy is found in the symbolic goods of the state. English is designated the *official* language and

Setswana the *national* language. The name of the country, as well as the choice of national language, reflects the dominance of the Tswana culture unequivocally. However, at independence the symbolic affirmation of "who owns the country" was remarkably muted and did not convey a strong cultural or ethnic message. The national stamp series that was issued to celebrate independence, for example, showed but four objects: the Botswana Meat Commission, the National Assembly, the State House, and Air Botswana.[33]

Accounting for the Strength of the State

Not all policies of the ruling BDP produced happy, equitable outcomes. Nor were they all intended to do so. Where the BDP sought equitable outcomes, such as with the Accelerated Rural Development Plan and the Post-Drought Recovery Program, it was able to secure them. Where its intention was to achieve other objectives, such as with the Tribal Grazing Land Policy (TGLP; see chapter 1), it formulated the policy so as to contain those objectives. (That the objectives of the TGLP were not achieved in full does indicate the limits of state strength and also reveals some of the strength of societally based groups who opposed this policy.)[34] What should be taken into further account is that a number of these policies, regardless of the equitability of their impact, have also resulted in the strengthening of the state. In this section the question of which policies strengthened the state and why, will be considered. Five sets of policy measures will be considered.

The first comprise the successful strategies of co-optation employed by the colonial authorities and later by the ruling BDP against early challengers such as Tshekedi Khama, Linchwe II, and Daniel Kwele. In all these cases, and somewhat subtly, a confluence of the career and personal interests of a member of a vital sector of society with that of the new Weberian bureaucratic state emerged. This is, according to Migdal, a key ingredient in effective state building. What is required is that "bureaucrats of the state . . . must identify their own interests with those of the state as an autonomous organization."[35] In the continental European context this shift occurred when the city burghers skilled in law and administration judged their own interests served better by the prince, representing an expanding state, than by the feudal structures. In

Tshekedi Khama's career shift, he pursued personal ambitions within the avenues offered by the state rather than avenues outside the state and against the state. This shift was soon to be emulated with immensely greater rewards by Sir Seretse and his hundred or so "new men," thus accelerating the state-building process in Botswana. As the new head of state, Sir Seretse ably deployed the same strategy later in co-opting Linchwe II and Daniel Kwele, again with results that strengthened the state.

Second, the strength of the state as an organization that can effectively assert itself through superior methods of social control is closely tied to the character of the public service. Three characteristics of the Botswana public service explain the strength and autonomy of the state: its composition, the socialization policies it is subject to, and the value orientation of some of its crucial personnel. In comparative African terms, an outstanding feature of the Botswana public service is the gradual way in which the colonial inheritance of a white, expatriate work force has been replaced by indigenes. In an accurate reflection of the technocratic priorities of the new rulers, President Khama declared in 1967, "We would never sacrifice efficiency on the altar of localization."[36] Subsequent policy has borne this out, and by the late 1980s the continued presence of large numbers of expatriates led to the conclusion that "political elites in Botswana have continued to place localization second to economic expansion and development."[37]

Given the numbers and placement of these expatriates (see chapter 1), their approach to dealing with issues of equity in the distribution of public goods would have been influential at any stage in independent Botswana's history. Detailed research into the policymaking process that produced the TGLP has revealed that concern with matters of equity is indeed more pronounced in the ranks of expatriate civil servants than among others. However, this analysis also shows the limits of the expatriates' influence: in this particular case they were able to shift the direction of the policy only up to a certain point. Beyond that point the core values and interests of the critical mass of the policymaking elite held sway. The elite acted as an autonomous interest group and were not moved by outside expert advice or by inside loyal opposition.[38] The more general finding is that the role of expatriates as upholders of the technical (and technocratic) standards of efficiency and effectiveness and also of social justice has been both consistent and influential.[39] Both these attributes contribute to the functioning of the civil service as an effective and autonomous corporate group insulated, but not necessarily isolated, from society.

The capacity of these expatriates to act as the equivalent of moral watchdogs in the public service can be explained by their structural position. As expatriates, they are foreigners, not Batswana. As temporary, contract appointees (some contracts lasting only two or three years), they are transients. Both conditions produce the effect of *gelding* (that is, depriving a person of ancestry, posterity, or both): with no ancestral ties to the population, and a slender prospect of creating kinship links in their short stay, they are unlikely to be susceptible to any social ties that would sway their loyalty from their contracting party, the state.[40] Denied of both ancestry and the opportunity to establish posterity, they can make an undiluted commitment to the corporate integrity of the state. Even opposition to state policies is bound to be expressed as decidedly *loyal* opposition.

The autonomy of the public service has been further enhanced through deliberate policies of socialization. Specific policy measures have been introduced in the civil service to prevent ethnic loyalties from asserting themselves: "Staff are routinely rotated around the country without regard to ethnic identity. Promotions are not governed by concern for ethnic balance. To further combat parochialism, the Ministry of Education places better secondary students, most of whom will enter the civil service, at residential schools outside their home districts."[41] The combined effect of these measures is to create a corps of public servants who are both competent in a technical sense and legitimate in a political sense of being seen as fair, not as parochial, and without regional, cultural, or ethnic bias. These measures enhance the capacity for social control by the state in strengthening almost every dimension of its capabilities. Legitimacy adds to the capacity of the state to penetrate society and to regulate social behavior with the aim of extracting resources. Efficiency adds to the capacity of the state to extract resources and reappropriate them competently.

The third source of strength of the state is the legal system. The system of a dual but subordinate legal system, with the Roman-Dutch and English law as the dominant components and the customary law as the subordinate components, was formalized with the institution of indirect rule in 1934. By protecting the customary courts of the *lekgotla* assemblies after independence, the state effectively merged the established rules of social control with those of the modern constitutional system. This merging has had the effect of making traditional, established, indigenous survival strategies largely compatible and congruent with those prescribed by the modern legal state.[42] Moreover, it has been done in such a way that the powerholders in the established system, the chiefs, were weakened as political entities, the modern powerholders were strengthened, and the continuity of established practice was largely retained. The modern state was built not by destroying the preexisting system of social control, but by effectively taking it over and harnessing it to the overarching set of rules of the modern system. The *kgotla* system strengthens the modern system by adding to it the legitimacy of the traditional. Given the institutional reach and depth of these assemblies throughout the rural areas of Botswana,[43] the dovetailing of these legal structures with those of the modern constitution has added greatly to the ability of the modern state to penetrate society, regulate social behavior, and extract resources.

The fourth source of strength of the Botswana state is in the effects of its interventionist policies. In some cases these highly intrusive policies were built on traditionally established codes of behavior, thus ensuring some continuity with the preexisting system of social control. At the same time, the policies effected greater penetration by the state into society. The TGLP is a case in point. This policy, aimed at securing formal private ownership of grazing land, appears diametrically at odds with the customary practice of communal ownership of land. But "under Tswana customary law, open surface water was free to be used by anyone who wished. Where water was obtained through the expenditure of capital and labor, as in the case of dam construction and well-digging, people were able to keep that water for their own personal use. . . . Once . . . they had invested in the water source, they gained essentially private rights over the resource. By locating their cattle posts some distance away from those of other people, water source owners were able to gain *de facto* control over the grazing surrounding their wells."[44] This aspect of customary law provides a crucial link in making the traditional survival strategies compatible with those imposed by the modern state. The TGLP, which aimed at making land a commodity and commercializing property, turns this de facto practice into de jure state policy. Again the legitimacy of the practice sanctioned by customary law is carried over into the new set of rules.[45] In addition, the process is accompanied by, and requires legal entitlement through, officially registered title deeds or lease agreements, which are administered by the state.[46] Thus, quite apart from the commercial aims of the policy, greater penetration by the state, especially into rural society, is effected. Similar bureaucratic penetration has resulted from the implementation of the Accelerated Rural Development Plan and the Post-Drought Recovery Program. Even the self-help housing scheme in Old Naledi has its bureaucratic component: land tenure is regulated through the issuing of an official certificate of rights to every qualified plot occupant.[47]

A fifth and final source of strength for the state is found in certain regime rules. The constitution stipulates that no public servant, teacher in a state school, employee of a parastatal, or member of the House of Chiefs is eligible for election to the National Assembly.[48] Those persons are not even allowed to take leave of absence during election campaigns.[49] This rule has three significant effects. First, it reinforces the demarcation between state and regime. Personnel of the state who wish to seek elected positions within the regime are confronted with a clear-cut choice of career change. They have to resign their positions if they want to stand as candidates. This inhibiting factor serves to increase the autonomy of the state, because it adds to the insulation of the public service corps from party politics. Second, the rule reserves a substantial portion of the educated middle class for careers in the state and denies them careers in the regime. This reserved pool of expertise (one-third of the population employed in the formal sector work for the state)[50] again adds to the strength of the state. A third effect is to make co-optation by the state an effective strategy. When Daniel Kwele and Chief Linchwe II took up positions in the state, they *by law* forfeited all opportunities to engage in electoral politics as candidates. Apart from Chief Linchwe, who retains considerable influence in Mochudi,[51] one of the potentially most influential figures who could threaten the ruling BDP is Ian Khama, son of the late Sir Seretse. But "the government has Khama somewhat more effectively trapped than Linchwe in that he is a brigadier in the army."[52] The third effect of this rule that affects the strength of the state is the differential penalties it has on the political parties. The requiring of English fluency (speaking and reading) and monetary deposits by candidates and the prevailing bias against women taking leadership roles in politics shrinks the effective recruiting pool outside the civil service. It has been calculated that the recruiting pool may be as small as 2 percent of the voting-age population.[53] Political parties therefore have little choice but to seek new candidates from the ranks of the public service. Because the ruling BDP has the greater chance of success at the polls, its new candidates recruited from the public service face less risk than candidates of the opposition parties face. BDP candidates who lose can at least hope for another political appointment. This effect consolidates the coherence of the ruling coalition and adds new members who are already imbued with corporate loyalty to the state.

These rules that delimit the state from the regime and restrict access to political candidacy are part of a wider set of constitutional rules that restrict and inhibit patterns of contestation within the political arena of Botswana politics. Voter turnout is influenced by citizenship qualifications, the minimum-age requirement of 21 years, and registering procedures that stipulate that a new roll of voters be drawn up for every election; in addition, there is no absentee voting. The electoral outcome is influenced by the effects of the first-past-the-post electoral system within single-member districts and the malapportioning of these districts.[54] It has also been claimed that freedom of assembly and association has become unduly restricted by laws such as the Trade Unions and Employer's Organizations Act and the National Security Act. Finally, the Botswana Police monitor the urban meetings of political parties, apparently giving special care to the behavior of the opposition parties.[55] The overall effect of these measures is to restrict the level of contestation in Botswana. Unrestrained public contestation is limited to a small sector of the society, those with the highest education and with private-sector employment. The state is strengthened because the ruling coalition is the base of recruitment. Like-minded individuals are more apt to be recruited from this base than from a society-wide base. The state is also strengthened by shielding the ruling coalition from the greater public demands that a system of unrestrained contestation would generate. The capacity for state social control is enhanced through the elite's greater coherence and the state's insulation from societal demands.

If the strength of the state in Botswana is the result of these deliberate policy choices, why did the state builders make these choices and not others? Why the apparent coherence in the direction of policy choice, and why the consistency in the substance of policy content? J. Stephen Morrison has put a persuasive case that the answer is to be found in the *ethos of state action* that guides elite actions in the making of public policy. This ethos was established in the late colonial and early independence era through the formal and informal negotiations that resulted in the creation of the Botswana Meat Commission (BMC). Because cattle were the emergent state's primary industry and no other state, regime, or parastatal institutions had been established yet, this bargaining process produced the "essential formatting" for subsequent state-building enterprises as well.[56] The three early sets of protagonists were the officials of the Commonwealth Development Corporation (CDC); the colonial authorities and the emergent nationalist leaders (represented by Sir Peter Fawcus and Sir Seretse Khama respectively); and the biracial elite private cattle ranchers. The three groups approximated the later trilateral coalition of interests that buttress the current ruling coalition: foreign and donor capital, the state, and the private economic sector.

Early negotiations to establish a viable cattle economy took place in a context of scarcity, crisis, fear, and threat. *Scarcity* was felt in the absolute poverty that made the country the third poorest in the world at that time. The *crisis* for the cattle industry lay in the loss of regional markets (South Africa and Southern Rhodesia in 1956), recurrent outbreaks of foot-and-mouth disease from 1957 through 1965, and drought. The *fear* was fear of racial conflict given the presence of influential white racist farmers in the Tuli, Tati, and Ghanzi blocks, with separatist ambitions. The immediate *threat* to a commercially viable cattle industry was the BPP with its radical socialist objectives. Acute awareness of these forces generated the self-negating prediction that "recognition by elite categories, white and black alike, of their respective need for one another (and the CDC) [was necessary] if they were to avoid what each individually imagined as a catastrophic alternative."[57]

What enabled all parties to convert this shared perception into a mutually profitable bargain was the astute leadership of Fawcus and Khama and the overall condition of interdependence, described as mutual hostageship: "The interplay among the major actors ultimately yielded positive results because during the entire period their interests remained interlocked. . . . Each remained quite dependent upon the others, at the same time that each possessed resources permitting it to impose conditions upon its entry into the new institutionalized bargain. The result: the three became mutual hostages of one another."[58]

During the bargaining process Sir Seretse employed a number of notable tactics, each with success. One was to make room for face saving by the CDC officials, who had to concede to the nationalization of the industry. He did so by inviting Cater, the CDC executive officer, to become the first chairman of the BMC. He secured the collective esteem of the nationalists in the BDP by insisting that the BMC become a nationalized, monopolistic parastatal, symbolically indicative of a new era with new owners of the country. And he used one of the paradoxes of power that derive from interdependence—that power is based on giving. The Botswana Meat Commission Act officially declared the industry under the control of a parastatal, but it also ensured that the BMC would be run on commercial principles. It secured state sponsorship for the infrastructure (roads, abattoirs, veterinary services, etc.) needed to make cattle farming profitable. Later it secured access to European markets and, through the TGLP, the potential for more privately owned ranching land. In the longer term, these concessions to private elites only bound them closer to the state as the state became the crucial party in ensuring their commercial viability. This dependence became a source of strength for the new state.

The immediate outcome was the establishment of the BMC, nationalized, yet running on commercial principles. Foreign and donor capital won by securing profitable conditions for investment. Private elites won by gaining sponsorship from the state to ensure the conditions to operate profitably. The state won by securing, in principle, recognition as the ascendant party in securing the deal: "Most significant, the rule emerged that any resolution of the industry's difficulties was to be in *national* terms, brokered by state authorities."[59] A fusion of interests took place. State building and the promotion of a commercially viable cattle economy became inseparable. From this specific set of negotiations emerged the general ethos of state action: "The primacy of commercial criteria, the high value placed upon compromise, stability, security and the systematic accommodation of competing interests, and . . . durable patterns of elite interaction—linking bi-racial elite producers, state authorities and external interests."[60] What initially applied to the cattle sector became the norm for the whole modern economy: to avoid the-state-as-market. Instead of the cattle economy being plundered for private gain, it was deliberately nurtured, subsidized, and supported for profitable gain by individuals within the state who, along with private-sector elites, were entrepreneurs in their own right. A profitable private-sector economy yielded revenue for state building and profits for the elite in their capacity as commercial operators. A final component of this ethos was added in the early 1980s, when the self-financing rule for private and public enterprises was substantially modified, and it became accepted that the state had to finance a safety net for those who lost out in an economy running on technocratic priorities.[61]

The general logic of the state builders' ethos of state action went as follows: (1) They reached a consensus on the basis of shared commercial priorities. (2) They were aware of and appreciated the constraints inherent in pervasive conditions of scarcity and at the same time accepted the need for discipline and deferred gratification. (3) They made appropriate institutional arrangements to separate the private and public sectors and gave each sector adequate rules to enforce the discipline that is necessary when resources are limited. In addition (4), they realistically assessed regional and global forces and made an astute bargain between the constraints and the opportunities presented by those forces. Thus the state builders achieved effective results in the first 25 years of independence.

THE STRONG SOCIETY

Rampant crime, looting, civil violence, and social decay are not hallmarks of Botswana society. Evidence of these or any other indicators of a breakdown in social control are hard to find. The norms that regulate social behavior appear secure. Limited reports of abuses, such as youths ridiculing the elderly headmen who lead some of the informal customary courts, do indicate that norms are under strain, but they do not indicate collapse.[62] Given the social dislocation normally associated with rapid modernization and the speed with which Botswana has been modernizing since independence, more disruption and a concomitant loss of societal social control might be expected.

Instead, in the communities that experienced those disruptive forces most intensely, premodern social rules survived. Research shows that among first-generation migrants to Gaborone who occupied relatively affluent positions, many retained their rural links.[63] Similar findings apply to the poorest sector of the Gaborone population in Old Naledi.[64] One research report showed that an informal power structure in Old Naledi, reminiscent of the *kgotla* structures of the rural towns, also quickly emerged.[65] These findings point to the conclusion that the modernization process did subordinate the political institutions of the tribal Tswana kingdoms without destroying the kingdoms' social structure. Social control has been retained and is still being exercised through the traditional social institutions.

If the society is strong, then is it also undivided and civil? In considering the social divisions within society the debate on class versus ethnic affiliations is relevant. At issue is the social impact of the large socioeconomic inequalities in Botswana society. The relative and absolute differences between the rich and the poor, partly counterbalanced by the rising standards of living for all and the equitable distribution of public goods such as rural infrastructure and drought aid, have been described in some detail. In a sense, the question is whether the cup is half full or half empty.

Jack Parson has consistently taken the view that the cup is half empty; the social inequalities in the country are overwhelmingly significant because they reveal the basic structure of society. He argues that these inequalities in Botswana are due to a process of class formation and that the ameliorative impact of redistributive policies and trickle-down effects has not altered that structural division. Therefore, the importance of class formation and the primacy of Marxist class analysis are posited.[66] The primary classes in Botswana are identified as the "peasantariat" (created through "the transformation of a pre-capitalist tributary *peasant*ry into a colonial peripheral capitalist semi-prole*tariat*")[67] and the ruling class, consisting of the "agrarian petty-bourgeoisie" and the "educated bureaucratically based petty-bourgeois strata," who joined in forming the BDP.[68] Having argued that these are the primary social classes in Botswana (and they are undeniably visible as social categories), he is then led to the finding that the peasantariat has yet to *act* as a social class.[69] This behavior is explained largely by the effects of the redistributive policies of the ruling BDP and the persistence of "social ties" based on tribal and/or ethnic loyalty. Yet the general conclusion remains that overtly class-driven politics may assert itself in Botswana in the future, although the format of such actions is left unspecified.[70]

The view that the cup is half full instead of half empty is strongly presented by Morrison, who offers the "counterfactual proposition" that the truly significant fact about Botswana is the state's response to the social inequalities that emerged from capitalist modernization: "Were the Botswana state, however flawed, not as successful as it has been thus far—were an effective industry with access to lucrative external markets not created—I seriously doubt that ground level realities in Botswana, particularly in the countryside, would not be now far worse, in equity and other terms."[71] Public programs were executed that never challenged the status quo, but could "nonetheless assure water, education, drought relief and other developmental essences which most states in Africa, of whatever ideological hue and whatever avowed intentions, have simply failed to deliver."[72] This perspective denies the structural qualities that Parson assigns to the Botswana society and casts the state as an autonomous actor that, through deliberate policies, has thus far prevented class formation from becoming salient.

The other obvious contender for the status of primary social cleavage is ethnicity. Parson does note that electoral choices have been shaped by ethnic concerns,[73] but he considers the ethnic factor an intervening variable, temporarily weakening the ultimately more durable and determining causal link between class (independent variable) and electoral choice (dependent variable).[74] He advances the working hypothesis that the weakening of these social links will lead to a decline in support for the BDP; in his analysis of the 1989 elections he found initial evidence of such a decline, in the form of alienation and abstention from voting. John D. Holm takes ethnicity to be a fully independent variable in explaining electoral choice[75] but also records a peculiar form of "exit" from electoral politics into abstention among the socially mobilized population. The explanation for this exit is in the cutting of social links with the traditional rural-based political system and, by implication, with ethnic ties.[76]

Two questions remain. First, If ethnicity is a stronger predictor of political choice than class, why has ethnicity not turned Botswana into an ethnically divided society? The immediate answer is that the strength and autonomy of the state and its ability to deliver public goods on a nonethnic, nonregional basis, as well as other deliberate measures to depoliticize ethnicity, produced this result. Second, Why have the poor wage-earning and/or unemployed Batswana not yet acted as a self-conscious political entity, as a social class? In the absence of any other theoretically informed answer, the proposition will be put that it is so because Botswana remains a strong society. The established rules of social control that mitigate against individual Batswana seeing themselves as part of, and loyal to, a social class or ideological grouping, have not been destroyed or displaced through massive social dislocation. These rules still bind society into identities that do not assert the primacy of class or ideological affiliations. Where these norms do weaken, the response is only apathy or alienation, because no new competing survival strategies and rules of social control have taken hold and created new social and political solidarities. Parson's prediction might be realized if Botswana society were so weakened that the established rules of social control became inoperative without being replaced by similar, functionally equivalent ones. In such a society, political and social mobilization along class or ideological lines might well yield new social and political lines of division.

The continuity with traditional society not only contributed to the strength of contemporary Botswana society, but also serves in maintaining its civility. Civility in Botswana is not maintained through conventionally defined civil society, because the organizational embodiment of civil society—that is, substantial interest group diversity—is conspicuously absent. Only one daily newspaper (owned by the state) has persisted, along with about 10 periodicals and weeklies. Only one trade union federation and one employers' federation is listed.[77] Nor do these organizations vigorously resist domination by the state over society or protect the autonomy of society from increasing penetration by the state.[78] In a survey of interest group activity only three groups were found to maintain permanent offices, and only two consistently lobbied policymakers in pursuit of their own objectives.[79] When the interest groups do act, they tend to prefer approaching civil servants and bypassing elected representatives. And on the whole, interest group activity appears to have little impact on elected representatives, who prefer to make direct contact with the public through the *lekgotla* assemblies.[80]

Given the weak institutional presence of organized interest groups and their low impact on society, which agents uphold the norms of civility? Who civilizes society? The institution of the *kgotla*, both as a public assembly and a customary court, serves this function. Tswana customary law makes the practical distinction between criminal and civil law. The latter "establishes *inter alia* the private rights of people in regard to personal status, property, and contracts; and provides for redress, if such rights are violated, by compelling restitution or compensation." Criminal law "treats certain acts not merely as injuries to individual persons, but as offences harmful to social life generally, and therefore deserving of punishment."[81]

The 1934 proclamations that inaugurated indirect rule also compelled chiefs to record the cases brought before the customary courts. (In some communities, such as the Bangwaketse, recording of cases was common practice already.) On the basis of these records Isaac Schapera was able to analyze (in an article published in 1943) the balance of civil and criminal cases from a total of 1,591 cases. He found not only that civil issues predominated, but also that delicts (defamation, insult, assault, seduction, adultery, damage to property, theft, sorcery, and rape) outnumbered every other single category of issues, including penal offenses, contracts, property, and domestic and personal status. From the 1,866 issues involved in these cases (some cases dealt with more than one issue), no fewer than 726 dealt with delicts.[82] In a later study that deliberately replicated the study by Schapera and employed the same classificatory scheme for the analysis of issues, similar findings were made in the court records for the villages of Kuli (1946–67) and Kalkfontein (1962–66) in Ghanzi district. Private delicts, "the protection of person and property from attacks of one kind or another," accounted for nearly three-quarters of all issues.[83] And in yet a further survey (which used the records of all the customary courts for the country for 1961–70 and again closely followed the Schapera study) it was found that delicts were comprising 70 percent of the judicial load versus the 39 percent recorded by Schapera.[84] Delicts of this kind deal with the essence of civility as defined by Shils, that is, with "the moral dignity of others."

Over a number of decades, then, evidence shows that the *lekgotla* customary courts played a vital role in maintaining civil order. Herein lies a crucially significant dimension of constitutional evolution in Botswana. The incorporating of the customary courts into the modern polity protected the mechanism for maintaining, safeguarding, and repairing the social fabric that makes the society civil.[85]

The strength of the Botswana society is explained by factors that prevented the social order—and concomitant survival strategies and rules of social control of the Tswana kingdoms—from being dismantled and eliminated. The first factor is the Mfecane, which affected the Tswana kingdoms without decimating their populations or obliterating their social orders. Instead, the kingdoms centralized and consolidated into coherent political and social units, increasing their capacity for social control. The colonial experience was the second factor. Colonial imposition was executed virtually by request, instead of by force, with almost no immediate social disruption. This imposition of "benign neglect" had its virtues. The colonial regime made minimal penetration into established society through infrastructural projects. Benignity (from the drawing of district boundaries to the policy of indirect rule) resulted in political penetration with allowance for the established social order. And third, the region had not, since the Mfecane and despite numerous droughts, been subjected to massive social dislocation through disease or other natural calamities. Warfare to gain independence, defend borders, or maintain internal unity has yet to occur.

While good fortune presented these favorable conditions, deliberate policy measures strengthened the society in confronting the disruptive forces it had to confront. The social order could prevail against the potentially dislocating effects of drought and rapid modernization. Not even decades of large-scale labor migration to the South African mines destroyed the Tswana social order. The social safety net in the form of drought aid, urbanization policies, and the like had a buttressing effect. The structural strength of society also resulted from policy choice, which after independence followed through on the colonial pattern of removing from chiefly institutions their direct political power but retaining their public and social influence, authority, and esteem. Herein lies the significance of the House of Chiefs, which is generally denigrated in the academic literature. This institution stands at the apex of the pyramid of rules of social control, which starts with the informal, unwarranted customary courts. It is important not only for its political symbolism but also for its social significance, symbolizing the enduring presence of the rules of social control of Tswana custom and law.[86]

STATE, SOCIETY, AND DEMOCRATIC STABILITY

The predominance of the metropolitan power over society was asserted in the colonial era. The precedent that policy initiatives are taken at the institutional center was also established before independence. After independence the state builders extended these two trends, penetrating society so effectively and comprehensively that challenges to public authority from beyond the institutional reach of the state have been effectively precluded. Challenges are invariably conducted within the boundaries and opportunities dictated by the state, that is, within the constitutional limits set for citizens. Thus exit from the state has been made so unattractive as to be almost unavailable. The salience of citizenship and the hegemony of the state have been accomplished. This strength is the result of fortunate circumstances as well as of deliberate policies by the ruling coalition, who, guided by the general logic of their ethos of state action, did not squander opportunities and dealt with constraints constructively.

Within this strong state the ruling coalition occupies sites in both the state and the regime. The regime is clearly demarcated as one site within the state, offering a career trajectory to incumbents quite separate from that of the rest of the state. The elected

representatives occupy these positions and, along with the traditional leaders, the bureaucracy, and the private-sector business
and farming elite, comprise the ruling coalition. Since constitutional rules limit public contestation, it is clear that in electoral
politics the state is not at stake. To change the guiding ethos of
state action, more than an alternation of electoral incumbents is
required. Instead, the instrumentalities of technocratic public policies are at stake. (The reader is bound to object by now that this
does not satisfy the fundamental requirement of democratic participation in offering the electorate *real* choices. The answer is that
democratic methods are effective only in addressing instrumentalities anyway, and that the basic issues, such as what the appropriate unit of democracy should be, cannot be settled by democratic choice. Democracy presupposes consensus on, or acquiescence
with, a number of basic issues. It is no surprise that democracy has
flourished in societies where these basics have been agreed on).

The technocratic priorities of the ruling coalition resulted in
public policies that eventually yielded a highly solvent state with
substantial revenues at its disposal. The temptation to succumb to
the-state-as-market has been largely (but not entirely) resisted.
Instead, the happy convergence of the commercial and electoral
interests of many of the crucially influential individual members of
the ruling coalition with the imperatives of state building shaped
the priorities for spending that revenue. The need to pursue social
justice, as demanded by the autonomous bureaucracy; the incentive to create a state in which private profits could be made; and
the incentive to win elections resulted in the state's largely equitable expenditures on physical and social infrastructure. The
expenditures had two results that further strengthened the state.

The first result was a greater penetration of the society by the
state, which enhanced its capacity for extraction and for realloca-
tion of resources. The second was greater mobilization of electoral
support for the ruling BDP. The consistent electoral support gained
in this way reflected the legitimacy not only of the BDP but also of
the ruling coalition and the state. The currencies of social control
that state leaders can assemble consist of compliance with state
rules, participation in state-designated structures, and legitimacy.
Legitimacy is the most valuable of these currencies, as it "is
more inclusive than either compliance or participation. It is an

acceptance, even approbation, of the state's rules of the game, its social control, as true and right."[87]

The strong society was created by historical and geographical good fortune as well as sound public choices. It maintains rules of social control that embody the norm of consensus, which is sought through public debate and participation; communication and consultation; and tolerance for diverse opinion. These rules of social control strengthen the democratic process and emphasize respect for public authority, deference to hierarchy, and restraint in demanding public goods.

PART II

ZIMBABWE

The Strong Society and Weakening State

❋ 3 ❋

RHODESIA:
THE CONTEST FOR HEGEMONY
IN A DIVIDED SOCIETY

Rhodesia, like South Africa, could throughout its existence be confidently classified as an undemocratic regime. More strongly contested is whether the society was divided and, if so, where the lines of division were. The literature on the politics of Rhodesia and postindependence Zimbabwe is dominated by whether class or ethnicity has determined the political choices and actions of the opposing forces since the advent of the colonial era. If volume of print could serve as a yardstick for proof, then the case for the Rhodesia-Zimbabwe drama as class conflict (and therefore, to be explored through class analysis) would be virtually beyond dispute. However, in this study other criteria are taken into account.

The building of the Rhodesian state, the formative impact of that state on the emerging society, and the effect of the confrontations between political forces battling for hegemonic ascendancy on both the state and society are the focus of this chapter. The legacy of this contest has been a longer-term impact on the potential for democracy in the successor state and society of Zimbabwe, which will be explored in the next chapter.

The populations between the Zambezi and Limpopo Rivers in the immediate precolonial era were largely Shona-speaking peoples whose ancestors migrated south from central Africa and established themselves among the earlier Stone Age inhabitants. From this mix of cultures on the watershed plateau between the two river systems a number of significant cultural and sociopolitical units emerged, which have appropriately been called "plateau states."[1] A much-disputed prehistory exists about the exact origin of the creators of the Mutapa, Torwa, Rozwi, and especially Zimbabwe states and how they relate to the contemporary inhabitants and culture of the region. (These rival interpretations have been used to buttress a number of claims about rightful ownership of the country and about who was there first, claims that are typical of ethnic politics.)

The cultural, demographic, and political landscape of the precolonial era was even more dramatically reshaped by the Mfecane in this part of southern Africa than in the neighboring Tswana territories. After his decisive break with Shaka Zulu in 1821, Mzilikazi and his followers gradually moved north in search of a new territory. At first they settled north of the Vaal River, but after being defeated by the Boers under Hendrik Potgieter in 1837, they moved farther north, eventually settling near the site of the present town of Bulawayo, asserting immediate dominance over the local Shona-speaking Kalanga people. The Shona speakers named them the Ndebele, and their language came to be known as siNdebele. The strongest force in the rest of the plateau among the Shona-speaking people was then still assembled around the Rozwi state, over which Mzilikazi (and his successor, Lobengula) established "a loose zone of Ndebele influence," requiring "no more than that his authority should be recognized and tribute in cattle be paid."[2] However, Ndebele dominance was always tenuous, reaching its peak by 1873 and rapidly shifting in favor of the Shona speakers after 1879.[3]

British imperial interest in the region accelerated in the mid-1880s, fueled by persistent rumors of profitable gold deposits. Cecil John Rhodes was the pivotal figure. In 1888 Rhodes managed to obtain the controversial Rudd Concession from Lobengula, which formed the basis of the 1889 royal charter granted to his British South Africa Company (BSAC), in terms of which the right to occupy and rule most the plateau was granted. Effective rule was secured when the Pioneer Column invaded the region in 1890, rapidly followed by a British order in council (in 1891) declaring

Mashonaland (inhabited by the mostly Shona-speaking peoples) a British protectorate. BSAC control over Matabeleland was provisionally obtained through military defeat in 1893 and secured with the subjugation of both Shona and Ndebele forces after an abortive rebellion in 1896–97. Formal control over the entire region by the BSAC was enacted with the Southern Rhodesia Order in Council of 1898.[4]

The eastern boundary of the embryonic state reflected mutually agreed domains of influence of the British and Portuguese imperial powers and was established by treaty in 1891. The southern boundary followed the agreed-on boundary (the course of the Limpopo River) between the former Ndebele kingdom and what was still the South African Republic, as it was known after 1858. The only noteworthy boundary delimitation was in the west, where for some time it was considered probable that all Bechuanaland would eventually be transferred to the BSAC. In 1895 certain areas were actually transferred, but transfers were stopped and later rescinded after objections were raised by Tswana chiefs. Had these objections not been upheld, the demographic and political history of both countries would have been profoundly affected. As it was, the boundary was drawn to follow as closely as possible the territories of the Ndebele and Bamangwato kingdoms.[5]

By the early part of this century the cultural complexity of the population of the territory had been established. Within the black population the Shona speakers were numerically dominant, followed by the siNdebele-speaking Ndebele people. Each group consisted of smaller linguistic groupings, largely on the basis of differences in dialect, with the Karanga, Zezuru, Manyika, Korekore, Rozwi, and Ndau as the major Shona subgroups, and the Ndebele and Kalanga within the siNdebele ranks. Still smaller groupings— Tonga, Venda, Hlengwe/Shangaan, and Sotho—made up the other black linguistic minorities.[6] The white settler society has throughout this century been a numerical minority but has been at different times either economically influential, politically influential, or both. The size and internal composition of the white minority have fluctuated with its political fortunes and have been affected by large-scale immigration and emigration. By 1901, however, whites had established a resident population of more than 11,000, and whites dominated domestic politics until 1980.[7] The BSAC venture was motivated not only by imperial ambitions (opening up the road to the north) but also by commercial objectives. The promise of gold deposits, and even speculation about a second Witwatersrand, provided much of the initial driving force for conquest and colonization. These promises were not fulfilled, but a diverse mining sector, and later—especially after World War II—substantial manufacturing and commercial farming sectors were developed. Throughout the colonial era, the modern economy was closely tied to the international economy through investment capital, ownership, and foreign markets. This overall mix of cultural diversity, political conquest, and a modern economic core provided the context for the distinctive kind of state building that emerged in the territory during the colonial era.

THE RHODESIAN STATE

The State and Regime

After the 1898 order in council, the area under the jurisdiction of the BSAC was officially known as Southern Rhodesia. In 1923 it became a crown colony under the same name, and in 1965, after the Unilateral Declaration of Independence (UDI), the then incumbent Rhodesian Front Party insisted on calling the country Rhodesia. In 1979 it was briefly renamed Zimbabwe-Rhodesia after a new constitution was enacted, and only in 1980, when Britain officially granted independence, did the state of Zimbabwe come into existence. According to the conventions of the international system of states the entire period up to 1980 must therefore be considered "colonial." However, the de facto constitutional momentum—which accelerated after 1923 with the granting of "responsible government" and peaked with UDI in 1965—resulted in organizational action that resembled the imperatives of a state more than those of a colony under the sovereignty of a metropolitan power. Many analysts have shown awareness of this ambivalent status by referring to the "colonial state"[8] or "settler colonial state,"[9] contradictions in terms that nonetheless accurately convey the dynamics of the political process up to 1980. In similar vein this text will refer to the *Rhodesian state* for the period 1923–80.

The most striking (and undisputed) feature of the constitutional enactments of 1923, 1953, 1961, 1965, and 1969 and their attendant legislation is the racial bias in favor of whites and against blacks. The laws did not always discriminate explicitly but almost invariably did so by effect, thus often inviting analogies to the South African constitutional and legal doctrine and practice of apartheid.[10] What is not so clear cut is whether Rhodesia should be considered an example of a state built and run by and for a dominant class, or whether it represents an ethnic state. The main contours of this state-building project will be described briefly before that question is addressed.

British policy toward Rhodesia between 1897 and 1922 was led by the assumption that a single future southern African federation was in the making, in which the white settlers, British and otherwise, would rule. Thus, "with a united South Africa as the goal of British policy and the conciliation of Dutch and British colonial opinion a decisive factor, segregation of the races was the basic assumption on which Rhodesian society was established."[11] The first representative legislative council, established under BSAC rule, set the example for most of the subsequent constitutional legislation: the franchise required property and literacy qualifications, a requirement that was not directly racially discriminatory but in effect restricted the vote to white settlers. Only 51 black Africans qualified on the first electoral roll.[12] Restrictive legislation on African movement into the towns, masters and servants laws controlling labor relations, and a hut tax (passed in 1894 to draw Africans into the monetary economy) further entrenched settler dominance. In addition, legal sanctions to maintain social distance between white and black (such as penalties for interracial sexual relations) were enacted.[13]

The prospects for a larger southern African federation receded in 1922, when the Rhodesian electorate in a referendum declined to join the Union of South Africa. Instead the country was annexed as a crown colony in 1923, and legislative and executive powers were given to the electorate, except on matters dealt with by the Native Department, which were subject to approval by Parliament in Westminster. The British settlers' expectations of eventual self-government under the so-called Durham Formula—as in Cape Colony in 1872, Natal Colony in 1893, the Transvaal in 1906, and Orange Free State in 1907—were probably further strengthened when Rhodesia was placed under the Dominions Office when it was established in 1925.[14] In all the above-mentioned cases, the essentially white colonial electorates gained definitive control of the political process. In practice, Rhodesia was nearly a self-governing dominion, for the convention was soon established by which all legislation on Africans was initiated by the Rhodesians and enacted after being cleared with Britain.

Before 1953, legislation that set many of the definitive characteristics of the Rhodesian state was passed. Voting requirements in elections for the Legislative Assembly were again based on property ownership and literacy. The Land Apportionment Act of 1930 effectively divided the country into European and African areas of occupation, ownership, and communal life. The Industrial Conciliation Act of 1934 protected white artisans from black competitors and created a de facto color bar. The Education Act of 1930 made education compulsory for European children, but not for African children. On the lands allocated for African use and ownership, the Native Land Husbandry Act of 1951 dictated agricultural practices. This and other ostensibly benign laws such as the Native Development Fund Act and the Native (Urban Areas) Accommodation and Registration Act consolidated the dominance of the settlers and their state, society, and economy over the African population.[15]

In 1953 Southern Rhodesia joined with Northern Rhodesia and Nyasaland in establishing the Federation of Rhodesia and Nyasaland under the slogan of "partnership" for greater biracial cooperation. Each territory held its first elections to the Federal Assembly under its own voting laws, which in Southern Rhodesia at that time required literacy plus income or property. By 1953 only 429 of the 1,000 eligible Africans had cared to register. The various attempts to give practical effect to the notion of partnership by accommodating the interests of Africans floundered as European and African interests came increasingly to be seen as fundamentally inimical. Politicians had to walk the tightrope of persuasion, knowing that "the arguments which reassured the Europeans alarmed the Africans and the arguments which might persuade the Africans disturbed the Europeans."[16]

Inevitably, the interests of the mostly white electorate prevailed over those of the mostly disenfranchised Africans. Efforts to increase Africans' access to the vote (however marginally) were rejected by the territory's white voters and reversed by the Federal

Electoral Act and Constitution Amendment Act of 1957, which again raised the qualification thresholds and split the electorate into two categories. One set of voters, who qualified on a high threshold and in effect constituted the white voters, were registered on the so-called general roll and elected 44 of the 59 representatives. The special roll, with a much lower threshold, in effect comprised mostly African voters, who elected eight "special African members" to the Legislative Assembly. African opposition to these machinations led to the formation of the Southern Rhodesia African National Congress, also in 1957, which in turn was met with repressive security legislation, most notably the Preventive Detention (Temporary Provisions) Act, the Unlawful Organizations Act, the Emergency Powers Act, the Native Affairs Amendment Act, and the Law and Order (Maintenance) Act, all of which were passed in 1959. The 1961 constitution followed, virtually ending British powers of supervision over the country; with rising African resistance, the federation dissolved in 1964.[17]

The 1961 constitution modified the franchise again by renaming the general roll the "A roll" and the special roll the "B roll," retaining the differential qualifications. The A roll would elect 50 representatives in "constituencies," while the B roll would elect 15 representatives in "districts." An intricate system of cross-voting added to a devaluation of votes in an ostensibly color-blind electoral system still produced an outcome of 50 representatives elected by mostly white voters and 15 elected by mostly African voters, from an electorate that from 1962 to 1977 represented less than 0.3 percent of the African population of voting age and almost half of the non-African population.[18] The theoretical possibility of an African majority on both rolls remained, but calculations at the time ranged from a 15- to 100-year evolution to achieve such ascendancy.[19]

The 1965 election, in which the Rhodesian Front Party won all 50 A-roll seats and secured 79 percent of the A-roll votes, gave new impetus to the direction of state building in Rhodesia.[20] After the 1965 Unilateral Declaration of Independence a new constitution was enacted, which removed the blocking effect of racial referenda on future constitutional changes that had been entrenched in the 1961 constitution. With this done, a new constitution was passed in 1969 reserving the A roll explicitly for European, Asian, and colored voters, and the B roll for Africans. The A-roll voters were to elect 50 members to the lower House of Parliament and the B-roll voters 8, 4 each from Matabeleland and Mashonaland. Eight other African representatives were elected by an electoral college made up of chiefs, headmen, and councilors, again 4 each from Mashonaland and Matabeleland. The theoretical possibility of an African majority of voters was removed by placing an upper ceiling of parity on the African electorate, which could be achieved only incrementally as their tax contribution rose to equal that of non-African voters. The electoral process was also changed to eliminate the cross-vote and devaluation procedures and the single prefer-ential vote that was briefly introduced in 1962. The racial cast of the system was completed by stipulating that every representative (parliamentary as well as local government level) be elected by its own racial group. In the Senate, African representation was again on a linguistic basis (usually condemned by critics as a tribal basis). The Council of Chiefs acted as an electoral college to elect 5 Matabele and 5 Mashona senators.[21]

While constitutional power was thus secured, the further imposi-tion of a racially discriminatory grid onto society and economy pro-ceeded. A series of laws culminating in the Land Tenure Act of 1969 sought to comprehensively "segregate Africans from all other races in the occupation of land, and to divide the country as a whole into large white and black dominated areas."[22] Control over how Africans should conduct themselves in their designated "tribal trust land" was extended through the Constitution Amendment Act of 1967, the Tribal Trust Lands (Control of Irrigation Schemes) Regulations of the same year, and the Tribal Trust Land Development Corpo-ration Act of 1968. The movement of Africans into urban areas was increasingly subjected to control through the Local Government Areas (General) Regulations of 1964; the African (Urban Areas) Accommodation and Registration Act; and the equivalent to the infamous South African pass laws, the African (Registration and Identification) Act. Social segregation of races within towns was made possible by the Municipal Amendment Act, also of 1967, empower-ing local authorities to require separate public amenities. In the eco-nomic sphere, state surveillance of trade union actions was extended through the Industrial Conciliation Amendment Act of 1967.

Finally, as the challenge to the Rhodesian state escalated into armed confrontation, a series of security laws was enacted. These consisted primarily of numerous amendments to the Law and Order (Maintenance) Act, the Emergency Powers Amendment Act of 1967, the Emergency Powers (Maintenance of Law and Order) Regulations of 1970, and the Official Secrets Act of 1970.[23]

The overall picture shows that at the national level "the Rhodesian Front had a coherent theory of maximizing European political power"[24] wherever possible through segregationist policies. However, this coherence did not extend to local government institutions. When the high commissioner for South Africa established a system of magistrates courts for Mashonaland in 1891, he instructed that the law of Cape Colony be applied. That was basically Roman-Dutch law, modified by elements of English common law, and became the basis on which the Rhodesian legal system was built.[25] This legal system had to be imposed onto the Shona- and siNdebele-speaking peoples, who before colonization had their own legal systems. The way this was done provides a striking contrast with colonial Bechuanaland.

The traditional Shona political systems consisted of autonomous chieftaincies subdivided into wards under subchiefs and again under headmen. Political authority was vested in the chiefs, who through the spirit mediums represented the authority of the ancestral spirits and embodied their wisdom. Customary law, which stipulated codes and norms derived from the founding myths of the chieftaincy and from the collective wisdom of revered ancestors, was applied through a chief's court. Major disputes between chieftaincies were settled not through civil war but through a process of secession and fission, which led to a continual process of proliferation of chieftaincies. The Ndebele had a more centralized kingdom, with power concentrated in the king as supreme judge and military commander, assisted by three councilors and two councils. A regional division of the territory under chiefs and provincial military leaders, each commanding a regiment, supplemented the central authority. The latter positions, once established, usually became hereditary.

The imposition of colonial rule through military conquest in 1893 and 1896 completely destroyed the traditional Ndebele political structure. The BSAC created a new structure by appointing some of the old provincial chiefs and regimental commanders as chiefs and, below them, a series of headmen. This process was highly selective and arbitrary and at times an inaccurate replication of the original system, as not all appointees were traditionally recognized chiefs, and some traditional chiefs were not appointed. The Shona political structures remained intact, and the proliferating of chieftaincies continued into the colonial period. There were 150 recognized Shona chiefs in 1902, 271 in 1911, and 330 in 1921. Again the process of recognition was selective and did not mirror the existing traditional structure.[26]

The creation of a modern legal-bureaucratic state required a territorial base for local government. The areas designated by the Land Apportionment Act were therefore divided into wards, each under the jurisdiction of an appointed chief. In Matabeleland after the destruction of the traditional system, creating wards caused less dislocation than in Mashonaland, where the new ward boundaries were imposed onto existing, operative boundaries and dissolved them.[27] The modern bureaucratic state's imperatives of efficiency could not accommodate the proliferation of chieftaincies through fission, which was generic to the Shona structure. The equivalent of the moving frontier could not form part of the bureaucratic landscape of the modern state. Once ward boundaries had been laid down, therefore, the number of appointed chieftaincies (mostly Shona), was reduced again. Of the 323 appointed chieftaincies in 1914, 89 had been abolished by 1951.[28]

Administrative order also required clarity in the procedures of succession of hereditary positions. The traditional Shona method was an adelphic form of succession, operating on the general principle that "after the founder of a chiefdom dies, his sons succeed in turn. When the last of the filial generation dies the eldest son of the founder's first son ought to succeed, followed by the eldest son of the founder's second son and so on." This procedure is complicated by another rule stipulating that "no man of a junior generation ought to succeed whilst a man of a senior generation is still alive."[29] With the precolonial method of solving this problem—secession—foreclosed, the builders of the modern Rhodesian state could not rise to the challenge of codifying the adelphic method of succession into the Roman-Dutch legal system. Instead, they recommended that a system of primogeniture replace the existing Shona method. Once again, imposition, instead of merging and dovetailing the established with the modern, became the method of state building.

The legal incorporation of the chiefs proceeded through a number of stages, fluctuating between direct and indirect rule. Until the early 1920s the chiefs were subjected to direct rule from the political center, with effective power over the African populations in the hands of the native commissioners. Chiefs were allowed to hold their courts, but the courts were not officially recognized, and all civil and criminal jurisdiction remained in the hands of the native commissioners. The emergence of African political organizations in the towns prompted the state to bolster the powers of the chiefs. In 1931 "native boards" were established, with chiefs and headmen as ex officio members. These were succeeded by the councils in 1937, to which were given powers of taxation in 1943, and eventually by the bodies created through the Native Councils Act of 1957.[30] The chiefs also received a measure of civil jurisdiction for their courts through the African Law and Courts Act of 1937.[31] During a brief interlude from 1957 to 1963 when fully elected councils were introduced, the chiefs were reduced to being only judicial officers. When the Rhodesian Front came to power it quickly returned to the chiefs their political functions.

The position of the chiefs as figures of authority within the Rhodesian state was precarious. They were the meeting point of two sets of rules of social control, each a potential source of authority. As chiefs they were part of, in Matabeleland, an entire newly fabricated system of imposed "traditional" authority. The network of norms, codes, rules, and mythology comprising the traditional network of social control from which they drew their authority was virtually dismantled in the process of conquest. The Shona chiefs were marginally better off, having retained this structure, but their traditional legitimacy was eroded through the ward boundaries and methods of succession imposed by the Rhodesian state. Their second source of authority, as official representatives of the state, placed them in an even more vulnerable position. As officials of the state they had to administer a new set of rules that dictated enormously harsh strategies of survival for the people they represented. As a result, their status among their people was further undermined. As representatives of their people they had to convey that resentment to their superiors in the state. The response of the state was to increase the coercive powers of the chiefs, which undermined attempts at state building: "Whilst the chief's power may be increased in terms of his ability to coerce people—his personal authority tends to diminish in direct relation to this increase."[32]

This situation was in vivid contrast to colonial Bechuanaland, where the chiefs gradually lost their functions as political representatives but retained their social status and influence as respected, authoritative societal leaders. The strength of that association ensured that individuals retained that status even when forced to step down from formal chieftainship. Having entered modern competitive party politics (albeit as *former* chiefs) they could still draw on both sources of authority, which complemented rather than undercut each other. The outstandingly successful examples were Sir Seretse Khama and Bathoen II. In Rhodesia and independent Zimbabwe there are no comparable examples of chiefs who succeeded in electoral politics.

During the 1960s the process of forming African councils was accelerated, and the number rose from 52 in 1962 to 153 in 1972. By 1967 the accepted practice was that these members were nominated by the chiefs, not popularly elected.[33] The Council of Chiefs and Assemblies Act of 1961 continued this trend, bringing the chiefs (in equal numbers from Matabeleland and Mashonaland) into the central government, where they were also to serve as the electoral college for electing chiefs to the Senate. The Tribal Trust Land Act of 1967 restored their role in the allocation of land, and the Constitution Amendment Act of 1967 allowed for the granting of criminal jurisdiction to the chiefs' courts. In 1969 the new legal system was inaugurated, comprising a triadic but subordinate system and drawing the customary law into the Roman-Dutch and English law of the modern Rhodesian state.[34] The lowest pillar in this triad consisted of "tribal courts," which applied customary law only, and in a limited jurisdiction of cases. Appeal from this set of courts for civil cases went to the second pillar, the district commissioners' courts, and from there to the first pillar, the Appellate Division of the Rhodesian High Court. An outline of this court system is presented in figure 3.1.

The crucial point here is that what comprised the "customary law" these courts were to apply was determined mostly by the district

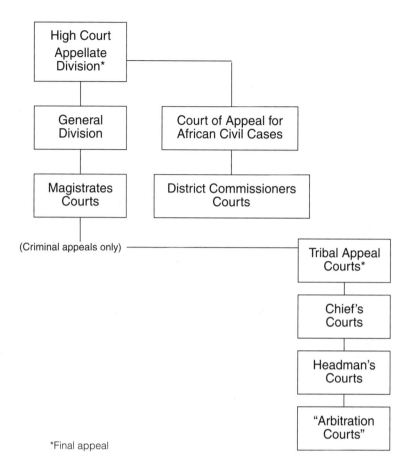

Figure 3.1 — Judicial Structure of Zimbabwe at Independence, 1980

Source: Adapted from Andrew Ladley, "Changing the Courts in Zimbabwe: The Customary Law and Primary Courts Act," *Journal of African Law* 26, no. 2 (1982): 96, figure 1. Copyright © Oxford University Press. Used by permission of Oxford University Press.

commissioners' courts, and especially the influential Court of Appeal for African Civil Cases.[35] Overall, the assessment has been made that this court system "entrenched a particular European view of African society" and that "these courts adopted narrow views of customary law and arguably did more to 'ossify' than reform the law, in the light of changing social conditions."[36] Again the contrast with Bechuanaland and independent Botswana is striking. There the chiefs were the initiators of change in customary law, a function they retained after independence.

The state's inability to achieve social control by reconciling customary law with the modern legal system is epitomized by the different approaches to the phenomenon of witchcraft. The Witchcraft Suppression Act of 1899 stipulated that accusing anyone of witchcraft was as great an offense as practicing it. To avoid prosecution, people resorted to one of the remaining customary defenses—killing those whom they suspected of being witches, thus exposing themselves to prosecution for murder. The basic assumption of this act and its supporting legislation on murder is that witches do not exist and that belief in witchcraft incites people to commit homicide and therefore must be dealt with accordingly. But, as has been elegantly argued, witches represent evil forces and are pivotal in defining the moral and social order in traditional Shona society, along with the benevolent ancestral spirits, the *mhondoro*.[37] This belief system is an extremely powerful instrument of social control. The inability of the Rhodesian state builders to make it part of the state system of social control would prove a crucial strategic weak point in the state and would be used with telling effect by hegemonic challengers.

Public Goods

A state thus constituted was clearly geared to deliver public goods favorably to the European powerholders at the expense of the largely powerless African population. And it did. The most apt overall characterization of state action before formal independence is "socialism for the whites," wherein "the state sought to provide an economic life for Whites that was basically shock-free with a near guarantee of an extraordinarily high standard of living."[38] The result was systematic racial inequality in the delivering of public goods, which consistently violated the twin criteria of jointness of supply and nonexcludability in almost every sector of public choice.

These results were most highly visible in the distribution of land. The series of laws that culminated in the Land Tenure Act of 1969 allocated 44.95 million acres of land to the European population and 44.94 million acres to the African population.[39] Given that the Africans then numbered about 4.75 million and the former only about 250,000, the actual distribution was highly skewed. Since African land ownership was mostly communal and the Europeans' was entirely private, the absolute land inequality was even more skewed. On this basis it has been calculated that by 1965 about 28,197 whites owned 33.7 million acres of farm land while 2.5 million Africans were the collective "owners" of a similar amount of land, for an actual per capita white-to-black land ownership ratio of 88.5:1.[40]

The cumulative impact of such inequality was that by 1982, 5,500 large-scale European farms comprising 36 percent of the land, employing 300,000 people, and carrying 1.5 million overall were producing 68 percent of the country's total agricultural output. This situation contrasted sharply with the 8,000 small-scale African farmers on land with private tenure (called the African Purchase Area) who were producing 4 percent of the output from land that carried 168,000 people, and even more sharply with the 675,000 peasant household farmers on communally owned land that had a population of 3.76 million and yielded 28 percent of the total agricultural produce.[41] By 1965 almost half of these African lands (then known as tribal trust lands) were already classified as overgrazed[42] and generally overpopulated. According to some calculations reported in 1978, some areas were exceeding their carrying capacity by as much as 250 percent.[43] This inequality of land ownership prompted further cumulative inequalities in capital ownership to emerge, and by the late 1970s one report had it that non-Africans controlled 88 percent of the productive capacity of the economy.[44]

Inequality of opportunity extended into the field of education, where the ratio of public expenditure on white versus black education by 1976 stood at almost 12:1.[45] What was not legislated in these matters was achieved through informal discriminatory practices, especially through an informal color bar in employment practices and in the taking on of African apprentices.[46]

One of the most highly visible areas of discrimination was in public-sector employment. Although the 1898 ordinance in terms of which the Rhodesian public service was established contained no formal discriminatory employment measures on the basis of race, the merit requirements effectively precluded Africans from entry. Racial discrimination was formalized only with the 1931 Public Services Act, reserving the established posts for whites. This condition was retained in the 1939 and 1944 acts and was relaxed only when Rhodesia entered the federation.[47] Even then entry was extremely limited, and by 1959 only 16 Africans had been placed in the top grade of the federal civil service. In 1961 the formal discriminatory clauses were removed from the Public Services Act, but with the ascendancy of the Rhodesian Front the recruitment of Africans to the civil service was virtually stopped. The practical effect was that the number of Africans in the service fell from 1,652 in 1965 to 802 in 1969.[48]

The compound effect of "socialism for the whites" was a chasm between the black standard of living and that of the other racially designated categories of Rhodesians. By 1965 the wage gap exceeded the ratio of 10:1, and in 1972 the average wage rate of whites stood at R$3,632 versus the average of R$332 for Africans.[49] Another report places the per capita income of whites, coloreds, and Asians in 1977 at R$6,156 and of Africans at R$588.[50] The disparity in overall incomes is also shown by the fact that of the 70,661 registered taxpayers in 1967, only 596 were Africans.[51]

STATE-SOCIETY INTERACTION

Were such public policies, which piled up privilege in favor of Europeans at the expense of Africans, the actions of a state created by a dominant class and working for that class? Or was it an ethnic state, implementing the objectives of a dominant ethnic group and reflecting the concerns of an ethnic group perceiving itself to be under threat? And what has the societal response been to those state actions? Given the pervasive presence of the class interpretation of politics in the literature on Rhodesia/Zimbabwe, the logic of the method used here to assess this explanation needs to be spelled out in some detail.

At question is whether ethnicity and class can logically claim to be an *independent variable* that explains the *dependent* variables of choice and action in the politics of Rhodesia and Zimbabwe. The criteria for deciding this question are logical, empirical, and theoretical.[52] The logical criterion requires that an independent variable, if it is to act as a causal variable, precede a dependent variable in time. One way of examining a time sequence is to consider the attributes of the variables. Variables that consist of *properties* (such as race, age, or place of birth) have greater claims to permanence than those that consist of *dispositions* (such as attitudes, opinions, and values), and the latter cannot plausibly be a causal factor in creating the former.

The empirical criterion of a causal relationship is association. Changes in the independent variable must correlate with changes in the dependent variable. When both ethnicity and class associate with the dependent variable, each relationship must be checked for spuriousness. This is done by examining whether the relationship with one of the independent variables holds up when the effect of the other is controlled for. If changes in the variables are measured with quantitative data and cover a large number of cases, then this can be done through statistical techniques. When qualitative data on one or a few cases are available (as they usually are with Rhodesia/ Zimbabwe), the controlling effect can be achieved through subcategory analysis. To control for the causal effect of ethnicity, the relationship between political choice and action (as the dependent variable) and a number of different classes *within* the ranks of one ethnic group must be examined. If the relationship falls away, then the association between class and the dependent variable is spurious. To control for the causal effect of class, the relationship between the dependent variable and two or more different ethnic groups *within* one class must be measured, and if it does not persist, then the association between ethnicity and the dependent variable can be considered spurious. (A variation that applies the same logic of method is to measure whether or not class solidarities extend across ethnic boundaries, or whether ethnic unity can transcend internal class differences, and if these affiliations cross-cut, to register which becomes salient and under what conditions.)

The theoretical criterion is that a coherent, plausible, persuasive rationale can account for the existence, or predict the absence, of a measured association. Even more important would be a rationale explaining the association that appears contrary to the central expectations of the theory, and how such a rationale measures up to that of competing explanations predicting the actually measured association.

Since both ethnicity and class are dispositions derived from more permanent properties (cultural categories that denote real or presumed descent in the case of ethnicity, and economic categories that reflect wealth and structural positions of exploiter or exploited within a given economic system in the case of class), the logical criterion on its own rarely yields clear-cut answers on the strengths of the rival claims to explanatory sufficiency. And since for many decades in Rhodesia/Zimbabwe these properties were closely related, so that the relevant social categories (but not necessarily the dispositions) largely overlapped, the immediately visible phenomenon has been of coinciding and mutually reinforcing social divisions between largely affluent white people and mostly destitute black people. The result has been covariation of rival independent variables with the dependent variable. The political choice and action by each of the opposing sides could equally plausibly have been motivated for one by the fact that it is rich or white, and for the other by the fact of being black or poor.

What remains to be done is to expand the empirical base and assess the accompanying rationale of each theoretical approach. The empirical testing ground has to be expanded to find behavior that fits the explanatory framework of either one of the theories, but not both. The theoretical testing ground must be brought down to questions such as how the class rationale can account for social categories that conform to classes but do not act as such, or social aggregates that do not conform to the definitional criteria of classes but are nonetheless classified as such, and how social categories that have all the attributes of ethnic groups but act otherwise can be accounted for by the ethnic rationale.

The contested ground then becomes the class rationale of *false consciousness,* expressed as "ideology," whereby people are duped by others into accepting that they are not a class but something else, such as a race, ethnic group, nation, or tribe. These identities are taken to be false because they are manufactured by the politically dominant forces, and are therefore contrived instead of authentic. When leaders advance false identities among their own people they are considered to be pursuing either their own material interests (in which case "tribalism then becomes a mask for class privilege")[53] or power. This rationale must stand up to the critique that it fails to pay what Peter Berger has called *cognitive respect*, that is, "that one takes with utmost seriousness the way in which others define reality," and "the recognition that no outsider, including the outsider who possesses power, is in a position to 'know better' when it comes to the finalities of other peoples' lives."[54] Second, and closely related, is the need to answer why these ideas and identities, especially if they are "clearly" false, take hold and prevail in the marketplace of political ideas against the competition offered by "true" class identities. Third, comparative evidence has shown many instances of ethnic movements that have pursued objectives in the face of economic penalties and to the detriment of their own prospects for power.[55] Finally, ethnic groups have consistently sought to implement measures that have little if any bearing on material or power advantages but have great significance in terms of status, prestige, and presumed rank.

The ethnic rationale has to stand up to similar scrutiny. Cognitive respect requires that ethnic dispositions not be assigned to social categories simply because they have the cultural attributes from which such identities are typically constructed. When class affiliations and interests outbid the attractions of ethnic solidarity in the marketplace of identities, and when the pursuit of collective esteem is channeled through nonethnic associations instead of exclusive ascriptively defined interest groups, it has to be accounted for. In this and the following chapter, claims for the primacy of ethnicity or class in the case of Rhodesia/Zimbabwe will be weighed against these criteria, where appropriate.

The first question then is whether the categories of people who have been labeled as classes have indeed acted *like* classes, or *as* classes.[56] This question includes two others. The first deals with the empirical matter of boundaries. Do class solidarities transcend other social cleavages, especially ethnicity, or not? In the Rhodesian case this would be important with respect to the white-black divide as well as the Shona-Ndebele cleavage. The second deals with the equally empirical matter of actions. Do the objectives that are pursued reflect class interests only, or do they reflect ethnic concerns? An ethnic explanation must field similar questions. On the matter of boundaries, do the purported ethnic solidarities transcend internal class differences yet heed cultural differences relevant to the subjective content of the proclaimed identity? And with respect to actions the question is whether people are acting *like* ethnic groups or *as* ethnic groups.

Did class interests succeed in straddling the white-black divide? The overwhelming finding is that they did not. The white and the black workers did not find a common cause and instead organized themselves in racially defined trade unions.[57] The white and the black commercial farmers did likewise.[58] Nor could a political party based on class interests raise these shared concerns above those of race. The Southern Rhodesia Labor Party, formed in 1943, recruited its African members in a separate African Headquarters Branch, yet so many white members were incensed that the party split, with the breakaway Labor Party excluding Africans from membership.[59] No significant, thoroughgoing biracial interest group emerged in the Rhodesian era up to 1980. Where the state did not legislate for separate, racially defined institutional representation, the dynamics of the society ensured that outcome through informal discriminatory practices such as the informal color bar in the field of industrial relations.[60] In this sense both white and black Rhodesians were encapsulated into social institutions that demarcated two rival and parallel incipient whole societies.

If the ultimate primacy of class interests is claimed, then how can 90 years of colonial rule in which class formations were expressed only *within* racially defined categories be explained without conceding that concerns other than class weighed heavier in the calculations of both African and European Rhodesians? One part of the answer is obviously that the racial grid of laws and policies imposed by the Rhodesian state prevented an authentic class consciousness from emerging and finding organizational expression. One way of testing this answer would be to control for the effects of state policies. The historical pattern of events in Rhodesia provides for two such opportunities. The first is found in the challenge to the Rhodesian state by the nationalist forces. The substance of that revolt was directed against the racial ordering of society. And if the fundamental structure of the conflict had been class based, then surely the organizational shape of this challenge would reveal it. An even stronger confirmation of the presumed class-driven societal divisions should be expected to emerge from the state-society interaction of independent Zimbabwe, freed entirely from the racial strictures of the Rhodesian state. Both these possibilities are examined later on.

The second part of the answer is some variation of the rationale of false consciousness, in which the visible racial prejudice that upholds an informal color bar, for instance, is considered to be the mask for class privilege. Only one authoritative interpretation of one aspect under discussion can be considered. In explaining the racial solidarity and prejudice of white mine workers against their black counterparts, Ian Phimister concluded that "the basic conservatism of the white mine workers was partly a consequence of their class interests being dependent on some degree of a job color bar, a device incompatible with broader working class solidarity. But the matter went deeper than that. The job color bar itself was a response to the exploitation color bars of the employers (which extended the structural insecurity of white workers), but, because the overall profitability of the mining industry rested on cheap African labor secured by the exploitation of color bars, in the last analysis the very existence of the highly-paid white mine workers depended on those same exploitation color bars."[61] White miners, in other words, were operating as "prefabricated collaborators" with the mine owners to keep a system of exploitation going within which they benefited as the "aristocracy of labor": the economic benefits they gained from the system "obliged them to defend the *status quo* and such defence enhanced their value to the mining companies."[62] Their actions elicited an equivalent response: "African workers themselves were quick to repay the compliment and they, too, never struck in support of white miners."[63]

Both white and black miners acted therefore *like* classes, each group defending and advancing its own economic interests against the other's, but they could not possibly be said to have acted *as* classes (or more correctly, as *a* class), because the pursuit of economic interests (by the white workers), in Phimister's own analysis, required of them a strategic choice that entailed the fracturing of class solidarity along racial lines. The pursuit of economic interests by groups along racially defined boundaries and at the expense of class solidarity therefore does not mask class privilege but rather exposes the ease with which "authentic" class consciousness could be outbid by competing solidarities in the marketplace of group identities.

The second important potential fault line that class solidarities had to transcend is the Shona-Ndebele cultural divide, which also served as a potential ethnic rallying point. Again the major findings point in one direction. For most of the colonial era the Shona and Ndebele speakers *did not* diverge into culturally distinct organizations. With the odd exception this pattern did not emerge in the black trade union movement.[64] Again with but one exception, bicultural solidarity marked the evolution of organizations representing the interests of black commercial farmers.[65] Nor did the interest groups representing the mostly urban dwellers, such as mutual aid societies and other voluntary associations, display a prominent Shona-Ndebele split despite their sometimes obvious "tribal" or regional character.[66] In this sense, therefore, the Shona speakers and the siNdebele speakers did not coalesce into two opposing incipient whole societies. The outstanding exception to this pattern was the extensive civil violence that erupted in 1929 in Bulawayo Location between Ndebele railway compound residents and other non-Shona migrant workers on the one side, and Shona speakers on the other.

How does the class perspective account for this cross-cultural solidarity as well as for the notable exceptions? The solidarity is explained by the shared experience of being drawn into the modern economy *as workers* and by the common interest that was created by this structural position. This explanation has to be tested against the counterargument that the common structural position that generated shared interests was, rather, the domination by the Rhodesian state, with the social and economic rules it imposed. To control for this factor the interest group pattern in independent Zimbabwe after the demise of the Rhodesian state will be examined.

A different kind of explanation is given the violently hostile Shona-Ndebele confrontations in Bulawayo in 1929. Again only one authoritative interpretation of what may be taken as a test case will be examined. Ian Phimister and Charles van Onselen have, through an exhaustive empirical description, traced how the initial confrontation was triggered by gangs attacking civilians and how this criminal violence rapidly escalated into civil conflict comprising Ndebele and northern migrants on the one side against Shona speakers on the other. The question raised by the sequence of events is why the initial nonethnic conflict developed so rapidly along ethnic fault lines. Their answer, according to Phimister and van Onselen, is that the conflict came to reflect an "index of working class frustration and despair," an "intra-working class conflict" of "workers against workers" reflecting "internalized or displaced aggression."[67] The observable pattern of conflict exhibits the features of "class suppression," in which the absence of class awareness (defined as "the common awareness of a shared interest") is explained away by the presumed effects of ideology in the form of "ethnicity and race prejudice," which involves the "deliberate manipulation of racial feelings by a group, usually the dominant group (and/or) as the result of a belief system developing a force independent of material interests in the narrow sense." In short, false consciousness. In this case the trigger for the communal violence is narrowed down to a single sentence, on which the entire explanation hinges: "The corruption and favouritism which for so long had characterised the Location management ensured that many Ndebele believed the rumour that in return for £8, the Native Department had granted the Shona permission to attack them."

This proposition is no explanation at all, but it does merit close examination. It pertinently restates the problem: Why does the ideology (of ethnic solidarity) succeed in being more persuasive than "the common awareness of a shared interest"? What persuasive chord is struck by inflammatory rumors of preemptive ethnic violence, and why do these rumors prevail over the supposedly greater formative strength of class interests? What kind of collective psychology can explain why corruption and favoritism can be so compelling in making such rumors persuasive? The class rationale of Phimister and van Onselen offers no answer, but on the basis of comparative evidence, this particular case typifies a context where a subordinate ethnic group that has been occupying a niche in the economy of a relatively advanced region feels threatened by the immigration of ethnic strangers and responds with xenophobic aggression.[68]

If an ethnic perspective applies to the Rhodesian case, then the question of boundaries is whether ethnic solidarities could succeed in transcending internal class differences yet remain true to the cultural criteria in terms of which the proclaimed identity is expressed. In the case of the dominant white minority, the question is whether the whites acted *as* an ethnic group or *like* a racially defined group of people bent on the pursuit of privilege. A number of features of white unity reflect an ethnic character. The dominant factor shaping this identity was the shared perception of threat. According to one in-depth study, the strongest force shaping white consensus was "an awareness of the fundamental precariousness of their position as white settlers in a black land." Political supremacy was matched by psychological insecurity: "Power was matched by fear, arrogance by anxiety, disdain by suspicion."[69] Given their demographic position, this was understandable. In the early 1950s, when the black-to-white balance was as favorable as it would ever be for Europeans, Africans outnumbered them 16 to 1. By the 1970s the ratio had widened to 22 to 1.[70] In response the whites not only created social and cultural boundaries along the lines of race, they did so in a way that affirmed their own superiority, dignity, status, and prestige and denied the same to the Africans.[71] Such exhibitions of racial prejudice matched by practices of discrimination marked the extent to which the Rhodesian society was lacking in the most basic civility.

Although the perception of the "black peril" was a powerful unifying force by itself, what is striking is the ethnic substance of the threatened minority's core identity. By the early 1920s the white population was exhibiting "a certain persistence in its social patterns: tending to be born in Southern Africa; tending to be English-speaking and pro-British; and tending to look to Britain, English-speaking South Africa, or the rest of the Empire for supplementary population inputs. Already by 1921 there seemed to emerge a self-centered 'Rhodesian-ness.'"[72] This identity generated social rejection of whites of other cultures, especially the Afrikaners, and to a lesser extent, continental European migrants.[73] Concern for maintaining the core values of this identity found expression in debates about the proper contents of school curricula and in the maintaining of social norms that inhibit nonconformist behavior.[74]

The result was the emergence of a core community of ethnics in which internal social differences were overridden by a common culture and identity despite the continuing large differences in wealth within their ranks (by 1976 more than half of the taxable income paid by farmers was generated on 271 of the 6,682 farms).[75] Within these ranks cordiality, friendliness, and hospitality marked social behavior. Civility was an in-group matter only.

The actions of white Rhodesians also reflected ethnic concerns. An early political expression of this distinctive Rhodesian-ness in white politics was the 1922 referendum, rejecting political unification with the Afrikaner-dominated Union of South Africa, which arguably had similar "class interests." And by the early 1960s this core identity as a rallying point for white-black perceptions was consolidated in the political solidarity, cohesion, and electoral success of the Rhodesian Front Party, which had succeeded in tapping what has been described as their "collective will" in support for UDI.[76]

The white Rhodesians also put the state they had constructed for themselves into use to take care of their ethnic anxieties. Their need to affirm their own worthiness and deny the moral dignity of Africans was enacted in legislation that implemented what can be called "petty segregation." Such laws, epitomized by the regulation that forbade Africans from using urban sidewalks (they had to walk outside the curb), had little to do with economic gain, but a lot to do with humiliating one set of people and publicly and symbolically announcing their inferior status.[77] Even where legislation did not enforce status differences, such as in the civil service after 1961, government policy ensured such outcomes. In 1969 a cabinet minister gave assurances that within the civil service, appointments would be made so as to ensure "that no European should be in a position where he should unwillingly have to accept an order from an African."[78] The social safety net provided by the state for the so-called poor whites has also been interpreted in terms of this ethnic psychology: "All these governmental services had as their underlying aim the desire to insure that white settlers escaped indigence and its denouement, the fall from racial grace."[79]

The Rhodesian concern about foreign white immigrants who did not share their core culture was taken care of by the 1946 Aliens Act, "which would enforce a quota whereby aliens would only be allowed to comprise five to ten percent of 'British' immigrants, subject to the control of an immigrants' selection board which would maintain the 'right standards.'"[80] This law was significant not only because little economic (or, if one prefers, class) interest could be derived from it but also because it was passed despite the precarious demographic position of the white minority. Matters of identity at that stage outweighed even strategic and power considerations. Finally, in symbolic terms the white Rhodesians answered the question about who owns the country in explicit ethnic terms. Not just whites, but a particular kind of white people owned it. From the Beit Bridge in the south to Fort Victoria, into Salisbury along Jameson Avenue, and up to Victoria Falls on the northern border, the symbols of the state bearing the name Rhodesia were permeated by indicators of a specific heritage, kinship, and descent.

On the basis of the above analysis, then, the balance of judgment leans toward the interpretation that the Rhodesian state was an ethnic state, created by the white Rhodesians who at their core were an ethnic group. The logical, empirical, and theoretical strength of the case for considering Rhodesia a state representing the class interests of the white Rhodesians acting as a class dissipates under scrutiny. To persist in arguing the case for the primacy of class involves "doctrinal gymnastics" akin to those performed by many politicians in ethnically divided societies who engage in "a redefinition of ethnic positions in para-class terms."[81] "The use of class when no class exists," as one scholar has warned, "is a sort of soft Marxism, wanting to have the benefits of Marxian analysis without having to carry the burdens."[82]

THE CONTEST FOR HEGEMONY

The Challengers

Briefly, the revolt against, and the eventual displacement of, the Rhodesian state went as follows. The immediate forerunner to African nationalist opposition was the City Youth League in Salisbury in 1955. In 1957 the league became part of the newly established Southern Rhodesia African National Congress (SRANC) with Joshua Nkomo as president. SRANC was banned in 1959, to be succeeded by the National Democratic Party (NDP) the following year, again with Nkomo as leader. The NDP was also banned the following year and the Zimbabwe African People's Union (ZAPU) was immediately formed, once again with Nkomo as leader. When

ZAPU was banned in 1962 it relocated to Tanzania, operating as the People's Caretaker Council, while internal opposition to Nkomo led to the formation of the Zimbabwe African National Union (ZANU) in 1963. Both ZANU and ZAPU established armed wings, ZANLA and ZIPRA, respectively. Armed confrontation between ZANLA and the Rhodesian state started with the "battle of Sinoia" in 1966. In 1971 the African National Council was formed under the leadership of Bishop Abel Muzorewa, operating as a political party inside the country, while the Front for the Liberation of Zimbabwe (FROLIZI) was formed outside from former ZANU and ZAPU members. In December 1972 ZANLA infiltrated from the northeast to establish a war zone. By 1975 Robert Mugabe had established himself as the undisputed leader of ZANU. The war escalated rapidly during the 1970s and by the middle of the decade had taken on a definitive pattern, with ZIPRA operating from Zambia into the northwest part of the country and ZANLA operating from Mozambique into the northeast, with only Nkomo and Mugabe commanding guerrilla forces. In 1979 the warring parties were brought to the negotiating table, where the Lancaster House agreement was concluded. That agreement led to formal independence in 1980. Mugabe and Nkomo then joined forces as the Patriotic Front (PF), renaming their parties to ZANU-(PF) and (PF)-ZAPU, respectively. The first elections were won by ZANU-(PF) under the leadership of Robert Mugabe.

The immediate question for interpretation is whether this revolt was driven by class formations or rather by ethnically defined, delineated, and inspired movements. The answer will be sought along two lines of inquiry. The first is to look at the boundaries of the various political organizations. Who were members of which, and what were the criteria of allegiance? The second explores the kinds of appeals with which support was mobilized. Were the grievances against the Rhodesian state expressed in terms of class interests, or in terms of ethnic themes? The boundary question will be taken up first.

The actions of the Rhodesian state made for the emergence of either class or ethnic revolt. The sharp lines of privilege and poverty drawn along the white-black racial divide set the context for class-driven organizations to use. The administrative boundaries of the Rhodesian state also shaped the context for ethnic mobilization. The Land Apportionment Act reinforced the white-black division, the hallmark of the colonial era. The African Purchase Area allowed for increased per capita incomes for some African farmers, thus establishing potential economic cleavages within the black population. The consolidation of a larger Shona identity was made easier first by the development of a standardized orthography for the six dialects (Korekore, Zezuru, Manyika, Ndau, Karanga, and Kalanga), each with a regional base. Later, in 1955, a single standardized Shona alphabet made it easier to straddle these internal boundaries. The Shona-Ndebele boundary was strengthened by the creation of seven provinces, further consolidated into Mashonaland and Matabeleland, which eventually became regions represented at central governmental level. This division was further strengthened by the quota system of representing the chiefs in government. The 1961 legislation made for equal representation of chiefs from Matabeleland and Mashonaland, thus not only overrepresenting the Ndebele, but again emphasizing that they were representing different communities.

The dynamics of organizational politics within the nationalist organizations that successfully challenged the Rhodesian state has been accounted for in detail by Masipula Sithole on the basis of ethnic loyalties.[83] The initial 1963 split from ZAPU, which led to the forming of ZANU, is not attributed to ethnic motivations, but rather to dissatisfaction with the leadership of Nkomo. The creation of FROLIZI, however, is accounted for by ethnic tensions between Shona and Ndebele as well as within the Shona ranks. FROLIZI was formed by the Chikerema group from ZAPU and the Shamu-yarira group from ZANU, who joined in creating a party that was dominated by Zezuru-based Shona speakers. ZAPU was left in exile as a mostly Ndebele (Kalanga) party, and ZANU in exile as a largely Shona (Manyika and Karanga) party. Violent internal confrontations between these groups led to the death of more than 250 ZANU guerrillas by early 1975 and to the eventual demise of the Manyika group of the party. In 1976, after the further split from ZANU by Ndabaningi Sithole and the ascendancy of Mugabe, the party became dominated by a Zezuru and Karanga group. Sithole has defended this interpretation against the rival thesis—that the old guard leaders were petit bourgeois and therefore tribalistic rather than young, radically pure leaders—on empirical grounds.

It cannot be shown that the leadership core of any of the national-ist organizations was composed exclusively, or even predominantly, of individuals who would fit the profile of either petit bourgeois or non-petit bourgeois.[84]

The kind of appeals that mobilized partisans to challenge the Rhodesian state can also shed light on the class or ethnic character of their identities. Easily the most outstanding feature of the authoritative accounts of the resistance to the Rhodesian state was the mobilizing role attributed to the spirit mediums, a practice that was also present in the revolts of the 1890s and early 1900s.[85]

Spirit mediums are explained by Shona cultural links with the land. In the account of David Lan (based on his work in the Dande district), land belongs to the first occupants, who acquire the status of "autochthons"—those who have the closest association with, and are in every sense part of, the territory. This status is reserved for the spirits of the most senior and most original of all the deceased chiefs. The ZANLA guerrillas established themselves as the authentic autochthons, embodying the spirits of the ancestors, and therefore true owners of the land, versus the chiefs, who had been co-opted into the state as civil servants. Politically, the ZANLA guerrillas used this status to establish themselves as a legitimate and ulti-mately benevolent force, fighting a war for the good of society against the evils of the Rhodesian state and its policies.[86] From there the final step was to eliminate the chiefs through assassina-tion and take over their functions—notably witch finding, which was prohibited by the laws of the Rhodesian state.[87]

The question is what kind of identity is invoked by this process. Lan does not ponder this matter deeply but is convinced that the rural populace of the Dande district was persuaded by the ZANLA interpretation that the war was being waged as a class, rather than ethnic, conflict: "The enemy was defined as racism and the struc-tures of exploitation, rather than as individual members of the white population," and so it follows that "the return of the land could only be achieved by the victory of one class rather than of one ethnic group over another."[88]

Terence Ranger (on the basis of his research in the Makoni dis-trict of Mashonaland) also concludes that the rural peasantry need to be "regarded as a class in itself."[89] This consciousness was revealed in their behavior and their choice of strategies, which reflected an understanding of the economic system in which they were caught up.[90] The peasants' grasp of the importance of possessing and controlling the land, the crucial economic resource for survival, was further strengthened by the system of belief embodied in the spirit mediums: "Spirit mediums were significant to peasant radical consciousness precisely because that consciousness was so focused on land and on government interference with production: above any other possible religious form the mediums symbolized peasant right to the land and their right to work it as they chose."[91]

Yet, in the social, moral, and mythological order of which the spirit mediums are a part, both these scholars describe ancestry, kinship, descent, and genealogy as the most vital ingredients in settling the question, Who are the true owners of the land? The answer conveyed by the spirit mediums was profoundly ethnic: "The people whose ancestors bring the rain own the land."[92] The vital message the ZANLA guerrillas conveyed was not class identity; rather, they merged their identity with the kinship network represented in the *mhondoro*: "What the guerrillas have learned to say is: 'our ancestors bring the rain therefore we own the land.' In other words they have become autochthons or rather super-autochthons, as the military vanguard of a nation of autochthons, of all the original displaced but authentic owners of the land . . . in opposition to the conquerors, the white population of Rhodesia."[93] The identity is ethnic to its core: the imagery and symbolism convey not an identity shaped by class-based exploitation by any economic system or economic interests in the land, but identity that flows from ownership claims to the land on the basis of descent, genealogy, and kinship.

The final indicator that the challengers to the Rhodesian state were ethnically motivated is found in the range within which these appeals found resonance. Both Lan and Ranger found that the spirit mediums' appeal reached across the boundaries of chieftaincies within the Dande and Makoni districts and elsewhere in Mashonaland and thus provided ZANU with a platform for mobilizing support that transcended immediate lineage divisions. But the platform could not extend beyond the Shona-speaking regions of the country.[94] The ancestors of the Shona—and not of the Ndebele, Shangaan, Sotho, or Venda—figured centrally in the cosmology invoked by the ZANLA guerrilla forces. The non-Shona groups were involved in the revolt, and they did call on ancestral spirits, but not the same ones the Shona invoked.

The challengers to the Rhodesian state therefore mirrored the incumbents in their ethnic dispositions. To insist on calling them classes is to revert to reclassifying ethnic phenomena in para-class terms and to engage in analyses that resemble "soft" Marxism. The dispute over the identities of the adversaries is, however, for the purposes of this study, important only up to a point. What in the final analysis divides a society is not the identity of the antagonists, but the kind of claims they bring into the contest. In this matter the opposing scholars previously cited are in agreement. ZANU developed into a party that defined itself by an uncompromising position toward the Rhodesian state and a demand for nothing less than the complete transfer of power to a newly constituted state ruled by an African majority.[95] This demand was conveyed to the Rhodesian state in many forms, often as a demand for *surrender* as a condition for the end of the war.[96] The guerrilla promise to "free the land from the grasp of the whites" and the offer of "a Zimbabwe returned to its original and rightful owners"[97] also implied a fundamentally transformed state, not only in composition but also in purpose: "a state that would back black farming against white, rather than the other way round."[98] White Rhodesians recognized what they saw and accurately assessed the zero-sum quality of the competing kinds of statehood, peoplehood, and democracy being advanced by the opposing political formations. All parties appeared to be aware of the hegemonic nature of the stakes in the conflict, but although the defining features of the Rhodesian state and regime were explicitly demarcated, the contours of the contending regime model were not. The notion of socialism was outlined vaguely to the rural populations of Dande and Makoni, and apparently it was understood almost in millenarian terms as "the name of the good one," which was to replace the oppressive Rhodesian state at the successful conclusion to the war.[99]

The Civil War

This hegemonic contest can be accurately described as a civil war. Each of the rival military forces with its political organization drew support and manpower from specific segments of the population, sought compliance from its own support base, and tried to eliminate compliance with the opponent's laws, rules, and policies. Each tried to displace the other instead of finding accommodation for the other's aims and objectives. The respective populations resembled incipient whole societies. No civil institutions crossed the white-black racial divide, and an ethnic core identity bound the white population across other social divisions. The African populations—despite the common denominator of oppression, which created shared conditions of deprivation—coalesced into ethnically demarcated political units and mobilized and controlled their supporters accordingly. The contest was between rival institutions of social control, the Rhodesian state versus the hegemonic challengers. In this contest the rural populations themselves, even more than the territory, became the contested terrain. The impact of this violent confrontation[100] on society and on the Rhodesian state, and its legacy for the successor state of Zimbabwe have to be considered. Given the outcome of the war, the impact on the Rhodesian state is not surprising: the state rapidly weakened the longer the war proceeded. The impact on the strength of society is less clear cut. Both will be discussed in turn.

The state constructed by the white Rhodesians was relatively large; public-sector expenditure in 1972 amounted to 40 percent of total expenditure in the economy.[101] Coupled to the enhanced legal capacity to intervene in the economy, which was introduced after UDI in 1965, the state was strong in its capacity for controlling society and economy.[102] Control was exercised with measurable effect on the African population. In containing Africans' movement to the urban areas, the Africans (Registration and Identification) Act was so vigorously applied that the population of Highfield township was reduced from 100,000 to 70,000 by the end of 1964.[103] In penetrating African rural society the state exhibited its strength in rapidly expanding the number of African councils between 1962 and 1972 and later in the war, relocating up to 750,000 people into so-called protective villages.[104] That the dominance of state over society during the 1960s resulted in compliance but not necessarily in acquiescence was reflected in a declining number of prosecutions under the existing security laws.[105]

The limits on the strength of the Rhodesian state were set by the features that defined it. Because it was an ethnic state, the acquisition of that most precious currency of social control—legitimacy—

could be safely made from only one sector of the population, the white Rhodesians. The ethnic outsiders, those who received the least in public goods from the ethnic state and whose status and dignity suffered continual denigration, therefore became the contested terrain. From these ranks rose the challenge to the state: transformation of the state through armed insurrection and insurgency warfare, and assertion of a network of social control to rival that of the Rhodesian state and to displace it. In setting out to displace the Rhodesian state, ZANU and ZAPU confronted the local government system of the Rhodesian state, composed of district commissioners, appointed chiefs, and the triadic court system, which drew customary law into the legal system of the modern state.

The Rhodesian state tried to isolate the insurgent guerrillas from the local population by forcibly relocating them into protective villages.[106] The insurgents tried to destroy effective rule by the state in the rural areas by establishing so-called liberated zones[107] with an alternative parallel legal structure[108] and by physically eliminating the chiefs,[109] the immediate representatives of the state. In this contest of coercion, the rural battlefield by the end of the 1970s was marked by the almost complete breakdown of the school system and the extension of martial law into most of rural Rhodesia.[110]

By the end of the war the Rhodesian state was decisively weakened through a decline in legitimacy as well as coercive power. The guerrilla forces showed a concomitant rise in strength. To what extent this strength was composed of coercive abilities or legitimacy or a combination of both remains disputed. Research from the Dande and Makoni districts finds that the guerrillas, through their endorsement by the spirit mediums, attained unquestionable legitimacy.[111] Other findings from research done in the Mutoko district concluded instead that coercion by ZANLA was decisive in accounting for its ability to countervail the Rhodesian state.[112]

The important point for the purposes of this study is not to find a conclusive answer to the above dispute but to note the impact on society of the contest between two sets of institutions, both aiming to assert exclusive social control over the rural population. The overall effect of this contest, through the tactics mentioned above, was large-scale social dislocation and hardship, which weakened rural society significantly. Moreover, the war created opportunities for previously submerged tensions within rural society to emerge, and the ensuing attempts to change some of the most basic social role definitions in Shona society further weakened the established system of social control.

It has been found that in the Mutoko district of Mashonaland, the youth associated with ZANLA guerrillas not so much to engage in the war as to challenge the strictness of their parents' control. The war also created a power vacuum within which poorer villagers could use the guerrillas' instructions to report on collaborators and sell-outs as a smoke screen to attack wealthier members of the community whom they envied. Women, resentful of the abuse they received from husbands, sought the guerrillas as superior sources of authority to discipline their husbands. Finally, the war created opportunities for commoners outside the officially recognized chieftaincies to try to gain political control over the incumbent chiefs by participating in the village committees. The overall conclusion "that peasants, even during the anti-colonial war, ranked coming to terms with their internal enemies as far more pressing and more worthy of risks than eliminating the white state"[113] supports the interpretation that the contest for hegemony between rival political and military forces created a process of social change in which the fabric of rural society, and the rules of social control embedded therein, was placed under enormous strain. To the extent that the social fabric gave way under this strain, society was effectively weakened.

Negotiations

Many attempts were made to settle the Rhodesian conflict through negotiations. Failure marked all until the Lancaster House negotiations of 1979. That agreement ended the existence of the Rhodesian state and inaugurated its successor, the state of Zimbabwe. From the perspective of this study, three questions are important. First, why did the numerous early attempts at negotiated settlements fail? Second, what can account for the success of the Lancaster House negotiations? Third, did the Lancaster House agreement dissolve the contest for hegemony and lay the basis for the creation of an autonomous state?

The early attempts are memorable more for their dramatic locations than for their substantive results. Negotiations failed on HMS *Tiger* in 1966, on HMS *Fearless* in 1968, on the Victoria Falls bridge in 1975, and at Geneva in 1976. Other, less geographically spectacular attempts failed too: attempts by the British government in 1971 (often referred to as the Home-Goodman effort), and the 1977 Anglo-American attempt (the Owen-Young plan of 1977). These failures were obviously a function of bad faith by one or more of the negotiating parties. Robert Blake describes Ian Smith's approach to the *Tiger* and *Fearless* talks: "Negotiating to him meant seeking an agreement on his own terms and wearing the British Government down till they were accepted."[114] However, willingness to make concessions must accompany the desire to reach a settlement if the good faith requirement is to be met. Smith clearly was not willing to make concessions, and at times, such as during the Victoria Falls talks, apparently preferred no agreement at all.[115] This lack of good faith follows from the hegemonic quality of the stakes being negotiated and was also demonstrated in ZANU's frequent insistence (at the 1976 Geneva Conference) that the Rhodesian state surrender as a precondition for negotiations,[116] a compliment returned by Smith in setting the conditions for ZANU and ZAPU to attend the negotiations for the "internal" settlement of 1978.[117]

The various proposals that implied the notion of surrender not only reflected bad faith but also created loss of face. The Kissinger proposals (from which the Geneva Conference flowed) provided for Rhodesian control of the armed forces during the transition process. This offended ZANU and ZAPU, requiring them to submit to an illegal regime. The Vance-Owen plan proposed the opposite: the armed forces would be composed of ZANLA and ZIPRA members. This plan alienated the Rhodesian military leaders: "Not only was their pride wounded by the connotation of surrender, it was a practical matter as well."[118] Given the theoretical perspective used in this study, the order of importance of these objections must be reversed: not only was the composition of the armed forces a practical matter, but more important, it was also a matter of pride. Armed forces are important practical as well as symbolic indicators of who owns a country and, as such, are valued badges of collective esteem. Both peace proposals failed to make accommodation for this crucial psychological need, and on this point both of them failed.

In a sense, therefore, the negotiating events that preceded Lancaster House can be taken as prenegotiations. Prenegotiations contribute to the reaching of a settlement by contributing to all the parties fundamentally redefining the conflict and the conceivable outcomes, thereby creating a contract zone within which a range of mutually profitable agreements can be found. Such a redefinition gradually took place in the ranks of the incumbents of the Rhodesian state: "Though unsuccessful, the 1976–1979 diplomatic efforts had helped change the Rhodesian scene dramatically. Smith, in accepting the Kissinger plan, had at least acknowledged the possibility of majority rule within a few years."[119] Whether a similar process was occurring within the ranks of ZANU and ZAPU is less clear.

Success eluded all third-party efforts, though, as long as all the major antagonists "perceived that their alternatives were superior to any likely political settlement."[120] By the end of the 1970s these options had narrowed considerably, owing to the constraining effects of two sets of dependence relationships. The dependence of the Rhodesian state on the global economy for maintaining its resource base and, ultimately, its capacity to wage war was effectively exploited by the major international states through economic sanctions.[121] To escape this punishment, an agreement at Lancaster House had to be clinched. In a regional economy such punishment could not easily be meted out within national borders only, and the Rhodesian state also helped to distribute the economic hardships of sanctions to neighboring Zambia and Mozambique, which were providing bases for ZIPRA and ZANLA, respectively. The leaders of those states, especially President Samora Machel of Mozambique, put pressure on ZANU and ZAPU to reach agreement at Lancaster House. The mutually hurting stalemate, keenly felt by the military command on both sides,[122] was also felt by these frontline states.

An additional vital part of the motivation that moved all parties to the agreement was the perception that each would emerge as the victor from the first elections.[123] Superficially at least, that perception contributed to the appearance of a non-zero-sum outcome to the contest at the conference, which Lord Carrington, as the chair, took great trouble to preserve.[124] It also swayed President Machel of Mozambique, who, when Mugabe still resisted signing the agreement at the end of the conference, sent him this message: "Electoral victory was assured. . . . If he did not sign the agreement, he would be welcomed back to Mozambique and given a beach villa where he could write his memoirs. In other words, as far as Mozambique was concerned, the war was over."[125]

The actual convergence of opposing views to a final document stipulating the conditions of cease-fire, transition, elections, and the constitution was also effectively induced through the strategy and tactics of Lord Carrington. The British decided, in effect, that in the absence of a mutually perceived contract zone they would unilaterally define such a middle ground, present it to the parties (or, it seems, confront each party with it), and then seek concurrence on it. Finally, numerous face-saving measures deployed by the third-party mediator rescued the negotiations from potential deadlocks. By far the most significant face-saving action of all, however, was made by Robert Mugabe at the end of the transition process. Having won the first election, and on the eve of taking power in the new state, he appealed on national television: "Let us join together. Let us show respect for the winners and the losers. There is no intention on our part to victimize the minority. We will ensure there is a place for everyone in this country. I want a broadly based government to include whites and Nkomo."[126] A few days before, Mugabe had magnanimously offered the command of the new state's army to General Walls, who had commanded the forces of the Rhodesian state. That act hinted at the dissolution of the contest for hegemony between the forces who had defended and opposed the Rhodesian state. What remained less certain was the question whether Lancaster House had created a new arena in which a new set of contenders would vie for hegemony. The dynamics of such a process would once again decisively shape both state and society in independent Zimbabwe.

✤ 4 ✤

ZIMBABWE: RECONSTITUTING STATE AND SOCIETY

A decade after Zimbabwe became independent under the Lancaster House constitution, the country has not (unlike Botswana) built up a track record that can be comfortably classified as wholly democratic. In the 1988–89 Freedom House annual survey of political rights and civil liberties the country is described as "a one-party state with the trappings of a parliamentary system." On the scale of political rights, which ranges from a low score of 7 to a high of 1, it gets a rating of 6 (versus Botswana's rating of 2), and on the scale of civil liberties with the same range its rating is 5 (compared with Botswana's rating of 3).[1] The limited democratic success of the country cannot be assessed only by looking for how much or how little democracy there is. The qualified democratic rating generally given to Zimbabwe also invites the two further questions: Why is the country not more democratic? and Why is it as democratic as its current status reveals? The general literature on independent Zimbabwe has not focused directly on these questions, and it tends to be dominated by analyses of the extent to which the socialist expectation created by the first generation of state leaders has been realized. In this study, these analyses are considered only to the extent that they bear on the dimensions of state-society interaction outlined in the appendix. The aim of this chapter is also to explain why the Zimbabwean regime has neither evolved into a full democracy nor lapsed into a fully authoritarian regime.

The newly independent state had a population of 7.5 million people living in an area of 391,000 square kilometers (roughly the size of Montana). As in Botswana at independence, the overwhelming majority (77 percent) still lived in the rural areas by 1982, although this percentage was down from the 1965 figure, 86 percent. A demographic trend similar to Botswana's was that both the overall population growth rate and the rate of urbanization were accelerating; 51 percent of the population in 1982 was under the age of 15.[2] The Shona speakers outnumbered the siNdebele speakers 4 to 1, and both groups outnumbered the smaller African cultural minorities and the 37,000 Asians and coloreds.[3] By far the most significant demographic change in the immediate post-independence years was in the size of the white population. The cumulative impact of the civil war on white morale and the subsequent change in statehood with its attendant uncertainties resulted in a major emigration. From an all-time high of 275,000 in 1979 the number of whites declined to 260,000 in 1980 and 80,000 by 1983.[4]

The segregation policies of the Rhodesian state from 1910 to 1964 had displaced up to 283,000 Africans from the land.[5] The civil war aggravated the social dislocation that goes with forced population removals. By the end of the war 1.2 million people (nearly 20 percent of the population) had been displaced. Some 228,000 fled as refugees to Mozambique, Zambia, or Botswana. Almost 400,000 fled to the urban centers, and up to 750,000 were relocated into the 220 "protected villages" in the countryside. The rural infrastructure had also suffered from the war. About one-third of the cattle in the African lands died by the end of the war. Of a total of 1,800 dip tanks, 1,600 were destroyed or damaged, as were 64 causeways and bridges, 1,830 boreholes, 425 dams, and 40 airstrips. Even more important, 2,000 rural schools had been destroyed or damaged, and 9,000 of the total 13,700 rural small businesses were completely demolished. More than 700 square kilometers of minefields in the border areas had to be cleared.[6] These visible signs of destruction obscured the damage done to the social fabric in breakup of families, drug addiction, alcoholism, and financial destitution on both sides.

At independence Botswana was the third poorest country in the world, having only the most rudimentary economic infrastructure in place. By contrast, the Rhodesian legacy to the new state builders was a relatively complex and resilient economy. Although the prospects of profitable mining initially lured the British South African Company into occupying the territory, the core of the modern economy was subsequently built around manufacturing and agriculture. At independence the manufacturing sector employed 15 percent of the formal work force and contributed 24.8 percent of the GDP.[7] By early 1980, 1,366 manufacturing entities were producing more than 6,000 different products.[8] The agricultural sector was generating 12.4 percent of GDP by 1979 and providing 34 percent of formal employment.[9] With the agricultural activities in the communally owned lands taken into account, it has been calculated that more than 75 percent of the country's population were dependent on agriculture for their livelihood. The modern commercial component of the agricultural sector still dominated production, yielding 80 percent of the output and 95 percent of the marketed produce.[10] The mining sector ranked only third in size, contributing 7.9 percent of GDP and employing 6 percent of the formal work force.[11] Like the manufacturing sector, mining was a complex and diverse enterprise. By 1978, 186 different entities were mining 40 minerals commercially, although a few large companies dominated.[12] The remaining large sector of employment was the state; public administration accounted for 8 percent of formal employment.[13]

This modern economy became subjected to comprehensive economic sanctions by the international state system after UDI in 1965. Despite this adversity the economy grew at first, with GDP per capita rising annually by 3.5 percent between 1965 and 1974.[14] Eventually the pressure from outside and the effects of the civil war took their toll, and GDP for 1975 declined by 1 percent, for 1976 by 3.5 percent, and for 1977 by 7 percent. By the end of 1978 it was estimated that real per capita incomes had slumped by 25 percent of what they were at the end of 1974.[15] This economic decline froze or exacerbated the inherited inequalities created through decades of racially biased, unequal economic development. Black unemployment exceeded 20 percent in 1975, and the overall ratio of white to black incomes remained at 10 or 11 to 1 throughout,[16] with 60 percent of the income going to the wealthiest 4 percent of the population.[17]

The other structural features of the Rhodesian economy also remained intact through the statehood transition. The size of the state as an active participant in the economy did not change significantly. Total expenditure by the state in 1967 stood at 27 percent of GDP and increased steadily to 35.8 percent by 1976,[18] and by 1980 the private-sector share of total expenditure was down to 63 percent.[19] The major dimensions of dependence that characterized the Rhodesian economy were carried over into independence. The dependence of the state and society on the small number of white commercial farmers who produced the bulk of the nation's food remained unchanged. The community that had occupied 8,716 farms in 1968 held only 6,110 in 1979; more than a thousand farmers left this sector during the war years.[20] Within this shrinking farming community, dependence was accentuated by wide disparities in farm size and productivity. Roger Riddell reports that in 1976 as many as 2,000 white farmers were technically insolvent and that the most productive 28 percent of the farms (which covered 77 percent of the white land area) yielded 79 percent of the white farming output, which in turn was 80 percent of the national output.[21] In 1978 the most productive 1,100 of the 4,500 white farmers who grew maize were delivering 60 percent of the national maize crop.[22]

The dependence of the economy on foreign capital investment was high from the start of colonial industrial development,[23] as was reliance on imports and exports. During the UDI years and under the impact of sanctions, the economy's external dependence gradually shifted more to South Africa, both as a source of trade and as a source of investment capital.[24] At independence, South Africa was receiving 18.4 percent of Zimbabwe's exports and providing 32 percent of its imports,[25] and South African capital assumed an increasingly large component of the two-thirds foreign ownership of Zimbabwe's economy.

The most damaging impact of sanctions on the UDI economy was carried over into independence. Toward the end of the 1970s the fixed capital formation in the agricultural and manufacturing sectors fell dramatically and started to lag even in replacement and improvement of mining-sector machinery.[26] This was the start of technological decline, the long-term damage from which began appearing much later, "when investment-starved industrial subsectors began to reveal a comparative backwardness that seriously threatened their survival in export markets."[27]

The political inheritance of the Zimbabweans was a state weakened by war, international isolation, and domestic illegitimacy, and an internal governmental infrastructure greatly damaged at the local level by civil war and the attempts of rival military and political formations to gain control over the rural populations. But transition to the Zimbabwean state did not, however, smash the institutional framework of the Rhodesian state.[28] The state's major instruments of legal control—most notably those that controlled the economy and the security apparatus—remained intact. These two sets of institutional mechanisms would dovetail well with the intentions of the Zimbabwean state builders and would bear strongly on the evolution of the state, society, and democratic politics in the first decade of independence.

RECONSTITUTING THE STATE

The first Zimbabwean elections were won with a clear majority by ZANU-(PF) under the leadership of Robert Mugabe. ZANU had fought the civil war under the banner of socialism, which was primarily a symbolic reference point to delineate the old Rhodesian order from the prospective new, better, and qualitatively different Zimbabwean state. The ZANU-(PF) party constitution of 1984 formalized the ideology of the party as the pursuit of "a socialist state in Zimbabwe based on Marxist-Leninist principles," a statement repeated in the party's 1985 election manifesto.[29] The party has claimed that this explicit ideological commitment sets ZANU-(PF) apart from the other political parties in the country.[30]

Such forthrightness about ideological principles has not been matched with clear policy blueprints for transforming the state and society according to the mold of Marxism-Leninism. Broadly derived objectives relating to land redistribution, restructuring of the economy, establishment of a one-party state, and state control over the mass media and education were not accompanied by policy documents on how to achieve them. That omission has left analysts without clear yardsticks for judging the policy measures implemented during the first decade of independence and has left them in a quandary as to whether ideology, though explicitly stated by ZANU-(PF), plays any role in policy formulation at all. The interpretation that ideology did and still does matter in the sense of delimiting broad parameters for policy measures but rarely as a source for detailed directives has been argued convincingly.[31] Also persuasive is the interpretation that the Marxist-Leninist components of this ideology were chosen selectively to fit into the overall project of using the state to transform the society and the economy.[32]

The new state was shaped primarily by the constitution negotiated at Lancaster House. This Westminster-type constitution provided for a bicameral parliamentary legislature consisting of the House of Assembly and the Senate. The House comprised 100 members, of which 80 were elected on a common voters' roll. The other 20 seats were elected by white Zimbabwean voters from a separate roll. The Senate comprised 40 members: 14 were elected by an electoral college consisting of the members of the House who were elected from the common roll; 10 were elected by an electoral college consisting of the House members elected from the white roll; 10 were chiefs elected by the Council of Chiefs; and the remaining 6 were appointed by the president. The maximum term of office of the parliament was set at five years. The reserved white seats in both houses were entrenched for seven years. The executive consisted of the prime minister and the cabinet, with the president as a ceremonial head of state.[33] The constitution was superior to the parliament and was the supreme law of Zimbabwe, the locus of sovereignty, and the site of hegemony.

One of the striking aspects of continuity with previous Rhodesian constitutions was the retention of ethnic representation. The Council of Chiefs elected 5 chiefs from Matabeleland and 5 from Mashonaland to the Senate.[34] The passage of this provision at Lancaster House was noteworthy also for the fact that "none of the nationalists at the Lancaster talks either advocated or criticized retention of this structure. Once presented, it was accepted as if by conditioned habit."[35] Another stipulation that ensured continuity with the past was the provision that prohibited the state from expropriating private property. Instead, exchange of property to the state had to be on a "willing buyer, willing seller" basis. This measure was entrenched for 10 years and ensured that private property and the modern capitalist enterprise sector of the economy remained in place.

Within these constraints the ruling ZANU-(PF) began reconstituting the state, society, and the economy. At their disposal was the public service structure of the old Rhodesian state, which was retained by its brief successor, the Internal Settlement Constitution (1979) of Zimbabwe-Rhodesia. The top positions in the public service remained occupied by the personnel recruited under the rule of the Rhodesian Front, but the Muzorewa internal settlement government did start recruiting more Africans into lower-level positions. Of the 40,000 public servants in 1980, 29,000 were black, but in the higher echelons of the 10,570 so-called established officer ranks, only 3,368 were black.[36] A number of white officials within these ranks exhibited what have been described as "dubious loyalties" by an analyst, who noted that "several Ministers were quick to report the use of administrative discretion to oppose or delay the implementation of new policies."[37] The Lancaster House constitution provided a mechanism for dealing with such a politically intolerable situation within the executive. The so-called Presidential Directive (section 75[2] of the constitution) allows the president to give policy directions to the Public Service Commission so as to achieve "a suitable representation of the various elements of the population in the Public Service" and was put into use to combat this problem.[38] The effect was dramatic. Three years after independence the number of white "established officers" had dropped from 7,202 to 4,495, and the number of blacks had risen to 17,693.[39] Even with an expanding public service the proportion of black officials in these ranks rose to more than 88 percent by 1984.[40] With the dramatic increase in the overall size of the public service to 95,000 from the independence level of 40,000—the new positions being filled mostly by blacks—the composition of the public service was changed substantially within a decade of independence.[41] Large-scale change notwithstanding, there were also some important continuities, especially in the security-related bureaucracies, where some of the top positions remained in the hands of individuals appointed by the Rhodesian state.[42] The crucial question for state strength, state autonomy, and democratic stability would lie not only in the changing composition of this corps of personnel but also in the role they played in shaping public policy after independence.

The Lancaster House constitution placed few obstacles in the way of a fundamental restructuring of local government under the newly established Ministry of Local Government and Town Planning. The new system differed from the old in two fundamental ways. First, it eliminated the racial basis of representation and administration, and second, it removed the chiefs from the system of local government and replaced them with a fully elected system of representatives similar to that of independent Botswana. With the scrapping of the Land Apportionment Act, the tribal trust lands became known as communal lands. The District Councils Act of 1980 provided for 55 popularly elected district councils to replace the 220 African councils (many of which had ceased to function during the civil war anyway). Below these councils two further levels, the ward development committees and village development committees, served the district councils as elective and administrative units, respectively. In the formerly white farming areas, elected rural councils were established. Both these types of bodies fell under the relevant appointed district administrator (formerly district commissioner), the chief executive officer. The Urban Councils Act of 1973 was amended in 1980 to provide for 16 nonracially elected bodies to govern the urban areas. The next step was the Provincial Councils and Administration Act of 1985, which established eight provinces, each with a provincial governor appointed by the central government and a provincial council consisting mostly of appointed officials and indirectly elected representatives. The most recent reform was an attempt to merge the mostly white rural councils into the entirely black district councils through the 1988 Rural District Councils Act.[43] A schematic presentation of this system of local government is presented in figure 4.1. The impact of this set of institutions on the strength of the new state, especially on its penetrative and extractive capabilities and its democratic quality, is taken up later in the chapter.

The new constitution recognized the same sources of law that had served the legal system of the Rhodesian state, namely, the Roman-Dutch law of Cape Colony, with its component of English law, and the customary law of the African population. At the national level the constitution provided for the separation of powers, and so the judiciary's primary function was the interpreting and applying of existing law. An important body established by the constitution was the Judicial Service Commission, empowered to

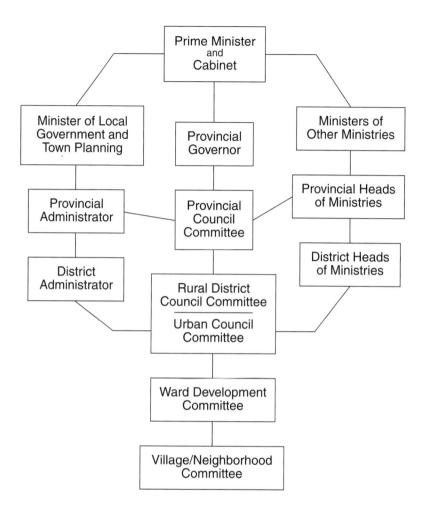

Figure 4.1 — Provincial Councils and Administration in Zimbabwe

Source: Adapted from Kamiel Wekwete, "The Local Government System in Zimbabwe: Some Perspectives on Change and Development," *Planning and Administration* 15, no. 1 (spring 1988): 26, figure 1. Copyright © International Union of Local Authorities. Used by permission of the Publisher.

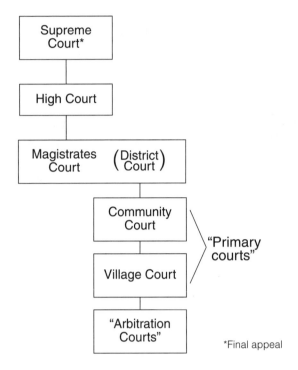

Figure 4.2 — Judicial Structure of Zimbabwe, February 1983

Source: Adapted from Andrew Ladley, "Changing the Courts in Zimbabwe: The Customary Law and Primary Courts Act," *Journal of African Law* 26, no. 2 (1982): 96, figure 2. Copyright © Oxford University Press. Used by permission of Oxford University Press.

advise the president on the appointment of judges to the higher courts and of presiding officers to the lower courts. The Rhodesian triadic-but-subordinate court system was replaced early on by a more streamlined system (figure 4.2) intended to integrate the customary and general sets of law.

The High Court has unrestricted jurisdiction over persons and matters in the country, and it can review all actions of lower courts. The Supreme Court is a court of appeal for the High Court and has a similar range of jurisdiction. Both sets of courts are presided over by judges. Magistrates courts have more limited jurisdiction in both civil and criminal cases and are presided over by magistrates who are appointed by the Public Service Commission. The Customary Law and Primary Courts Act of 1981 and the Customary Law and Primary Courts Amendment Act of 1982 scrapped the previous customary court system and established a new set of primary courts. Under these acts, customary law, restricted to civil cases, is applied when parties agree to it or when it appears appropriate. Village courts are primary courts of the first instance and can hear only civil cases. Community courts are primary courts as well as courts of appeal from village courts and also have limited criminal jurisdiction. Both sets of courts are presided over by a presiding officer who is a public servant appointed by the minister of justice, and both are accompanied by assessors appointed from a list prepared by the minister.[44]

The main difference in the status and application of customary law in Zimbabwe versus Rhodesia is that it is not forcibly compartmentalized anymore. Customary law is allowed to move closer to general law, and in this regard it has been concluded that "in general, . . . the overall effect of the various elements of the definition of customary law in the Customary Law and Primary Courts Act is one of 'freedom'—allowing customary law to find its own limits on a case-by-case basis."[45] The implications of merging these two sets of rules of social control into a single state-driven set of rules for state strength and democratic practices are considered later in this chapter.

By the end of 1982 almost 1,500 village courts and more than 50 community courts had been established. The Ministry of Justice trained and appointed all the presiding officers for the community courts, as stipulated by the letter of the law. In the case of village courts, however, the presiding officers and their assessors were elected at public meetings through a show of hands. The ministry generally did not turn down these names when they were submitted for confirmation. Thus, unlike Botswana's chiefs, Zimbabwe's chiefs lost their status as officers in charge of the customary courts, as they only rarely (with the apparent exception of southern Matabeleland) were returned to these positions by election, being seen by electors as "collaborators" with the former Rhodesian regime. The implications of this trend for state-society interactions will be taken up later in the chapter.

In the security establishment, continuity with the Rhodesian state was more marked than in almost any of the previously discussed sectors of state institutions. The armies of ZIPRA, ZANLA, and the Rhodesian state were merged and integrated into a single force without great difficulty, albeit only after the February 1981 uprising by ZIPRA was quelled with the loss of 300 guerrillas.[46] Continuity in the security bureaucracies was effected by retaining some of the strategically placed officials of the Rhodesian state. Legislative continuity was ensured by retaining the 1960 Law and Order (Maintenance) Act and the 1960 Emergency Powers Act. The latter has been extensively used; more than 60 new emergency regulations were issued in the first four years of independence. The 1975 Indemnity and Compensation Act, reportedly labeled "fascist" at the time by the nationalist movements, was scrapped in 1980 but reappeared as the Emergency Powers (Security Forces Indemnity) Regulations in 1982.[47] The insulation of the security establishment from surveillance and control by parliament continued, and high budget allocations through the 1980s rounded off a process not so much of state reconstitution but, rather, of state maintenance. An explanation of this continuity in state building is offered later in the chapter.

Finally, the new state announced its qualitatively different status through a set of symbolic changes that proclaimed black ownership. The official name "Republic of Zimbabwe" swept away the name of the conqueror Cecil John Rhodes and exalted the largest indigenous civilization of the area during precolonial times.[48] Likewise, Salisbury was renamed Harare, Fort Victoria became Masvingo, Hartley was renamed Chegutu, and Vila Salazar (on the Mozambiquean border) was changed to Sango.[49] The civil war, instrumental in the change of ownership, received symbolic recognition in the changing of Jameson Avenue in Harare to Samora Machel Avenue and the replacement of Rhodes and Founders Day with Heroes Day (May 6).[50] The second message contained in the symbolic trappings of the new state was the Shona identity of the new owners of the state. Thus far the political and religious institutions of the other African cultural entities have contributed little to the symbolism of the new state.[51]

The constraints initially imposed on the Zimbabwean state builders by the entrenched clauses of the Lancaster House constitution were dismantled as soon as the seven- and ten-year restrictions were passed. In 1987 the 20 reserved seats for whites in the House and the 10 seats in the Senate were abolished. Those House seats would be filled from then on by an electoral college comprising the remaining 80 members of the House, and the entire House would elect the 10 senators. In the same year the position of prime minister was replaced by an executive presidency with a six-year term of office. In 1989 the Senate was abolished, and the House was enlarged to 150 members, 120 of whom were to be elected by universal suffrage, 8 appointed by the provincial governors, and 12 appointed by the president, and 10 chiefs were to be elected by the country's chiefs. In 1992 the Land Acquisition Act scrapped the "willing buyer, willing seller" principle, enabling the state to expropriate agricultural land on its own terms.[52]

RESHAPING THE SOCIETY

From the outset, the ruling ZANU-(PF) government was intent on using the state to reshape the society. Because the ideological goals were vague, the state structures described above were an important constraint inhibiting societal change. Nevertheless, substantial changes were made in the Zimbabwean society through public policies during the first decade of independence. In one of the most detailed analyses thus far, Jeffrey Herbst has examined a number of policy outcomes, the locus of decision making, the extent to which ideological considerations carried the day, and the extent of state autonomy in policymaking. In looking at policy outcomes alone, the record shows that the Zimbabwean state builders made some substantial achievements.

The most immediate policy priority was land redistribution. In November 1982 the government published a broad plan to resettle 162,000 families, requiring the purchase of 9 million hectares of land from white farmers. The only actual detailed target with accompanying budgetary support, the resettling of 15,000 families in three years, was achieved in due course. Resettlement has continued slowly, and 162,000 total resettlements is still the target. The actual record of slow, gradual resettlement is therefore, according to Herbst, indicative not of policy failure but of meeting specific targets. The larger target should be seen, according to him, as an expression of intent, not as a policy blueprint.[53] By 1990, 52,000 families had been resettled on 3.3 million hectares.[54]

State control of producer prices for agricultural products was another policy priority. There the new rulers took over the institution set up by the Rhodesians—the Agricultural Marketing Authority, a government parastatal. Within this framework they succeeded in controlling prices in favor of those producers (such as black growers of small maize crops and sorghum) whom for ideological reasons they considered important, despite deft lobbying tactics from organized producers and huge subsidy costs to the state.[55]

Other changes in the distribution of public goods produced similar outcomes. The racial inequalities that epitomized the Rhodesian state were strikingly visible in the field of public health care. By the late 1970s public expenditure on health was so skewed that approximately R$144 per year was spent on every white person versus to R$31 on each urban black citizen and R$4 on each rural black citizen. To deracialize public health service and provide more equitable rural health facilities, a new institution—the provincial medical director (PMD)—was set up within the new provincial framework. The PMD received requests for the siting of new health centers from village and ward development committees, coordinated them, and sent final recommendations to the Ministry of Health, which made allocations in liaison with the Treasury. By deconcentrating decision making to the lowest level of government, the government eliminated regional, and therefore ethnic, biases and also eliminated regional backlogs (such as in northern Matabeleland) in providing health centers to the rural populations.[56] By the end of 1987, 224 such new centers had been completed.[57] Another innovation was the passage of the Traditional Medical Practitioners Council Act in 1981, which enabled traditional healers and spirit mediums to engage legally in their vocation. This step was especially important because of the crucial symbolic and mobilizing role spirit mediums had played in the civil war, and because up to 80 percent of the population of the country was still using traditional medicine in the mid-1980s.[58]

Through the Minimum Wages Act of 1980 the minister of labor gained control in the setting of wage levels for anyone receiving remuneration. The evolution of wage determination within this institutional framework did not automatically lead to employees turning the tables on employers with the government on their side. Yet a gradual, incremental rise in wages roughly equal to the inflation rate did at least allow employees to hold their standard of living against rising costs, while beneath them the economic safety net constructed by the state was extended.[59]

In addition, the educational system was deracialized and expanded[60] and the legal status of women in society was redressed, largely through the Legal Age of Majority Act of 1980 and the Matrimonial Causes Act of 1985.[61] In all, these policies were significant achievements for the new state in changing the way public policies were formulated and public goods were distributed. This process contributed to the deracializing of society and inserted a larger measure of equitability in state provision of benefits to society.

THE DYNAMICS OF STATE-SOCIETY INTERACTION

Comparison with Rhodesia is useful to some extent in judging the new Zimbabwean state's strength as an institution of social control—that is, in judging its capacity to extract resources from society, regulate the social conduct of the population, and penetrate society and reallocate resources, all on its own terms and not those of other social institutions.

The most visible signs of state weakness—widespread lawlessness, civil disobedience, and tax revolts—did not characterize the new state's first decade. For the most part, citizens complied with the laws. Not all officials of the state followed suit, however. Allegations of widespread corruption by government officials (the so-called Willowgate scandal) culminated in an official judicial inquiry that led to the resignation of five cabinet ministers and one provincial governor in 1989.[62] There has also been speculation that ZANU-(PF) fractured along clan and regional lines into a patronage system that undermines strict law abidance by state officials and the enforcement of discipline by senior political leaders.[63] Given the weakness of the data, one is unable to discern whether the resulting power relationships approximate Migdal's configuration of *triangles of accommodation* or Rothchild's model of *hegemonial exchange* (see the appendix for more on this subject).

Certain features of the new state seem to make for greater potential penetration of society than the Rhodesian state achieved. The bottom-tier local institutions, the village and ward development committees, are almost indistinguishable from ZANU-(PF) structures at this level,[64] and they therefore provide institutional reach for the state into these sectors of society. Yet through removal of the chiefs from the local governmental system a different source of social control was forfeited. It has been observed that "as a result of the removal of chiefs, there has also been a sharp decline in the yield of the development levy (formerly the poll tax) which used to be collected by traditional leaders but now has to be collected by the district council."[65] Greater penetration may have been achieved, but a decline in the extractive capacities of the state has been the price.

In the new system of courts, state penetration is enhanced by making the presiding officers of the community court paid civil servants and reserving the right of the state to veto the appointment of presiding officers for the village courts. Overall control is also bolstered by the fact that the state constitutes these primary courts by warrant and maintains surveillance over them through the official body called the Inspectorate.[66] Removing judicial authority from the chiefs maintains and builds on continuity with the wartime so-called people's courts or comrades' courts established by ZANLA.[67] And through the drawing of customary law closer into the legal and institutional body of general law and the dismantling of the rigid racial boundaries between the administration of the two legal systems, a greater merging of these two sets of rules of social control becomes possible. In practice, this process has yet to achieve its potential. It has been found to perpetuate inconsistencies between the two legal systems, leading to a conflict of laws between general and customary law.[68] It has been criticized for imposing Shona-Ndebele customary law onto the other cultural minorities in Zimbabwe, thus creating a conflict of laws within the overall body of customary law.[69] And it has been accused of abandoning the essential socialist political direction taken by the former people's or comrades' courts.[70]

The last important institutional innovation that could strengthen the state was the change in the status of the spirit mediums. Legalizing (and thus decriminalizing) their activities through the Traditional Medical Practitioners Council Act greatly reduced the clash between the customary and modern rules of social control that marked the Rhodesian state; at the same time, however, legalization also extended state control into that realm. The act established the Traditional Medical Practitioners Council and gave legal status to the Zimbabwe National Traditional Healers Association (ZINATHA). The council must maintain a register of all traditional medical practitioners who are allowed to practice either as a traditional medical practitioner (usually as a herbalist or diviner) or as a spirit medium. The act also allows for such persons who do not hold to the standard of the council to be expelled, in effect giving the state the prerogative to dictate who qualifies as a true spirit medium and who does not—a policy that offends the very definitive qualities of spirit mediums in the first place.

The similarity between the structural problems confronted by the Rhodesian state builders and their Zimbabwean counterparts (and the irony in that similarity) has been superbly captured by David Lan: "In effect the Traditional Medical Practitioners Act entrenches in law precisely that control over the mediums that political authorities of the past, whether chiefs or district commissioners, attempted to enforce in order to discredit mediums who opposed them. The state emphasizes its own 'descent' from the ancestors thus minimizing the importance of that other technique by which the *mhondoro* are represented on earth, possession."[71] Recognizing this threat from the state for what it is, Lan reports that a senior spirit medium, speaking in trance in 1982, sent a warning to the new rulers: "It was, he said, the *mhondoro* who had enabled the present government to come to power. If they failed the people and therefore failed the ancestors, the *mhondoro* would transfer their authority elsewhere."[72] Spirit mediums' dissent with government policy has ranged from refusal to apply for ZINATHA membership[73] (they object to being aggregated with herbalists and diviners) to active support for squatters who have illegally occupied land. A report registering similar findings of dissent concludes that by the mid-1980s "the complex authority of rural leaders was something no one at the top truly controlled."[74]

These above-mentioned issues have yet to coalesce into major societal challenges to the strength of the Zimbabwean state. Two other issues have in the first decade of independence presented actual challenges of great significance and with clear hegemonic implications to the state. The first arises from the adversarial relationship between ZANU and ZAPU, and the second from attempts by the ruling ZANU government to use the state to gain control of and reshape the economy.

The so-called Matabeleland problem started with the alleged discovery of an arms cache inside Matabeleland big enough to equip a battalion of soldiers. Tensions increased with the dismissal of (PF)-ZAPU leader Joshua Nkomo from the cabinet and the arrest of two ex-ZIPRA commanders, Dumiso Dabengwa and Lookout Masuku. Those actions, combined with the desertion of 4,000 soldiers from the national army in 1982 and the rise in violent criminal assaults and murders inside Matabeleland, led the government to send the national armed forces into the region on a so-called antidissidence campaign.[75] The primary instrument was the Fifth Brigade, trained by North Korean instructors and widely reported to have been recruited exclusively from Shona-speaking ranks.[76] The primary target was (PF)-ZAPU, which the government accused of organizing and controlling these activities (but the accusation was never proved). The overall outcome of the campaign, executed under protection of the Emergency Powers (Maintenance of Law and Order) Regulations, was at least 1,500 Ndebele deaths in 1983, the disappearance (and presumed deaths) of more than 100 ZAPU leaders in 1985, the widespread detention without trial of hundreds of civilians, and evidence of gross abuse of human rights through the torture of detainees in the infamous Stops Camp at police headquarters in Bulawayo.[77]

What triggered this overzealous political and military response to a primarily criminal problem? One investigation cites the incompatibility of the ideological disposition of ZANU-(PF) and its inherited structural position in the new state of Zimbabwe as the prime cause. As a party of liberation, ZANU had always been engaged in a contest, not only with the Rhodesian state but also with ZAPU. Intense suspicion about ZAPU's true agenda during the war had, according to this interpretation, led some ZANU politicians to believe that "Nkomo's long-term plan, aided and encouraged by the Soviet Union, was to watch while the white settler bull elephant and the ZANLA rhinoceros fought almost to a standstill and then move in his more conventional forces to establish a victorious position over both the other armies."[78] ZAPU was therefore seen as a hegemonic adversary rather than an ally in wrenching hegemony away from the Rhodesian state. In Masipula Sithole's view, had the Lancaster House process not stopped the war and "had the Smith regime been run out of Salisbury by ZANLA guerrillas, it is conceivable ZIPRA would have occupied Bulawayo and the two forces would have engaged each other in the Midlands, beginning a worse civil war than the scattered skirmishes witnessed in Matabeleland."[79] Even after the Lancaster House process and the independence elections, the victorious ZANU found its old opponent as much of a potential threat as ever.

To this one must add Sithole's interpretation of ZANU's intentions: "It is doubtful whether ZANU(PF) would have cooperated fully had it lost the election to either ZAPU or to some coalition. In fact, given that its guerrilla force controlled a good three-quarters of the countryside, it is reasonable to predict that all hell would have broken out."[80] ZANU-(PF)'s overriding intent to achieve hegemony was not dissolved during the Lancaster House process, nor by the conversion of warfare to electoral contestation. Rather, elections merely became another avenue to achieving hegemony. Since ZANU-(PF) had won the elections and its only remaining obstacle was (PF)-ZAPU, it is easy to share the conclusion that the heart of the Matabeleland problem was that "the regime has ascribed goals to dissidents that are congenial with its *own distinctive interests* in consolidating state power and entrenching Z.A.N.U. hegemony in the political system" (original emphasis).[81] The Matabeleland campaign therefore must be seen as part of the process of consolidating the hegemony of the Zimbabwean state. It was conducted European style, reminiscent of the way state builders in 17th- and 18th-century Europe had extended their jurisdictions through imposition and displacement, primarily by means of military power.[82] The dynamics of the process that led to the Matabeleland campaign as well as its outcome held crucial implications for the movement toward a one-party state, the merging of state and party, and political tolerance—all of which would have impact on the democratic quality of Zimbabwean politics.

The second major test of state strength during the first decade of independence was in the economic arena. The immediate task of the new rulers was to address the racial inequalities in the economy and bring equity into the distribution of public goods. The results, especially in health care and education, have been impressive.

Infant mortality declined rapidly from 120 per 1,000 live births in 1980 to 83 per 1,000 by 1982, and life expectancy rose from 51 years in 1970 to 57 years in 1985.[83] Enrollments at educational institutions have also skyrocketed. By 1988, primary school registrations were 35.8 percent above the 1980 figures; at secondary schools, 771.5 percent above; and at technical colleges, 623.7 percent above.[84]

This expansion in opportunities and welfare has not been matched by growth in wealth. During the first decade of independence the annual growth rate in GDP was 2.9 percent, distinctly less impressive than Botswana's 11.3 percent. GDP per capita for 1990 was U.S.$1,970, which again compares poorly with Botswana's U.S.$4,300 for the same year.[85] When population growth is taken into account, the increase in wealth has been negligible; the GDP per capita in real terms (at 1980 prices) for 1990 was only marginally above that of 1980.[86] The extent of this stagnation in the economy is revealed by the fact that per capita real consumer spending for 1986 was 29 percent lower than that for 1976.[87]

As a result, the educational system has been delivering more potential employees than the economy can absorb: by late 1987 the economy was generating only 19,300 new jobs annually[88] and 1991 graduates were expected to number more than 300,000. The unemployment figures rose throughout the decade, rising from 11 percent in 1982 to 18 percent by 1987 and an expected figure of 23 percent for 1991.[89] Restated slightly differently, another estimate is that by the 1990s only 10 percent of the 300,000 annual school-leavers would find employment in the formal sector of the economy.[90]

This inability to induce the economy to generate wealth results from and is part of the overall attempt by the new rulers to use the state as *the* instrument to gain control of the forces that shape the economy. Analyses of this aspect of Zimbabwean macroeconomic policies tend to measure policy success by the extent to which the state builders set out to build a Marxist-Leninist state and economy and reneged, or set out to achieve lesser socialist aims and succeeded or failed. Conclusions differ widely. In one view, the Zimbabwean state submitted to the forces of imperialism and global capitalism and made growth a higher priority than equity.[91] Another view holds that the state's placing a higher priority on control of economic forces and redistributive priorities than on growth has prevailed.[92] Determining which view is correct is not the precise focus of this study. What matters here is to gauge to what extent the economic policies of the state affected the strength of the state as an institution of social control vis-à-vis societally based actors, and eventually how these policies and their outcomes have affected the democratic quality of Zimbabwean politics.

The overall direction of policy has been to assert greater state control over the economy. The cumulative result of the state's expanding role in the economy can be measured in the decline of the private-sector share of domestic expenditure—63 percent in 1980 but down to 44 percent by 1989.[93] Behind this control has been marked hostility toward capitalist enterprise, foreign investment, multinational corporations, and white-initiated economic endeavor.[94] The overall result has been a cycle of public finance policies and outcomes that have left the state increasingly insolvent.[95] This insolvency has impact on every dimension of state capacity for social control. A stagnating economy meant the tax base did not expand, and so the extractive capacities of the state were adversely affected. Creating stronger regulative institutions to counteract these effects only aggravated the problem by further inhibiting growth. When the state lacks expanding resources to reallocate to society as public goods, its ability to penetrate society is correspondingly diminished. Taken together, these outcomes point to a crucial weakening of the state. When the additional impact of these policies on the legitimacy of the ruling party is taken into account, the causal link between state strength and democratic practices can be made. This argument is presented in the last section of this chapter. Before that, one additional dimension of the state has to be explored.

To what extent is the evolving Zimbabwean state autonomous from societally based forces? Or is it the instrument of racial, ethnic, or class-based social formations? The first social cleavage of importance is the white-black divide. The end of the civil war and the ascendancy of ZANU-(PF) to power in the new state ended the white-black armed hostilities that had left more than 40,000 casualties. Prime Minister Mugabe's immediate declarations of reconciliation toward the white population and his including of white members in his cabinet have been seen as vital in securing and consolidating civil order in subsequent white-black relations and in the fact that more than 80,000 whites remain in the country. Reconciliation rather than retribution has indeed prevailed.

Closer examination reveals that white-black amicability rests on an implicit bargain, the terms of which are dictated by the ruling ZANU-(PF). According to Herbst, this bargain, "which is never discussed publicly, but is understood by almost everyone, is essentially that the whites who are now economically active can stay, continue to operate their businesses and farms, and lead the colonial life they are accustomed to for the rest of their lives. Their children, with two exceptions, must leave."[96] The excepted fields are agriculture and wildlife tourism, where whites' continued presence and dominance are tolerated. This intriguing proposition is partially confirmed by the observation that the whites who do remain in public service tend to be recruited into the Department of Wildlife in the Ministry of Tourism and Natural Resources.[97]

The further suggestion is that the state implements this bargain through systematic antiwhite discrimination in access to credit, government purchases, and tenders for public enterprises. Creating "socialism for the whites" required such discrimination by the Rhodesian state. To achieve "socialism for the blacks" would require the same from the Zimbabwean state. Partial confirmation of this proposition can be found in the functioning of the Indigenous Business Development Center (IBDC), established to aid black businessmen, and whose director, a close relative of President Mugabe, "was perceived to have personal ties that enabled members to gain preferential access to business licenses, bank financing, and foreign exchange."[98] Since most whites are denied an economic future in the country, emigration becomes their remaining option, and thus, "by discouraging White society from increasing its numbers, the government has the assurance that within a generation Blacks will, through attrition, gain control of the economy."[99] Herbst has expressed himself well pleased with this bargain, and considers it part of the ongoing success of post-independence reconciliation. Viewed in ethnic terms, however, this bargain is nothing less than a slow-motion, benign, long-term policy of expulsion, and its overall content is to deny the whites in Zimbabwe a continued existence as a community. Furthermore, the most emphatic message contained in this bargain is that ownership of the country is reserved for black Zimbabweans. The rest can remain as temporary lodgers, but only on terms set by the owners.

If this is a black African state, is it also a Shona state? The first site where ethnic preferences can be revealed in the dynamics of state-society interaction is in the distribution of public goods. The available data on the distribution of public goods—specifically, those relating to rural public health centers—do not reveal any bias against the siNdebele-speaking population of Matabeleland, as was noted earlier. Where these goods have not reached remote cultural minorities, such as the Tonga of the Zambezi Valley, ethnic mobilization (through the institutional channel of the Binga District Council) has been found to be employed, in part, as an extractive mechanism to gain benefits from the state.[100]

The second potential indicator of ethnic preferences can be found in the field of electoral choice. The three elections thus far have all produced large ZANU-(PF) majorities. In the inaugural 1980 election the party won 57 of the 80 seats on the common voters' roll; (PF)-ZAPU was a distant second with 20 seats. In 1985 this majority was extended to 64 ZANU-(PF) seats, with (PF)-ZAPU an even more distant second with 15 seats. In the 1990 election, after the merger of (PF)-ZAPU into ZANU-(PF), the party swept into an unchallengeable electoral position, having taken 116 of the 120 seats in the newly reconstituted House of Assembly. The newly formed opposition party, the Zimbabwe Unity Movement, could win only 2 seats. The 1980 elections were contested under the rules of party-list proportional representation without regional constituencies, and the subsequent two elections under the rules for first-past-the-post majorities in single-member constituencies. The general finding on the role of ethnicity in the 1980 and 1985 Zimbabwean elections is that it revealed that "the particular course taken by its nationalist politics and the role of the two guerrilla armies before 1980 produced a split which assumed a largely ethnic form in 1980, and this has been deepened in 1985."[101] This appears to be the case although ethnic issues were virtually absent from the electoral rhetoric of the major parties.[102]

The 1990 election did not reveal the same social division. With the merging of (PF)-ZAPU and ZANU-(PF) the institutional channels for expressing this division disappeared. The election outcome was marked by a low turnout of 54 percent, sharply down from the 95 percent turnout of the previous two elections. The number of spoiled papers almost doubled to 5.5 percent for the parliamentary elections and 5.7 percent for the presidential elections. The unified ZANU-(PF) did secure a landslide, taking with it all the Matabeleland constituencies, but its 78 percent of the total vote was down from the 93 percent the two parties combined had garnered in 1985. Residual pockets of ethnic and regional support remained in the Binga constituency (the site of Tonga support) and among the Ndau and Manyika groups within the ranks of the Shona speakers—despite the fact that ethnic issues did not feature highly in any of the party's agendas. The general pattern of turnout is to be expected from an election whose outcome was a foregone conclusion, but it also revealed a decline in the legitimacy of the regime.[103] The overall conclusion is that ZANU-(PF) has throughout the independence era retained its ethnic core of supporters but has not been reduced to the status of an exclusively ethnic party. Instead it has gradually extended its support base beyond the boundaries of its traditional preindependence support.

No clear-cut confirmation of the Zimbabwean state as a Shona state is therefore possible. What needs to be explored more energetically is whether it is becoming increasingly a ZANU-(PF) state with whatever ethnic support groups the party has. The merger (or rather, incorporation) of (PF)-ZAPU into ZANU-(PF) is part of the project of establishing a one-party state, which is part of the larger project of merging state and party. Both projects have been part of the overall ideological goals of ZANU-(PF) for many years. And those overall goals have informed the expressed aims of creating a politically partisan public service, asserting the primacy of the party over the government, and practicing intolerance toward political opponents.[104] The actual convergence between party and state structures at the level of village and ward development committees has already been noted. The extent to which the Fifth Brigade has been invested with the ZANLA symbols and military doctrine and the military infused with ZANU-(PF) philosophy and personnel is also relevant.[105] And one case study shows the extent to which rural farm workers have failed to distinguish between ZANU-(PF)–sponsored worker committees and government institutions of the same name.[106]

Against this evidence must be weighed the findings that in numerous policy decisions at national level, the locus of decision making was in the state bureaucracy instead of the ruling party and the actual decisions were made on the basis of technocratic considerations instead of ideology. But even the most technical considerations must be judged, assessed, and measured against prior goals derived from normative yardsticks. Louis Picard's detailed research findings on the yardsticks for policymaking used by state officials in Botswana are crucial to assessing state autonomy in that country, but no such research is available for Zimbabwe. In the absence of additional research on the partisan status of the central-level bureaucrats in Zimbabwe and the impact of their party affiliation on decision making, the question of the autonomy of the Zimbabwean state cannot be explored further. What can be said is that it has no corps of public service personnel even remotely equivalent to the gelded expatriates of Botswana. Instead, the Fifth Brigade can be taken as their polar opposite.

The strong and weak points in the state outlined above are an inverse mirror of the strengths and weaknesses of the society. The weakness of the state in failing to capture the authority structures built around chiefs and spirit mediums mirrors the strength of societal networks of social control in resisting incorporation by the Zimbabwean state builders. Even the most basic administrative unit in the rural areas, the village, is still based on clan and kinship ties despite the chiefs' loss of formal authority.[107] At a different level, the inability of the state to reshape the economy on its own terms and to move the major economic actors to generate wealth on those terms also indicates societal strength in resisting rules of social control contrary to those under which the enterprises were established. Interest group formations are far more complex in Zimbabwe than in Botswana, given the former's more diverse economic structures and history of conflict. The major social cleavages (ethnicity, class, and gender) all find expression in the social issues of the country, yet none of them assumes such importance as to divide the society into permanently hostile "incipient whole societies," which marked the interest group structure of Rhodesian society.[108] What is visible at the political level is the absence of the norms of civility with respect to political tolerance and democratic practices. The best-publicized case of civil violence occurred after the 1985 election results were made known. Members of the ZANU-(PF) Youth League and the ZANU-(PF) Women's

League violently attacked supporters of (PF)-ZAPU, causing personal injury and property damage.[109] Within the interest group
formations of the society, one study has also found a largely
undemocratic organizational culture: "The institutional culture of
smallholder unions in Zimbabwe shows that non-state organizations reproduce the syndrome of arbitrary executive power that
ails the highest levels of government."[110] The conclusion is that
these institutions are unlikely to serve as the recruiting base for
those who would uphold a democratic political culture in Zimbabwe; interest group diversity does not automatically signal the
establishment of a civil society.

THE STATE, SOCIETY, AND DEMOCRACY

The low rating Zimbabwe receives from the Freedom House annual
survey of political rights and civil liberties (cited at the start of this
chapter) is not hard to explain. All three election campaigns have
been marked by intolerance, intimidation, and violence. In 1980
ZANU-(PF) refused to let other parties campaign in the areas it
had secured during the war.[111] In 1985 and 1990, as ruling party,
it is said to have used violence and intimidation against opponents.[112] During the 1990 campaign it was reported that the ruling
party made extensive use of the state media in campaigning against
opponents.[113] In the field of public policy the extensive systemic
discrimination by the state in the allocation of import licenses,
credit, and official tenders, as claimed by a number of analysts,[114]
also undermines the democratic character of the regime. The aspect
of regime structure and public policy most damaging to democracy, however, is that the new state retained and extended the security structures of the Rhodesian state and then applied them similarly. The extension of the state of emergency, the brutal military
campaigns in Matabeleland, the continuing practice of detention
without trial, and the widespread use of security legislation epitomize the undemocratic character of Zimbabwean politics.

Undermining of democratic politics—official intolerance toward
electoral opposition, economic discrimination against whites and
private-sector enterprise, and extreme reaction against perceived
extraconstitutional opposition in Matabeleland—is the result of the
ruling party's deployment of the state since independence. What

caused the ruling ZANU-(PF) to use the state in this way? The answer provided by Ronald Weitzer is that a sense of insecurity within ZANU-(PF), which follows from the multiparty constitutional framework negotiated at Lancaster House, led to exaggerated fears about the threats to the new state and to the party's own incumbency.[115] But what generated such exaggerated fears of the security threat from the opposition? Weitzer offers a structural explanation: repressive measures were used to limit democratic opposition because they were available; they "invited" continued abuse of state powers and were "conducive" to repressive strategies and outcomes. To this he adds an interest calculation. The new rulers, like the Rhodesians before them, are primarily concerned with ideological control, maintenance of order, defense, economic viability, and consolidation of state power. Their overriding objective has been to consolidate ZANU-(PF) hegemony, and the merging of state and party would be the culmination of the entrenchment of party hegemony.

What the above explanation fails to take up is why these interests and not others were pursued. One explanation would be continuity: the rulers of both the Rhodesian state and the Zimbabwean state commanded ethnic parties and were concerned with the construction of ethnic states. This explanation would also account for the exaggerated security fears felt by ZANU-(PF). Ethnic politics invariably entails a psychology of anxiety, that is, unrealistically perceived fears. The Rhodesian state, as an ethnic state, was built to respond to such fears, which proved to be a self-fulfilling prophecy. By extension it could then be argued that the Zimbabwean state as a Shona state, and ZANU-(PF) as an ethnic party, would easily accept a state geared to perceived threat, for each would share the psychological predisposition of the previous incumbents.

That interpretation is not offered in this study, as it has been argued in this chapter that ZANU-(PF) cannot be considered an exclusively ethnic party and that the Zimbabwean state, which may well be becoming a ZANU-(PF) state, still does not exhibit the defining features of an ethnic state. Instead, the explanation for the sense of insecurity that spawned unrealistically perceived threats and gave impetus to policy measures that undermined democracy in Zimbabwe can be found in the particular *ethos of state action* with which the new rulers took power at independence. Although no original research has been done on such an ethos to compare with the work of John Stephen Morrison on Botswana, the outlines of such an ethos can be pieced together from literature cited in this and the previous chapter.

This ethos was shaped primarily by ZANU's formative experiences from 1963 to 1980. The event that led to the establishment of ZANU was the banning of ZAPU in 1962. From that crisis evolved a split in the nationalist ranks over strategy, tactics, and purpose, which persisted into independence. Neither the common enemy nor the shared overall objective of liberation could bridge the divide, and when ZANU was formed in 1963 it was intensely adversarial to ZAPU.[116] Soon a leadership dispute developed, centered on specific individuals. An ethnic and regional division gradually arose, as argued in this and the previous chapter, without being explicitly expressed. The second and equally important formative relationship was with the Rhodesian state, the ruling Rhodesian Front party, and its leadership under Ian Smith. This equally intense adversarial relationship was conducted through war and negotiations and was substantively proclaimed by ZANU in an ideology of socialism. A number of scholars have pointed out that ZANU's socialism was primarily an ideology of opposition, vague in its guidelines and almost devoid of blueprints for a new order, but distinct enough to delineate the hated old order from the promised new one.[117]

At independence ZANU-(PF) took power in the new state after having defeated both its opponents at the ballot box. But to a party whose raison d'être had been shaped by a virtual zero-sum perception of conflict with both these antagonists, the electoral victory was exceptionally unsatisfactory. Given their fundamentally adversarial operational ethos, the structural position they found themselves in was nearly intolerable. Both their opponents were still in the political arena, and both found protection under the rules of the Lancaster House constitution. (PF)-ZAPU was entrenched in Matabeleland with an electorally proven power base and, initially, still had its army and weaponry. The Rhodesian state was no more, but the component parts from which it had drawn its strength during the war were still there. The leaders of the Rhodesian Front (an almost all-white political party), the white community, their economic system—all remained in place in the new state and were constitutionally protected. The most offensive aspects of this economy, namely, the operative rules of private ownership and profit and the supportive forces of foreign capital investment and multinational corporate activity (increasingly of South African origin), remained untouched. This structural position was not particularly unique and did not differ much from the situation in which the Botswana Democratic Party took power at independence in Botswana. What made it intolerable, however, was ZANU-(PF)'s adversarial ethos. In that sense, the two primary enemies of ZANU remained undefeated.

The ZANU ethos was rapidly converted into a state ethos. At ZANU's disposal now was the state, a new instrument with which to continue the pursuit of its twin objectives. To subdue the opponent (PF)-ZAPU, the adversarial relationship was easily converted into a relationship of the state versus lawless dissidents; hence, the Matabeleland campaigns with the Fifth Brigade in the forefront. The security structures inherited from the Rhodesian state were well suited for the task and were readily taken over and expanded. The reformulated ethos of state action continued to inform the substantive goals: the merging of the two parties, the closer integration of state and party, and the eventual establishment of a one-party state. The first two of these have duly been achieved, with the attendant erosion of democracy.

The remaining forces that embody the old adversary represented in the Rhodesian state are less tangible and have proved more difficult to subdue through state action. The reformulated substance of the ethos driving ZANU against this opponent has taken the form of a policy goal called "socialism for the blacks."[118] This goal entails using the institutional channels of state control over the economy set up by the Rhodesians, expanding them, and modifying them where needed; the prosperity generated by the economy will then be delivered disproportionately to black Zimbabweans through state intervention—a mirror image of the "socialism for the whites" practiced by the Rhodesian state. This broadly defined objective of state action has shaped policy in land resettlement, agricultural pricing, foreign investment, minerals marketing, educational and health restructuring, and recruitment into the public service. The policy ethos remains essentially adversarial; the state appears to be battling fundamentally antagonistic, hostile, and malevolent forces.

The ethos of state action that guides state leaders in Botswana found early expression in the process of establishing the Botswana Meat Commission (BMC). Those negotiations were not only an early operational expression of an evolving ethos, they were also a formative experience in consolidating and institutionalizing these early vague ethical and normative guidelines. The similarities and differences in the process of establishing the Minerals Marketing Corporation of Zimbabwe (MMCZ) highlight the contrast between the state leaders in the two countries.

As the first parastatal in the newly independent Botswana, the BMC was acutely important to the country symbolically, representing the ascendancy of the new state and its elected leadership in the only sector of the economy that was then considered viable in the modern world. The cattle industry embodied the social values of the traditional Tswana kingdoms, the commercial aspirations of the modern biracial farming elite and the foreign capital investors, and the political ambitions of the modernizing politicians. Zimbabwe's mining industry was equally laden with symbolic significance. Mining prospects had brought the Pioneer Column of Cecil John Rhodes into the country in the first place, and the mining sector can be considered the founding industry in Zimbabwe's modern economy. Throughout the Rhodesian era the mining industry relied almost entirely on foreign capital investment, had repatriated profits out of the country, and had been subject to ownership and control by foreign companies, the top personnel of which had been almost entirely of European descent. In short, it was an encapsulation of the forces ZANU had been fighting since 1963.

In 1982 the government decided against nationalizing the mining industry and instead established the MMCZ as a parastatal marketing agency. All mining companies were compelled to sell their products to the corporation, which found buyers and negotiated the selling price. After taking a commission it distributed money back to the producers. In return, broad control over rates of production, stockpiling, and the like was extended to the industry. The industry strongly opposed this initiative and responded to the draft bill with detailed, clause-by-clause proposals, all of which were explained and defended in person by the president of the Chamber of Mines to the permanent secretary of the ministry. The outcome, according to Herbst, was that "*every* suggestion made by the mining industry was rejected and that the very few changes in the draft Bill made before it became law had the effect of tightening it up and rendering it even more unfavorable to the industry. Mining company officials express doubt that the government was even interested in the mining industry's suggestions" (original emphasis).[119]

This episode of state building in Zimbabwe encapsulates an ethos of state action as much as the establishment of the BMC in Botswana did, revealing the general priorities of state leaders who view the modern economy in adversarial terms. This view induces them to place state intervention and control above commercial criteria. It leads them to judge regional and global dependence relationships as a source of threat, not (as their Botswana counterparts did) as a source of potential benefits. In general, they respond defensively to the international environment. Unlike the state leaders of Botswana, the Zimbabwean state builders appear to be less concerned about the constraints imposed by the pervasive economic scarcity that characterizes the subcontinent and to show little concern for constructing an economic order on the basis of multisector elite bargains. They seem prepared to put equity before growth, despite the costs involved. And, in contrast to the BDP under Sir Seretse Khama, ZANU-(PF) was not and is not prepared to build state strength gradually, through a slow process of the incorporation of elites from different sectors of the society and economy.

This ethos has left the Zimbabwe state leaders ill equipped to make decisions that will lead to their goal of a more prosperous economy and society. Their immediate aim after independence was to rectify the racial inequities the Rhodesian state had imposed: thus, the goal of equity. With that goal went the aim of making people equally better off. Both objectives were effected through measures such as buying up white farmland, subsidizing food prices, and extending health and educational facilities, thus giving practical content to the policy of socialism for the blacks. The difference between this and the previous policy of socialism for the whites was that the whites had numbered 250,000, but the blacks numbered more than 8 million. This far more expensive project could be sustained only by expanding the resource (that is, tax) base. Socialism for the blacks in the long term presupposes economic growth.

The ZANU-(PF) leadership's ethos of state action led them to some crucial miscalculations about the policies needed to generate growth. They were unable to accurately weigh the consequences of other ideological goals such as escaping dependence on the South African economy, lessening dependence on foreign capital, controlling foreign investment, and dictating minimum wages. In trying to meet those objectives they effectively inhibited growth, stifling job creation and expansion of the tax base. The forces to which they responded defensively are the ones that, if deftly managed, are the key to growth and prosperity. The big picture, obscured from them by the prevailing ethos, is that in the global economy of the late 20th century, African states are rarely in a position to dictate the terms of creating wealth and prosperity in their domestic economies. Nor could they see the even bigger picture, which requires state leaders to jettison the adversarial ethos that views domestic, regional, and global economic forces in hostile terms.

The effect of these miscalculations has been the state's gradual but cumulative inability to muster the resources it needs to sustain its goal of socialism for the blacks. By drawing more resources from the economy than could be sustained in the long term, it progressively undermined the basis of its own solvency. Economic stagnation and decline merely extended the conditions experienced by the Rhodesian economy. By the end of the first decade of independence, both the economy and the state had been weakened by the inability to generate wealth.

The pressures for change in macroeconomic policy came from external agencies as well as from domestic conditions, primarily those generated by unemployment. Change came in the form of increasing acceptance of technocratic criteria as the yardstick for policymaking, and it culminated in the policy document "Zimbabwe: A Framework for Economic Reform 1991–95," released in early 1991. This document amounts to a complete capitulation to technocratic considerations of the kind that prevail in Botswana, a fundamental reversal of policy objectives, and a basic reorientation to regional and global economic forces.[120] To what extent this document also reflects the collective resolve of the Zimbabwean state leaders remains unclear.[121]

The political cost of these combative economic policies has been a decline in legitimacy, that vital component of social control and indicator of state strength. Because of the closeness between the state and the ruling ZANU-(PF), opposition to party policies has impact on the state as well. The taunt by the Zimbabwe Unity Movement in the 1990 election campaign, that "the people have gained nothing from ten years of independence,"[122] not only reflects badly on the ruling party but also strikes at the heart of the weakness of the state that ZANU-(PF) has built and is occupying. It pinpoints the inability of the party to use the state to achieve its overriding objective of controlling the economic destiny of the country. Economic ownership of the country is still in the hands of the forces that sponsored the Rhodesian state. The present rulers' repeated failures to achieve this objective, which was stated so explicitly in terms of their prevailing ethos, not only reveal their weakness but also generate the continuing sense of insecurity that has been identified as the source of undemocratic practices.

This sense of insecurity cannot be addressed by ever greater electoral victories or by decimating real or imaginary opposition through repressive security measures. The insecurity stems from the judgmental yardsticks with which state leaders in Zimbabwe measure the regional and global forces that affect the domestic economy. The yardsticks of Botswana's state builders' ethos of state action allowed them to gauge their own strengths and weaknesses and to act accordingly in dealing with regional and global forces. The results have been impressive. The Zimbabwean state leaders, imbued with a different ethos of state action, assessed essentially the same forces differently and acted with far less impressive results.

The gradual shift toward a more technocratic set of policy yardsticks has in some ways exacerbated the legitimacy problem of the state. In the mid-1980s the labor officer of the state intervened in a conflict between a commercial farmer and his laborers. A micro-level study of the incident reports the laborers' dismay over the officer's siding with the farmer in the dispute. They had expected him to act otherwise, because "he represented a government which had achieved autonomy for the indigenous people and had promised to change the relationship between farm workers and owners." In addition, "there was the belief that, when all was said and done, the land belongs to the ancestors and therefore to the people, a belief which is articulated both at grassroots level when the ancestors are invoked at party meetings as well as by the Party leaders at national level."[123] In practice, the laborers found the labor officer acted according to the imperatives of state building set out by his superiors: securing the productive farms so as to meet internal food demand, maintain a stable image abroad, maintain the value of the currency, and the like. From the perspective of these farm laborers this new set of imperatives represented a fundamental capitulation; they saw the government as having "adopted the laws of the land of their predecessors in office and put aside those observed by their ancestors perhaps forever."[124] In the farm laborers' view, the structural adjustment policies that follow from the 1991 economic policy document (which was drawn up with assistance from the World Bank and the International Monetary Fund) would remove ownership of the land still further from the ancestors and deliver it into the hands of the global state system. This is the crux of the legitimacy problem of the Zimbabwean state and the source of the insecurity among the state leaders who have thus far undermined democracy in Zimbabwe.

PART III

SOUTH AFRICA

From Apartheid to the
Autonomous State?

✻ 5 ✻

THE APARTHEID STATE AND
THE DIVIDED SOCIETY

The dominant theme in the literature on South African politics is, as in the case of colonial Rhodesia, the primacy of class analysis in accounting for an ostensibly racial conflict. In South Africa the debate has tended to focus primarily on the relationship between capitalism and apartheid and to a lesser extent on related subjects such as Afrikaner nationalism and the class/racial/ethnic character of the antiapartheid movements. The major lines of debate as well as the minor ones address the question of the character of the South African state, albeit sometimes indirectly. This study engages these debates to the extent that they are relevant to the variables of state strength and weakness, state autonomy and partisanship, societal civility, and the lines of cleavage that divide society.

The chapter provides a state-centered analysis of apartheid, concentrating on how the state went about distributing public goods. The emphasis in analyzing state-society interaction is on the attempts by the builders of the apartheid state to comprehensively restructure society along racial lines. In assessing the strength of the apartheid state, the capacity of the state to exert social control over all the people affected by its vast project of social engineering is examined. Finally, the impact of this state-driven project on the strength of society is considered.

Unlike Rhodesian state building, in which independence was a definitive watershed between two distinct eras of state building,

151

the zenith of apartheid-style state building is not easy to pinpoint. One view considers 1968 as the year when National Party power crested.[1] Another finds 1970 the culmination of apartheid oppression.[2] The passage of the 1983 constitution could also serve as a high point. All of these could serve as benchmarks without necessarily being decisive turning points. This chapter closes with events leading into the mid-1980s.

THE CONTEXT

The construction of the South African state as a distinct political unit started in 1910 with the merging of the four British possessions, Cape of Good Hope, Natal, Orange River Colony, and the Transvaal, into the Union of South Africa, a self-governing entity with the status of a dominion of the British commonwealth. The character of this entity had already been decisively shaped by a number of key historical events.

The first notable feature of the Union was the absence from its constitutional structures of those with arguably the strongest claims to being direct descendants of "the first South Africans." The San (Bushmen) and Khoikhoi (Hottentots) were resident populations in much of southern Africa when the Bantu-speaking peoples, migrating southwest, entered the region around 550 A.D. These groups—and, later, colonizers from the Dutch East India Company who established their base in Cape Town in 1652— effectively wiped out the San, while the Khoikhoi merged with the increasingly complex population of Cape Colony under Dutch rule.[3] With that they effectively lost their significance as a demographic, social, economic, cultural, or political unit in South Africa.

The second feature of the Union was the strong demographic, economic, and cultural presence of the various Bantu-speaking peoples and their lack of corresponding political weight. The Mfecane led to the consolidation of kingdoms and chieftaincies among the Zulu, South Sotho, Swazi, West Sotho (Tswana), Venda, and Ndebele speakers, complementing the already established chieftaincies among the Xhosa-speaking population of the South Nguni.[4] These political units came into severe conflict with the Afrikaner republics (Orange Free State and South African Republic) established by white colonists who left Cape Colony in the early 1830s under political protest against British rule.[5]

The Afrikaner republicans took a well-established sense of racial superiority with them into the interior.[6] In the later independent Afrikaner republics, whites therefore ruled exclusively; Africans were not even considered for citizenship. Meanwhile, the colony Cape of Good Hope became a British possession in 1806, followed by Natal Colony in 1843. From 1870 to 1906, British rule was extended over the remaining chiefdoms, kingdoms, and republics. The African entities were brought under imperial rule through a mixture of military subjugation and diplomatic machinations,[7] as well as by means of what has been described as "psychological conquest."[8] The Afrikaner republics succumbed only after waging a three-year war (1899–1901) with both conventional and guerrilla warfare against a British force of nearly 450,000 troops. The Afrikaners fought and lost what they called the Tweede Vryheidsoorlog (Second War of Liberation), and the way they lost it would be remembered by future generations of Afrikaner nationalists, including those who constructed the apartheid state. The British responded to the guerrilla tactics of the republics with a scorched-earth policy, burning almost 30,000 farmsteads and 20 villages. Women and children were forcibly taken off the land and relocated into so-called concentration camps, where epidemics led to almost 28,000 casualties, more than three-quarters of whom were children under the age of 16.[9] After the war the two republics became British territories known as the Transvaal and Orange River Colony.

By the first decade of this century the political arena was occupied by a victorious imperial power, keen to consolidate its possessions; embittered and humiliated Afrikaner nationalists; and a subject and largely quiescent black majority. The National Convention was the formative event in the state-building process that culminated in the South Africa Act of 1909, through which the Union was established. The composition of the convention and the resolutions passed by it reflected the power equation in the subcontinent. Only white parties sent representatives. No representatives of the subject African population were invited to attend, and no strong case for their interests prevailed. Instead, the citizenship arrangements in each of the former colonies (now provinces in a decentralized unitary political system) were allowed to continue into the Union. This meant a qualified nonracial franchise in Natal and the Cape, through which a small number of blacks gained access to the vote, and a whites-only franchise in Transvaal and Orange Free State. The parliamentary system of the Union was to become an arena within which only the white electorate would compete for power.[10]

The constitution of the Union contained a clause enabling the British monarch to transfer the High Commission Territories as well as Rhodesia (then still under administration of the British South Africa Company) to the Union by enacting an order in council. The boundaries of the High Commission Territories were drawn in such a way that large populations of Sotho, Swazi, and Tswana speakers became residents of the Union with the attendant implications for citizenship. These options were never exercised and fell away when the Union became a de facto sovereign state in 1931 with the enactment of the Statute of Westminster and the 1934 Status of the Union Act.[11]

APARTHEID: STATE AND REGIME, ECONOMY AND SOCIETY

The evolution of state and society in the first decades after union was strongly influenced by the guidelines for racial policy set by the South African Native Affairs Commission, appointed by Lord Milner in 1903. The commission made four recommendations: (1) that land ownership be divided by race into exclusively white and black areas; (2) that dormitory towns, called "locations," be established for blacks adjacent to but distinct from towns in the white areas of land ownership; (3) that education for blacks be focused on agricultural and industrial vocations rather than on the classic liberal arts; and (4) that political separation be implemented, including separate elections, separate voter rolls, and separate institutions with separate jurisdictions.[12]

Segregation

These recommendations formed the basis of the legislation and policies of the 1910–39 era, described by Giliomee and Schlemmer as "classic segregation,"[13] similar to the Rhodesian racial policies. The Natives Land Act of 1913 set aside about 7 percent of the country for exclusive black ownership, effectively precluding blacks from owning property in the remaining 93 percent of the country.[14] The Native Trust and Land Act of 1936 extended the land of the "reserves" to 13 percent of the country, which still remained far short of the white-to-black land ownership ratio that existed in Rhodesia. The Natives (Urban Areas) Act of 1923 (as amended in 1930) required that white local authorities provide segregated housing for Africans and create separate revenue accounts for the administration of Africans in the white areas. The act also empowered authorities to implement measures to control the influx of Africans to towns, a precursor to the "pass laws." These provisions were strengthened in the Natives Laws Amendment Act of 1937. The Mines and Works Act of 1911 and the amended version of 1926 instituted a color bar in the mining industry, and the Industrial Conciliation Act of 1924 effectively prevented Africans from joining legally recognized labor unions. The Native Administration Act of 1927 set up special courts for Africans in which African customary law would apply to civil cases; it also allowed for the official recognition of chiefs.

Regime modifications were introduced in 1930—when the franchise was extended to white women but not to Coloreds or Africans—and in 1931, when the property and income qualifications for white men in the Cape and Natal were removed. The Representation of Natives Act of 1936 removed African voters in Cape Province from the common parliamentary roll and placed them on a separate roll from which they had to elect three white parliamentary representatives.[15]

This policy was implemented in a population of exceptional cultural diversity. Centuries of colonization, migration, conquest, and dispersal had created a population of at least 23 linguistic communities with European, African, and Asian ancestry and with adherents to animistic, Christian, Muslim, and Hindu religions.[16] Unlike both Botswana and Zimbabwe, South Africa has no single dominant linguistic community. Few of these criteria moved the legislators, however, and the prime legal categories were based on race. The categories would be formalized in the next era of state building: apartheid.

Apartheid

Leaving aside the questions of interpretation for later in the chapter, apartheid can be understood as a way of ordering state and society and as a state-driven system of social control. Far exceeding Rhodesian-style segregation in ambition, apartheid aimed at comprehensive communal, economic, and political control of subject populations and was engineered in every dimension by relocating selected categories of people.[17]

The enabling objective was to extricate the categories of people who were to be subjects of the planned social engineering from the social, political, and economic center of society. The Population Registration Act of 1950, the most fundamental of apartheid laws, established those categories. The act (as amended) defined two basic categories of people: "whites" and "Africans." Individuals who fit neither category were assigned to the residual category "Colored"; of the numerous subdivisions that were allowed, the most prominent was "Indian/Asian." The official criteria for classification were based on descent, "appearance," and "general acceptance." In both principle and practice these definitions did little justice to the cultural complexity of the country or to people's self-definition. Instead, classification became a function of administrative decisions.[18]

The other major legislative pillars of apartheid were the Prohibition of Mixed Marriages Act of 1949, prohibiting multiracial marriages; the Immorality Act of 1950, outlawing interracial sexual relations; the Group Areas Act of 1950, establishing the administrative infrastructure for separate urban residential areas and business premises on the basis of race; the Separate Representation of Voters Act of 1951, removing the Colored voters from the parliamentary roll (it passed only in 1956 after a long legal battle); and the Reservation of Separate Amenities Act of 1953, authorizing the state to establish separate public facilities for the different races. It was stipulated that the doctrine "separate but equal" did not apply to this act.

The political objective of apartheid was racially defined state building. The apartheid state builders subdivided the African population into 10 so-called national units, or "homelands," largely on the basis of linguistic criteria: 1 each for the North Sotho, South Sotho, Tsonga, Tswana, Venda, Swazi, Ndebele, and Zulu, and 2 for the Xhosa. The state-building process was initiated with the Bantu Authorities Act of 1951, which activated tribal authorities and made the chief the pivotal source of authority. The Promotion of Bantu Self-Government Act of 1959 upgraded these structures as autonomous but still subordinate regional bodies, while the Bantu Homelands Citizenship Act of 1970 and the Bantu Homelands Act of 1971 made it possible to expand them into full ministates with elected legislatures, executive and judicial branches, and bureaucracies with police forces and miniature armies. By 1975 eight such "homeland" governments had been established, and in 1976 the formal leadership of the Transkei took the final step to "sovereign independence."[19] This was followed in 1977 by Bophuthatswana's "independence," sealing the constitutional fate of the luckless Setswana speakers, who ended up on the wrong side of the Limpopo River and were thus locked into a state-building trajectory vastly different from that of their kin just across the border in Botswana. Venda also took the independence course in 1979, as did Ciskei in 1981. The international community of states speedily announced its nonrecognition of these claims to statehood. With this final step went the essence of statehood, that is, citizenship. By accepting independence, the citizens of the "independent homelands," whether living in South Africa or not, lost their claims to South African citizenship. Those inside South African territory became legal aliens without civil rights or claims to public goods made available by the state, and subject to deportation back to the "homelands."

No room was found for Coloreds and Indians in this statebuilding scheme. They were considered South African citizens, albeit of a lesser status, and were assigned to racially defined, territorially separate, and politically subordinate institutions within the common area. The Colored Persons Representative Council Act and the South African Indian Council Act, both of 1968, provided for such bodies at national level, and the amended Group Areas Act did so at the local government level. The 1968 Prohibition of Political Interference Act declared mixed political parties illegal, thus sealing off Colored and Indian politics from the political center.[20]

The South Africa Act of 1909 provided for a sovereign parliament in which the legislative, executive, and judicial functions were closely modeled on the Westminster system. Writing the constitutional principle of the legislative sovereignty of parliament into the act deprived the judiciary of constitutional authority over parliament, and the constitution was made subject to the authority of parliament. As is often the case, parliamentary sovereignty in South Africa evolved into party dominance. After the Statute of Westminster was passed in 1931, Britain lost all potential influence on the South African parliament, even though the country achieved republican status only in 1961.

The National Party (NP), which won every election from 1948 to 1989, used its constitutional position of strength to enact measures to change not only the character of society through the apartheid measures outlined above, but also the character of the state and the regime. The laws governing the franchise were changed to ensure a whites-only parliamentary electorate by 1956 (as described above). The autonomy of the courts was whittled away; power became more centralized in the parliamentary executive and was eventually delegated to bureaucrats.[21]

The character of the state was shaped markedly by the security legislation the NP created. The NP built on some of the laws of the segregation era. The first Riotous Assemblies Act was passed in 1914, restricting public gatherings. The Bantu Administration Act of 1927 extended these restrictive provisions. After 1948 the Suppression of Communism Act of 1950, with its numerous amendments, further widened the state's scope of action against opposition and gave an exceptionally wide definition of communism. The Unlawful Organizations Act of 1960 allowed the state to ban organizations (it promptly banned the African National Congress and the Pan Africanist Congress), and the General Law Amendment Acts of 1962 and 1963 provided for declaring a state of emergency and detaining leaders. State control of sources of funding from organizations operating outside the country was made possible through the Affected Organizations Act of 1974.[22] In regard to security the South African state came to resemble its Rhodesian counterpart closely. Many of these laws delegated executive decision making to security bureaucracies, which were comprehensively restructured under Prime Minister (later State President) P. W. Botha in the national security management system.[23] During the 1980s these bodies became the crucial centers of state decision making in confronting the challenge from extraparliamentary movements.

In 1983 parliament passed a new constitution, in terms of which the tricameral parliament was introduced in 1984. This parliament was unique in its three racially delimited legislative chambers for whites, Coloreds, and Indians. A functional division of jurisdiction was made between "general affairs" and three categories of "own affairs," and four executive structures (including bureaucracies) were established to implement policy for the four "interests." In addition, the built-in majority ratio of 4:2:1 in favor of the white representatives, a selective application of the Westminster majoritarian principle, ensured NP dominance.[24] The 1983 constitution can be seen as the constitutional high point of apartheid, for it incorporated the most basic principles of apartheid in such a way as to effectively merge state and regime. From then on, any fundamental change in either one would require equally drastic change in the other.

This entire system of state and regime was constructed within a legal system similar to that of Botswana and Rhodesia. The colonial inheritance of Roman-Dutch law, to which were added elements of English law (especially in regard to administration of justice), formed the basis of the legal system, and African customary law was given limited recognition as a subordinate source of law.[25]

The economic and communal objectives of apartheid entailed not only that people be moved to and from specific places, but also that they behave in prescribed ways. The job color bar was extended into the building industry through the Native Building Workers Act of 1951. The Industrial Conciliation Act of 1956 extended this form of social control even further by making it possible to reserve almost any position exclusively for whites.[26] In addition, the Bantu Education Act of 1953 was intended to eliminate direct competition between African and white labor by providing different curricula in the schools, thus effectively confining Africans to the lower ranks of the occupational pyramid.[27] The economic and communal objectives of apartheid (as well as the political ones) required halting the rapid urbanization of the rural poor blacks. The NP had at its disposal the Bantu (Urban Areas) Consolidation Act of 1945, the basis of the infamous "pass laws." To it they added the Bantu Laws Amendment Act of 1952, making the carrying of "reference books" (passes) compulsory at all times. Further restriction on the movement of Africans was engineered through the Physical Planning and Utilization of Resources Act of 1967 requiring industries to obtain ministerial approval to expand their African labor force.[28]

The outline above gives but the barest description of the legislative pillars of the apartheid state. In her study of laws directing race relations up to 1976, Horrell described 331 different enactments, while Giliomee cites a study reporting that by 1978 there were 4,000 laws and 6,000 regulations affecting the private sector of the economy.[29] This gives some indication of the extent to which apartheid was a state-driven system of social control. The qualitative difference between Rhodesian segregation and apartheid is further revealed in the detailed prescriptions that provincial ordinances and municipal bylaws set out in terms of the above laws. These amounted to minutely specific state-directed survival strategies—ways of earning a living and coping.

The legal constraints on entrepreneurship illustrate the point. African shopowners outside the homelands were considered to be in charge of temporary enterprises and in the process of relocating in the homelands. They were therefore denied the right to establish companies or partnerships, to conduct more than one business, and to establish African-owned financial institutions and wholesale concerns. In 1968 it was also stipulated that they were not allowed to operate from more than one premise or to sell goods to non-Africans living outside the African residential areas.[30]

These kinds of prescriptions extended into other fields of endeavor as well. Regulations released in 1957 required white taxi license-holders to carry only white passengers; Johannesburg and Durban bylaws allowed black passengers to use only the back row of seats in the upper deck of buses; and in 1965 the Cape Town City Council received special permission for Colored people to attend symphony concerts in City Hall if separate booking offices, entrances, exits, seating, and restrooms were provided.[31] Even the most extreme aspects of survival had to be coped with in terms of race: separate ambulances were normally provided for blacks and whites, except in emergencies; in hospitals, black nurses were allowed to care for whites only when no white nurses were available.[32]

APARTHEID: PUBLIC POLICY AND PRACTICE

Population Relocation

One of the most directly visible effects of the implementation of apartheid laws was on settlement patterns. The Group Areas Act divided the urban landscape racially. Nearly 80,000 Colored families and 38,000 Indian families were required to move from their homes to other residential areas versus 2,000 white families from 1950 to the mid-1980s.[33] These relocations also affected people's livelihoods. Thus 1,965 Indian traders and 129 Colored traders had been removed from their premises by the end of 1978 and told to reestablish elsewhere, versus only 21 white traders.[34] The overall effect was fragmented cities, not merely racially segregated ones as in Rhodesia, and by 1987 only 10 percent of the urban population were still residing outside the more than 1,300 proclaimed group areas.[35] Africans were relocated under a battery of laws, bringing the total number of people removed from their homes under duress from 1960 to 1983 to 3.5 million.[36] "Influx control" was the term for inhibiting the urbanization of the rural African poor. Forced removals complemented these control mechanisms by returning previously urbanized populations to the homelands. Between 1950 and 1990, 1.4 million Africans were resettled this way, with almost catastrophic implications for the rural population density.[37]

Wages, Incomes, and Standards of Living

The cumulative impact of physical relocation, inadequate education, and the job color bar was that blacks settled to the bottom tiers of the socioeconomic pyramid—which was already sloping steeply from rapid economic modernization. The statutory color bar, threats from powerful white unions, and the pervasive threat of legal actions by the state closed far more occupational avenues for blacks than the legislative restrictions alone did.[38] The overall impact on the occupational structure of the labor force is shown in table 5.1.

The resulting distribution of income by race was obviously very unequal. Table 5.2 shows that before 1970, whites received more than 70 percent of total personal income. This point must be considered against the background of their numerical minority, which became even smaller as the century progressed. In 1911, Africans numbered about 4.0 million, whites 1.2 million, Coloreds 0.5 million, and Indians about 150,000. By 1970, Africans were just over 15 million, whites 3.7 million, Coloreds slightly over 2 million, and Indians about 600,000.[39]

Table 5.1. Racial Contribution to Occupations, 1960 and 1980

Occupation	Year	Whites	Coloreds	Indians	Africans
Professional/	1960	67%	7%	2%	23%
technical	1980	57	8	4	31
Managerial/	1960	87	1	3	9
administrative	1980	91	2	3	4
Clerical	1960	88	3	3	6
	1980	60	8	6	25
Sales	1960	61	6	14	18
	1980	44	8	8	40
Service	1960	7	13	2	78
	1980	11	10	1	78
Agriculture	1960	7	7	1	85
	1980	5	8	–	87
Production/	1960	19	11	2	68
laborer	1980	16	13	3	69

Source: Merle Lipton, *Capitalism and Apartheid, South Africa, 1910–1986* (Cape Town: David Philip, 1986), p. 406, table 7. Copyright © Ashgate Publishing Limited. Used by permission of the Publisher.

These inequalities can be expressed in various ways; McGrath, for example, calculated that in 1970 the richest 10 percent of income earners were receiving 57 percent of the total personal income and that whites comprised 97 percent of that upper bracket of income earners.[40] Overall, societywide inequality (expressed as a Gini coefficient) for South Africa in 1975 stood at 0.68, which McGrath judges to be "higher than the Gini coefficient estimated for any economy for which family or household income data is available."[41] (By comparison, the Gini coefficient for the developed Western countries ranges between 0.35 and 0.40.) By 1992 this figure was down to 0.60, according to official estimates,[42] but still markedly higher than the figure for Botswana— 0.55 in the late 1980s. These differences varied by sector but were probably highest in the gold mining industry, where the white-to-black ratio for income in 1970 stood at 20.9:1.[43]

Table 5.2. Racial Shares of Total Personal Income

	1924–25	1946–47	1960	1970	1980
Whites	75.0%	71.3%	71.2%	71.9%	59.9%
Africans	18.0	22.2	21.4	19.3	29.1
Coloreds	5.0	4.5	5.5	6.5	7.6
Indians	2.0	2.0	1.9	2.3	3.4

Source: Merle Lipton, *Capitalism and Apartheid, South Africa, 1910–1986* (Cape Town: David Philip, 1986), p. 408, table 9. Copyright © Ashgate Publishing Limited. Used by permission of the Publisher.

Within these broad racial categories is hidden the dramatic rise in white Afrikaners' incomes and standard of living. In 1910 the per capita income ratio of Afrikaners to English was 1:3. Unable to compete effectively in the modernizing industrial economy of the Union, they fell even farther behind, and by the 1930s the so-called poor white problem was largely an Afrikaner phenomenon. But through a remarkable resurgence the income gap between Afrikaans and English speakers narrowed to 100:211 by 1946, to 100:156 by 1960, and to 100:141 by 1976.[44] This was the result not only of astute Afrikaner enterprise and entrepreneurship, but also of the active intervention of the state, by that time firmly occupied by the NP.

To retain perspective on the bigger picture it must be pointed out that the economic deprivation of blacks was relative, not absolute. In the first 50 years of the Union, real income per person grew annually at a rate of 1.8 percent.[45] From the 1920s, real per capita incomes of blacks grew steadily and, according to one calculation, more than doubled from 1920 to 1970 and quadrupled by 1980.[46] Another estimate is that real wages of blacks increased almost five-fold from 1920 to 1970.[47] The probable exception, unvalidated because of incomplete data, is the African population of the homelands, who probably experienced absolute deprivation.[48] The overall effect of rising black wages was not only that the racial distribution of income changed markedly from 1970 to 1980 (see table 5.2) but also that the overall inequality in the economy evened out. Calculations have shown that whereas the top 20 percent of income earners were receiving 77 percent of the national remuneration in 1970, they were receiving only 61 percent by 1980.[49]

Public Goods

The unequal allocation of public goods by the state, so much the hallmark of the Rhodesian state, also characterized the South African state. The principles of nonexcludability and jointness of supply were violated consistently in decades of public spending. Education is a striking example. The colonial inheritance of a white population with a European cultural approach to formal education versus an African population with no such disposition was perpetuated by the rulers of the Union. By 1920 the result was already great disparity: 78 percent of eligible white children attended school, but only 14 percent of Africans did so.[50] Unequal public spending continued into the apartheid era, and by 1975 the overall white-to-black per capita ratio of spending on pupils was 15:1.[51] Finer dimensions of racial bias are hidden within this aggregate figure. The teacher-to-pupil ratio for whites in 1978 was 1:19.7; for Indians, 1:27.2; for Coloreds, 1:29.2; and for Africans, 1:49.2.[52] To gauge the cumulative impact on education one has to add to the effects of budgetary discrimination the qualitative differences created by overcrowding, communal poverty, inadequate infrastructure, legal harassment, and different curricula and administrative systems.

The overall effect was predictable. The illiteracy rate for whites has been calculated at about 2 percent; for Indians, just less than 13 percent; for Coloreds, 18 percent; and for Africans, nearly 30 percent.[53] The rates of attrition in the schools also differ dramatically. Calculations are that only 4 of every 100 children who started school in 1969 completed school by the end of 1978. However, 69 of every 100 whites did so.[54] The momentum of these inequalities and the fact that black schools became centers of political revolt and resistance after 1976 are reflected in the graduation rates. In 1991 the white graduation rate was 96 percent; Indian, 95 percent; Colored, 83 percent; and African, 41 percent.[55]

Public spending on social pensions,[56] public housing,[57] and health and welfare[58] followed a similar pattern, with similar results. Perspective on public expenditure can be gained by comparing the racial aspects of taxation, government expenditure, and population.

According to the data of Servaas van den Berg, whites contributed 77 percent of the tax burden in 1975 and received 56 percent of government expenditure while comprising only 17 percent of the population. Coloreds and Indians, who together made up 12 percent of the population in 1975, contributed 7 percent of the taxes and received 16 percent of government expenditure. Africans, who by then were 71 percent of the population, contributed 16 percent of the tax and received 28 percent of government expenditure. Restated in per capita figures, whites received R516 in government expenditure per person, Indians R227, Coloreds R206, and Africans R61. Van den Berg's interpretation of these data is apt: he argues that these figures "reflect the fact that Whites have contributed more to taxes than the benefits they have received from government expenditure, yet they have received far more generous benefits than their numbers alone warrant."[59]

Not only are public service appointments a highly sought-after public good, but the way this good is distributed also shapes and reflects the character of the state. In the early decades after Union, white English speakers dominated the public service. In 1912 they occupied 85 percent of these positions.[60] Black South Africans were considered for only the lowest positions, and white Afrikaners did not have the skills to compete for the top positions. Under the NP the size of the public sector grew rapidly, total state activity increasing from 23.3 percent of GDP in 1946 to 41 percent in 1985.[61] By 1976, 60 percent of the whites in the public sector as well as in the parastatal sector were Afrikaans speakers.[62] The overall picture was white dominance, as can be seen from the fact that whites comprised only 36 percent of the government labor force in 1970 but received 72 percent of the total wages, whereas the African component of 50 percent received only 16 percent of the wages.[63]

Citizenship, indicating formal membership in the state, is the basis for making claims on the other public goods made available by the state. Without citizenship, no such claims can be made. With the "independence" of the Bophuthatswana, Ciskei, Transkei, and Venda homelands almost 9 million Africans lost their claim to South African citizenship, technically became foreigners subject to deportation, and lost any grounds for presenting claims on the public goods of the South African state.[64]

STATE STRENGTH

The apartheid project required an exceptionally strong state. The legal enactments of apartheid comprised an extraordinarily wide set of state prescriptions for how people should behave, where they should live and work, and which survival strategies were to apply to whom. In short, it was an enormous project of social control. The number of people who were moved within urban areas and from urban areas back to the rural homelands, can indicate how many people's lives were directly and drastically influenced by apartheid laws and how strong the state was in enforcing patterns of behavior on people.

Another measure of state strength is the extent to which it enforces compliance with its rules of social control. The data from one study reveal that from 1916 to 1984 as many as 17,745,741 Africans were arrested and/or prosecuted under the influx control laws. Other major control measures were the trespass and tax laws. Under the latter only, 4.5 million Africans were prosecuted from 1920 to 1979. Taken together, the calculation is that under pass laws and the related tax and trespass laws more than 26 million Africans were prosecuted from 1916 to 1982.[65] These data support the conclusion arrived at by Donald Rothchild that the apartheid state, at least into the mid-1970s, was a relatively strong state.[66]

But was the state strong enough to reshape South African society into the mold envisioned by the legislators? In physical relocating of people, the rate of African urbanization slowed down significantly, from 6.4 percent in 1946–50 to 3.9 percent in the 1960s, largely through the effect of influx control.[67] Nonetheless, the size of the urban African population still increased from just over 500,000 in 1911 to almost 6.4 million in 1980.[68] This growth reflects the limited success of apartheid's overall state-building objectives. The state may have been strong, but it was not strong enough.

Other indicators of the state's strength were its responses to organized resistance against apartheid from within South Africa and its ability to mobilize support for apartheid within the homelands. From union in 1910 until the mid-1970s, the state was able to measure up to all antiapartheid challenges from the African National Congress, the South African Communist Party, the Pan Africanist Congress, and related organizations.[69] The early forms of organized resistance—deputations, letters of protest, delegations to relevant government ministers, and petitions—generally met with indifference or arrogant disregard.[70] Stronger resistance, from the civil disobedience of the Defiance Campaign in 1952 to the sabotage tactics of the post-Sharpeville era, were contained by the bureaucracies and the enabling legislation of the state's security establishment.[71] (The Soweto revolt of 1976 arguably marks the turning point in this dimension of state ascendancy.)[72]

The extent to which the state could mobilize active support from the subject population within the homelands would contribute significantly to state strength. The rapid construction of the ministates in the homelands and the occupation of the political and bureaucratic positions created within them seem to indicate there were some willing clients in apartheid state building. Closer examination reveals some flawed state building, similar to that in Rhodesia.

In 1956 the Bantu Authorities Act was put into effect in the Transkei through Proclamation 180, establishing indirect rule and creating a local government system for the Transkei based on the authority of the chief. (In complete contrast, the following year saw the end of this style of local government in Bechuanaland.) The entire homeland was subdivided into districts and allocated to chiefs. Where no chiefs came forward, the government ethnologist apparently succeeded in "finding" them, which is reminiscent of the Rhodesian machinations in identifying chiefs.[73] These chiefs became local-level executive officers of the state and, like their Rhodesian counterparts, immediately found themselves at the center of the clash between two qualitatively different systems of rule: "The civil service chief now has to implement laws without the approval of his people, and a wedge is thereby driven between him and them. It is as if two opposed ideological systems meet in one man—the universalistic, impersonal norms of modern bureaucracy, and the particularistic, diffuse, highly personalized norms of close-knit kinship, based on the traditional structure."[74]

More fundamental, the new role of the chief was completely foreign to the established position of the Xhosa-speaking chieftains. Their traditional role was equivalent to that of a constitutional monarch, fulfilling the ritual, moral, and symbolic roles of embodying the unity of the community, removed and insulated from the daily distributive politics of who gets what when and how. The homeland state builders were unable to marry the rules of modern representative and bureaucratic states to the traditional rules of social control that revolve around the chiefs. Cast in their new roles as executive officials and charged with implementing often unpopular policies, the chiefs in the Transkei were placed in an intolerable position, the contradictions of which they could not solve. They faced either inevitable loss of legitimacy or becoming central figures of resistance and revolt against the state. Both outcomes weaken the state, and both occurred in South Africa, as they did in Rhodesia.[75]

The administration of customary law would be another vital weakness of the apartheid state. The commissioners courts, set up in terms of the Bantu Administration Act of 1927, provided for the settling of civil cases between Africans under the customary law by legal practitioners supposedly skilled in these laws. In practice, skilled practitioners were the exception. Many commissioners had never studied customary law, and where such courses were available, the subject matter did not receive the respect it required. One authoritative assessment holds that "often precepts of customary law will be forced into the procrustean bed of European legal notions and as a result the law and custom that is supposedly being applied is warped into a grotesque image of that which it is supposed to reflect."[76]

A far greater calamity befell the customary court system when in 1957 it was given criminal jurisdiction over the pass and influx control laws. Given the massive number of cases, the enormous cultural divide between the accused and the court officers, the nature of the law being administered, and the overall harsh environment of this cutting edge of apartheid, these courts rapidly degenerated into parodies of juridical fairness. They first lost the procedural requirements safeguarding the accused and then became conveyor belts for the administering of injustice. In one case study it was found that a court heard 38 cases of pass law contraventions in just over 90 minutes, averaging less than two and a half minutes per case.[77] The contrast with the *kgotla* customary courts in Botswana can hardly be more extreme. There the court is the crucial institution for maintaining civil society, but in South Africa the courts served to legalize the opposite: mass relocations, family breakdowns, and economic hardship followed from the sentences enacted in this inhuman way. This system of courts was scrapped in 1986, but by that time a key element in the challenge to the apartheid state had been formed: an alternative system of so-called people's courts.

Enthusiastic voluntary participation in the institutions created by the apartheid state was evident only in the white parliamentary and local-level bodies. At national level the NP won every election from 1948 to 1989, with the biggest margin of victory in 1977. The party discipline of the NP also probably contributed to the coherence of the various government departments entrusted with implementing apartheid. Tension between some departments certainly did arise, but not to the extent of affecting the strength of the state.[78] The sustained electoral victories of the NP, the internal cohesion of the party, and the integrated functioning of the apartheid bureaucracies can probably be accounted for in part by the invisible helping hand of the Afrikaner Broederbond. Established in 1918 as a facilitator of white Afrikaner interests, it became a secret organization in 1921, thus complicating matters in ascertaining its precise role. The authoritative interpretation holds that the Broederbond was a crucial agent in integrating the leadership in the different Afrikaner "civic" and political bodies, thus ensuring unity of purpose, organizational coherence, and the capacity to mobilize support for the party and the state.[79]

The subordinate institutions within which Coloreds, Indians, and Africans were required to participate failed to generate much voter involvement. The Colored Labor Party succeeded in dismantling the Colored Persons Representative Council from within by winning the 1969 and 1975 elections and then refusing to conduct the business of the council. In both elections the turnout was low, at 35.7 and 25.3 percent of the total potential electorate, respectively.[80] Data on homeland election returns are not adequate to assess voting turnout, except for the Transkei, where a high turnout in the 1963 elections slumped dramatically in 1973.[81]

The institutions created in the era of reform apartheid did not generate substantially higher rates of participation. The Tricameral Parliament, the regional services councils, and the fully elected "black local authorities" all established new, representative, but still subordinate, institutions. The 1983 black local authorities elections, held in 29 townships, produced an average turnout of 21.1 percent.[82] The inaugural elections for the Colored and Indian chambers of the tricameral parliament registered a percentage poll of 30.9 and 20.3 percent of registered voters, respectively. With the low level of registration taken into account, the votes as a percentage of all eligible voters amounted to 17.8 and 14.25 percent, respectively.[83]

In sum, the overall strength of the apartheid state can therefore be measured in the currency of enforced compliance and low levels of voluntary participation and legitimacy among the subject populations. Only among the white electorate could its strength be measured in terms of legitimacy, voluntary support, and unenforced compliance. The disparate proportions of social control lead to Johnston's proposition that South Africa may be a case where "a strong state exists within a weak one." Johnston concludes that by the end of the 1980s South Africa represented "a particularly hard case, since it does indeed have serious domestic security problems, but it also has a narrowly diffused but strong and durable sense of identity and purpose, and powerful, resilient institutions."[84]

Johnston's proposition about the flawed strength of the South African state is further illuminated by analyses of the extent to which the character of the state is the product of class or of ethnic forces. Arguably the most convincing presentations of these two perspectives are made by Dan O'Meara and Hermann Giliomee.[85] The entire field cannot be dealt with in this chapter, and so only these two analyses are described and assessed in terms of the logical, empirical, and theoretical criteria outlined in chapter 3.

O'Meara, concentrating on the 1934–48 era, explains the ascendance of the NP and the implementation of apartheid as the actions of a class alliance to exploit labor for the benefit of employers and the owners of capital. His overall assessment is that it duly succeeded: "Apartheid was much more than a policy to advance the interests of NP supporters. More fundamentally, it in effect secured the interests of the entire capitalist class, enabling all capitalists to intensify the exploitation of African workers and so raise the general rate of profit."[86] Giliomee finds that the gradual electoral advance of the NP was the result of growing Afrikaner nationalism and that the policies of apartheid were used as a flexible instrument in service of the larger objective: Afrikaner unity and power.

However, the apartheid state builders of the 1950s perceived these two objectives as almost completely intertwined: "Without a privileged position the Afrikaners could not survive as a separate people; without safeguarding the racial separateness of the people a privileged position could not be maintained."[87] Apartheid legislators were therefore intent on securing the objectives of ethnic nationalists, not those of a capitalist class.

Both explanations meet the logical criteria for independent variables. Ethnic identities and material interests are both dispositions that result from ascriptive cultural properties and structural properties of wealth or poverty and from relations between the exploiter and the exploited, and both were formed prior to the rise of Afrikaner nationalism. O'Meara accuses Giliomee of offering Afrikaner ethnicity as a timeless given, therefore collapsing the independent and dependent variable through stealthy definitions and thus ensuring perfect association and correlation between cause and effect.[88] This is an invalid criticism, for it relies on an eccentric reading of Giliomee's own work and completely ignores the joint work by Giliomee and Elphick (see note 6).

As with the Rhodesian case, both explanatory frameworks muster ample empirical evidence of association between independent and dependent variables. O'Meara finds strong evidence of conditions that generated material concerns among the Afrikaans-speaking farmers in the Transvaal, the Cape, and Orange Free State; among sections of the white Afrikaans industrial labor force; and among Afrikaner middle-class entrepreneurs and capitalists. These Afrikaners became the core constituency for the NP. Likewise, Giliomee finds ample evidence of the spread of Afrikaner nationalist ideas and the electoral success of the NP. On close examination Giliomee does find a glaring lack of fit in one sector of O'Meara's data: wine and wheat farmers in the Cape stood to gain little if anything in economic terms from supporting the NP. Yet they were among its staunchest supporters.[89] This point not only weakens the overall strength of the association, it also erodes the authority of O'Meara's other empirical claims.

What is required therefore is a check for spuriousness of association. As with the Rhodesian case, this can be done only through subcategory analysis. If Afrikaner ethnicity is the independent, explanatory variable, it must hold under conditions of multiclass solidarity within the ranks of the ethnic group. Here O'Meara's own data provide telling evidence against the class factor as an explanatory variable. He shows in convincing detail how the NP succeeded in building an electoral support base extending *across* class lines within Afrikaner ranks. For the class factor to survive the same test for spuriousness, it would have to be shown that class solidarities did extend across the lines of ethnic membership. Again O'Meara shows that none of the white Afrikaners in the class categories mentioned above (farmers, industrial labor, small-scale entrepreneurs—or, if you prefer, petite bourgeoisie—and capitalists) sought the company of their counterparts in the ranks of the white English or black populations in forming a political alliance equal or even close to that of the NP during the time under examination. Yet O'Meara insists on calling the support base of the NP nothing more than a *class alliance* despite the fact that the common denominator is Afrikaner identity and—with the exception of the Cape farmers—economic interests.[90] By refusing to call this formation an ethnic group, he probably commits the obverse of concept stretching, that is, concept shrinking.

The heart of the matter is the pursuit of economic interests by the NP on behalf of its constituents, however named, through the apartheid state. Classes and ethnic groups strive for material prosperity for different reasons. O'Meara and Giliomee offer sharply contrasting theoretical interpretations. They differ, first, on causation. For O'Meara the pursuit of Afrikaner unity in nationalist ideology was a means to secure material interests: "Its predominant message held that the material interests of the various classes could only be secured through *volkseenheid* (unity) at all levels of social intercourse."[91] O'Meara is in effect arguing that the Afrikaners were acting *like* an ethnic group but were in reality a class. Giliomee interprets the causal relationship in the opposite direction. Material elevation was seen by Afrikaner nationalists as the crucial means of securing unity: "The poor white issue . . . was interpreted in a specifically nationalist way: 'Save the poor whites and assure the future of the Afrikaner nation and the white civilization.'"[92] For Giliomee the NP only appeared to be behaving *like* a class, but at a deeper level of motivation it was acting *as* an ethnic group.

O'Meara is unswervingly insistent that material interests alone drove the Afrikaners to support the NP and, through it, to create the apartheid state as a class state. Giliomee suggests that other ambitions preceded these material aspirations and were served by them. At this point, however, his analysis falters. He hovers uneasily between a modernization theory of ethnicity—in which ethnicity is a handy lever with which to mobilize people in the pursuit of power, status, and wealth in the competitive arena of industrial modernization—and a psychological theory in which "psychosocial fears and needs" are the primary driving forces.[93] If the Afrikaner nationalists of the 1930s and 1940s had only material interests, or deeper psychological needs, this research does not tell us so. O'Meara takes us no further than the first issue and does not even consider the second. Giliomee does point to the second but does not present enough data to state conclusively that Afrikaners' economic aspirations were driven by the need to assert and display their group worthiness, their collective esteem and dignity, and their ability to transcend the humiliation of military defeat and socioeconomic backwardness. The definitive study of Afrikaner ethnicity, revealing this deeper source of psychological gratification behind ostensibly materialist ambitions, remains to be done.

There are other features of the apartheid state that would be explicable if the state were characterized as an Afrikaner ethnic state. Apartheid was not only about separating people into discrete spatial domains. Built into these measures were also constant humiliation and denial of dignity, which make sense only in terms of ethnic politics. The enforcement of the Immorality Act, the Mixed Marriages Act, and the Population Registration Act entailed the public scrutiny of intimate social and family relationships and the passing of judgment on what is acceptable and what is not. Transgressors became victims of intolerable psychological manhandling through the legal process. The law preventing mixed marriages is particularly instructive. From 1930 to 1950 the number of such marriages was declining, and between 1943 and 1946 fewer than 100 such marriages were concluded, compared to the annual total of about 30,000 marriages between white couples.[94] There was therefore no need for such a law to control social behavior or, for that matter, to maximize profits. In terms of ethnic politics, however, it did serve the important function of denigrating nonwhite South Africans. In a negative way it bolstered the status of whites by publicly denying dignity and worth to blacks.

Countless other discriminatory laws also embodied this message, some more explicitly than others. An example of the most explicit was the bylaw, virtually identical to the Rhodesian one, stipulating that "coloured persons are prohibited from walking on sidewalks of the streets or any stoep serving as a sidewalk." This bylaw was put into effect in one instance to prosecute a lawfully operating Colored shopkeeper who used the sidewalk to get to the office of his bookkeeper.[95]

The apartheid state's symbolic features, like the Rhodesian state's, reveal the labels of ethnic ownership. After 1948 the names of towns, airports, dams, and bridges increasingly resembled lists of the key figures of Afrikaner nationalism. The so-called master symbols of the Afrikaner ethos were also embedded into the curricula of South African school textbooks.[96] Another highly illuminating demonstration of the psychology of ethnic symbols and imagery is found in the destruction of Sophiatown, Johannesburg. This African residential area was a long-established center of anti-apartheid resistance and was rezoned for whites in 1954, thus removing the anchor of African social and political presence from Johannesburg, the country's industrial heartland. The rezoned white suburb was renamed Triomf (Triumph).[97]

Both class and ethnic analyses succeed in outlining the precarious foundations of the strength of the South African state. The resources of the state as an institution of social control were increasingly drawn from a more tightly demarcated section of the population. As the ideology and legislative program of apartheid unfolded, the need for state social control increased, given the dictates of the legislators. As the practice of apartheid unfolded, vastly divergent survival strategies were offered to those considered to be white and to those considered to be not white. Given the enormous penalties and hardships built into the survival strategies the apartheid state offered to blacks, the incentive not to comply with them also increased, once again necessitating greater state social control. Being geared to enriching only one small sector of the population at the expense of the others increased the state's capability to exert social control over the beneficiaries of state actions (through legitimacy and voluntary compliance and participation). At the same time, however, the state's capacity to exert social control over the others decreased, except at escalating costs; in the absence of legitimacy and voluntary participation, compliance had to be enforced. Costly social control could be sustained only as long as the state remained solvent, held its single small site of support, and retained its legitimacy in the eyes of its white constituents.

The state's need for solvency to sustain expensive forms of social control points to the importance of examining the relationship between the apartheid state and the system of capitalism in South Africa. This analysis has been intertwined with the ethnic/class dispute outlined above. Briefly, the positions in the debate have been taken up by class analysts of various Marxist shades on the one side and liberals on the other. The class analyses argued that capitalism and apartheid evolved as essentially compatible institutions and practices, with apartheid creating and maintaining the conditions for profitable capitalism. The liberal analyses tended to present capitalism and apartheid as incompatible in principle, with capitalism functioning on the operative principles of economic liberty and the rationality of market forces, and apartheid on the fanciful blueprints of racial ideology. In the longer term, they predicted, capitalism would prevail and contribute decisively to the demise of apartheid.

Crucial to the issue of state strength is the extent to which South African capitalism and apartheid were merged in a coherent system of social control under the auspices of the state. The class analysts would conclude that cohesion was achieved and that apartheid served capitalism. Liberals would argue that cohesion was not achieved, and that apartheid and capitalism existed as two fundamentally opposing sets of rules. The third position presents the relationship as symbiotic: each needed the other, yet neither was able to incorporate the rules of the other into its own system on its own terms.[98]

In terms of this study, the question would be posed somewhat differently. Capitalism and apartheid are elaborate systems of social control that offer survival strategies to individuals—ways of earning a living, coping, and even prospering. If capitalism and apartheid were merged in a single system of social control, then they would not present divergent, competing survival strategies; compliance with the one would not undercut the effective working of the other. One of the most striking demonstrations of the incompatibility of the capitalist and apartheid survival strategies on offer, and the immensely greater attractiveness of the one over the other, is the finding on the earning capacities of urban African migrants in the late 1970s. Data have shown that an illegal migrant from Bophuthatswana who found six months' employment in Pretoria and then spent six more months in jail on a pass law contravention would still on average be increasing his living standard by 56.9 percent over what it would have been if he had remained in the homeland. An illegal migrant from Lebowa who went to Johannesburg and went through the same experience would on average still raise his living standard by 170 percent, and a Ciskei citizen illegally migrating to Pietermaritzburg and going through the same process would effect an increase of 468.5 percent in his living standard.[99] To enforce the survival strategies offered by apartheid against such economic incentives would require enormous capacities of social control. During the 1980s the apartheid state would experience a rapid decline in such capacities, running out of manpower, resources, and resolve, more or less in that order.

APARTHEID SOCIETY

If the apartheid state had been omnipotent, then South African society would have conformed to the blueprints written into law and thus with the watertight divisions defined by race and language. The fact that the society did not do so can be accounted for by at least two other factors that also shaped this society.

The first was the concern of the Afrikaner nationalists for emulating the institutional structure of Dutch society and building Afrikaner unity and strength through a policy of deliberate *verzuiling* (institutional segmentation and encapsulation), aimed primarily at establishing a clear Afrikaans-English divide within the white population.[100] The second, and countervailing, formative factor was the deliberate societal resistance to apartheid social engineering at all levels. The social impetus was initially to resist state attempts to fragment society and to hold onto social ties that bridged the racial divide. The attempt at white Afrikaner *verzuiling*, that is, encapsulation of Afrikaner social life in an exclusive set of interest groups, was very successful, but the attempt to impose similar patterns of social interaction onto other population categories was only partially achieved.

The resulting pattern of interest group (or "civic" body) diversity exhibited the following features by the early 1970s.[101] First, a number of voluntary associations were established to take care of the interests of a specific group. This was most noticeable within Afrikaner ranks and was the product of deliberate attempts at *verzuiling*. Second, government measures put pressure on some associations to become uniracial, or to establish racially defined branch structures. This was done in particular to labor unions and the library, nursing, and scientific associations.[102] Third, friction within mixed associations led to the establishment of rival associations based on race or cultural affiliation. This occurred when the inclusive student body NUSAS (National Union of Student Associations) split along Afrikaans-English lines and again later along the black-white racial division. The same process occurred when the Union of Black Journalists established themselves independent of the South African Society for Journalists in 1973.[103] These kinds of actions are fully understandable given the strong aversion between various racial and cultural groups in society.[104] Fourth, a number of mixed associations had prevailed despite the forces ranged against them. By 1969 there were still more than 40 mixed labor unions, and other socially prominent bodies such as the South African Institute of Race Relations and the Christian Institute of South Africa continued to operate in the face of hostile government actions.[105]

The effects of this emergent interest group structure on the structure of society were threefold. First, efforts at *verzuiling* were so successful as to provide virtual autonomy in everyday Afrikaner social life: "A child born into an Afrikaans family could move from the cradle to the grave within the framework of Afrikaner organizations: Afrikaans nursery, primary, and high schools; in the place of the Boy Scouts, the Voortrekkers; the equivalent of the Chambers of Commerce, the Afrikaanse Sakekamer; and then a variety of cultural organizations."[106] This was done so effectively that the Afrikaner social encapsulation was typified as "popular social communalism."[107] Second, the parallel sets of social institutions made by and for Afrikaans and English whites were eventually matched by a third set of institutions constructed by and for blacks.[108] These social institutions effectively performed the "socialization of isolation," thus cementing new generations in their respective opposing camps.[109] Under apartheid ideology this response seemed desirable at first, because it reflected acquiescence and thus effective control, but such bodies became institutional rallying points of resistance to the state and regime, complementing the townships, which became sites of resistance and revolt.[110]

The parallel but antagonistic interest group structures that encompassed political, cultural, economic, religious, and sporting activities eventually demarcated the boundaries of rival, "civil" societies. These institutional lines of opposition represented the divide in South African society more accurately than the identities of ethnicity or the interests of class were able to. Membership in these rival sets of "civic" bodies was seldom rigidly restricted to racial, cultural, or class criteria. Instead, the common denominator was the shared position on the character of the South African state. During the 1980s these positions were further defined by alternative conceptions of what the future South African state should be, and divisions in society were thus deepened. In this process the middle ground of civic bodies based on equal dignity and respect became progressively eroded.

The impact of apartheid-style social engineering on the social fabric of communities was predictable. By 1976, 1 in every 6 members of the Colored population and 1 in every 4 of the Indian population had been subjected to relocation under the Group Areas Act, versus 1 in 666 whites.[111] This massive state intervention in family life is indicative of one of the general effects of apartheid: dislocation through the disruption of family and communal life led to an inevitable weakening of the social fabric of these communities. Rapid industrial modernization, a socially disruptive process in any case, was exacerbated in South Africa through apartheid policies, which piled stresses onto black South Africans and cushioned the whites from the same disruptions.[112] The weakening of the social fabric among black communities could be easily measured in the escalating social pathologies of crime, drug abuse, and family breakdown.[113]

CONCLUSION

The apartheid state as it evolved into the early 1980s could by no means be described as an autonomous state. It was a highly partisan state in which public goods were distributed differentially in favor of white South Africans, presenting an even more clear-cut example of "socialism for the whites" than Rhodesia. The unique character of the apartheid state was found not only in the highly unequal value of citizenship but also in the creating of elaborate subordinate institutions for the subject populations, who were denied full citizenship.

The character of the partisanship within the state cannot be clarified conclusively. The incumbents of the state, assembled in the ruling NP, behaved to a large extent like a class but certainly not as a class. Instead, many features of the state and numerous aspects of apartheid policies are explicable in terms of the repertoire of ethnic politics. Although the definitive analysis of the ethnic character of Afrikaner politics in the apartheid era remains to be done, available research points to a stronger case for an Afrikaner ethnic state than for a class state.

This partisan character provided the state's immediate source of strength, enabling it to assert enough social control to extensively shape the society into the mold outlined by the apartheid legislators. The potential weakness of the state can also be traced back to the partisan character of its societal base. Legitimacy, the most valuable currency of social control, eluded the apartheid state builders.

If the apartheid state can be described as a "strong state within a weak one," then so can the society be described as having a strong and a weak component. Because white communities were shielded from the disruptive forces of rapid capitalist industrial modernization through the protective policies of the state, social cohesion could be reestablished after the devastation of the imperial wars at the turn of the century. The black communities, on the other hand, had to cope with the same forces and also with the further stresses of removals, relocation, and resettlement. The result was a marked weakening of networks of social control within black communities.

The society thus created was divided, but the lines of division did not correspond neatly to the cleavages of race, culture, or class. Instead, the fault lines were drawn along the contours of support for, or opposition to, the South African state. As the impact of the state spread across the political, cultural, communal, social, recreational, and economic dimensions of society, so did the response to state actions. The resulting cleavages are revealed in the associational boundaries of the various "civil societies," which constructed interest groups throughout all of the dimensions of society named above. As the opposition to the state intensified, the defining rallying points for each of the antiapartheid "civil societies" became more clearly associated not only with opposition to the state but with a vision of the alternative preferred state and society as well.

✼ 6 ✼

THE CONTEST FOR HEGEMONY

South Africa appears to be a less promising prospect for democratic success than either Botswana or Zimbabwe. From the standard checklist of preconditions for successful democratization, a very unfavorable prognosis emerges.[1] South Africa has more cultural and ethnic diversity than Botswana and Rhodesia, and, unlike both of them, it has no single numerically dominant linguistic community. South Africa has felt the destabilizing effects of rapid industrial capitalist modernization as much as the other two countries have in this century, with the exception that modernity penetrated the social fabric of African life in South Africa far more comprehensively on account of the greater scale of urbanization, population growth, decay of rural subsistence agriculture, and escalating unemployment. The rapid economic growth did generate wealth, but the wealth is less evenly distributed than even in Botswana. The middle class of potential democrats remains small and predominantly non-African.

South Africa was not the beneficiary of colonial policies of benign neglect. On the contrary, energetic policies of imperialism led Britain into the Boer War, which has been described as the longest, costliest, bloodiest (with 22,000 British casualties), and most humiliating war Britain fought between 1815 and 1914.[2] That war concluded a long process of imposition and shaped the context for white rule for most of the 20th century.

The apartheid experiment in social engineering exacerbated the most unfavorable effects of both capitalist modernization and the colonial heritage. Far more than the Rhodesian experiment of segregation, apartheid entrenched power and status in the hands of a white minority, concentrated wealth in a predominantly white middle class, and elevated the significance of race as the basis of discrimination by the state. The rapid capitalist development of the country also bound its economy into that of the region, yet it was not Botswana or Rhodesia/Zimbabwe but South Africa that became the dominating power in the regional network of interdependence. The greatest vulnerability of South Africa's economy was its dependence relationship within the global economy, where it shares the peripheral status of its two neighbors. Finally, as with the other two cases, the prospects for democratic success in South Africa have been shaped by the nature of the contest for power inside the country and its impact on the strength of the state and society. That contest is the subject of this chapter.

THE DEEPENING OF DIVISIONS WITHIN SOCIETY

The construction of the apartheid state did not go unchallenged. The passage of the South Africa Act of 1909 was met with dignified and restrained protest in the form of an African deputation to London led by the white parliamentarian W. P. Schreiner. Similar deputations to the Cape Town parliament, letters, and petitions followed the legislation of 1913, 1919, and 1936. The organizational dimension of the response was the formation of the South African Native National Congress in 1912, renamed the African National Congress (ANC) in 1923. The early leadership, described as a "black bourgeoisie," pursued the objective of being included in the political center because they expected liberal principles in the constitution and liberal practices among the white powerholders to be expanded.[3] The legislation of the first three decades of Union reflected the opposite trend, however, and conveyed the message to Africans that "they were not part of the South African community, that European interests were not bound together with African, and that there was no longer any community of interest between Europeans and Africans."[4]

The formation of the ANC Youth League in 1944 provided additional impetus for a change in strategy and tactics. Under the intellectual (and organizational) leadership of Anton Muziwakhe Lembede, the Youth League formulated what became known as the "Africanist" perspective. The league's fundamental premise was "that Africans comprised not *a* nation within the boundaries of South Africa, but in fact were, by right of indigenous origins and preponderant numbers, *the* nation, and the only nation, entitled to claim and to rule South Africa" (original emphasis). This basic principle of peoplehood held further implications for the ideal envisioned character of statehood, democracy, and the distribution of power in South Africa: "if Africans were the rightful owners of the country, whites would have to be made to vacate the seats of power and relinquish what they have stolen."[5]

With these internal pressures the old guard of the ANC leadership launched the 1952 Defiance Campaign, a strategy of civil disobedience deliberately challenging the apartheid laws of the state.[6] The drawing up of the Freedom Charter followed in 1955; the somewhat ambiguous document expressed the old guard's ideals and objectives, which were based on an inclusive South African concept of peoplehood but nonetheless differentiated clearly the position of the mainstream ANC "Charterists" from the Africanists. The Africanists split off from the ANC and established the Pan Africanist Congress (PAC) in 1959, then began a bidding competition with the ANC. A direct confrontation with the state ensued, ending in the Sharpeville tragedy and the banning of the ANC and PAC. Both continued in exile while their newly established military wings, Umkhonto we Sizwe (MK, as it is generally referred to in South Africa; the direct translation is "spear of the nation") and Poqo (which can be taken to mean "Africans alone"), respectively, moved into armed confrontation with the state.

In exile the ANC cemented its alliance with the South African Communist Party (SACP) at the Morogoro conference of 1969.[7] The two made a joint commitment to what were later called the four pillars of the struggle: the mobilization of the international community to isolate South Africa economically, politically, and culturally; mass mobilization within South Africa; the building of underground structures in an effort to make the country ungovernable; and the increase of "guerrilla warfare and sabotage, i.e. of the 'armed struggle.'"[8]

The SACP further elaborated on "colonialism of a special type" as the appropriate diagnosis of domestic politics in South Africa and the "two-stage revolution" as the necessary remedy. The first stage, described as the "national democratic revolution," was to be led by the ANC, and for the second stage, the "socialist revolution," the SACP appropriated for itself the leadership role.[9]

During the 1970s and 1980s these objectives were pursued with some vigor. The armed struggle peaked in 1988 with 281 guerrilla attacks.[10] Mass mobilization was led by the United Democratic Front (UDF) and focused on rent, school, and consumer boycotts. The goal of ungovernability was pursued, again with the UDF in an important role, through attacks on the institutions of black local authorities (see chapter 5) and the erection of alternative structures called "street committees."[11] The international isolation of the country was largely achieved through sporting, diplomatic, and comprehensive economic sanctions.

The state response to this rising challenge was *reform apartheid* in the 1970s and early 1980s and, later, the counter-revolutionary *total strategy* offensive. The constitutional products of reform apartheid were primarily the tricameral parliament established in 1984 and the regional services councils (1985). The general consensus among analysts is that these regime modifications were intended as vehicles of co-optation, drawing subject populations into the formal decision-making process but still leaving them unable to decisively affect the outcomes of the policy-making process.[12] Communal reform apartheid entailed the relaxation of control measures over multiracial sport and the deracialization of public facilities such as elevators, parks, buses, trains, theaters, and libraries. Greater autonomy was given to the owners of hotels and restaurants as well as to tertiary educational institutions to determine their own criteria of admission.

In the economic terrain the statutory color bar was dropped, African and mixed labor unions were legalized, access to apprenticeships for Africans was improved, and restrictions on black entrepreneurs in the urban centers were lifted:[13] "The impact on income distribution was dramatic: from 1970–82, real wages for Africans in manufacturing and construction rose by over 60 percent, compared with 18 percent for whites; on gold mines real wages for Africans quadrupled, while those for white miners rose by 3 percent; on white farms real wages for Africans doubled between 1968/9 and 1976. As a result the white share of personal income declined from over 70 to under 60 percent, while the African share rose from 19 to 29 percent."[14] Public spending also shifted markedly during the era of reform apartheid. In the field of education, for example, the ratio of white-to-black per capita spending disparity decreased from 51:1 in 1975 to 7.6:1 in 1985 and 5.4:1 in 1987.[15]

The counterrevolutionary *total strategy* entailed activating the national security management system; declaring successive states of emergency from 1985 to 1989; and allowing for the banning, deportation, or detention of persons and the banning or restriction of the activities of organizations deemed to be a threat to the state.[16] These measures, like those of earlier emergencies, were put into immediate effect and resulted in the banning of no fewer than 98 organizations (in both South Africa and the "independent homelands") between 1950 and 1988[17] and, according to one source, the detention of as many as 73,000 individuals between 1960 and 1988.[18]

Three important comments must be made about the structure of this state-society conflict, all of which throw light on the dividedness of South African society. First, the conflict was about hegemony, and subsumed within that issue were concerns about identity, status, and wealth. Second, each of the contending formations embodied significant sectors of society, thus drawing its own "civic" bodies into partisan conflicts. Third, the conflict did not involve a bipolar configuration in a state-versus-society confrontation; instead, from a multiply divided society a number of contestants emerged to contest the hegemonic claims of the state. Each of these propositions will be considered in turn.

The hegemonic quality of the challenge to the apartheid state can be read from the fundamentally different conceptions of peoplehood and democracy held by the major challengers and by the incumbent National Party (NP) government. For the extraparliamentary anti-apartheid challengers to implement their own visions of democratization and nation building would have required constructing a state qualitatively different from that run by the NP. This anti-apartheid challenge was composed of a number of organizations, some of which (such as the UDF) even had internal ideological differences. Nonetheless, a number of shared features of their perspective can be noted.[19] First, the definitions of democracy usually stressed the themes of distributive justice (democracy is about outcomes, not procedures, and the only just outcome is one that measures up to the requirement of equity) and populist participation (democracy requires a radically egalitarian social order in which the unrestrained participation of "the people" can reveal the popular will, which elected leaders, as delegates, are mandated to implement).

Second, the appropriate strategy for democratizing was seen as a comprehensive program of insurrection. This strategy was conveyed through a range of concepts, not all of them fully compatible. The ANC stressed the *armed struggle*, the SACP the *two-stage revolution*, and the UDF the concepts of *ungovernability* and *people's power*. All of these concepts involve displacing the structures of the apartheid state and imposing new state structures as basic to the process of democratization.

Third, the nation-building vision of this perspective was guided by the conviction that South Africa is a single, nonracial nation, even if only a nation-in-waiting. This nation, so it was argued, is entrapped in the distorting structures of apartheid institutions and can be unified only by deliberately dismantling such structures and rectifying the misguided values, preferences, and allegiances of apartheid. The new democratic state is considered the agent of nation building, which may have to entail Jacobin-style methods of "liberatory intolerance."[20]

The economic priorities of these challengers were shaped by their definition of democracy. If the measure of democracy and distributive justice is equity, and a hallmark of South African society is the extraordinarily unequal distribution of opportunities and wealth, then it follows that redistribution of wealth is the appropriate priority for socioeconomic development and democratization. The state, through its active intervention in the economy on behalf of the poor, is again seen as the agent of development and democratization. By the end of the 1980s, then, the conflict was less about which constitutional rules should apply within the state than about what features should define the state within which a new constitution should be embedded.

The second structural feature of the state-society contest of the 1980s was the fact that each major adversary took with it into the political contest a particular sector of society through the mobilizing agents of "civic" bodies. The range of such bodies, which

Table 6.1. Early UDF Affiliates

	Transvaal	Western Cape	Natal	Other	Total
Student	11	23	9	4	47
Youth	14	270	15	14	313
Worker	8	2	4	4	18
Civic	29	27	24	2	82
Women	7	20	3	2	32
Religious	2	4	5	6	17
Political	5	9	10	0	24
Other	17	3	7	5	32
Total	93	358	77	37	565

Source: Tom Lodge, Bill Nasson, et al., *All, Here and Now: Black Politics in South Africa in the 1980s* (Cape Town: Ford Foundation, David Philip, 1991), p. 51, table 1. Copyright © Ford Foundation. Used by permission of the Publisher.

mobilized Afrikaners behind the NP into the position of state power, was described in the previous chapter. The alliance of ANC, UDF, SACP, and the Congress of South African Trade Unions did likewise. Many civic organizations affiliated under the UDF, which was the primary catalyst for mass mobilization during the 1980s. The diversity of this affiliated membership across the range of interest groups usually associated with civil society can be read from table 6.1.[21]

Many of these organizations had come into existence before the formation of the UDF in 1983 and were established within townships to confront the state on specific local issues such as rents and bus fares. Through the UDF they came to have a bearing on national-level politics and the overriding issue of state transformation. Not only overtly political bodies thus entered the contest for hegemony, but what are more accurately described as rival "civil societies" also came to confront one another on the most basic issues of state and society.

The other notable structural feature of this conflict is that the adversaries squared up not in two sociopolitical formations but in several, representing the multiple faultlines within South African society. Within the state the fault lines between the NP establishment and the predominantly English liberal and capitalist establishment persisted. As the politics of reform apartheid evolved, the white right wing's position became more distinct from the NP's. Within the antiapartheid bodies, the Charterist and Africanist division remained, and the co-optees of reform apartheid also came to be seen as a distinct formation in the political contest. These formations, consisting of political, civic, cultural, and economic organizations, are seen by the political elite of the country as distinctive objects of political sympathy or distrust, and even since the "normalization" of politics in 1990 these divisions within society remain. This partisan alignment of civic bodies along the principal political divisions is reflected in the attitudes of South African elites. The attitude clusters represented in a factor analysis of elite attitudes done in 1992 (table 6.2) illustrate these multiple political divisions with their attendant civic components.[22] The sample consisted of 2,282 positional elites selected on the basis of their leadership positions in the various institutional sectors of South African society. The sectors from which they were drawn are agriculture (99 individuals), labor (129), the bureaucracy (200), big business (190), academia (148), the political right wing (148), the legislature (361), local-level politicians (156), extraparliamentary politicians (310), media (140), parastatals (94), the Convention for a Democratic South Africa (139 delegates not already represented in any of the above sectors), churches (143), and the military (74).

It is worth emphasizing that none of these clusters of institutions can be compartmentalized into rigid racial, class, or ethnic categories. The interest group diversity of South Africa rapidly became more multiracial and multicultural as the policies of reform apartheid took effect. Within a number of them, pockets of distinct ethnic or class-based organizations can be found, but no easy labeling of their overall character is possible. These formations are less easily described by the identity of their members than by their demands about the appropriate character of the South African state and society.

THE WEAKENING OF THE STATE

The apartheid state was weakened from within by officials and elected representatives who engaged in actions beyond the limits set by the laws of the state. Corruption—the use of public funds in contravention of the laws of the state—was a widespread phenomenon. Most widely known was the scandal about the use of secret funds by the Department of Information, which led to the resignation of State President B. J. Vorster in 1978.[23] During the 1980s, allegations of the misuse of public funds in the subordinate homelands of Transkei, Ciskei, KwaNdebele, and Lebowa became the subject of official commissions of inquiry, and the allegations were confirmed in the latter two cases.[24]

Dirty tricks by the state, in the form of illegal actions against the political opposition, are not easily verifiable. However, circumstantial evidence is not hard to find. Most infamous are the deaths of political prisoners in detention; the death of Black Consciousness leader Steve Biko in 1977 is the best known. According to one source, 68 such casualties occurred from September 1963 to August 1988.[25] Accusations that the security forces operated death squads have persisted into the 1990s, but neither an official inquiry nor a standing commission of the National Peace Accord could find evidence of any such operations.[26] The best-substantiated action of this kind by members of the state in their personal capacities thus far was revealed in the so-called Trust Feed murder case: a police officer was found guilty on 11 counts of murder after admitting to executing an attack on a UDF stronghold in 1988.[27] Less violent but still in the realm of dirty tricks was the government's admission that it clandestinely funded the Inkatha Freedom Party (IFP) in 1991.[28]

From outside, the state was weakened by a number of forms of resistance. Organized civil disobedience took the form of the 1989 Defiance Campaign, targeting segregated hospitals, beaches, and buses.[29] Far more extensive was the gradual but persistent unorganized civil disobedience of thousands of ordinary black South Africans who simply stopped following the apartheid prescriptions in an attempt to devise workable survival strategies for themselves. Civil disobedience of this order accelerated the collapse of urban and communal apartheid as much as organized resistance did.[30] It also stimulated the rapid growth of a parallel economy operating beyond the control of the state. According to one estimate released in 1992, up to 3.5 million people of an economically active population of 14.3 million were employed in the informal sector of the economy.[31]

Table 6.2. Factor Analysis: Elite Attitudes toward Civic and Public Organizations

Organizations	Factor 1 "State"	Factor 2 "Alternative State"	Factor 3 "Liberals"	Factor 4 "Right Wing"	Factor 5 "Co-optees"	Factor 6 "Africanist"
Broederbond	.79115					
Federasie Afrikaanse Kultuur*	.78040					
NG-Church (Dutch Reform)*	.75515					
Afrikaanse Handelsinstituut*	.71416					
Afrikaans Press*	.70027					
SA Broadcasting Corporation (TV)	.68375					
National Party	.65142					
House of Assembly	.63156					
SA Defence Force	.59076					
Big business	.58399					
Civil service	.56656					
State president	.52991					
SA Agricultural Union*	.52527					
Courts	.50961					
Confederation of SA Trade Unions*		.76303				
Umkhonto we Sizwe		.76131				
African National Congress		.73014				
National Education Coordination Committee*		.72499				
SA Communist Party		.72217				
Civics*		.71612				
SA Council of Churches*		.71445				
Soweto People's Delegation*		.71345				

People's Defense Committees*	.68695					
Alternative media*	.58123					
Democratic Party		.70286				
Institute of Multi-Party Democracy*		.68552				
Urban Foundation*		.65821				
Inst. Democratic Alternative for SA*		.59861				
SA Chamber of Business*		.59861				
English Press*		.55936				
Afrikaner–Weerstandsbewegings			.82217			
Conservative Party			.79499			
Afrikaner–Volkswag*			.76401			
House of Delegates				.66530		
House of Representatives				.64587		
Homeland leaders				.53779		
Inkatha Freedom Party				.51365		
Azanian People's Organization					.7398	
Pan African Congress					.7364	
National Council of Trade Unions*					.5265	
Percentage of variance	28.9	17.3	6.9	3.5	2.7	2.7

*Institutions normally found in civil society.

Source: Hennie Kotzé and Pierre du Toit, "The State, Civil Society and Democratic Transition in South Africa: A Survey of Elite Attitudes," *Journal of Conflict Resolution* 39, no. 1 (March 1995): 27–48 at 40–41. Copyright © 1995 Sage Publications. Used with permission of the Publisher.

The challenge to state social control presented by tax revolts is aimed at a fundamental state claim to sovereignty, and inability to quell these revolts signals crucial state weakness. The rent and service charge boycott of black local authorities started in 1984 and by 1986 had spread to 53 townships.[32] The boycott was most widespread in the Transvaal, where by 1991 only 33 percent of dues could be collected. By 1992 many of these actions were still operative, and the total amount outstanding was nearly R1.58 billion.[33]

State tolerance of private armies and paramilitary forces that challenge state claims to sovereignty also indicates a weakening of state power. When the PAC and ANC were unbanned in 1990 they did not disband their military wings, the Azanian People's Liberation Army (APLA) and MK, respectively. The ANC did suspend the armed struggle in 1990 but refused to reveal its armed caches, while the PAC continued its armed campaign, even with its newly acquired legalized status. The ANC then announced in December 1990 that so-called people's defense committees would be established in black townships to ensure the physical safety of residents. The white right-wing Afrikaner Weerstandsbeweging (AWB) followed suit in early 1991 by establishing a new military wing, the Ystergarde (Guards of Steel), to be recruited from the ranks of former defense force and police personnel.[34] The National Peace Accord—signed in September 1991 by the NP, ANC, SACP, and IFP but not by the AWB and PAC—explicitly prohibits the maintenance of private armies (section 3.7, paragraph 3.7.3) but as of early 1994 had not yet been effective in disbanding any one of these units.

Another crucial challenge to the state was in the form of so-called people's courts, erected to enact informal justice in the black townships. Unlike some of the earlier informal township courts, these were not merely complementary parallels to the formal judicial system. The courts established by UDF affiliates were parallel and antagonistic to the state, "part of a broad national movement that sought to transform the state itself"[35] through "a deliberate effort to replace the organs of the state and in so doing transform political relationships."[36] The state recognized this challenge and with some measure of success sought to suppress the continued existence of these courts, which during 1985 were estimated to number more than 400.[37]

Armed confrontations with the state escalated through the 1980s, with the ANC's armed struggle reaching its most intense level in 1988. After 1990 the ANC's suspension of the armed struggle officially stopped the MK confrontation with the state, but attacks by APLA continued, and police officers and soldiers of the South African Defence Force were singled out as targets. In 1992 alone 122 policemen died in such incidents, up from 81 in 1990.[38]

The most tangible success of the insurrectionary project against the state, and the most visible indicator of the weakening of the state was the extent to which the state structures called black local authorities collapsed. These bodies, set up to administer African townships, were constituted with elected councils; elections were held in 1983 and 1988. The councils and councilors became a prime focus of attack by the UDF-ANC allied township organizations. The 1988 elections were countered with a boycott so successful that only a 25.1 percent official turnout was registered.[39] Individual councilors and their property were subjected to physical attacks; 111 such attacks were recorded in the first half of 1990.[40] These attacks, coupled to the campaign by CAST (Civic Associations of the Southern Transvaal) to bring about the collapse of the black local authorities, resulted in many councilors resigning. By the end of 1990, 40 percent of the authorities had ceased functioning, and by March 1991 the number had risen to 48 percent.[41]

A final indicator of the decline of state social control is found in crime rates. In 1990, serious crime rose by 8.53 percent over the previous year, the highest annual increase in a decade. In 1991, it rose by 9.8 percent, sustaining the trend of the previous year. During 1990, armed robberies increased by more than 27 percent, and in 1991, by a further 16 percent. The overall number of infringements of the law for 1991 rose by more than 15 percent over 1990.[42] Although not overtly political in nature, these actions do indicate the extent to which people were prepared to act in ways other than those prescribed by the state through its laws.

In assessing how weak the state had become by the early 1990s, one has to consider the extent to which insurrectionary goals and counterrevolutionary targets on both sides were *not* achieved. The ANC was successful in its military campaign of "armed propaganda" but failed to achieve a generalized insurrection.[43] Nor were liberated zones established or dual sovereignty achieved on a more or less permanent basis.[44] The state was strong enough to do little more than protect its core interests and institutions against the insurrectionists.[45] "Although security action weakened the extra-parliamentary opposition and welfare action *won the hearts and minds* of a small number of blacks, this low-intensity conflict phase of total strategy succeeded in *managing* rather than *destroying* political opposition" (original emphasis).[46] In short, the mutually hurting stalemate had set in. The resilience of the state in meeting these (and earlier) challenges has been ascribed to its capacity for innovation as well as to apartheid institutions having modified and adapted to changing conditions of adversity.[47] The inability of the state to maintain its almost omnipotent position of the late 1960s has been accounted for by a combination of manpower shortages, declining resources,[48] and weakening resolve.[49]

THE WEAKENING OF SOCIETY

The creation of the apartheid state substantially weakened some sectors of South African society. The resistance against the state, like the revolt against the Rhodesian state, contributed further to the weakening of *all* sectors of society. The decaying of the social fabric can be gauged in part from crime statistics. Cases of rape in the white population in 1990 rose by 23.7 percent over 1989. Within the overall population, reported cases of sodomy rose by 15.47 percent; incest by 24.22 percent; and stealing of children, 20.44 percent over the previous year. In 1991, cases of both incest and indecent assault again rose by more than 10 percent, and reported cases of child stealing rose yet another 29.35 percent.[50] It became increasingly difficult for perpetrators to distinguish between political and criminal violence, as both became indispensable components of the survival strategies of the urban youth trying to cope with the dislocation of township life. This merging of criminal and political intent came to be epitomized by the emergence of so-called *comtsotsis*, gangs of youths surviving through violent actions against both the state and township society.[51]

The weakening of all sectors of society as measured in family breakdown accelerated in the 1980s. By the early 1980s white families still appeared to be fairly cohesive, if one looks only at rates of illegitimacy. The 1980 figure for whites was 5 percent illegitimate births versus 15 percent for Asians, 43 percent for Africans, and 52 percent for Coloreds.[52] Yet between 1978 and 1982 the divorce rate for whites increased by 47 percent, and by 1982 the probability was that 1 out of every 2.24 white marriages would fail—one of the highest divorce rates in the world. (No immediate causal link between the changing political environment and white divorce rates can be shown, but it is an intriguing correlation.) In the same year the official divorce rate for Coloreds stood at 1 in 4.5 marriages and 1 in 8.8 for Asians.[53] No comparable figures for Africans exist, because they may marry under customary law, making direct comparisons impossible. Yet a vast literature does confirm the rate of African family breakdown through the adverse conditions created through apartheid (see chapter 5).

These conditions of family dissolution amid rising political turmoil profoundly disturbed the pattern of childhood socialization. Where African families did not break up completely, the status of parents, especially of fathers, came under increasing threat.[54] This further undermined their position as role models for children to emulate, leaving the street experience of socialization through confrontation with the state as the dominant formative agent.[55]

This growing adult-youth divide found political expression when some of the "people's courts" run by youthful practitioners of informal "justice" took on cases of complaints against adult members of the community (such as a dispute between husband and wife). The response to such actions by one court in Cape Town was outrage: "For youths who were unmarried, and who by implication understood nothing about such matters (as they had not yet been initiated) to pronounce that a man had to leave his mistress and return to his wife, was deemed to be challenging the entire basis of the cultural norms widely supported in the broad community."[56] In the Mamelodi township of Pretoria, the adults established their own informal court, roughly compatible with traditional customary courts, to confront the social and political challenge of rebellious youth.[57]

Official figures report that between 1984 and 1986, 300 children (that is, youths under age 18) were killed by police actions, 1,000 were injured, 11,000 were detained without trial, and 173,000 had awaited trial for some time, while being held in custody.[58] The psychological damage done through stressful experiences such as these is not easily captured in aggregate statistics. Qualitative research nonetheless gives adequate insight into the scope of the damage that has been done.[59] The conclusion most relevant to the future strength of both state and society and to the prospects of democratic stability is that these children were socialized into rejecting the entire legal system, not just the offensive apartheid laws.[60]

SOCIETY AS A CONTESTED TERRAIN

The level of social control in the black sectors of society receded with the weakening of the state and of core social institutions such as the family, creating social space in which new institutions of social control could emerge and existing institutions hitherto constrained by the state could expand. From the late 1970s to the early 1990s, both of these trends occurred. The result was the emergence of a pattern of social control not predicted by the theoretical perspective outlined in the appendix: a weblike pattern of social control (at local level) in which society became a terrain contested by numerous antagonistic institutions, yet within a society that still had to be characterized as weak. The first set of institutions comprising the "progressive" organizations associated with the UDF-ANC antiapartheid alliance has already been discussed in this chapter. Foremost in this regard was the youth-based "comrades" movement, which emerged in organizations that were distinctive to the region or urban area where they were located yet were all characterized by the populist idiom of the antiapartheid establishment and involved in the politics of "the struggle."[61] The people's courts that became aligned to UDF structures also formed part of this loose configuration of institutions.

The second set of local institutions, primarily located in the shantytowns on the urban periphery, were constructed by the newly arrived migrants from the rural homelands. These informal political structures, typically comprising a system of committees, were engaged in regulating social and political conduct, raising levies or dues from shackholders, executing policing and "judicial" functions, and above all controlling access to the community. Early examples of these structures have been found in the shantytowns of Johannesburg in the 1940s and 1950s,[62] in the Cape Town area of Crossroads from 1976,[63] and in the Witwatersrand from 1983.[64] Since recent urban migrants were close to the culture of the rural areas, these informal political structures tended to be rooted in the shackholders' tribal codes and can therefore be described as less "progressive" and more "traditional." Yet they remained principally antagonistic to the state as long as the pass laws remained in effect and were vigorously applied. The informal courts run by adults who set up these structures were, however, viewed with less hostility by the state than were the populist people's courts, because they were usually closely aligned either to community councilors or to tribal or homeland authority structures and thus tended to be viewed as complementary to the formal legal system of the state.[65]

The third set of distinctive local-level organizations was the hostels. These units were established for single male migrants under the apartheid presumption that they were seeking only temporary work in the white urban areas and therefore needed only temporary accommodation. A recent survey identified 402 hostels countrywide with an estimate of 604,000 beds.[66] Hostel dwellers established informal authority structures as survival strategies for coping with overcrowding, family dislocation, poverty, and the unfamiliar urban landscape. Again the rural experience provided the basis for the new structures.[67] In 1968, aspects of this authority structure were formalized through measures published in the *Government Gazette.* This power structure centered on the elected *izibonda,* or headmen, usually men of high social status according to traditional cultural yardsticks.[68]

Interwoven within all of these structures is an adherence to selective aspects of rules of social control associated with traditional rural African life. The practice of traditional healing through herbalists and diviners has not only persisted despite the modernizing effects of rapid capitalist industrialization but has even flourished in modern urban settings.[69]

These beliefs and practices became vital ingredients in the survival strategies of different parties to the conflict in contemporary South African society. Not only did the more traditionally oriented members of the African townships make use of them, but so did the more progressive organizations. Thus we find reports of "comrades" resorting to *muti* to strengthen them for confrontations with the state or community-based opposition.[70] *Muti* are special empowering medicines made from specially selected herbs and specific body parts of animals and humans. The more esoteric the ingredients, the more potent the medicine. The more intense the confrontation, the greater the need for powerful medicine. In these confrontations the beliefs and practices of witchcraft also came to be used by the youthful opposition against established conservative communal authorities. Increasing numbers of so-called medicine murders, in which the victims' bodies are used to manufacture such medicines, and the burning of witches therefore accompanied the civil strife of the 1980s and early 1990s.[71] The exact scope of these activities is hard to ascertain, but newspaper reports suggested that the market for *muti* in South Africa had grown so large as to sustain a cross-border traffic in human body parts.[72] Whether these practitioners were true believers or just skillful entrepreneurs cynically employing deep-seated beliefs for their own gain is disputed. The state, however, is clear on the matter. The Witchcraft Suppression Act of 1957 (as amended in 1970), like the comparable Rhodesian legislation, forbade both the practice and the accusation of witchcraft. These aspects of township survival strategies therefore not only embroiled different communal actors in conflict with one another but also brought these parties into conflict with the state.

A situation of numerous tenuously institutionalized social organizations vying for community control, established social institutions being substantially weakened, and state control receding opened up opportunities for potential strongmen to engage the state (and other national political actors) in consolidating their own power. The potentially mutually profitable exchange was outlined by Mike Morris and Doug Hindson, writing in 1992: "The ANC, Inkatha and, increasingly the agencies of the central state, are forced to operate through the local warlord or youth power centers to gain power locally. Equally, local power groups turn for support to regional and national organisations: Inkatha and the homeland or national government on the one hand and the ANC national structure on the other."[73] They do not cite data to substantiate this proposition, but limited research provides some confirmation.

An analysis of the power struggles in and around the Crossroads shantytown settlement in Cape Town provides the only detailed confirmation of the repertoire of actions to be expected from strongmen to date. The career of Johnson Ngxobongwana shows his skillful tactical allegiance with the antiapartheid establishment and against the state while influx control was still applied. Then he adroitly aligned himself with the state against the UDF-affiliated comrades, eliminating them in the infamous *witdoek* war of 1986, which left 60 dead and 70,000 refugees fleeing Crossroads. In this emerging triangle of accommodation the state won (by getting people to relocate away from Crossroads and by eliminating UDF influence in Crossroads); the local authority won (by retaining a reliable and conservative set of agents for the daily administration of Crossroads); and Ngxobongwana won (by trouncing his immediate opposition in Crossroads). The state then equally skillfully drew him into the formal structures of local government when Crossroads became a black local authority. He became the duly elected mayor, and the state's implementor, R. Schelhase, became the acting town clerk. Ngxobongwana's reign ended when one of his recalcitrant headmen, Jeffrey Nongwe (an emergent strongman), drew the newly unbanned ANC into his own camp and forcibly evicted Ngxobongwana from Crossroads in 1991.[74] Nongwe then unilaterally founded his own ANC branch, and by 1993 a steadily deteriorating relationship ensued with the official ANC Youth League branch of Crossroads.

Further support for the Morris-Hindson proposition can be found in the data on the warlords of Natal.[75] Although that research is not explicitly guided by Migdal's conceptual framework, the data reveal local powerholders with some control over communities, which the powerholders offer as a valued resource to national-level players in exchange for consolidating their own positions.

A hallmark of the way control over society is contested is found in the persistently high levels of violence in South Africa since 1985. Deaths due to political conflict in the country had by the end of 1993 approached a total of 14,000 casualties.[76] A widely held explanation offered by Lauren Segal is the "general theory that it is the disintegration of apartheid which is the cause of the contemporary escalation in violence."[77]

The perspective employed in this study allows for the explication of the above theory through a number of more detailed propositions. The first proposition is that the violence is in part a function of the deepening of divisions within society, that the rising stakes in the conflict culminated in a confrontation between adversaries intent on gaining hegemony. The second proposition is that the violence is in part a function of the weakening of the state, leaving a vacuum of social control, thus creating opportunities for other actors to assert themselves. Given the fact that so many different communally based organizations tried to step into this newly vacated social space, the result was intense competition for social control in the receding phase of overall rule setting by the state, and hence the emergence of violent contestation. The third proposition is that violence is in part a function of the weakening of society, that the rising normlessness created both conditions and incentives for violence, both criminally and politically inspired. The fourth proposition is that violence is in part a function of triangles of accommodation, that both national and local political actors strive to assert social control in local communities through weakly institutionalized bargains, which are contested by rivals trying to do the same. These triangles of accommodation serve to link local conflicts with the national contest for hegemony, thus intensifying the former and extending the scope of the latter.

The weakening of state-directed rules of social control over group identities culminated in 1991 with the scrapping of the Population Registration Act. Within the contested terrain of society a number of the new political formations assumed new identities or were assigned new labels, some of which appeared to have a distinctive cultural content. Attempts at interpreting these phenomena lead to a resurgence of the debate on ethnicity. The most prominent objects of analysis have been the ethnic character of Zulu nationalism, as represented by the IFP and the group dynamics of predominantly Zulu-speaking hostels on the Witwatersrand, and that of the white right wing, where numerous organizations claim representativeness.

Limitations of space here make it impossible to discuss all relevant research, but a few trends will be highlighted.[78] First, some analysts reject the apparent emergence of postapartheid ethnicity with evermore elaborate versions of the claim of false consciousness. The leading example must be this one: "The *false self* is compliance to an enforced environment. It is a defensive adaptation to an impoverishing and constraining environment, by which the individual is frozen into failure. . . . A marked characteristic of present-day

South Africa is the pervasiveness of compliance on cognitive, intellectual and emotional levels. The persistence of ethnic, national and racial *false selfs* implies a collusion with—or surrender to—forms of identity that are assumed to be givens, immutable and irresistible" (original emphasis).[79] Why ethnic identities should by definition qualify as being false, but not other competing identities such as class, worker, or even citizen, is not considered. It could be argued that, depending on context and salience, all of these identities could equally well be thus limited.

Second, microlevel empirical research by analysts who pay cognitive respect to their respondents has recorded as authentic the fact that the respondents do hold ethnic identities, which provide meaning to their circumstances.[80] Third, among those who recognize these ethnic phenomena, the trend is to explain them in terms of the modernization theory of ethnicity, which interprets ethnicity as a useful mobilizing instrument for the collective pursuit of wealth, status, and power.[81] The weakness of this theory becomes most apparent in the analyses of the ethnic forces within the white right wing.[82] One account correctly notes the correlation between economic backwardness and right-wing sentiments among whites and then argues that economic growth will weaken the attractiveness of ethnic cohesion as economic uncertainties fade.[83] This leaves the researchers unable to account for the fact that right-wing politicians offer various plans of secession to their followers, all of which promise even greater economic sacrifice and hardship than the conditions of the early 1990s. These hardships, though well recognized, still get substantial support from white ethnic groups. An adequate explanation of right-wing ethnicity needs to draw on the theory that demonstrates that economic hardships are interpreted as a loss of esteem and that further economic sacrifices are accepted as long as the redemption of collective status through political self-determination and ownership of a state is held as an achievable future prospect.[84]

NEGOTIATIONS

The crucial breakthrough to formal negotiations on a new constitution occurred with the unbanning of the ANC, PAC, SACP, and 33 other organizations on February 2, 1990, by the new state president, F. W. de Klerk. Nine days later, Nelson Mandela was released from prison, having served 27 years of a life sentence for treason.

During the ensuing prenegotiation phase the commitment to compromise was rapidly formalized. The first agreement to this effect was the Groote Schuur Minute, a bilateral agreement signed in May 1990. This was followed by the Pretoria Minute, in which the ANC agreed to the suspension of the armed struggle and the release of political prisoners and the granting of indemnity to affected persons were settled. The D. F. Malan Accord of early 1991 further strengthened these agreements, and a multilateral attempt at trust building culminated in the signing of the National Peace Accord in September 1991. Major nonsignatories were the PAC and the AWB. To date this remains the most comprehensive attempt to construct a nonaggression pact between the major national political players inside South Africa.[85]

The ANC/SACP alliance, joined later by the Congress of South African Trade Unions (COSATU), entered into the negotiation process with an agenda shaped by its populist perspective on the appropriate kind of state, regime, and society, as outlined earlier in the chapter. The NP, by contrast, pursued an agenda informed by technocratic preferences. Its socioeconomic priorities were growth over equity and stability over unrestrained participation, so as to protect the modern sector of society where most of its supporters are located. The NP still conceived of South Africa as a nation of multiple minorities and thus saw democracy as power sharing among such communities in which none would be able to dominate the others.[86] The right wing (both black and white, represented by the Conservative Party [CP] and IFP) insisted on the concept of a multitude of nations and placed even greater stress on the need for minority protection, while the liberal agenda tended to focus less on minority protection and more on the entrenchment of individual rights.

The Convention for a Democratic South Africa (CODESA) inaugurated formal constitutional negotiations by a multiparty forum of 19 delegations, which first met on December 20, 1991. Notable absentees were the PAC and the CP, both claiming that participation would "sell out" their supporters. CODESA established five working groups with a brief to report back in May 1992. Working group 2, assigned to deal with general constitutional principles, deadlocked on a single item with the ANC and the NP on opposing sides and failed to produce a report. The ANC then withdrew from formal negotiations and set in motion its campaign of mass action. Tensions escalated, especially with the Boipatong and Bisho shootings, and only in September 1992 were bilateral negotiations between the ANC and the government resumed at which the so-called Record of Understanding was concluded.[87] Bilateral discussions were continued in a secret *bosberaad* (bush summit) in December 1992, followed by another one in January 1993.[88]

In 1993 a number of highly significant events and outcomes occurred. First, in April 1993 multiparty negotiations were resumed and the ANC's proposal for a two-stage process of transition was accepted. This in effect amounted to a complete endorsement of the Record of Understanding, which committed the ANC and NP to enact the transition through the democratically elected Constituent Assembly as the appropriate constitution-making body. Under the terms of the transitional constitution, the Constituent Assembly had to function as the interim parliament from which an interim multiparty "government of national unity" had to be assembled.

Second, the transitional constitution, which is to last for the five years ending April 27, 1999, was agreed on in November 1993. Agreement was also reached for elections to be held on April 27, 1994, and for the termination of the status of the independent homelands. This agreement was rejected out of hand by the Freedom Alliance, established in October 1993 and consisting of the IFP, the CP, and the governments of Ciskei and Bophuthatswana. In December 1993 the tricameral parliament passed the new constitutional bill, and on January 1, 1994, the people of Ciskei, Transkei, Venda, and Bophuthatswana automatically regained South African citizenship.

Third, the United Nations ended formal economic sanctions against the country and South Africa regained access to World Bank and International Monetary Fund (IMF) facilities. And fourth, the government and the PAC agreed to end hostilities between APLA and the state.

The state-society perspective employed in this study requires that five questions guide the analysis of these negotiation events: To what extent was the outcome shaped by specific tactics in the use of power? Has the criterion of good faith been met? Were adequate measures for face saving deployed? Has the contest for hegemony been resolved with the establishment of an autonomous state? And finally, Does the new constitution provide for the rebuilding of the strength of the state?

Power and Tactics

The Record of Understanding contains major concessions by the NP and, conversely, formalizes substantial gains by the ANC in getting a commitment from the NP to the principle of an elected constituent assembly. The mass action campaign of 1992 thus appeared to yield clear-cut results and allowed the ANC to score a decisive victory at the negotiating table.

The power-dependence perspective can be used to explain the power behind the tactic of mass action. By the end of the 1980s, 95 percent of semiskilled and unskilled labor in the wage sector of the economy was still being done by blacks.[89] The ANC-SACP-COSATU alliance draws much of its support from these ranks, with COSATU alone having 1.2 million members, and it succeeded in implementing a general strike on August 3 and 4, 1992, in which between 2.5 and 4 million people took part.[90] To the extent that the modern economy is dependent on this category of labor, the alliance controls a vitally needed commodity and a source of bargaining power. The hospital strike of 1992 demonstrates the point vividly. Hospitals are indispensable, as are the people who run them; without alternative sources (of facilities to take care of the ill) and employees (nonstriking workers), and with full country-wide support, the strike could have yielded the maximum actual power to the party in control of this valued scarce commodity.

The mass action campaign targeted the modern sector of society. It was carried out by populists whose foremost priority is the equitable redistribution of wealth. This priority places them in a position of dependence on the wealth-producing sector of society, which generates the goods that are to be redistributed. This modern sector also contains pockets of strategically placed people on whom the wealth-creating capacity depends. In the agricultural sector 12,000 white farming families produce 75 percent of the country's food (not unlike the situation in Zimbabwe in 1980).[91] By the end of the 1980s, 91 percent of managers in the modern sector were still whites, and a study released in 1992 claimed that whites and Asians were responsible for 97 percent of job creation in the modern sector of the economy.[92] These kinds of data figure in the calculation that if all the whites and Asians in the country with access to foreign passports exercised the option of leaving, the country's economy would collapse.[93] Mass action did not produce this outcome, but in tandem with a decade of rent and school boycotts, economic sanctions, and labor strikes, it has elicited the *investment strike*. Gross domestic fixed investment dropped by 8.5 percent in 1991 from the previous year,[94] and by another 10 percent in real terms during 1992.[95] In addition, GDP in real terms had declined every year from 1987 to 1991.[96] With less wealth to redistribute, the prospect of meeting populist promises dwindles and the dependence of future populist rulers on the wealth-generating sector of the economy, from where the NP draws much of its support, increases. Concomitantly, the long-term potential bargaining power of the wealth-producing sector increases.

The NP, as incumbents of the state, used their control over institutions to further their own interests. One way of doing so was to try to control the process of transition, a tactic that was skillfully thwarted by the ANC.[97] The other primary tactics—deracialization, privatization, commercialization, and restructuring—all entail fundamental changes to the character of the state. Deracialization included the removal of the legal cornerstones of apartheid, including the Group Areas Act, the Population Registration Act, the Natives Land Acts of 1913 and 1936, and the Reservation of Separate Amenities Act, which allowed for further deracialization of hospitals, secondary and tertiary educational institutions, and public amenities. Deregulation entailed the withdrawal of the state from the economy by privatizing some parastatal corporations, commercializing others, and deregulating control over entrepreneurial activities. Major restructuring of the police and the defense force took place, in which a number of top officers took early retirement.[98]

These tactics must be assessed against the background of the strategic thinking that led the NP into negotiations. A number of analyses have argued that the NP's decision to enter into formal negotiations with the ANC was based on the calculation emerging from the Afrikaner Broederbond that "the most important prerequisite for Afrikaner survival was the acceptability of a new constitution for the majority of the population."[99] The NP went into formal negotiations confidently, "firm in its conviction that the outcome of negotiations would strengthen the existing state, and that the NP had the means to ensure that it would play a meaningful role on all levels of government both during the transition and thereafter."[100] This confidence was bolstered by the perception that a new, benign international order would emerge after the demise of the USSR and other communist regimes in central Europe: "In the government's perception, the ANC without Soviet backing was a containable force."[101] The strategic calculation was therefore to manage the transition in such a way as to deradicalize the ANC and moderate it to such an extent that it could be accommodated in the newly restructured and deracialized state, which in turn was to be firmly reembedded into the international system of states. This system of states, in the post–Cold War era, had become so strongly geared to the rules of a capitalist, private enterprise political economy that the NP felt secure about the ANC's inability to realign a future South African state in any other direction.

At face value, therefore, many of the structural changes to the state may appear to be driven by a commendable, albeit long overdue, elimination of discriminatory apartheid measures. Tactical implications go much further, however. The immediate implications were that some of the most visible emotive targets against which the ANC-SACP-COSATU alliance could mobilize had been removed from the arena. The state became less visibly an *apartheid* and *Afrikaner ethnic* institution. The longer-term tactical implication was to make the state more compatible with the norms of the newly emerging post–Cold War system of states. These norms favor the NP's technocratic priorities of growth, capitalism, and privatization, and are hostile to the ANC's populist priorities of state-driven redistribution and COSATU's explicit commitment to socialism. Binding the state into this global system locks the modern sector of the economy, on which future ruling populists will be so dependent, into structures and processes beyond the boundaries of the state itself and beyond the control of a single ruling party, irrespective of election returns. Economic ownership of the country, much like that in Zimbabwe, would then become partly vested in forces operating within the global economy.

When South Africa regained access to the IMF and World Bank facilities, on their terms, and Mandela publicly committed the South African economy to growth priorities, a crucial step was taken toward achieving this long-term goal of the NP. Unilateral state action thus subverted attempts to level the playing field by firmly securing the economic arena within the wider landscape of the global political economy—a landscape inhospitable to populist policies and socialist ideals.

Good Faith

CODESA failed, according to one interpretation, "because the two main contenders were convinced they would win. . . . Fundamental disagreement remained on the meaning of negotiations and its legal framework, on what had to be negotiated, and on the transitional institutions and the timetable of the process."[102] A concurring interpretation argues that both parties lacked the "strategic realism" necessary for substantive negotiations, so that "when CODESA finally met, the parties still faced each other with the expectation that they could outmaneuver the other behind closed doors and then emerge from the cloisters to present their prize to their waiting followers."[103] In sum, they entered formal negotiations on constitutional matters without having successfully concluded the crucial phase of prenegotiations. The mythologies of "liberation" and "total strategy" were still in place. From the start, then, CODESA was about talking the opponent into submission, about negotiations in bad faith.

The sources of such intent in the ANC-SACP-COSATU alliance can be traced back to its intellectual tradition of resistance, revolt, and struggle. The SACP's 1989 official program, "The Path to Power," for instance, explicitly argues that a link must be seen between negotiations and insurrection: "There is no conflict between this insurrectionary perspective and the possibility of a negotiated transfer of power. . . . *Armed struggle cannot be counterposed* [sic] *with dialogue, negotiation and justifiable compromises, as if they were mutually exclusive categories.* Liberation struggles have rarely ended with the unconditional surrender of the enemy's military forces. Every such struggle on our continent has had its climax at the negotiating table, occasionally involving compromises judged to be in the interests of revolutionary advance."[104]

Other documents are more ambivalent. The following example from a 1990 ANC document titled "The Road to Peace" illustrates the point: "Negotiations involve enemies attempting through dialogue to find a solution to their conflict which is mutually acceptable." Yet, "negotiations are not an alternative to struggle. They are part of an ongoing struggle, whose outcome will be decided less by what happens at the negotiating table, as by what happens away from it."[105] This formulation can be interpreted as part of the difficult process of turning around the party faithful to follow a new line diametrically opposed to what has been sold to them as the final truth. The new truth, so to speak, must therefore be couched at first in the familiar jargon of the old.

Bad faith from the ruling NP is more easily detected in its dirty tricks than from official documents. The "Inkathagate" debacle is a case in point. By funding the antisanctions campaign of the IFP, the government was not addressing an issue with a nonpartisan countrywide impact, as it claimed to do, but was using public funds to support one agenda with a bearing on this dispute at the expense of others. The Inkathagate incident demonstrates the general bad faith behind the tactical impact of unilateral state actions: the governing NP used resources at the disposal of the state to which it had exclusive access to alter the bargaining context in its own favor. Such actions allowed the NP to be both umpire and player at the same time, and to tilt the playing field in its own favor.

The mass action campaign that followed the breakdown of CODESA and culminated in the fatal shootings at Bisho, where demonstrators broke ranks and scores were killed by Ciskei security forces, appears to have been a profound learning experience that "instilled a sense of humility, sobriety and realism in both government and ANC leaders."[106] The mutually hurting stalemate was relearned: the ANC realized that it had to contribute to stability during the transition, and the government digested the inescapable fact that the ANC was indispensable to the effective management of state and society during the transition.

These realizations became the basis for the ANC-SACP-COSATU alliance's acceptance of the need for power sharing[107] and for the NP to relinquish exclusive control of the state (as acknowledged in the Record of Understanding). The cementing of good faith was probably consummated behind closed doors at the two *bosberaad* meetings in December 1992 and January 1993. Future scholarship may well reveal that these two gatherings were the pivotal events in the overall process of transition. When multiparty negotiations resumed in 1993 they were driven by the joint resolve of the NP and the alliance, embodied in the decision rule of "sufficient consensus"—a peculiar South African invention, which in practical terms meant that proposals were carried as long as the NP and the ANC supported them.

Face Saving

The bilateral process of establishing good faith between the governing NP and the ANC alliance was not matched by a similar process with regard to the IFP and the CP, arguably the strongest remaining players in the field. ANC and IFP relations at national level remained adversarial despite their January 1991 bilateral agreement to end violent confrontations. At the local level, the rural areas—especially in southern Natal—remained the most violent of the contested parts of South African society; both the ANC and the IFP registered hundreds of casualties.[108] For the reasons given earlier in this chapter, the national attempts at peace between these two parties had little effect on confrontations among the locally based power centers.[109] The IFP nonetheless became one of the inaugural signatories to the National Peace Accord in September 1991.

The alienation of the IFP from the political mainstream was rapidly accelerated by certain decisions made at CODESA. Arguably the most important was the decision not to grant the IFP's request for the Zulu king, Goodwill Zwelethini, to be awarded full status at CODESA.[110] The objections centered on logistics: so many other traditional leaders were around that the presence of all of them would swell CODESA to unmanageable proportions. No evidence can be found that the objectors (or their academic analysts) considered or were even aware of the more fundamental symbolic stakes riding on this request. The parties at CODESA were, in Friedman's apt phrase, "reluctant reconcilers," and at such an early stage of the proceedings, preventing the loss of face to any party was of the utmost importance. Furthermore, a party of delegates that claimed to represent ethnic communities (as did the IFP) and requested the admission of their monarch (the embodiment of that identity) was bound to experience the refusal of the request as the utmost humiliation, loss of collective dignity, and a public demonstration of contempt. CODESA strategists and academic commentators alike too easily discounted the IFP's outrage as small-minded nit-picking. Few showed any awareness that the most valuable of public goods in ethnic psychology—honor, dignity, and respect—could have been distributed equitably at CODESA without too great a burden being placed on the taxpayer.

State Strength and Autonomy

To what extent do the new regime rules contribute to the strengthening of the state, and to what extent does the passage of the new constitution indicate a dissolution of the contest for hegemony? The constitution provides for a bicameral parliament consisting of a 400-person National Assembly and a 90-person Senate. The National Assembly is elected directly on the basis of a system of party-list proportional representation; the Senate, indirectly by the nine newly created provinces. The National Assembly elects, by majority vote, an executive president who acts as head of state. Each party obtaining more than 80 seats in the National Assembly is also entitled to nominate an executive deputy president. The cabinet is composed proportionally of all parties obtaining 5 percent or more of the vote in a national election, and collective decision making is to be conducted in the "spirit of consensus."

Each of the nine provinces gets a provincial legislature, also elected on the basis of proportional representation. These bodies were to have concurrent powers with the national government to make laws on issues set out in a schedule of the constitution; however, an amendment to the constitution in early 1994 gave provinces exclusive, rather than concurrent, powers. Each province is governed by a provincial executive council consisting of a premier and 10 executive members comprising all parties that win at least 10 percent of the seats in the provincial legislature.

The constitution allows for autonomous third-tier local government bodies in which traditional leaders are to be accommodated as ex officio members. On the provincial level there is a House of Traditional Leaders, and at national level, a Council of Traditional Leaders.

The Constitutional Assembly consists of the National Assembly and the Senate sitting in joint session. In drafting the final constitution they are bound to a set of constitutional principles set out in a separate schedule of this constitution, and it will have to be adopted by a two-thirds majority. Should this not be achieved, a number of deadlock-breaking mechanisms will come into effect, ending with a national referendum requiring a 60 percent majority. The Constitutional Court has final jurisdiction over matters relating to the interpretation, protection, and enforcement of the constitution at all levels of government.

One obvious source of strength for the state lies in the undeniably democratic character of the constitution, which should gain legitimacy among the millions of previously disenfranchised South Africans. The potential weakness may stem from disgruntled minorities who may feel threatened by perceived majority domination. Such minorities, especially if strategically located within the state or the modern sector of the economy, could once again weaken the state through strategies of "ungovernability."

A second potential source of strength is in the ample room being made for traditional leaders at all three levels of government. In that respect, this constitution exceeds the constitutional accommodation allowed for traditional leaders in both Botswana's and Zimbabwe's constitutions. Should this representation be adequately effected and be accompanied by imaginative modernization of customary law within the legal system of the state, a key requirement for strengthening the state will have been met: that existing rules of social control be made compatible with and supportive of those prescribed by the state. The crucial challenge facing proponents of customary law is to make it compatible with international standards of human rights as represented in the Chapter of Rights in the new constitution. Major issues that stand out in this regard are the status of women and children and the matter of property rights.[111]

The accommodative capacity of the measures recognizing traditional leaders is closely tied to the autonomy given to local and provincial authorities. The federal characteristics of the provinces are equally important to other threatened minorities. The exact status of these second- and third-tier bodies cannot be accurately assessed at the time of writing, and their evolution will probably be shaped by a number of test cases that are bound to be brought before the Constitutional Court. That they were considered inadequate by the traditional leadership of the Zulu-speaking people was made clear in a memorandum presented to State President de Klerk in a meeting with King Zwelethini on January 17, 1994. In the document an objection is raised to naming the combined Natal province and KwaZulu homeland region as the "Natal" province in the new constitution. This, the king said, "renders it so alien that we must reject it. It amounts to the expunging of the very name of my kingdom from the constitution of South Africa. This has sent shockwaves throughout the psyche of every one of our Zulu subjects." That the failures of CODESA were replicated in the transitional constitution was also made crystal clear to the state president, who was informed of "the hurt that you, as head of state, have inflicted on us as Zulus . . . in allowing us to be humiliated in this way by people who never once conquered us in any war. . . . What is being done to us is something far worse than what our British conquerors did to us. . . . Even though there was a history of conflict between my people and your people, Mr. President, not one Afrikaner leader has in all history ever attempted to do to us what has now been done to us, to completely obliterate us as a people from the face of South Africa."[112]

The above sentiment suggests that for some minorities, at least, the newly reconstituted state will not be taken as a legitimate arena within which to conduct the daily politics of who gets what, when and how. Instead, as in the apartheid era, the character of the state itself will be the issue of contestation. Does the same apply to the major antagonists in the contest for hegemony, that is, the NP and its support groups, and the ANC alliance? Will the presumed understanding and good faith created between these two formations prevail and form the cement to bind constitutional rules into a "living constitution" within which politics is to be conducted?

The constitution is only a five-year transitional one, so the era of constitution making is not yet over. The elected parliament is to act as constitution-making body for this (final?) set of regime rules, which has to be passed with a two-thirds majority. The inaugural election of April 1994 was therefore to be a highly contested one, and the ANC alliance was the only possible candidate to reach that two-thirds majority. Regardless of election results, all parties are still bound to the principles set out in the constitution and to the surveillance of the Constitutional Court. There are therefore clear rules restraining future constitution makers, and a measure of autonomy has been built into this and future constitutions, which insulates them to some extent from electoral contests and changes in incumbency. But any such set of insulating rules is subject to attrition by politicians bent on unilaterally redefining the state and capturing it on their own terms. What matters, therefore, is the disposition of the new leaders of the democratic South Africa. Their ethos of state action is bound to shape the character of the postapartheid state and its democratic prospects as much as the newly negotiated constitutional rules are likely to.

CONCLUSION

An analysis of the dynamics of state-society interaction in post-apartheid South Africa and the impact thereof on the quality of democracy will become possible as events unfold. The study thus far supports the proposition that the superior democratic character of democracy in Botswana over that of Zimbabwe can be accounted for in part by the strength of Botswana's state and society. The analysis in this chapter has shown that in the contest for hegemony that resulted from the revolt against the apartheid state, both society and state have been substantially weakened. The chapter therefore closes with the proposition that to secure democratic stability and viability, both the state and the society of postapartheid South Africa will have to be strengthened. In the next chapter this proposition is explored further.

PART IV

TOWARD
SUSTAINABLE
DEMOCRACY

❋ 7 ❋

THE INCENTIVES FOR
SUSTAINING DEMOCRACY

"**S**ustainable development," we are told, "meets the needs of the present without compromising the ability of future generations to meet their own needs."[1] Analogously, then, sustainable democracy would mean that democratic practices should be judged against the yardstick of performance as measured in resilience and persistence, especially when democratic practices are established in adverse conditions and from their inception are under threat from hostile forces. To the perennial question, How much democracy and what kind of democracy are appropriate? the response must then be, As much as, and the kind that, can function in such a way as to provide future generations with opportunities to maintain and expand these very same democratic practices. Democracy in Africa is a rare phenomenon, and even the strongest examples such as Botswana are flawed when measured against abstract conceptual yardsticks only. But flawed democratic practices that can be sustained are always potentially open to improvement and enhancement. This perspective guides the assessment of the democratic prospects of the three states under discussion.

THE SUSTAINABILITY OF DEMOCRACY IN BOTSWANA

The persistence of democracy in Botswana is in some measure tied to the durability of certain sustaining factors. A decline in this sustenance could threaten democracy. The most important sources of potential breakdown are in the ecological constraints confronting the cattle economy, the internal discipline and cohesion of the ruling coalition, and the destabilizing forces generated by the regional context and the global context. The potential impact of change in each of these sectors on the democratic process will be considered in turn.

The nature of the state, the society, and the democratic process in Botswana is closely intertwined with the country's cattle economy. If the cup is considered half empty, then a measure of the inequality of this economy and this society is that nearly half of the people do not own any cattle. If the cup is considered half full, it is significant that half of the population *do* own cattle. This economy, and the social and political relations tied to it, has been sustained historically by an ecological presumption embodied in the notion of the "moving frontier." The core assumption of the traditional land tenure system is that "there will be enough land for all."[2] The traditional response to shortage of grazing land has therefore always been to open up new grazing areas, mostly westward into the Kalahari.[3] As long as this could be done, communal ownership of land for use by individuals for their private gain was ecologically sustainable.

This westward expansion accelerated as the technology and financing for the drilling of boreholes became more available. By independence there were an estimated 5,000 boreholes in the country, which rapidly grew to 8,000 in the late 1970s.[4] That increase and better veterinary support have led to a dramatic increase in the total number of cattle on the land: from about 1 million at independence to almost 3 million 10 years later.[5] This increase coincided with the closing of the grazing frontier and has unavoidably exceeded the carrying capacity of the land. One 1991 report notes that the entire eastern Kalahari has been covered by boreholes located less than five miles apart.[6] The result was large-scale environmental degradation, visibly measurable in the dramatic rise in overgrazed land from 2 percent of the country in 1975 to 25 percent in 1986.[7]

Neither public policy nor private incentive had been able to overturn this trend by the early 1990s. When resources are communally owned but are made available for private profit, individuals tend to be driven by incentives that invoke the tragedy of the commons: "The problem is that for each marginal increase in the size of the national herd the benefits flow to the owner of the marginal animal, while the costs, in the form of deterioration of the range, are borne by the community as a whole. Thus an individual cattle owner always has a net incentive to increase the size of his herd."[8] The only escape from this logic is through public policies that apply restraint to all and effectively protect the commons.[9] By the early 1990s, no such policy response had emerged.[10]

The cattle industry once again epitomizes a general trend in the political economy of the country: Industrial modernization, if pursued indefinitely and without restraint, threatens to destroy the human environment. The threat to the ecological balance of the commons is arguably most critical in the emerging contest for water between the mining complexes and the local communities.[11] Increasing demands have to be met with limited resources, and increasing scarcity is exacerbated by a worsening in the quality of the resource base. The protection of the ecological commons is a public good, which therefore requires the state to secure it through the mutual compulsion of its laws. This is the classic problem of scarcity, and a weak state that fails to meet this challenge directly threatens democracy: "Intra-elite competition may increasingly become a zero-sum affair, as a steadily deteriorating commons heightens the need for survival benefits to be distributed among the poor majority. Under stress from such pressures, the regime could break down; alternatively, it might become more authoritarian."[12] Inherent in this forecast is the implication that polarization could be in the form of class, ethnic, and/or regional divisions.

The second source of threat to democracy is in the unravelling of the internal discipline of the ruling coalition. A defining feature of the ethos of state action that informed the state-building process in Botswana has been the ability to resist the temptation of the-state-as-market. By the mid-1980s this discipline started to slide. In the Botswana Meat Commission (BMC), that microcosm of the modern economy, the discipline of strict technocratic management had been maintained by "the parastatal's lynchpin, its white authoritarian manager."[13] When this top position was localized, a continuance of policies to keep costs at the BMC as low as possible and deliver the greatest profits to producers could be expected only through the appointment "of an extraordinarily tough and locally unsympathetic individual. As it was, it did not occur."[14] The result is that costs at the Lobatse plant rose tenfold from 1973 to 1984, and employment of administrative staff rose from 164 in 1976 to 434 in 1984.

The biggest cost factors were salaries and perquisites for this expanding labor force. The explanation offered is that it became politically impossible for a Batswana manager to do what a white expatriate manager could do: resist demands from society to make the state itself a public good to be distributed. A continued decline of such discipline is bound to erode the autonomy of the state, and the distributive character of politics is then likely to increasingly become a matter of who in society will be able to capture which part of the state at the expense of whom. The implications for the emergence of deep divisions along class, regional, and/or ethnic lines in such a distributive contest are obvious, as are the implications for democratic stability.

The third source of threat to democratic practices in the country could be from within the region. The threat of belligerence from the former apartheid regime in South Africa is gone, supplanted by the threat of catastrophic failure in the process of peaceful change away from apartheid. If a reactionary white racist regime overturned the transformation of regime and state; or a radical black racist regime implemented revenge and retribution; or the state collapsed under internal civil strife and no single party gained ascendancy, Botswana could not escape from the resulting regional social and economic upheaval. Cross-border refugeeism, banditry, and terrorism would likely follow, along with the breakdown of the regional economic and social infrastructure, and the demands on the state to maintain civil order would increase dramatically. The strains of such events on the democratic process and the state itself can easily be predicted.

Global factors can also threaten the democratic future of Botswana. Favorable globally determined commodity prices, especially those of diamonds, and access to global markets, such as the European market for beef, are crucial factors in shaping the economic prosperity of the society and the solvency of the state. Neither can be guaranteed indefinitely,[15] and both strengthen the state (by ensuring its solvency) and legitimize democracy (by enabling the state to finance the provision of public goods).

Botswana's regional and global context comprises two distinct yet interlinked sets of economic networks within which Botswana has from precolonial times occupied a relationship of marked dependence. The significance of this condition is open to differing interpretations. One interpretation sees this dependence as a fundamental structural condition created by the global capitalist system. According to this interpretation the mature industrial capitalist economies stand at the center of this system and exploit those at the periphery—the latecomers, which cannot match the early industrializers in economic competitiveness. This exploitation is made feasible through the dependence of those in the periphery on those at the center. Africa in general and Botswana in particular are considered in the exploitable and exploited periphery.[16]

The crucial practical (and theoretical) question is whether this vulnerable and exploitable condition of dependence can be escaped. One way of doing so is to change the global structure of asymmetrical dependence. This would require the destruction of the "capitalist-world-system," which since the end of the Cold War appears to be a rapidly receding prospect. The other would be to withdraw from this system. Frank Baffoe thinks withdrawing is preferable and is prepared to offer a general recommendation for "development strategies designed to reduce [the] dependence on international finance and multinational corporate interests and more importantly to build internally integrated and balanced economies capable of providing for the basic needs of the people and providing expanded productive employment for the masses of their population."[17]

Whether this advice can produce self-reliance and prosperity (plus equity) has to be assessed against the general economic decline and escalating debt burden of African economies, which have resulted in *greater* need for foreign support. The overall process has made African countries "highly dependent on a variety of external actors. . . . This process, which some have referred to as *the new neocolonialism,* means intense dependence on the International Monetary Fund, the World Bank, and major Western countries for the design of economic reform packages and the resources needed to implement them" (original emphasis).[18] This increasing dependence is used with immediate effect by these agencies, which link explicit economic and political conditionalities to the providing of aid.

Within such a context, escape appears to offer highly unattractive returns. With both options foreclosed, dependency theory takes on the quality of a despondency theory. If these structural conditions are permanent and exploitative and cannot be transformed or escaped, one has to presume that exploitation of the working class in the peripheral African countries in general, and Botswana in particular, will endure indefinitely.[19] Likewise, when Botswana's spectacular economic growth is interpreted as no more than the result of shifting dependence from the narrow South African context to the broader global context, the inescapable conclusion is that economic deliverance is virtually unattainable.

A different interpretation of the facts of pervasive dependence is offered by Morrison: "Yes, but."[20] *Yes*, Botswana has had to confront its asymmetrical dependence on South Africa as a fairly permanent factor in its regional environment. *But* such dependence has been (and still is) fluid and contingent, which allowed policymakers to use it to their own advantage. The dependence on a hostile South Africa under a white racist regime was skillfully used to gain favorable access to European beef markets and international donor support for major projects.[21] At the same time, South Africa was not invited into a confrontation. Instead, skillful negotiations with that adversary resulted in a more favorable customs agreement and continued use of its transport facilities for import and exports. The overall assessment by Colclough and McCarthy supports Morrison's: "A delicate but fruitful balance has been maintained between South Africa's desire to remain on good terms with its moderate black neighbour, and the wish on the part of some western nations to support Botswana as a democratic, and obviously successful, non-racial alternative in this troubled part of the world."[22] Asymmetrical dependence, then, through astute policy response and initiatives, has been converted from a potential liability into an actual asset. These policy responses, which were guided by the ethos of state action of Botswana's leadership, have allowed Botswana to confront and exploit these regional and global challenges to democracy thus far.

THE EXTENDABILITY OF DEMOCRACY IN ZIMBABWE

Zimbabwe being less of a democratic success than Botswana, the question about Zimbabwe has less to do with sustaining its democracy than with extending its democratic practices. Yet the list of factors that affect Zimbabwean democracy is remarkably similar to the list of factors that influence democracy in Botswana.

The first factor inhibiting the extension of democracy in Zimbabwe is the constraint of land. The repossession of agricultural land through direct ownership by Africans at the expense of whites achieved preeminent symbolic significance during the civil war of the 1970s. In a sense, it came to symbolize what democratization was about. Zimbabwe's land resettlement program did change ownership to some extent. But this program cannot, in the longer term, resolve the problems of too many people on the communal lands exerting too much pressure on too few resources with the inevitable ecological maladies of overgrazing, soil erosion, and deforestation.[23] While the resettlement program that has removed some families from the overcrowded communal areas has been in progress, another 300,000 new families have been created in the same areas through a population growth of nearly 2.9 percent per year.[24] These policies will not in the long term release the ecological pressure on the communal lands, nor can they fully democratize the country by giving every rural African family a viable piece of agricultural land. But by continuing to view democratization in these terms, and to attempt to effect it through the redistribution of a finite resource, these policies inevitably assume a zero-sum character that puts a ceiling on further democratization and even threatens current democratic practices. As in the case of Botswana, ecological constraints bear on democratic prospects. And as in the case of Botswana, the state is the agency that has to confront the problem.

The land question is part of the wider problem of scarcity. If democracy is about the provision of citizenship of equal value to all by the state, which in part is about the equitable provision of public goods, then the availability of such goods is crucial to the extension of democracy. Availability of goods requires a solvent state able to manage the economy so as to generate prosperity, an expanding tax base, and a growing employment market. Zimbabwe's first decade of economic policymaking has been less successful than Botswana's. In accepting (or is it submitting to?) the Economic Structural Adjustment Program in 1991, Zimbabwe may have been rerouted to a new, more prosperous economic future, with positive implications for democracy.

The ability of the Zimbabwean state to generate economic wealth is bound to be shaped in part by the ability of state leaders to hold their own in the changing regional and global context of the 1990s. A failed transition in South Africa is bound to adversely affect the state and society in Zimbabwe as much as it would in Botswana. An equally negative impact can be expected from a failed process of transition and reconciliation in Mozambique. The politics of scarcity in Zimbabwe is profoundly shaped by regional economic factors that require regionally coordinated policy responses. Drought, energy shortages, water shortages, and transport bottlenecks are all regional issues, transcending the jurisdiction of any single southern African state.

If Botswana's track record on such challenges can be summarized as confronting, coping, and exploiting, then Zimbabwe's has consisted of challenging, failing, and acquiescing. The Zimbabwean policymakers challenged the international political economy by trying to generate economic growth on their own terms. They failed, and they contributed to that failure through poor judgment and inappropriate choices, with weak results. They were less sensitive than Botswana's state leaders to the conditions of scarcity; they were unable to respond with the same agility to the major drought of 1981–82, allowing wages to increase by 21 percent, and rapidly slid into major current account deficits, rising foreign debt, and economic growth—which tapered down to 1.4 percent in 1982 and –4.2 percent in 1983.[25] Toward the end of the first decade of independence the minister of finance was reported as conceding that on average, "Zimbabweans in 1989 were worse off than they were in 1982."[26] Another gross misjudgment of the international context was in the estimating of international aid, development loans, and reconstruction loans. Estimates based on the amounts promised far exceeded the amounts received, yet the estimated figures were used in the 1982 budget.[27] Similar poor judgments with concomitant weak results for the economy were the estimates of white business support for the projected socialist transformation of the early

1980s,[28] the estimates of growth rates in the early 1980s (and subsequent policy decisions),[29] and the economic confrontation with South Africa.

The acceptance of the five-year structural adjustment program signals public acceptance of the rules of the economic game of international agencies and capital, the erstwhile enemies of ZANU-(PF). The implementation of these agencies' terms is likely to raise tensions within society, for core interest groups who support the current rulers are bound to be adversely affected. One leading analyst has pointed out that "a structural adjustment programme might be hailed as a cure for the country's economic ills by international agencies, but those in Zimbabwe who are directly and adversely affected by it are reluctant to swallow the medicine of reduced social services, the lifting of price restrictions, abandonment of protective labor laws, cuts in the civil service and the dismantling of protection for industry."[30] If the structural adjustment program does not deliver the expected greater prosperity, greater turmoil and social instability could result, with adverse implications for the extending of democracy.

The last important factor bearing on Zimbabwe's democratic prospects is located in society. The most visible societal constraint on extending democracy in Zimbabwe appears to be the high levels of intolerance toward political opponents, a feature of 1980s politics that carried over into the election of 1990. Greater tolerance requires that norms of civility be extended across partisan boundaries, thus contributing to the civilizing of society.

THE VIABILITY OF DEMOCRACY IN SOUTH AFRICA

Botswana and Zimbabwe represent examples of democracy, both flawed, one somewhat more than the other. Both can be examined for their durability. In the case of South Africa, which at the time of writing is about to begin its first attempt at democratic rule, the more speculative question has to be asked, What is likely to contribute to sustaining South Africa's first democratic constitution?

The analysis of the preceding chapters suggests that both the state and the society will have to be strengthened to secure democracy in South Africa. The first requirement for democratic durability in South Africa is the restoring of citizenship as the salient identity for all the members of the society. Obligations must be reasserted on both sides: the state's obligation to award rights to people on the basis of which they can make claims against the state, and the citizens' obligations toward the state, particularly to pay taxes and obey the laws. Urban blacks have not been paying taxes for nearly a decade; crime has surged in every racial category. Both these trends are antithetical to democratic stability, and the state must halt them and turn them around. First, though, the rent and service charges boycott in the black townships will have to be effectively terminated.

The state will also have to extend its jurisdiction into the many urban shantytowns in which more than 7 million South Africans are currently living.[31] State authority must penetrate these communities in such a way that triangles of accommodation are broken down or prevented from forming and the autonomy of warlords and strongmen is squelched. Democracy requires that the laws of the state be compulsory, nondiscriminatory, and universal. Citizens in these shantytowns will have to be compelled to pay taxes to the state, not informal "dues" to self-appointed strongmen or warlords. And the coercive hold of informal protection rackets must be supplanted by the protection offered by the state.

Strengthening the state in this way will not suffice to curtail crime and lawlessness. Society will have to be strengthened by rebuilding the communities that have succumbed under the strain of apartheid and the revolt against apartheid. This task can be legislated only up to a point. Removing the coercive presence of apartheid-style social engineering will contribute to rebuilding communities as long as it is not replaced by another equally intrusive program of social engineering. Alleviating poverty and scarcity will contribute too.

The second major requirement for sustaining the democratic constitution will be to avert a revolt against the state by minorities. Such a revolt may adopt some of the "ungovernability" strategies used against the apartheid state: armed propaganda, civil disobedience, tax revolts, sabotage, guerrilla warfare—all with the aim of establishing liberated zones, dual sovereignty, and effective parallel rule beyond the boundaries of the state. Or the revolt can take on an explicit secessionary objective, with Zululand (roughly demarcated as eastern Natal north of the Tugela River) as one of the likely sites.

The restoration of the obligations of citizenship in the largely black communities is likely to be facilitated by the far greater legitimacy the new state leaders will surely enjoy initially. Dissuading minority revolts is bound to be more difficult, for legitimacy is likely to be withheld from the inception of the new constitution. Pragmatic policy measures to induce dissenting minorities to seek security within the boundaries of the state will have to be found. The statecraft with which such temptations were averted in Botswana may provide instructive lessons. Failing that, the remaining avenue is coercion. In that case Zululand may yet become another Matabeleland, with detrimental results for the democratic quality of regional political life.

The third requirement is that the state provide abundant public goods in an equitable manner. The need for equity is obvious. The need for abundance can be seen from the data on government social expenditure on housing, health, agricultural subsidies, education, and pensions by racial category in 1975 (figure 7.1).

The disparities in expenditure by race were noted in chapter 5. What is important here is where the *average* level of government expenditure would have stood (see the right-hand column of figure 7.1). An equalizing of expenditure across racial categories would have lowered the amounts received by whites dramatically, and even those of Coloreds and Indians, while raising those of Africans to a level still below that previously held by Coloreds. Van den Berg says that "parity at the average level in 1975 would have implied a more than 70 percent reduction in White benefits from government expenditure. Average social expenditure levels were even below the benefits received by coloreds. However, even real growth in social expenditure of as high as 5 percent per year for the last quarter of the century would still leave per capita social expenditure levels by the end of the century under 60 percent of 1975 white levels."[32] He concludes that "rising expectations . . . cannot be satisfied from existing resources."[33] The data also show the imperative for economic growth: without it, equity will bring a more even distribution of poverty for most South Africans and only a marginal improvement for the African majority. And even that can be lost if such drastic redistributive measures adversely affect the size of the state's tax base.

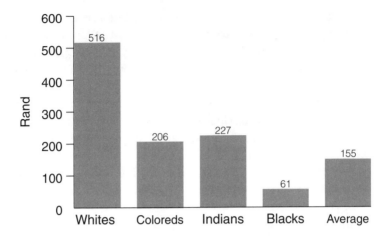

Figure 7.1 — Benefits from Government Social Expenditure on Different Groups, 1975 (expressed in 1980 Rand per person)

Source: Servaas van den Berg, "Long-Term Economic Trends and Development Prospects in South Africa," *African Affairs* 88, no. 351 (1989): 200, figure 13. Copyright © The Royal African Society. Used by permission of the Publisher.

The growth potential of South Africa's economy, like that of Botswana and Zimbabwe, is constrained by environmental factors. In these two countries the ecological frontier is drawn with respect to the availability of agricultural land. South Africa with its greater industrialization and urbanization, experiences numerous other dimensions of scarcity as well. Water is the most critical scarce resource for urban industrial development. The Pretoria-Witwatersrand-Vereeniging area is home to 42 percent of the country's urban population and produces 59 percent of its GDP, but the catchment area produces only 8 percent of the annual water runoff. Already water has to be diverted from Natal and Lesotho to maintain the industrial heartland. These schemes are projected to be sufficient only into the early 21st century.

Pollution in this region is also dramatic. The levels of acid rain in the eastern Transvaal highveld are equivalent to those of the northeastern United States and Europe. Attempts to cope with this problem first have to confront the fact that while Eskom (the para-statal responsible for electricity generation for most of the country) produces 60 percent of Africa's electricity, 70 percent of the population were still excluded from this network in the late 1980s. Up to 12 million of those excluded still relied on wood as their primary source of fuel.[34] A survey released in 1992 reported that of the 250 indigenous forests identified in KwaZulu in 1942, only 50 remained.[35] The Zulu king Cetshwayo was buried at a site deep in the Nkandla forest a hundred years ago; today his grave is more than a kilometer outside the perimeter of the trees.[36] Ecological pressure on the land is equally intense. Overgrazing has led to large-scale soil degradation; up to 55 percent of the country is threatened by desertification, and between 300 million and 400 million tons of arable topsoil are washed away annually.[37] Sustained growth will obviously require applying a thorough environmental ethic to all aspects of socioeconomic endeavor to protect the wealth-producing base of the country. Effective state measures to compel the protection of the ecological commons are also needed.

Measures of redistribution by the state tend to be effective when the relevant agencies and personnel inculcate fairness and justice within their operative ethos and assert these values in matters of policymaking. The influential role of the expatriate officers of the state in Botswana demonstrates this point clearly. Most personnel of the first democratic government in South Africa will have been recruited in the apartheid era; commentators generally consider these state officials wedded to the norms and principles of apartheid and therefore an institutional barrier to effective state-led redistribution; their removal is considered a matter of urgency.[38]

Empirical data confirm many aspects of this stereotype. The bureaucratic elite—that is, those occupying the top 350 public service positions in the central state departments—still did not include a single African in 1992. A 1992 survey of a sample of 200 of these officials reveals that they were overwhelmingly Afrikaans speakers (80 percent) and supporters of the NP (77 percent). They are seen by other elites to be closely associated with the cluster of institutions surrounding the NP (see table 6.2, chapter 6) and a large percentage of them (89 percent) express a high level of sympathy toward the institutions in this cluster. However, these officials tend to indicate that the organizations they are most opposed to are (in descending order) the PAC, SACP, AWB, and ANC. They also reveal greater political tolerance than elites from the military, agriculture, labor, and the churches. On policy matters they display divergent opinions. They are strongly opposed to redistributive policies such as more progressive taxation; not one respondent indicated this as a high priority. But they do see affirmative action as inescapable; 66 percent of them agreed with the statement "Any future government will have no choice other than to include large additional numbers of blacks at all levels in the civil service."[39]

The overall picture is therefore not one of monolithic, immovable opposition in the upper ranks of the public service to the policies of new rulers. The military elite is the most intolerant and may prove to be a more recalcitrant corps of state officials. It is almost equally strongly opposed to the ANC and PAC, and it commands a defense force with large racial imbalances in its personnel composition.[40] The molding of a unified defense force from the South African Defence Force, the four independent homeland armies, and the three liberation armies may become the most crucial step in constructing the kind of autonomous state needed to sustain democracy in South Africa.

The fourth requirement for sustaining democracy in South Africa is for new rulers to maintain a solvent state. This factor is also crucial in shaping the strength of the newly reconstituted state. The new state leaders will have to balance the need for accumulating funds with the need for maintaining legitimacy. A crucial source of weakness of the apartheid state (see chapter 5) was the state's inability to do so. The need for accumulation was met by protecting the modern capitalist sector of the economy and by limiting public expenditure on the disenfranchised black South Africans. This approach also secured legitimacy from the white voters, but that narrow base of legitimacy proved unable to sustain the apartheid state. The undemocratic character of the apartheid state in the end also proved to be its ultimate source of weakness.

The new rulers now find themselves in a uniquely different and difficult position. Being the first democratically elected government, with a vastly wider base of electoral support, it should easily meet the immediate requirements of legitimacy. The electorate, however, is drawn largely from the poor and has been mobilized by electoral promises of redistribution and restitution. To meet these promises the modern sector of the economy and society will have to be tapped for state funds. Excessive taxation measures (not to speak of the nationalization and expropriation of capital) would undoubtedly adversely affect capitalist enterprise and threaten the expansion of the tax base of the state, and the ability of the new government to meet its electoral promises on a sustained basis would decline. In that event, support at the ballot box is bound to wane. Exhorting the electorate to defer gratification carries the high risk of inviting outbidding by extremists who promise even greater and more immediate redistribution. Such promises could become compellingly attractive, setting in motion an ever tighter trade-off between legitimation and accumulation and giving a zero-sum distributive character to public policies. Only rapid economic growth and/or massive outside sponsorship of development and reconstruction programs can avert such an outcome. A decade of economic performance similar to Zimbabwe's in its first 10 years of independence is bound to put democratic institutions in South Africa under enormous strain.

The final requirement for democratic viability is to civilize South African society. By this is meant that (1) members of the contending "civil societies" who were highly adversarial during the 1970s and 1980s should reestablish interaction on a new basis. As citizens of equal status they should recognize one another's moral dignity. In practical terms, (2) overt prejudice and vilification on the basis of ascriptive criteria or partisan political affiliation have to be reduced, and institutional duplication by the parallel and rival economic, social, and cultural interest groups within the contending civil societies has to be eliminated. In addition, the civilizing of society entails (3) that the survival strategies of people in divergent positions of status, wealth, and power be made compatible. In practical terms, to cope, survive, and prosper, all citizens should be able to draw on and be accommodated within one embracing set of norms, values, and practices. This means more than equality before the law for everyone; it means standardizing the ways and means of successful endeavor and making them accessible to all citizens.

A crucial part of the transition process since 1990 has been to contain the political violence, much of which is enacted at community level. The centerpiece of the institutional response to violence was the establishment of the National Peace Accord by the major political players in 1991. The accord established the National Peace Secretariat, which is to oversee the creation and administering of regional and local peace committees (RPCs and LPCs). By mid-1993, 11 RPCs and 85 LPCs had been established, and 35 more were in the making.[41]

Early evaluations of the functioning of the LPCs show a measure of success in containing violence. Possibly more significant has been the socialization function performed by the LPCs. The assessment has been made that "the committees have . . . built regular lines of communication and confidence among erstwhile enforcers of apartheid, the security forces, and anti-apartheid forces in the communities. For many, these committees represent the first bridges across South Africa's deep and enduring racial divides."[42] Moreover, participants in these structures have been able to engage one another as community representatives with shared local identities and interests instead of as extensions of national political players; thus they were able to break the mold of entrenched confrontation that prevailed at the national level.[43] These breakthroughs are vital to historical enemies' recognition of one another's moral dignity and to the dismantling of firmly held negative stereotypes. What has not been recognized by analysts thus far is that the RPCs and LPCs, which have been given statutory status and are established in terms of the Internal Peace Institutions Act of 1992, are part of the state. And in that sense, the state is contributing to the civilizing of society.

One of the major divides remaining in South Africa is economic—not only the affluence-poverty divide, but also the institutional divide between the world of formal economic enterprise and the informal economy. The formal sector, the core of the modern economy, functions through the formal rules of legal contractuality and the informal conventions of private enterprise and corporate ethics. Networks—that is, "groups of people who help each other along in life, in ways that mystify and infuriate those excluded"[44]—form a vital component of success in this competitive arena. Networks are intricate survival strategies that all ambitious individuals have to master.

The survival strategies in the informal economic arena, on the other hand, are shaped by deprivation, uncertainty, disrespect for the state and its laws, and pervasive social and political upheaval.

Economic enterprise therefore tends to merge with crime and to operate outside a legal framework without the stabilizing effect of entrenched institutions that foster stable conventions and practices of acceptable behavior. Yet interest group activity has been a feature of black urban life since the earliest urban settlements; burial societies were the best-known form of economic association.[45] These organizations, so weakly institutionalized, rely almost entirely on the cohesion of networks to sustain them and to ensure continuity in their procedures and practices.

One of the most remarkable features of black urban life of the 1970s and 1980s was the mushrooming of *stokvels*. A stokvel is "a type of credit union in which a group of people enter into an agreement to contribute a fixed amount of money to a common pool weekly, fortnightly and monthly. Then . . . this money or a portion of it may be drawn by members either in rotation or in a time of need."[46] These bodies rely on voluntary membership, usually on personal recommendation, have no written agreements, and persist on the basis of members' trust, reliability, and honesty. Peer group pressure provides additional inducement to uphold the rules. According to one survey, 28 percent of Africans in the major urban areas (1.3 million people) were members of stokvels in 1991, which generated a monthly cash flow of more than R200 million.[47]

Given the fragile institutional base of the moneys thus collected, formal-sector financial institutions thus far have refused to accept the stokvel savings as collateral for home mortgages or capital loans to would-be entrepreneurs. In 1991, plans were announced whereby the National Stokvels Association of South Africa (NASASA) would channel a substantial portion of the stokvel savings into a unit trust fund managed by a major financial institution. The unit trust holdings would then be collateral for prospective home buyers.[48] The plan fell through, largely because NASASA was unable to raise enough funds from affiliated stokvels to make the project viable, but the concept retains its potential. If it had succeeded it would have dovetailed the survival capitalism of the townships, shantytowns, and squatter communities with the old-school networks and methods of corporate high finance. The potential reach of such a project is breathtaking: it would have meshed the survival strategies of South Africa's most desperately poor and marginalized people with those of the most sophisticated corporate entrepreneurs. The meeting of erstwhile enemies in new capacities as fellow citizens, the gradual breakdown of prejudice, the elimination of parallel civic institutions, and the integration of survival strategies represent promising beginnings in the long-term process of creating a civil society in South Africa.

The Appropriate Conditions for Sustainable Democracy

Establishing democracies in the adverse conditions of divided societies is not easy; sustaining them, even less so. One of the most authoritative recent treatments of this problem is by Donald L. Horowitz, who argues the need for an incentive-based approach to the democratizing of divided societies. His argument is developed in relation to South Africa, but it can also be applied to the wider context of this study.

Constitutional Rules

Constitutional rules are important when they serve as incentives "that operate on politicians and their followers, that harness their self-interest to the cause of intergroup conflict reduction, regardless of their personal feelings, that, in a word, make moderation pay."[49] Incentives for moderation are generated by constitutional rules that reward cooperation and penalize extremism. The incentives Horowitz considers most important for South Africa are the alternative vote electoral system and the federal system of government. Constraints, by contrast, involve guarantees against extremism without rewards for compliance.

In divided societies there are no self-evident reasons for parties with actual or prospective electoral majorities to submit to rules that make moderation pay. Why should they pursue self-interest through moderation instead of through hegemony? In the case of South Africa, as Horowitz points out, this is a very real consideration. Why should the ANC, with potential electoral dominance equal to that of the BDP in Botswana or ZANU-(PF) in Zimbabwe, uphold a constitution that protects minorities through regional autonomy—especially since some of these minorities have systematically exploited the majority through apartheid for four decades? Why not bend, break, or circumvent the rules instead and use the power thus gained to exact retribution and revenge? Where, then, are the incentives for the incentives?

Horowitz responds by arguing that the incentives for the incentives are generated by the *context* surrounding the political actors. Interests may remain consistent, but a changing political arena also transforms the "structure of the incentives" that informs the cost-benefit calculations of parties who must choose with whom to cooperate and whom to oppose. This study does not allow a great deal to be said about the appropriate constitutional rules for inducing moderation, but it does allow a lot more to be said about the contextual factors that can contribute to parties adopting policies of accommodation.

Regional Institutions

"The fact of the matter is that early, generous devolution is far more likely to avert than to abet ethnic separatism. Where a territorially based ethnic minority is politically out of step with other groups, uncompromising centralism in the guise of democratic majoritarianism will inevitably suppress that minority and provoke a reaction. Where, however, regional autonomy or federalism—on a territorial and not on a "homeland" basis—allows such minorities nationally to form majorities locally, the result is unlikely to be an aggravation of separatism."[50] The comparative evidence on Botswana and Zimbabwe bears out the validity of this proposition. In Botswana the early regional boundaries established in 1899 along the frontiers of the Tswana chieftaincies were retained in the independence constitution and provided the basis for regional governmental institutions. The resulting proliferation of sites of power open for electoral contestation has enabled opposition parties to consistently capture seats on the district councils even while the BDP retained its overall dominance of electoral politics at the national level.[51] With these boundaries as a framework demarcating electoral districts for parliamentary elections, national elections again represented regions, where opposition parties could and did gain representation. A similar kind of regional structure could easily be applied to South Africa.

Numerous other constitutional rules have been recommended for inducing cooperation, moderation, and the sharing of power among rival parties in coalition governments of divided societies.

None of them is found in Botswana. The district councils provide useful sites for regional representation, but they are not autonomous sites of power and are easily dominated from the center. The electoral system in use is the first-past-the-post, single-member-constituency–based rule rather than the recommended variations of proportional representation. Presidential rule instead of cabinet rule applies, and the president is elected by a simple majority of the legislature. These rules do not encourage multiparty representation, do not protect smaller parties, and are not conducive to vote-pooling majoritarian rule or consociational power-sharing rule. Instead, these rules favor the incumbent BDP and are likely to inhibit future alternation of ruling parties. The restrictive rules that limit contestation and participation are also likely to have a similar effect in future electoral outcomes.

Why, then, is the regional structure of representation and administration in Botswana significant? The first obvious reason is visible electoral representation. Winning minority representation in ineffectual district councils, or a few seats in parliament among an overwhelming ruling majority party has generally been discounted as having only symbolic value. But in ethnic politics, symbolic value can be immensely important. For a minority, to gain representation is to register the worthiness and collective esteem of the group, even though others still dominate.

A second reason is that the regional structures are the framework for state distribution of public goods. The regional structures are the instruments of public policies and the conduits for distributing public goods. Thus, when public goods are distributed equitably through the regional institutions, both regional equity and ethnic equity are achieved, and by extension, so is citizenship of equal value. Overall, these regime rules (along with the autonomous state) keep ethnic issues from achieving the intense importance that divides citizens into antagonistic, incipient whole societies.

During the Lancaster House negotiations over the Zimbabwean independence constitution, safeguards for the white minority were explored intensely, and allowances were duly made. A reviewer of the autobiography of Joshua Nkomo remarked, "It seems to be the fact that at no point during the prolonged Lancaster House constitutional discussions in 1979 did he [Nkomo] even raise the question of the possible desirability of instituting a measure of regional autonomy for Matabeleland."[52] The final outcome was a highly centralized constitution containing few incentives for the newly incumbent ZANU-(PF) to be moderate toward its Matabeleland-based (PF)-ZAPU opponents. Nor did the constitution provide strong constraints on the new rulers when they chose to use the Fifth Brigade to subjugate their real or perceived enemies in Matabeleland. From the limited data on the distribution of public goods (health services) through the newly created regional structures, it appears that these bodies can achieve equitable distribution *when the ruling party chooses to do so.* The overall assessment of regional structures in Zimbabwe is that they facilitate ZANU-(PF) dominance by serving as channels for the penetration of society and not as sites of regional autonomy. In the case of South Africa the matter is still in dispute. The passage of the 1993 constitution has only intensified the debate on whether the country needs more or less federalism.

The Autonomous State

The significance of the regional structure for the democratic quality of life of Botswana's average citizen, therefore, is contingent on whether the regional structure is the conduit for the actions of the autonomous state. And the autonomy of the state in Botswana, as was argued earlier, is a function of the specific character of the public service, with its expatriate sector that functions as a gelded corps of personnel; the deliberate socialization policies aimed at discouraging parochialism among the personnel of the state; the constitutional rules that separate the state and regime; and the ethos of state action that has directed the ruling coalition since before independence.

The evolution of Botswana's public service with its distinctive expatriate component is closely tied to the colonial history of the country, which has in this sense been uniquely different from Rhodesia's and colonial South Africa's. Most crucial to the position of the expatriates and to their influence has been the Botswana state's approach to localization after independence. The recruitment of such a corps into postapartheid South Africa or into contemporary Zimbabwe as a measure to promote state autonomy can be considered only on a very small scale. Given the prevailing conditions of scarcity and unemployment rates in these countries, the dictum that charity begins at home will be a guide to any prudent state leader in the foreseeable future in both countries. The condition of gelding will have to be created through imaginative constitutional rules. The socialization policies aimed at preventing parochial sentiments and practices from taking hold can be emulated, modified, and even extended, as can the kind of constitutional rules that separate the careers of administrative officers from those of politicians.

The basic features of the *Rechtsstaat*, or constitutional state, built into the interim constitution do provide a platform for the consolidation of an autonomous state, *should the new rulers choose to do so*. During the formal negotiations some effort was also made to find neutral symbols for the reconstituted post-apartheid state. A subcommittee was given the brief to find a new national anthem and a new national flag. The fact that sensitivity toward the issue exists is encouraging. Other smaller symbolic changes are also taking place. For example, new bank notes were introduced in 1992. The previous notes of all denominations displayed the image of Jan van Riebeeck, founder of the Dutch trading colony at the Cape of Good Hope in 1652, generally taken as the founder of white settlement in southern Africa. The new series of notes displays the Big Five: lion, leopard, elephant, rhino, and buffalo—politically neutral, and truly indigenous.

Incentives for the Incentives: The Context

In answering the question about where the incentives for the incentives are found, Horowitz restricts himself primarily to the changing context within which electoral politics is to be conducted. Whereas politics in South Africa once revolved around the antiapartheid movements versus the establishment, in the coming years the centrist parties (NP, ANC alliance, Democratic Party [DP], and a few others) will be defending negotiated regime change against both left-wing radicals and right-wing reactionaries. Therein lies the centrists' incentive for political moderation. Even with a new constitution in place and functioning, this configuration of a moderate center hemmed in by extremist flanks can be expected to prevail, because the center parties have an enduring self-interest in defending their incumbency through electoral cooperation. To be fair, Horowitz foresees cooperation extending beyond mere electoral matters, even to the coercive containment of violent challenges.[53]

The prospect of an electorally mutually dependent center where only a coalition of centrist parties can assemble a majority and no single party is strong enough to rule alone appears to be receding from the South African context. Why, then, should the electorally dominant ANC act with moderation once in power? In Botswana, incentives are absent. The BDP has ruled as a single party, having won every election since 1965. The same applies to Zimbabwe, where ZANU-(PF) is in an unassailable position. The striking difference is in how these two parties have used state power. The BDP has ruled over electoral minorities in a manner that in African terms must be described as exceptionally benign. ZANU-(PF) went the other way, epitomized by the brutal Matabeleland campaigns of the Fifth Brigade. What were the incentives for the BDP's moderation?

The major factor accounting for the autonomy and strength of the state in Botswana and for its democratic qualities is the particular ethos of state action that guides decision making in the ruling coalition. The particular conditions that shaped that ethos among the leadership of both the emerging nationalist politicians and the colonial administration, among both the white and the black large commercial cattle owners, and within the leadership of both the public- and private-sector enterprises were tied to the circumstances of a particular era in the evolution of the Botswana state. These conditions were unique and cannot be engineered elsewhere. The same *kind* of conditions can, however, be found in similar circumstances. Botswana's elites were responding to conditions of scarcity, to the "mutual hostageship" of high levels of domestic and regional interdependence, and to the pervasive constraints imposed by the international economic and political forces represented in the international system of states and their agencies. All of these conditions conveyed to the ruling coalition the narrowness in the margin of error for constructing a viable and democratic state in the southern African region. That awareness informed their ethos, with its technocratic economic priorities, its conservative fiscal and monetary policies, and its political preferences for order, legality, and constitutionalism. The incentives for moderation were thus not to be found in the context of electoral interdependence, but in a wider and far more complex set of dependence relationships that inhibit confrontational actions but also reward cooperative measures.

The formative experience of the civil war in Zimbabwe left the new rulers ill equipped to appreciate the incentives in complex interdependence relations. And, one has to add, in some crucially important cases of institution building, these incentives were absent. Compare again the circumstances surrounding the establishment of the Minerals Marketing Corporation of Zimbabwe (MMCZ) versus the Botswana Meat Commission. The private mining elite in Zimbabwe, unlike the cattle owners in Botswana, were not thoroughly biracial. The stakes were smaller: mining in the Zimbabwe of the 1980s was less important than the cattle industry was for Botswana in the 1960s. There was no fear of mineral markets collapsing. Above all, there was no inescapable mutual dependence. The multinational mining companies could relocate elsewhere, and the state could tap revenue from other sectors. But in the Botswana of the 1960s, the cattle industry *was* the modern sector and thus the only viable source of revenue for the state.

The conditions within which the negotiators in South Africa have been operating since February 1990 exhibit the structural features of complex interdependence. The supporters of each of the major political forces are located in the modern economy, where they are drawn into mutually dependent relationships that constrain their capacity to act unilaterally. The rapid economic decline of the 1980s, fueled by labor instability, economic sanctions, and civil violence, has exacerbated the problem of scarcity, as seen in poverty, a shrinking tax base, rising needs for social welfare, and increasing inequality. Since the end of the Cold War the rules of appropriate behavior being set by the major players in the global economy have become more explicit and stringent and less easy to circumvent. The terms of conditionality set by agencies such as the IMF epitomize this trend.

Each of these conditions can be engineered by policymakers to vary substantially. Greater mutual dependence can be created through sustained economic development, which pulls all sectors of the society into the modern economy. Greater scarcity can also be engineered through further economic embargoes, sanctions, and boycotts. (This would hardly be recommended as a policy option, however.) The mutual perception of scarcity can have a positive impact in that it creates a moment of crisis that draws adversaries together, but in the longer term democracy cannot flourish amid destitution. The rules set by major actors in the global economy are equally malleable and can be tailored to the particular context to induce the appropriate response. Taken together, these forces can have a decisive shaping influence on the ethos of state action that emerges in postapartheid South Africa, which in turn is crucial to the construction of a strong autonomous state and a democratic regime.

The inculcation of such an ethos is a learning process. Horowitz argues to the contrary—that is, that parties consistently follow their own interests and then learn that in the changing context they end up with new allies and incrementally changed interests.[54] But to calculate and recalculate appropriate strategies for such consistently held interests in domestic, regional, and global contexts, which are all subject to simultaneous change, and to appreciate the rewards and penalties built into relations of mutual dependence does require learning in the widest sense of the word.

The learning process set in motion in South Africa since February 1990 has produced some significant results. In the optimistic analysis by Herbert Adam and Kogila Moodley, enough learning has taken place to secure the "historic compromise" of a social-democratic outcome in which power sharing can be institutionalized and growth with equity can be achieved. This is made possible, they argue, by the major parties' grasping that they are in a condition of "mutual weakness."[55] Moreover, they argue that fundamental aspects of the mythology of apartheid and the mythology of liberation have already been abandoned and unlearned. Likewise, it can be argued that the convergence between elites on indigenous development priorities—empirical confirmation of such convergence has been found—reflects a convergence of even more basic values.[56] In the broadest terms, it reflects convergence on the kind of state and society these elites are prepared to endorse.

Practical demonstration of this convergence and of the general learning process was in the signing of the Overseas Private Investment Corporation agreement between the South African government (with multiparty support that included the ANC) and the United States on November 30, 1993. By contrast, Zimbabwe's refusal to sign until 1989 such an agreement came to serve as "a benchmark of Zimbabwe's refusal to collaborate with international capital."[57] This agreement—which allows foreign investors to take out insurance against political risks and the disruption of the movement of remittances—signals, as much as regaining access to IMF and World Bank funding, that convergence is being reached on the kind of state and economy South Africa is going to be in the international system of states.

Conclusion

Democratic rules and practices are embedded in the wider institutional framework of the state. States are embedded in the wider institutional framework of the global system of states and the context of the international political economy. Democracy requires institutions that can deliver a particular kind of equitable outcome: public goods of equal value. These public goods include the right to vote in competitive elections as a means to enter the contest for power, as well as the goods and services required for survival and prosperity. States exist and justify their existence on grounds that they can deliver public goods better than private individuals can. The public goods required by the peoples of southern Africa to ensure democratic stability, security, peace, and prosperity include not only the civic rights of access to power but also the age-old goods of protection against catastrophic droughts, the plundering and the degradation of the environmental commons, and the pervasive problems of scarcity. They also need protection against newer threats such as AIDS, virulent new strains of malaria, refugees, lawless and citizenless people armed with AK-47s, and the increasingly competitive and sophisticated international political economy within which a competitive edge will have to be found. In order to meet these challenges and secure democratic stability, very strong and resilient institutions will be needed. Strong sovereign states working closely together in the region with support from the global system of states will be required for this task.

✱ Epilogue ✱

The constitution accepted by the South African parliament on December 22, 1993, was strongly opposed by the Freedom Alliance. By then this alliance was composed of the governments of Ciskei and Bophuthatswana, and by the IFP, the CP (representing the white right-wing parliamentarians), and the Afrikaner Volks-front, an extraparliamentary, white right-wing movement. Their opposition extended to the transitional arrangements as well; they refused to serve in the Transitional Executive Council (TEC), entrusted to oversee the "leveling of the playing field" leading up to the elections.

The Freedom Alliance continued to negotiate informally on a bilateral basis with both the ruling NP and the ANC and secured a number of amendments to the constitution, which were taken through a special session of parliament in the last week of February 1994. These amendments generally strengthened the federal characteristics of the 1993 constitution and included the following changes: (1) The name of the Natal province was changed to KwaZulu/Natal, thus adding to the symbolic recognition given to Zulu ethnic identity. (2) Provinces were given exclusive rather than concurrent legislative powers, and greater financial and fiscal authority. (3) Provinces were also allowed to draw up their own constitutions, which need not replicate the national constitution in all its major features. (4) To meet the demands of the white right wing provision was made for the establishment of a Volkstaat Council, which is to pursue the matter of self-determination for communities within the jurisdiction of a single sovereign South Africa. (5) The federal nature of the reconstituted state was reinforced by the the Electoral Act, which allowed for two ballots in the election, one for national and one for provincial representatives.

These dramatic concessions put further pressure on the Freedom Alliance to enter the transition process and to contest the elections. Two weeks after this parliamentary session the public service of Bophuthatswana, after sustained pressurizing tactics by the ANC against the homeland's government, revolted against the authority of its president, Lucas Mangope. In the ensuing civil disorder, effective rule in the homeland collapsed completely. The South African government intervened in collaboration with the TEC and acted on the authority of the Restoration and Extension of South African Citizenship Act, which had returned to all homeland citizens their South African citizenship on January 1, 1994. A decree was passed on March 14 to nullify the 1977 Bophuthatswana constitution, dissolve its parliament, and appoint two joint administrators to the region, both of whom had to report to the TEC. The government also declared 52 magisterial districts as "unrest areas" subject to special security controls and placed Mangope under house arrest. All subsequent attempts to get Mangope to enter the election process failed.

The following week General Constand Viljoen, a leading figure among the white right wingers, broke ranks and registered the newly established Vryheidsfront (Freedom Front) as a party to contest the election. The CP refused all calls to follow. The following week the military ruler of Ciskei, Brigadier Gqozo, stepped down voluntarily, handing over his government to be taken care of by the TEC, and entered his African Democratic Movement into the election contest.

The same pressure brought by the ANC against Bophuthatswana failed to topple the KwaZulu government. Deadlock ensued, with the IFP refusing to allow electioneering in the territory and to register itself for the elections unless the matter of "Zulu sovereignty" was taken care of. Violent confrontations culminated in the "Shell House massacre" on March 29, when scores of IFP marchers were gunned down in downtown Johannesburg. This prompted the declaration of 11 more magisterial districts in the East Rand as unrest areas, and a full state of emergency in Natal and KwaZulu was declared on March 31. A formal three-way summit between government, ANC, and IFP delegations on April 8 again failed to secure IFP participation, but informal negotiations again proved more effective. On April 19 the final breakthrough was announced.

This agreement, by way of another constitutional amendment enacted by parliament a day before the election started, amounted to the following. In the first place, the section outlining the requirements for provincial constitutions would stipulate that they should "where applicable, provide for the institution, role, authority and status of the traditional monarch in the province, and shall make such provision for the Zulu Monarch in the case of the province of KwaZulu/Natal."[1] In turn, the IFP would take part in the election on both the regional and the national level and do its utmost to ensure a free election in the territory of KwaZulu.

Taken together, the two sets of constitutional amendments contributed to bolstering the federal character of the constitution. The second set of amendments further entrenched the traditional Zulu structure of authority. First, making the constitutional accommodation of the Zulu king compulsory for the KwaZulu/Natal province removed the matter from the arena of electoral politics. The status of the king is therefore entrenched irrespective of the election outcome in the province, and the traditional set of rules for the legitimation of political authority (that is, primogeniture) is kept distinct from the modern rule of electoral success. At the same time, the possibility of drawing the traditional rules of social control into those written into the 1993 constitution is also substantially improved. Second, securing the authority of the Zulu king entrenched the entire traditional structure of authority. The lower-order princes, chiefs, subchiefs, and *indunas* (headmen) forming the bottom sections of this pyramidal structure of authority also in effect gained constitutional protection. The overall result is a uniquely South African version of a constitutional monarchy within a federation.

The election campaign was further marked by problems of access for all the major parties. Local party supporters' intolerance for one another's campaigners, and institutional obstruction by organizations prevented conventional campaigning in many areas. These trends led to the general expectation that the three-day election would be marred by violence. This outcome was happily thwarted by the new South African electorate, and violence abated for the duration of the election.

The result of the election could hardly have been more fortuitous. The ANC emerged as clear winners with 62.65 percent of the vote, followed by the NP with 20.31 percent, and the IFP with 10.54 percent. All the other parties fared badly, with the Vryheidsfront getting 2.17 percent; the Democratic Party, 1.73 percent; and the PAC, 1.25 percent. The ANC also gained control of seven of the nine provincial legislatures, the NP captured one (Western Cape), and the IFP secured its home base of KwaZulu/Natal. Only the Big Three made it into the Government of National Unity.

The elections in a sense concluded the protracted four-year transition process. An immediate assessment of the outcome of this process in terms of the framework used in this study would read that the technocrats won the economic debate, the liberals won the constitutional debate, and the populists won the election. However, this does not convert into a three-way balance of power. If the electorally victorious ANC tries to implement wide-ranging redistributionist policies, it will be held back by the many inhibiting clauses in the constitution, which can be changed only with a two-thirds majority in parliament. Furthermore, the modern sector of the economy and society is supported by the many international linkages with the global economy, which favors technocratic priorities over drastic populist redistributive ones. In the reconstituted state the new leadership is bound to find formidable obstacles to implementing some of its promised policies.

The success of the transition process is in part the result of the two sets of constitutional amendments enacted in early 1994. Together they incorporated the most important recalcitrant minorities into the electoral process and into subsequent parliamentary politics. Insurrection by the white right wing was discouraged by acknowledging the Volkstaat notion. Secession was averted by granting KwaZulu/Natal special regional status. Both amendments strengthened the state by extending its jurisdiction over regions and peoples, by expanding its legitimacy, and by asserting the value of citizenship over group status.

Herein lie two valuable lessons for policymakers wishing to incorporate minorities through constitutional measures. The first is to take symbolic matters seriously. Recognition thereof provides emotional security to minorities at little cost to the taxpayer. Second, early and substantial devolution of power *does* have a moderating effect on conflict. Both these amendments will of course have to be buttressed by further appropriate policy measures to sustain the early profits of loyalty to the newly reconstituted state.

The policy priorities of the new Government of National Unity will be largely shaped by those of the senior partner, the ANC, which focus on the theme of national reconciliation and on its reconstruction and development program. The symbolic component of the state is a finely balanced blend of the old and the new, as revealed in the new flag and the use of two national anthems, "Die Stem van Suid-Afrika" (The Voice of South Africa) and "Nkosi sikelel' iAfrika" (God Bless Africa). Additional symbolic substance to the new order was provided at the first parliamentary session, where Nelson Mandela was elected president. The proceedings in the chamber were led by a Tembu praise singer dressed in the traditional Xhosa attire of beads, animal skins, and *knob-kierie*, who opened proceedings with a minute-long tribute to the new head of state. The theme of reconciliation was also carried by the new president into the inauguration ceremony on May 10, 1994. In his address President Mandela said, "The time for the healing of the wounds has come. The moment to bridge the chasms that divide us has come. The time to build is upon us."[2]

The reconstruction and development program presents policy proposals attempting to reconcile the objectives of growth and of redistribution, keeping the electorate happy, and at the same time protecting the tax base needed to keep the state solvent. In measuring up to this challenge the new rulers are bound to be placed under intense pressure by their constituents, who are likely to have less appreciation for the constraints within which the new leaders are operating and who may exert additional pressure on them to do away with such constraints. The first signs of such action appeared even before the new government took office.

The day before Nelson Mandela was sworn in as president the National Land Committee (NLC) called on the ANC to amend those clauses in the chapter on fundamental rights in the constitution that deal with the protection of property rights. The NLC claimed that these clauses, which stipulate that state expropriation of property be accompanied by "just" and "fair" compensation, effectively inhibit redistribution of land.

The capacity of the new leaders to meet demands such as this one for land while upholding the principles and practices of democratic constitutionalism will bear to a large extent on the strength of the state they reconstruct around them. A weak state is bound to succumb to dealing with this policy matter by going beyond the rules set for the rulers themselves. Dramatic demonstration of such state weakness was presented in the same week of President Mandela's inauguration. President Mugabe announced an official inquiry into revelations that land expropriated from white farmers had been leased to cabinet ministers, police chiefs, and other ranking public servants instead of to the landless peasants as promised.[3] This incident epitomizes the weakening of the Zimbabwean state and at the same time shows the test of strength before the South African state. Only a strong enough state can secure redistribution that yields restitution without retribution and reconstruction without corruption. On the outcome of this test also hinges the quality of democracy in the new South Africa.

✳ APPENDIX ✳

State Building and Conflict in Divided Societies

The role of the state as a potential, incipient, partial, or even wholly de facto autonomous actor in dealing with ethnic conflict that emerges from society has not been well researched; the work of Donald Rothchild is the major exception.[1] The state-centered approach that is used in this study aims to explore the relations identified by Rothchild within a more extensive framework. What is needed is a framework that allows for identifying state and society as distinct entities as well as making further distinctions within both state and society. The state-regime distinction identifies two separate sites where conflict-regulating rules can potentially be located. As for society, more than the presence of various ethnic groups needs to be identified. In particular, an analytical distinction must be drawn between divided and undivided societies, thereby enabling the intensity of ethnic formations to be examined in each of these categories. Furthermore, given the importance the Anglo-American intellectual tradition attaches to civil society as a source of democratic norms, values, and practices, a distinction is required between civil and uncivil societies, and propositions are required about the relationship between them and between divided and undivided societies.

To have such scope and depth, an analytical perspective would have to draw on the three distinct—sometimes divergent and ostensibly incompatible—sets of theory on state building, civil society, and ethnic conflict. A theoretical perspective that holds the state as the central concept, maintains the state-society distinction, and permits further analytical distinctions within state and society will serve to provide the basic framework. The theory of state-society relations presented by Joel S. Migdal in his book *Strong Societies and Weak States: State-Society Relations and State Capabilities in the Third World* (1988) will be used as a basis.

One of the shortcomings in Migdal's theory will be met by adding the state-regime distinction to the analytic components he identifies within the state. The second major shortcoming of his theory is that he fails to differentiate among various types of society *within* the categories he identifies. Merging aspects of the theoretical work devoted to civil society and ethnic politics with Migdal's analytic framework makes possible greater depth in the analysis of societal variables.

The third major gap in Migdal's work lies in the fact that he does not explicitly address what the requirements for democratic stability are in the universe of cases covered by his work. Although his own analysis implicitly points to themes that can be elaborated on in terms of democratization, he does not focus on them. In this study these themes are taken up and tied to the concerns with democracy that are present in the literature on civil society and on ethnic conflict. At the same time, Migdal's work can also contribute to these fields by emphasizing the state as the context within which components of civil society and of ethnically divided societies operate.

STATE, REGIME, AND SOCIETY

State and Society

Effective state building in Europe was achieved through the process of constructing "special-purpose organizations" for conducting war, collecting taxes, maintaining fiscal discipline, and enforcing law.[2] According to Migdal, modern states emerged dominant from the myriad of rival social organizations in medieval Europe, each intent on establishing, prescribing, and enforcing rules of social behavior, because of their superior ability to impose social control. The imperative for such control over populations arose from the need to survive in a system of states where the rate of elimination through warfare was very high. The capacity of states to mobilize populations into armies, extract taxes from them, and enforce the law on a continuous basis outstripped the comparative ability of other societally based social organizations to control people.[3] Furthermore, the special-purpose organizations of the state were made not only efficient but also highly distinctive through the "disciplinary methods of power" contained in their standard operating procedures.[4]

The social control that ensured state predominance in continental Europe entails a specific dimension of state power, which Michael Mann calls *infrastructural power:* the ability of the state to penetrate society and use the infrastructure of the state to direct and coordinate societal actions.[5] Migdal argues that effective social control thus defined requires states to be highly capable of extracting resources from society and regulating social relationships. These capabilities lead to the further capabilities of appropriating resources and penetrating society. Successful social control is reflected by three indicators: compliance (getting people to behave in ways they do not prefer), participation (repeated voluntary action within institutions run or authorized by the state), and legitimacy (voluntary acceptance of the myths and symbolic imagery with which the state justifies its rules of behavior).

These rules of behavior are constructed of rewards, sanctions, and symbols and, taken together, offer *strategies of survival* that are supposed to be relevant to conditions people confront every day. The state secures domestic hegemony when it attains compliance with its survival strategies at the expense of those offered by rival social organizations. Noncompliance, on the other hand, cannot be explained only in terms of corruption, criminal intent, or mental instability. It may also reveal a conflict over whose set of survival strategies is to be followed: those prescribed by the state, or those on offer from competing social organizations.[6]

The strong states, those with high capabilities, are more likely to succeed in achieving domestic hegemony. The measure of their success is the establishment of a unified network of social control. Social control is achieved by means of a universal set of rules that prescribe the conduct of relations between individuals and between them and the state. Indigenous law, if it is allowed to persist, is made congruent with law established by the state. Thus a single political status is established: citizenship, valid for all who qualify as members of the state.[7] By asserting this status through a single jurisdiction within its territorial boundaries, the state is able to assume hegemonic control over society and dictate its own survival strategies to all within its domain.

Weak states have less capacity for regulation, extraction, appropriation, and penetration and tend to fail in achieving these objectives. Other social organizations with their own survival strategies are therefore likely to retain a competitive edge. The weak state exists alongside its rivals as but one source of political allegiance and loyalty, and individuals and groups are under the compulsion of various contending survival strategies. Social control is fragmented among the rivals, and although the state may be acknowledged as having the juridical entitlement to claims of sovereignty[8] (which reflects the hegemonic quality of statehood), the empirical embodiment of its claim is absent: jurisdiction over the population and territory is multiple, the rules of the state are not universally applied, and citizenship is but one form of political status and not necessarily the most legitimate or valuable one.[9]

Of central concern to Migdal is why so many of the contemporary states outside Europe and North America have failed to assert themselves over the populations within their territorial jurisdictions. His answer is found in the structure of the society each state tries to subjugate. Strong societies, which exhibit a high level of social control, and weak societies, which exhibit a low level of social control, present contrasting contexts for state organizations intent on exercising domestic hegemony. In the strong societies of contemporary Europe the numerous social organizations converge to create a *pyramidal* structure of social control. These organizations have largely congruent rules and compatible structures. Strong states that gain hegemonic control over strong societies with pyramidal structures of social control do so by occupying the apex of the pyramid, and they succeed in dovetailing the societal survival strategies with those of the state.

The challenge to state predominance is found in strong societies that exhibit a fragmented pattern of social control, the result of a range of social organizations deploying incongruent sets of rules through incompatible social structures. These societies are *web-like*: no single strand of social control, but rather a network of strands, holds the social fabric together. "In weblike societies, although social control is fragmented and heterogeneous, this does not mean that people are not being governed; they most certainly are. The allocation of values, however, is not centralized. Numerous systems of justice operate simultaneously."[10]

The strands of social control in weblike societies are anchored around *strongmen*: individuals who, through their leadership positions in social organizations, succeed in offering viable survival strategies to their followers. Migdal argues that a specific historical sequence of unique events in Europe contributed to the dismantling of strong weblike societies. One of these events, the Black Death that swept through Europe in the 14th century, contributed decisively to the breakdown of the medieval networks of social control.[11] These events laid the basis for the creation of strong pyramidal societies and strong states. A different sequence of events in regions outside Europe and North America led to the creation of strong weblike societies. Strong weblike societies in Third World states present, in Migdal's view, some of the most severe obstacles for state builders intent on predominance.

Strong states that achieve predominance over strong weblike societies do so by breaking down the webs of social control and asserting the rules of the state. Many weak states have failed to emerge dominant from this environment, and they coexist with strong societal organizations under the leadership of strongmen who reinforce the fragmentation of social control by capturing parts of the state on their own terms. This is often accomplished through a process of bargaining that emerges from what Migdal calls the *triangle of accommodation*, which consists of state officials who formulate policy at national level, implementors (officials entrusted to oversee policy execution at the local level), and strongmen. Each of these bargainers holds a distinct power base but also operates under the considerable constraints that follow from their mutual dependence on one another. They come to coexist with one another through mutually profitable agreements. Whatever the substantive terms of such agreements, however, Migdal asserts that they almost invariably compromise state power. The end result is that strongmen succeed in consolidating precisely what state builders try to dismantle: multiple sets of rules of social control, each one of which is exercised within a parochial jurisdiction and results in discriminatory rather than uniform treatment for the citizens of the state.[12]

Strongmen's significance lies less in their individual power bases—which the state could dismantle if it chose to—than in the resulting weblike dilution of the power of the state. Imposing state rules over scores of strongmen is a costly option. The lower-cost option of coexistence through triangles of accommodation appears far more attractive.

Weak societies are defined by their low levels of social control. In weak societies, the prevailing strategies of survival advanced by social organizations are prone to collapse. These strategies find few adherents either because they have little bearing on actual everyday conditions or because the organizations that sponsor them are subject to internal strains or external pressures. Organizations that are undermined in this way have little power left, and social control becomes increasingly tenuous. Strong states easily dominate such societies. Weak states located in weak societies fail to establish new networks of social control where older ones have fallen into disarray. The end result is a lack of significant social control from any source whatever.[13]

State and Regime

When state leaders and strongmen confront each other in the contest for ascendancy, each reverts to a typical repertoire of stratagems and tactics. One of the tactical approaches open to use by state leaders is a variety of modifications to the regime format of the state. The first analytical gap in the Migdal framework can be filled by adding the state-regime distinction in order to distinguish different sites within the state. Migdal draws a line between state *leaders* and state *bureaus* and *agencies*, but it can be seen from his analysis that some of these bureaus and agencies are a product of specific regime types.

A *regime* comprises the values, norms, rules, procedures, and structures of authority that shape the ordering of power within and among the various organizational sites of the state.[14] The democratic, totalitarian, and authoritarian ways of ordering state power are indicative of distinctive regime types. Robert Fishman points out that while state and regime remain analytically distinct, their separateness is demonstrated when a change of regime can be brought about without altering other aspects of the state to any great extent.

In certain exceptional cases, however, the regime format requires a corresponding ordering of other basic defining characteristics of the state as well so that state and regime merge into a single indistinguishable unit. In these cases, a change of regime requires a reconstitution of the state as well. Fishman cites cases of personal rulership (sultanism) and the modern totalitarian state as contemporary examples of the state-regime distinction virtually dissolving.[15]

Various ways of securing state predominance have been deployed. The first such tactic identified by Migdal is the *big shuffle*, which consists of state leaders using their powers of appointment preemptively to effect a quick, unpredictable turnover of personnel in key positions within the regime and bureaucracy.

Nonmerit appointments, the second tactic, also have the objective of maintaining a coherence of interests between state leaders and their subordinates. Three categories of nonmerit appointments are identified: (1) appointments based on personal loyalty to state leaders; (2) co-optation of potential rivals (such as established strongmen) who may wish to build power centers within the state; and (3) the so-called ethnic bargain. The ethnic bargain is referred to as "a special sort of co-optation based on group identity"; the Lebanese National Pact of 1943 is held up as a prime example.

The third tactic is *dirty tricks,* ranging from illegal imprisonment of opponents to deportation, torture, and death squads.[16] Through these extreme tactics state leaders transgress and subvert the laws they need for effective state building. By abandoning law, state leaders set in motion a process of deinstitutionalization and thus undermine the project for which these tactics are deployed: the building of a state strong enough to impose its rules of social control over those of strongmen intent on operating beyond the laws of the state.

Civil Society and Democracy

The plurality of interest groups commonly found in modern, industrial, urbanized, and densely populated states is usually an indicator of civil society. The relationships between civil society and the components of "political society" (such as political parties); between civil society and primary social units such as the family; and between civil society and the state are also used as defining criteria.

Two definitional disputes characterize the literature on civil society. First is the relationship between the state and civil society. At issue is whether they are adversaries or congruent and complementary. Second is which voluntary groups are part of civil society and which are not. If some of the voluntary organizations that occupy the organizational space between the family and the state qualify as part of civil society and others do not, what are the criteria?

Both these disputes have a bearing on the link between civil society and democracy. If civil society is to prevail over the state, then it must serve as the source of democratic values, norms, and practices, and the logical sequence is for civil society to inaugurate the democratic regime and sustain it (if need be, against the state). If the state is to prevail, then the state must nurture the growth of civil society, establish the democratic regime, and act as the guardian of both.

As to the second dispute, the nature, composition, objectives, and methods of the voluntary groups who make up the ranks of civil society have a bearing on the causal link between social pluralism and democracy. The question is, When does social pluralism predict civil society, and when does it predict civil war?

Concern with what interest groups make up civil society—that is, concern with the defining attributes of civil society—is the focus of recent work by Naomi Chazan. Research by her and others has revealed an intricate pattern of associations emerging in the public sphere of postindependence African states.[17] These voluntary associations filled in the middle ground between the nuclear family and the state and thus seem to be potential building blocks for an emerging African civil society. Yet these structures emerged as the African state appeared to become more oppressive and authoritarian and at the same time increasingly powerless. Many of these African associational forms have therefore been interpreted as coping responses to a domineering yet ineffective state presence.

A typical coping strategy has been *disengagement*, in which people seek to organize themselves beyond the reach of the state. A striking form of disengagement has been the construction of economic, cultural, and juridical systems paralleling and competing with the state. At times these systems (especially in the economic sphere) have operated with some measure of collusion from state employees.

The scale of the parallel economy in Ghana, for example, can be gauged by the report that in the early 1980s up to two-thirds of the annual cocoa crop was being exported illegally.[18] The practices and guiding norms of these largely economic activities involved corruption, black marketeering, smuggling, embezzlement, fraud, and theft by state officials. The overall observable effect in Ghana "has been to make virtually everyone into a speculator, cheat, corruptor, or lawbreaker. Bypassing the rule of law has become a form of survival."[19]

This is hardly the ideal circumstance for nurturing democratic norms. Chazan has declared that "there is no axiomatic connection between the expansion of the voluntary sector and the consolidation of civil society in Africa."[20] The organizations that can serve as building blocks for civil society pursue limited, partial, and modest objectives and have clearly defined operating procedures and a distinct organizational profile. That profile includes "participatory structures, autonomous resources, technical expertise, and a discrete constituency (regardless of size)" and a tendency to have "a younger, relatively well educated leadership core." Such organizational attributes can be expected to favor the consolidation of "specific notions of authority, distributive justice, conflict resolution, and respect for the rule of law (at least within the group)."[21]

Chazan therefore provides a substantive description of civil society but does not isolate the common denominator that distinguishes the norms and practices of civil societies from those of the noncivil. She does not take up the question of what type of society generates the benign kind of voluntary association required for the construction of civil society and what type of society fosters the more malign associational forms that undermine the emergence of civil society.

Even more important, Chazan's analysis allows for the existence of states without civil societies. This raises questions about the causal link and the chronological sequence between civil society and the process of democratization. Can states democratize without civil society? Must construction of a civil society accompany the process of democratization? Must it precede democratization? Can it follow afterward? And finally, if civil society is missing, then what is the prime agent of democratization?

One part of one answer is readily available. The "civic community" is characterized by citizens who actively involve themselves in public affairs without seeing the public domain as an arena for the unrestrained pursuit of private interests only; who engage one another in this arena as political equals; who are tolerant of their opponents; and who are prepared to enter social arrangements on the basis of trust.[22] These norms are embodied in and reinforced by a set of social structures created to pursue what de Tocqueville called "the common objects of common desires," an observation that has been widely confirmed by the body of research in the tradition of the *civic culture*. The internal effect of such organizations is to entrench these norms of behavior. The external effect is to create a network of secondary associations with cross-cutting individual membership, which disperses social conflicts (instead of mutually reinforcing them) and thus contributes to democratic government. What needs examination is whether these norms and values can be expected to flourish in divided societies; whether such cross-cutting affiliations can be expected to form; and if they can, whether they function as moderating factors in social conflict.

The State, Divided Societies, and Civil Society

The Lockean tradition tends to view the state as a primary threat to liberty and therefore a force that democrats must contain. This view reinforces the notion that state and civil society are antagonistic forces, with one serving as the locus and protector of democratic values and norms and the other as the usurper thereof. Both Michael Bratton and Arnaud Sales have warned against such a rigid view and argue that the relationship between the state and civil society allows for congruence as well as conflict.[23]

Much of the current writing on this theme, however, is ambivalent if not contradictory, and lacking in conceptual clarity. Larry Diamond, for example, argues that civil society can serve as a countervailing force to the state and can also lend stability to the state.[24] Chazan notes that the emergence of civil society is most promising in African countries where "the institutional hegemony of the state has been rejected but its importance has been retained."[25] What these scholars point to is a variable relationship in which the strength of both societal formations and the state can vary and covary.

The need for a conceptual framework within which to describe these variations can be met by merging the definition of civil society offered by Edward Shils with the Migdal model of state-society relations and with aspects of the literature on ethnically divided societies.

Three main definitional criteria of civil society are isolated by Shils: "The first is a part of society comprising a complex of autonomous institutions—economic, religious, intellectual and political—distinguishable from the family, the clan, the locality and the state. The second is a part of society possessing a particular complex of relationships between itself and the state and a distinctive set of institutions which safeguard the separation of state and civil society and maintain effective ties between them. The third is a widespread pattern of refined or civil manners."[26] In this definition, emphasis is placed on the autonomy (and not on the independence) of civil society from the state: "The state lays down laws which set the outermost boundaries of the autonomy of the diverse spheres and sectors of civil society; so, civil society from its side lays down limits on the actions of the state."[27] Tradition, laws, and the constitution demarcate and maintain the boundaries of this autonomous sphere. The criterion of civility serves as a yardstick for the conduct of relations within society among individuals and groups and between individuals, social organizations, and the state.

The perspective on civil society contained in this definition can be explicated by means of Migdal's model of state-society interaction in the process of state building. First, not all strong societies are civil, but all civil societies are strong. The civil conduct of both private and public affairs is an expression of a high degree of social control, which is maintained through tradition, laws, and constitutional rules. This compatible triad of rules of social control not only ensures civility, it also indicates that a pyramidal structure of social organizations is working, with the state at the apex and with congruence existing between state and societal strategies of survival.

Citizenship is the primary indicator of an individual's formal membership in a state.[28] It is also the crucial qualification from which the status of civic persons and the guidelines for the conduct of relations among them are derived. The existence of civil society requires that the status of citizenship be invested with a very specific substantive content. Although Shils restricts the notion of civility to the conduct of good manners, it can be given greater conceptual depth by linking the status of civic persons to the body of rules subsumed under the category of *civil rights*.

Civil rights, which comprise a range of privileges, claims, duties, and obligations that individuals hold against the *state*, emerged not in the abstract but from specific conflicts in the process of European state building.[29] As state leaders yielded to these societal demands, essential adaptations to aspects of state organization and conduct followed. These changes led to the emergence of citizenship criteria that reflected these demands, and regime types that allowed for the execution of these demands. Civil society thus presupposes the salience of citizenship, which can emerge only when the state has drawn the entire population into a single common jurisdiction under a shared status of citizenship and a law that applies to all. This requires the exclusion of contending political loyalties, which presupposes the hegemony of the state.

When civility is conceptualized in these terms it can serve as a criterion for defining the substantive attributes of organizations that qualify for inclusion in civil society. This broader notion of civility is expressed in the norms of tolerance, cooperation, accountability, openness, trust, and respect for the rule of law within the organization and an appreciation of both procedural and substantive justice. It also serves as a criterion for differentiating the uncivil societies from the civil ones.

Strong weblike societies maintain structures of social control that tend to suppress the emergence of civil society. When strongmen succeed in imposing their own sets of survival strategies, the resulting tangle of societal rules inevitably becomes parochial, discriminatory, and even contradictory instead of universal. The value of citizenship is constantly open to question, and the comprehensive jurisdiction claimed by the state is continuously subverted. Because their respective survival strategies are incompatible, contending strongmen are not bound by common constraints in confronting one another or the state, and the civil conduct of public disputes becomes highly improbable.

Ethnically divided societies exhibit the essential characteristics of strong weblike societies. Ethnic identity consists of a distinct sense of a unique and collectively shared descent: "Ethnicity is based on a myth of collective ancestry, which usually carries with it traits believed to be innate. Some notion of ascription, however diluted, and affinity deriving from it are inseparable from the concept of ethnicity."[30] Presumed if not actually shared descent invokes the bonds of common ancestry, kinship, and family relationships, which are typically reflected in ethnic imagery and cultural attributes.

Ethnic groups are potentially powerful units of social control. Because of the emphasis on perceived bonds of descent, as expressed in family and kinship ties, the reciprocal obligations and prescriptions that bind family members are projected onto the entire ethnic group. In the view of Donald L. Horowitz, when different ethnic groups in a multiethnic state confront one another in an *unranked* system of stratification, where groups continually contest one another's claims for supremacy, status, and dominance in every social sphere, each ethnic group approximates an "incipient whole society."[31] In such unranked societies the overall pattern of societal social control conforms to a weblike rather than a pyramidal pattern. Although unranked multiethnic groups thus meet the first criterion set by Shils for inclusion into civil society (that is, being located between the family and the state), they fail to meet the other two criteria.

Ethnically divided societies are prone to fail in meeting the criterion of civility. The essence of civility, according to Shils, lies in the mutual recognition of the *moral dignity* of one's opponents in the course of public conduct: "It means regarding other persons, including one's adversaries, as members of the same collectivity, i.e. as members of the same society, even though they belong to different parties or to different religious communities or to different ethnic groups."[32] Civil conduct in these terms presupposes a very solid sense of "inclusive collective self-consciousness," which transcends other social cleavages and from which can emerge a shared notion of the common good, or public interest. In the absence of such civility, warns Shils, a society with a multitude of social bases can degenerate into civil war, the antithesis of civil society.

This criterion of civility is extraordinarily difficult to meet in ethnically divided societies, Horowitz argues, once the issue at stake becomes relative group worth and collective esteem. This elusive commodity is a function of social recognition that cannot be acquired through a process of self-assessment, and moreover, it is virtually indivisible: the dignity and worth of one's own group can be asserted only by relating to other groups to whom such dignity and worth are denied.[33] Civility, under such conditions, then becomes a yardstick reserved for in-group conduct, while relations with ethnic outsiders are not subject to the same restraints. Instead, the pursuit of collective esteem for one's own ethnic group almost requires that ethnic outsiders be treated with contempt and negative stereotyping, which tends to destroy the social fabric that nurtures and sustains civil society.

Ethnic groups in divided societies also tend to fail to meet the remaining criterion for civil society: the autonomy of the component units of civil society from the state. Ethnic groups that act as incipient whole societies are bound to insist on control over their own political future—which in such a context can be secured either by capturing state power at the expense of all other ethnic competitors or by seeking maximum insulation against a state that is under the control of hostile ethnic adversaries.

Control of the state yields both symbolic and tangible rewards. The symbolic reward lies in having the incumbents of state power affirm the group's worth in relation to all other subordinates within the state. An answer to the question Who owns the country? in favor of one ethnic group can be presented to the outside world. Relative group worth can be acquired only through affirmation and can be expressed only through entitlement. By occupying the vital sites of power in the state, the incumbent ethnic group (and by implication, its worthiness) is affirmed. The domestic and international recognition of such a state confirms and endorses the entitlement to such ownership. Symbolic endorsement of this ownership through coats of arms, flags, anthems, the name of the state, the official language, and the names of public buildings, dams, airports, and cities can all be given an ethnic content that conveys rightful ownership of the state.

Occupation of the state also brings concrete rewards in the form of control over public goods. The allocation of public goods (e.g., education, welfare, police protection) unlike private goods must meet two criteria: *jointness of supply* (the use of such goods by any one citizen must not preclude or prevent another from using it) and *nonexcludability* (no criteria should exist whereby some citizens are allowed to use such goods and others are prohibited from doing so). One of the reasons why states justify their societal hegemony and market their own set of survival strategies as superior to those of other societal organizations is their claim to be the only body capable of providing goods collectively that cannot be obtained through private endeavor. Yet when an ethnic group does gain control over the state and starts distributing public goods on the basis of ethnic preferences, jointness of supply is undermined (the resources of the state are used to educate, care for, and protect only one set of citizens) and nonexcludability is violated (ethnicity emerges as the dominant criterion for exclusion). Thus one of the most basic justifications for the existence of the state in the eyes of ethnic outsiders falls away.[34]

Control of the state also gives access to the regime. Changes in constitutional rules, the most vital component of the regime, can result in consolidating control of the state and forestalling the alternating of parties in power. When such constitutional rules are executed, the state ceases to be an autonomous actor and the state, the regime, and the incumbent ethnic group coalesce into a single unit of hegemonic social control. When ethnic outsiders try to distance themselves from such a state, the sphere of autonomy typically offered by the state to civil society is unlikely to be considered sufficient. Furthermore, the incumbents of such a state are likely to try to dismantle such boundaries between state and voluntary organizations in their attempt to assert state control over ethnic competitors. Under such conditions ethnic outsiders are unlikely to view the state as the guardian of civil society.

THE CONTEST FOR HEGEMONY

Migdal's model of state-society relations implies certain necessary conditions for successful democratization. The starting point is the Weberian definition of a state: a social organization that makes binding rules on a population within a given territory, using force to do so if necessary. A state therefore exists as an aspiring hegemonic force, competing with other social organizations for control over society. Aspirations to hegemony are reflected in the claim to sovereignty and enacted in the successful exercise of the infrastructural power of state social control.

A regime prescribes the various sites of hegemonic power within the state and sets out rules for the way in which such power is to be exercised. Constitutional rules typically embody the core of the rules that define the type of regime. Regime rules therefore guide and shape the hegemonic character of the state's domination of society. A contest for power between political adversaries in the society, conducted within the rules set by the regime and upheld by the state, therefore does not affect the basic state-society relationship. The hegemony of the state over society remains unchallenged and intact even when one set of regime incumbents is displaced by another.

However, when the opposing forces confront each other with irreconcilable regime models, wider issues are at stake. When a transfer of power from one set of incumbents to another entails scrapping an entire set of regime rules and replacing it with a fundamentally different one that would involve fundamentally redefining and reconstituting aspects of the state, the nature and character of state domination over society are at issue. A conflict between opposing forces with such agendas amounts to a contest for hegemony.

In a contest for hegemony at least three basic, interrelated issues are at stake: peoplehood, statehood, and regime requirements. The demographic unit within which conducting domestic societal politics is usually considered appropriate is the "nation," or the "people." Opposing social formations that conduct themselves as incipient whole societies have competing definitions of nationhood and peoplehood. In such cases, complications arise as to who comprises the "self" that has the right to self-determination, and which of the "people" should be consulted when the will of the people is to be taken as a guide for democratic politics. The statement of Sir Ivor Jennings, made in 1963, is still apt: "On the surface it seems reasonable: let the people decide. It was in fact ridiculous because the people cannot decide until somebody decides who are the people."

Furthermore, there are no standard agreed-on democratic methods for choosing which contender's definition of the appropriate democratic unit should prevail. The question of who chooses the choosers points to the need for infinitely prior assemblies to legitimize any democratically assembled choice on such matters.[35] This logically closed circle points to the limits of democratic theory in settling such basic disputes. The general authoritative conclusion by Robert A. Dahl is that "we cannot solve the problem of the proper scope and domain of democratic units from within democratic theory."[36]

Also at stake is the nature of statehood. The predominating questions are where the territorial boundaries should be drawn (the preeminent question facing those who argue for secession or irredentist policies) and who are citizens, subjects, and aliens. The disputes on peoplehood and statehood hold implications for the state's regime format. Ultimately, regime rules specify who qualify as citizens and who do not, and whether all citizens have citizenship of equal value or not. Constitutional rules spell out who will be consulted and in what way when the "people" are called on to express their "will" on public matters. Disagreements on these matters are bound to coalesce in divergent regime models, which in turn are derived from prior disagreement on the defining criteria of democracy. Each regime model can then be expected to be justified and legitimated in terms of its corresponding definition of democracy.

When hegemony is contested between opposing political formations that view themselves as incipient whole societies, the questions of statehood, which are usually dealt with in international treaties, need to be addressed as part and parcel of domestic politics. Herein lies the essence of the often-noted analogy between the politics of divided societies and of international society.[37] At the same time, the questions of regime requirements, which are the substance of social contracts, also have to be dealt with. From this perspective, then, the nature of the issues that are the subject of political confrontations indicates the true measure of the extent to which a society is divided. Shifting the focus to the nature of the issues and away from the identity of the conflicting parties makes possible a new perspective on the nature of what *divides* societies. The identity of the antagonists—ethnicity, in this case—is a contributing factor in that it shapes the formation of the opposing incipient whole societies, but it is also entirely conceivable (though not often likely) for a completely ethnically homogeneous society to be thus divided.

The point is that a divided society is not necessarily one in which the opposing sides are compartmentalized into neat and clear-cut ethnic categories. Nor does a divided society necessarily have its exact empirical lines of ethnic cleavage clearly established. The definition of a divided society goes beyond the identities of the adversaries. The demands of the opposing formations in terms of statehood, peoplehood, definitions of democracy, and regime models are the crucial indicators. For reasons argued above, these demands are most likely to occur in societies where ethnicity is intensely held.

Two kinds of strong state can emerge from a contest for hegemony within an ethnically divided society. The state either can be ethnically neutral, that is, autonomous, or it can be an ethnic state. In the former, a democratic regime can emerge, while in the latter it is virtually precluded. The essential difference lies in the quality of membership in the state (that is, citizenship) that is made available to the population under the jurisdiction of the state. Although Migdal does not address this matter directly, his analysis implies that citizenship of equal value is not necessarily forthcoming in all strong states. What is implied is that strong states are able to set the terms of who qualify as citizens, subjects, and aliens. If more than one category of citizenship applies, then the strong state can dictate the substance of citizenship within each category. Nor is it implied that everybody will be required to submit to identical strategies of survival. If the strong state chooses to be differential and discriminatory, then it is able to impose such rules. Likewise, if identical survival strategies are to apply to all, then a strong state is capable of asserting them.

In a contest for hegemony a dominant ethnic group is likely to find persuasive reasons for constructing a strong ethnic state. In an ethnic state the dominant ethnic group, the state, and the regime dovetail into a single hegemonic unit. The ethnic state, then, would fit in alongside the sultanistic state and the totalitarian state, in which the state-regime distinction virtually dissolves. Such a hegemonic configuration makes it possible for the incumbents to impose their own views on not only matters pertaining to membership (citizenship) and the regime format (rules determining the levels and range of participation and contestation), but also matters pertaining to societal autonomy (the official yardsticks of "civil" conduct and the social space reserved for "civil" society).

In asserting their hegemony, ethnic incumbents dictate to ethnic losers on every one of these issues in a way that dismantles or precludes the emergence of democratic regimes and of civil society. Hallmarks of the ethnic state are discriminatory rules of social control, loss of citizenship by entire categories of inhabitants, introduction of second-class and even third-class categories of citizenship for other inhabitants, and constitutional rules that limit the participation and contestation associated with the polyarchic regime type.[38]

The response is likely to mirror the imposition. Ethnic challengers who view themselves as incipient whole societies probably have the same ambitions as their opponents. Challengers of the ethnic state are likely to call for its destruction or partitioning or to take over the state and reconstitute its fundamental operative and symbolic characteristics. Their regime proposals are based on principles that diverge from the principles that inform the incumbent state and regime and, instead, correspond to the ideals of statehood they strive for. Prescribed spheres of autonomy in which ethnic subordinates are required to engage in the "civil" conduct of public life are also bound to be challenged through unilaterally declared "civil" space that rivals official demarcations. Likewise, officially sanctioned voluntary organizations are usually challenged by those who form a contending "civil" society parallel to and beyond the legal boundaries of the officially sanctioned one. The norms of conduct that define the civic culture—that is, public engagement, political equality, mutual trust, and tolerance—are equally likely to apply only within the ranks of the antagonistic formations, and the prospect of secondary associations emerging with membership that straddles the divide becomes very remote.

The strong autonomous state can be identified by the extent to which citizenship, rules of social control, and resulting survival strategies are applied to individuals within the state without discrimination. The state is neutral toward social differentiators such as ethnicity in determining criteria for membership to the state and in determining the substance and quality of such membership. Citizenship of equal value is available to all sectors of society.

The salience of citizenship over other competing social member-ships, however, is ensured. Democratizing a strong autonomous state requires adapting the regime so that citizens have access to unrestrained participation in and contestation for the political power *within* the state.

Democratizing a strong ethnic state requires dissolving the con-test for hegemony. This entails the following. First, the state must be strengthened further, for it is the only agency that can ensure that the value of citizenship transcends that of other contending social loyalties such as the ethnic group. For the state to supplant the ethnic group as the ultimate unit of political loyalty, agreement has to be reached on the substantive issues—all of which center on what the appropriate unit is for domestic politics. Questions of the substantive content of nationhood or peoplehood and the collective "self" that is to be accommodated within the sovereign state have to be settled. From this agreement must follow mutually accepted yardsticks for establishing who should qualify as citizens, subjects, and aliens. This entails the first step toward dismantling the ethnic character of the state.

For membership in the state to become more valuable than membership in the ethnic group also requires that the state allo-cate public goods in an ethnically neutral way: the criteria of joint-ness and nonexcludability must be upheld scrupulously. This requires that the administrative personnel of state departments be informed by a collective ethos of the public servant as a *civil* ser-vant that serves all citizens of the state equally well on the terms set by the laws of the state, not on the terms set by other social organizations. To be reconstituted so fundamentally, an ethnic state must acquire the attributes of an *autonomous* social organi-zation and strengthen its capacity to assert itself over societal com-petitors such as ethnic groups.

Advising concerted state building of this order as the first step toward securing democracy appears, at first glance, to run counter to the Anglo-American intellectual tradition. In that intel-lectual tradition the state is the greatest threat to liberty, and the containment of state power is the foremost priority in consolidat-ing democracy. Yet contemporary Africa provides vivid examples of cases where a decline in state power did not lead to the emergence of democracy.

Fellow African Claude Ake senses the causal link in Africa between state building and democratization that is being argued here: "In Africa, states are very paradoxical. They are very strong from one perspective and also very weak. Look at Zaire, one of the most authoritarian, repressive states but Mobutu probably controls less than 1/3, effectively, of Zairean territory. Even within those areas, the state has very little penetrative capacity. The state is largely absent, yet there is no democracy."[39] Ake's analysis, reported in a conference paper in March 1990, foreshadowed the riots of September 1991, when both soldiers and citizens went looting shoulder to shoulder through the streets of the capital city Kinshasa.[40] These events epitomize the kind of behavior that the framework outlined in this appendix predicts from a weak state in a weak society, where no rules of social control whatsoever are operative. These riots also underscore Ake's conclusion that "democracy is not, and can never be, a matter of weakening the state."[41]

Not only the strength of the state but, equally important, its autonomy must be established. Migdal stresses the need for bureaucrats of the state to see themselves as part of an institution, as having interests that are not related to or derived from their positions, and having wider commitments to societally based organizations of which they may be members. "Bureaucrats of the state, both those at the tops of agencies and the implementors in the field, must identify their own ultimate interests with those of the state as an autonomous organization." This is seen as a crucial step in the building of autonomous strong states, which "can emerge only when the shared notion that there should be an autonomous set of state interests exists, and when bureaucrats believe those interests coincide with their own."[42] Migdal posits that state autonomy is met when "state officials act upon their own preferences," not on those of societally based individuals or groups.[43]

This pattern of decision making can be encouraged by certain rules and practices that insulate (but do not necessarily isolate) the personnel of the state from the rest of society. Rules and practices that do so give effect to what Ernst Gellner has labeled the strategy of *gelding*: "The idea is to break the kin link by depriving the budding warrior/bureaucrat/cleric either of ancestry, or of posterity, or of both."[44] In the agrarian polities of an earlier age, various techniques were deployed, including "the use of eunuchs, physically incapable of possessing posterity; of priests whose privileged position was conditional on celibacy thereby preventing them from avowing posterity; of foreigners, whose kin links could be assumed to be safely distant; or of members of otherwise disenfranchised or excluded groups, who would be helpless if separated from the employing state. Another technique was the employment of 'slaves', men who, though in fact privileged and powerful, nevertheless, being 'owned' by the state, technically had no other legitimate links, and whose property and position could revert to the state at any time."[45] In the late 20th century, most state builders and their personnel would probably not consider most of these techniques conducive to esprit de corps! Constitutional rules are the major remaining mechanisms available to state builders for creating the conditions of gelding.

Within the state a similar distinction needs to be established. The second step in dissolving a contest for hegemony requires reestablishing the distinction between state and regime. In organizational terms each should be insulated from the other, so that a distinctive corporate character can emerge in the personnel ranks of each. Personnel of state departments, agencies, and bureaus that are organizationally separate from the regime have to develop a sense of autonomy and distinctiveness that matches and reinforces the organizational insulation between state and regime, once it has been established. A change in regime format and the regular alternation of personnel within the regime should not threaten or even seem to threaten the occupants of the other sites within the state. Positions within the regime and positions within the state *outside* the regime must be on two separate career trajectories and must be seen that way. Such an institutional and perceptual demarcation within the state lays the basis for effective democratization of the regime.

The third step is to establish constitutional rules that give effect to the principle of citizenship of equal value; secure the civil and political liberties in terms of which participation and contestation are delimited; and ensure that these rules remain functional within the contours of the societally based political loyalties that characterize an ethnically divided society.

The fourth step in dissolving a contest for hegemony is creating a civil society. The three preceding steps entail the construction of an institutional and attitudinal arena within which the voluntary organizations that make up the contending "civil" societies so typical of a divided society can be merged into a *civil* society. Within this framework—the concept of the contest for hegemony that has been described thus far—it is possible to return to the questions raised by Chazan on the role of civil society in the process of democratization.

The question raised but not answered by Chazan is which voluntary, grass-roots organizations can be expected to qualify as building blocks for a civil society that is congruent with and supportive of democracy. The answer is that in an unranked society in which other such formations are also operative, no organization qualifies that emerges from the grass roots of an incipient whole society. The pursuit of hegemony is exemplified in the endorsement or denial of group status and esteem; in the imposition of one vision of peoplehood, statehood, and constitutional rules to the exclusion of others; and in the discriminatory distribution of public goods. Politics of this nature precludes an inclusive view of the public interest or the common good, which is the foundation of a societywide context for the conduct of civility.

Civil society therefore cannot cause the dissolving of a contest for hegemony and the democratizing of a divided society. Instead, the construction of a civil society from the myriad of organizations in incipient whole societies must follow or accompany state building and the democratizing of the regime. "In Africa," notes Claude Ake, "civil society . . . is not . . . the prop of democracy. It is rather the manifestation of democracy."[46] The task of democratizing a divided society is therefore not merely to find a set of constitutional rules for a regime that gives citizenship of equal value to all (especially in the form of equally valuable votes); more fundamental, democratizing a divided society also means finding constitutional rules that strengthen, bolster, and secure the state, which is the body that issues citizenship in the first place. State building and the civilizing of society must precede, or at least proceed concurrently with, the process of democratization.

THE POLITICS OF NEGOTIATION IN DIVIDED SOCIETIES

Before any insights from the literature on bargaining and negotiation can be fruitfully applied to conflicts in divided societies, the nature of the bargaining problem in these societies has to be restated. The intriguing question is not What conditions enable a sound judgment to be made about which outcome will result from the bargaining process? It is, rather, What empirical conditions and prescriptive guidelines induce adversaries to engage in good faith bargaining when they would rather not do so?[47]

The bargaining problem thus restated implies that the necessary conditions for bargaining over hegemony in divided societies are more stringent than the conditions for other issues and other contexts. It implies first and foremost that all parties jointly accept that hegemony for any one of them is unattainable. Every party must explicitly acknowledge that it is not using the negotiating process to try to secure unilateral victory on its own terms and unconditional submission from the others. Negotiation cannot be converted into a tactical device for imposing any one agenda onto other parties. Instead, all parties must accept that bargaining is a joint endeavor to search for a mutually acceptable agreement on establishing a site of hegemony that is beyond the exclusive control of any one of the bargainers.

The following approaches to negotiation are relevant to divided societies. First, the social-psychological perspective on the impact of intangible issues relating to the loss of face highlights what Horowitz considers the definitive aspect of ethnic conflict: a contest for relative group worth and esteem. Adding the social-psychological perspective of J. Z. Rubin and Bert R. Brown shows that the threat of losing face is the most important intangible at stake not only in the conflict but also in the negotiating processes, where the collective esteem of each of the participants is at risk.[48]

J. S. Furnivall, one of the early analysts in this field, has noted that the interdependence and simultaneous antagonism of opponents in more or less permanent adversarial relationships is one of the remarkable structural features of divided societies. The phenomenon of antagonists who "mix but do not combine," who are increasingly drawn into the complex interdependence of economic modernization, is characteristic of virtually all contemporary divided societies, except only the most pristine cases of rural subsistence agriculture where each ethnic group still retains a wholly autonomous economic base. A critically important variable is the extent to which divided societies are modernized and the level of mutual dependence experienced by the adversaries within a given society.

This aspect is highlighted by the power-dependence approach of S. B. Bacharach and E. J. Lawler. The interdependence that arises from the uneven distribution of scarce and valued resources creates not only a source of conflict and potential for an amicable dissolution by exchanging resources but also the basis of a power relationship between the opposing parties.[49] If the parties choose to bargain, this power can serve as the basis of their bargaining power. Since this power relationship originates with the distributional pattern of scarce and needed resources, it is therefore outside any specific negotiating arena. Long-standing bargaining relationships are therefore characterized by ongoing power struggles in which enduring but changeable power relations extend from one negotiating event to the next.

The third theoretical perspective on bargaining and negotiation that is relevant to the context of politics in divided societies is the body of literature that analyzes the process in terms of a chronology of consecutive stages. These constructs tend to start with the opposing parties' decision to engage each other in formal or informal negotiations. However, as P. H. Gulliver has noted, this is a presupposition that does not always apply.[50] In cases of exceptional intractability the status quo may be considered more preferable than any foreseeable settlement. Reaching a mutually profitable bargain in such conflicts as these requires another crucial stage before formal negotiations begin: *prenegotiation*, or bargaining about bargaining.[51]

In this body of theory the question asked is What must be accomplished in this stage to ensure that conflicting parties proceed to the negotiating arena? The general findings thus far can be condensed into two.[52] The first relates to redefining the conflict, and the second to agreeing on and implementing mechanisms, procedures, and strategies with which to enact and consolidate some of the perceptual changes that ought to be brought about in redefining the conflict.

In redefining the conflict, all parties have to perceive that the outcomes do not allow only for winners and losers. In the metaphor of game theory, a *non-zero-sum* perception of prospective outcomes must take the place of a *zero-sum* perception. Once there is all-round acceptance on this point, all parties have to concede that outright victory on its own terms and unconditional surrender by the others is an unattainable objective. Instead, they must see other, more likely outcomes, such as all parties ending up doing fairly well together or doing badly together. On the basis of such an understanding, parties can and should construct a different view of each other. The other party is no longer seen as an enemy to be destroyed at any cost but as an opponent to be beaten in a fair contest under mutually accepted rules of the game.

One of the numerous ways of inducing this perceptual shift is to present an assessment of the costs of reaching an agreement versus the costs of not reaching an agreement. The presence of a *mutually hurting stalemate*, which is perceived as such by all parties and which outweighs the costs of reaching an agreement, is considered decisive.[53]

Mechanisms and procedures for testing, entrenching, and consolidating the mutual perception of such a redefinition of the conflict include the following. Cease-fires and moratoriums are usually considered temporary arrangements for managing deescalation. They can also be tests of the parties' ability to uphold the rules of good faith. Measures that consolidate support for negotiated settlements in both camps strengthen the parties' perceptual shift and shore up their position against extremists. Finally, agreement on a formula for addressing the substantive issue of indivisible goods also bolsters the position of parties who are ready to meet at the negotiating table.

Many of these general requirements have immediate relevance for conflicts in divided societies. For Arend Lijphart the principal factor that brings leaders in divided societies to engage in compromise is the mutual acceptance of the so called *self-negating prediction*.[54] This amounts to a mutual recognition that the conflict approximates a non-zero-sum game. Mutual awareness of the destructive potential inherent in unrestrained conflict in divided societies motivates rival political leaders to act preemptively to avert destruction by cooperating with one another and moderating their demands instead of escalating them.

If domestic hegemony is the substance of the dispute, prenegotiations should focus the formula for dealing with this almost indivisible commodity. Indivisibles are "goods that cannot be split physically into parts, and concerns that cannot be compromised on, without losing much of their intrinsic or perceived value."[55] Hegemony, being a relationship of pronounced and continuous dominance, fits this definition. According to Cecilia Albin, two conditions can facilitate dealing with disputes over indivisibles: first, softened perceptions of antagonism, fear, and mistrust between opponents; and second, expanded resources where appropriate. Two types of strategies are potentially viable, exchange strategies and functional strategies. The first consists of trading differently valued items: "Each party gives away something it values less and that is highly valued by the other, so that each ends up with those items it needs or values the most."[56] In functional strategies the parties "share or divide between parties, or delegate to an outside actor, a particular (the same) function of an indivisible good, the physical unity of which remains intact."[57]

In divided societies, the contested site of hegemony is the territorial state. A favorable exchange strategy might be the subdivision, or multiplication, of states—that is, of sites of hegemony. An exchange whereby each party acquires sovereign, undisputed (that is, hegemonic) control over the territory it considers its rightful sole property would settle the dispute over an indivisible and dissolve a contest for hegemony. The parties having agreed to such a formula, the tasks of negotiators would be to decide where the boundaries are to be drawn and settle related matters of detail.

If an exchange strategy is not feasible or desirable, functional strategies are the only remaining formula. Three types are possible: *sharing* ("to jointly exercise a function of the indivisible"), *division* ("to separately exercise a particular function of the indivisible"), and *delegation* ("parties agree to transfer a function of the indivisible to an outside actor"). Parties who contest hegemony within a single state cannot share or divide it. Sharing would amount to dual sovereignty, with each of the contending parties trying to exercise hegemonic claims in the same territory. Likewise, division would balkanize the state, with each party capturing a functionally delimited part of the institutional infrastructure. Neither of these strategies produces an outcome that effectively dissolves the hegemonic quality of the conflict.

What is at stake is who occupies which position in a relationship of superordination and subordination. The remaining strategy is for the parties to delegate—the site of domestic hegemony (the state) is not to be the exclusive domain of any one of the contestants. It could theoretically be occupied by a foreign power, which amounts to a request for (renewed) colonization.[58] Or the parties could agree to the construction of an autonomous state. The autonomous state as a site of domestic hegemony is beyond capture by any societally based formation on an exclusive and permanent basis. The contest for power is reserved for one site *within* the autonomous state—the regime. *Within the regime,* power, once captured, can be shared, distributed, dispersed, or divided in terms of any one of the many constitutional formulas available. The autonomous state, as the uncontested site of domestic hegemony, retains its character by upholding the state-regime distinction. If the contending parties agree to this formula, then formal negotiations can proceed in searching for mutually acceptable rules with which to establish and safeguard state autonomy, the state-regime distinction, and constitutional rules with which to define the regime format.

The Regional and Global Grid

Hegemonic contests conducted within the sites of states are not shaped only by domestic forces. Contending parties may muster support from beyond the boundaries of the state, and actors from outside the state may through their own initiative shape the context of the conflict or even directly influence the course of events through partisan support for one of the contenders. The dissolution of a contest for hegemony is also therefore open to influence by regional or global forces or both.

Different perspectives on how the international system shapes the context within which this autonomous state is to hold its own are ably summarized by Peter Gourevitch.[59] Two aspects of this system are kept analytically distinct: the international economy, and the international system of states. Although there are a number of divergent perspectives on the contextual character of the international economy, they share an emphasis on interdependence as the dominant feature.[60]

The first perspective, strongly associated with Alexander Gerschenkron, emphasizes the link between late industrialization and centralized state control. The basic proposition of this school is that a state's regime type, political coalitions, public policies, and character are affected by the character of the global economy at the time the state seeks to enter the competitive arena. Generally, the later a state enters, the more difficulty it has competing effectively. Each entrant is faced with new competitors, new rules, and new requirements for success and a competitive edge. For the Gerschenkronians, late entrants into the global economy are in a disadvantaged position.

The theories of dependency, core periphery, and imperialism are used to explain the proposition that the states at the center of the global capitalist economies are able to dictate the asymmetrical relations of interdependence under which late entrants enter and compete, thereby locking the peripheral states (which would include all African states) into more or less inescapable conditions. The rules of the game predetermine that late entrants will be the perpetual losers.

The liberal development school also recognizes the formative effects of interdependence that extends beyond the territorial jurisdiction of the state, but they do not see interdependence as inherently malign. Late entrants can play well and can play to win. The disadvantage of a late start can be offset by shortcuts to technology and access to development capital and established markets. Unlike the previously mentioned perspectives, the liberal view is that economic parity can be achieved with the full complement of democratic regime characteristics. The Gerschenkronians argue that centralization of state authority (presumably with a loss of democratic features) is the price to be paid for catching up. The dependency school sees the shift to authoritarian regimes as an almost inevitable outcome as the states at the periphery develop dual economies—one part modern, closely tied to and dependent on the global core, and another part internal periphery, also asymmetrically dependent on the domestic modern sector. Authoritarian rules serve to protect this modern domestic core against claims from the internal periphery.

The extreme view on interdependence, offered by theorists who focus on transnational relations, modernization, and "complex interdependence," is that the modern international environment has become so densely interdependent that states have effectively lost control over policymaking and that the well-being of domestic populations is increasingly shaped by forces beyond state boundaries, irrespective of the regime rules of the state. The neomercantilists and state-centered Marxists counter that this pervasive interdependence with its intrusive effects is not an unstoppable set of forces but a function of state policy and, therefore, of the deliberate or inadvertent choices made by state leaders. State actions are guided by national interest, for the neomercantilists, and by class interests, for the Marxists.

The international state system presents another set of forces that affect the domestic politics of states.[61] The theoretical perspectives mentioned above argue that the international economy generally tends to affect domestic politics indirectly through the binding and constraining effects of conditions of interdependence. Theories that emphasize the condition of anarchy within the state system point to actions that can have the most immediate impact: invasion, occupation, partitioning, and incorporation are extreme intrusions into domestic politics. The need to confront such threats has often been the major factor motivating state action. This concern is given much attention by Migdal, who puts it that a "prime motivation for state leaders to attempt to stretch the state's rule-making domain within its formal boundaries . . . has been to build sufficient clout to survive the dangers posed by those outside its boundaries, from the world of states."[62] Responding to these threats proved to be one of the major catalysts in the process of European state building.

The state-centered perspective outlined here leans toward the neomercantilist interpretation of economic interdependence on domestic politics and the anarchic interpretation of the international state system and its effects on domestic actions by state leaders. It also commits one to the state-centered answer to the question about which feature of domestic politics best explains state action in the international arena. State strength or weakness presents itself as the most important independent variable.

Gourevitch finds this kind of perspective has the shortcoming of offering an apolitical explanation for a political phenomenon. According to him, the strong state–weak state dichotomy obscures the fact that policymakers in both strong and weak states confront an international environment in which choices are available and options have to be exercised, and where the internal dynamics of building ruling coalitions around chosen policies has impact on domestic arrangements such as democratic rules, minority protection, and human rights. An adequate state-centered theory therefore has to measure up to the fact that "some leeway of response to pressure is always possible, at least conceptually. The choice of response therefore requires explanation. Such an explanation necessarily entails an examination of politics: the struggle among competing responses."[63]

Dependence relations do extend beyond national boundaries and have impact on domestic relations. Theory ought to be able to allow examination of how domestic adversaries locked in a domestic contest for hegemony can draw power from such regional or global dependence relations. The power-dependence framework of Bacharach and Lawler makes this possible. In this study an account is given of how actors have used such power in the domestic contexts of South Africa, Botswana, and Zimbabwe, and how they responded to the constraints as well as opportunities presented by mutual dependence that is intertwined with regional and global grids of interdependence.

✤ Notes ✤

Preface

1. For discussion of this "third wave," see Samuel P. Huntington, *The Third Wave: Democratization in the Late Twentieth Century* (Norman, Okla.: University of Oklahoma Press, 1991), pp. 24, 25.

2. Jean-Francois Bayart, *The State in Africa: The Politics of the Belly* (New York: Longman, 1993), p. 65.

Introduction

1. Robert D. Kaplan, "The Coming Anarchy," *The Atlantic Monthly* 273, no. 2 (February 1994): 44–76 at 48.

2. Huntington, *Third Wave*, p. 6.

3. Donald L. Horowitz, *A Democratic South Africa? Constitutional Engineering in a Divided Society* (Berkeley, Calif.: University of California Press, 1991), p. 240, footnote 1.

4. Richard Rose, "Comparing Forms of Comparative Analysis," *Political Studies* 39 (1991): 446–462 at 447; Arend Lijphart, "Comparative Politics and the Comparative Method," *American Political Science Review* 65 (September 1971): 682–693 at 685.

5. Lijphart, "Comparative Politics and the Comparative Method," 685.

6. The Economist, *Pocket World in Figures* (London: Economist Books, 1993), pp. 18, 24, 65, 204.

7. Ibid., pp. 17, 26, 27.

8. Arend Lijphart, "The Comparable-Cases Strategy in Comparative Research," *Comparative Political Studies* 8, no. 2 (July 1975): 158–177 at 164.

9. Joel S. Migdal, *Strong Societies and Weak States: State-Society Relations and State Capabilities in the Third World* (Princeton, N.J.: Princeton University Press, 1988), p. 22.

10. Rose, "Comparing Forms of Comparative Analysis," p. 458.

11. Ibid.

12. A historical perspective on this trend of growing economic linkages within southern Africa is ably presented in Jesmond Blumenfeld, *Economic Interdependence in Southern Africa: From Conflict to Cooperation* (Cape Town: Oxford University Press, 1992).

13. Patrick McGowan, "The World Political Economy Today and Tomorrow: Character, Trends and Implications for Southern Africa," in Anthoni van Nieuwkerk and Gary van Staden, eds., *Southern Africa at the Crossroads: Prospects for the Political Economy of the Region* (Johannesburg: South African Institute of International Affairs, 1991), pp. 16–53 at 48, table 1.

14. Erich Leistner and Pieter Esterhuysen, eds., *South Africa in Southern Africa: Economic Interaction* (Pretoria: Africa Institute of South Africa, 1988), p. 264.

15. David Moorhead, "Trade and Trade Promotion," in Leistner and Esterhuysen, *South Africa in Southern Africa*, pp. 89–105 at 100, Table 2.

16. Gavin Maasdorp, "The Southern African Development Co-Ordination Conference (SADCC)," in Leistner and Esterhuysen, *South Africa in Southern Africa*, pp. 70–88 at 86, table 2.

17. McGowan, "The World Political Economy Today and Tomorrow," p. 49, table 2.

18. Simon Baynham, "The New World Order: Regional and International Implications for Southern Africa," *Africa Insight* 22, no. 2 (1992): 84–94.

19. For an extended explication of the intricacies of this analytical perspective, see the appendix.

1. Botswana: Constructing State and Society

1. Huntington, *Third Wave*, pp. 20, 21.

2. John D. Holm, "Botswana: A Paternalistic Democracy," in Larry Diamond et al., eds., *Democracy in Developing Countries*, vol. 2, *Africa* (Boulder, Colo.: Lynne Rienner, 1988), pp. 179–215.

3. Louis A. Picard, *The Politics of Development in Botswana: A Model for Success?* (Boulder, Colo.: Lynne Rienner, 1987), pp. 142, 146, 147.

4. Horowitz, *Democratic South Africa?* p. 270.

5. Stephen R. Lewis provides a recent example of such a claim in "Policymaking and Economic Performance: Botswana in Comparative Perspective," in Stephen John Stedman, ed., *Botswana: The Political Economy of Democratic Development* (Boulder, Colo.: Lynne Rienner, 1993), pp. 11–26 at 12–14.

6. Donald George Morrison et al., *Black Africa: A Comparative Handbook*, 2nd ed. (New York: Paragon House, 1989), p. 376.

7. Q. N. Parsons, "The Evolution of Modern Botswana: Historical Revisions," in Louis A. Picard, ed., *The Evolution of Modern Botswana* (London: Rex Collings, 1985), pp. 26–39 at 27–28.

8. Morrison, *Black Africa*, p. 516.

9. N. J. Van Warmelo, "Grouping and Ethnic History," in I. Schapera, ed., *The Bantu-Speaking Tribes of South Africa: An Ethnographical Survey* (London: Routledge & Kegan Paul, 1937), pp. 43–66.

10. Lawrence Frank, "Khama and Jonathan: Leadership Strategies in Contemporary Southern Africa," *Journal of the Developing Areas* 15, no. 2 (January 1981): 173–198.

11. *Difaqane* is a Nguni word for "forced migration." See Monica Wilson and Leonard Thompson, *The Oxford History of South Africa*, vol. 1, *South Africa to 1870* (Oxford: Oxford University Press, 1969), p. 391.

12. J. D. Omer-Cooper, *The Zulu Aftermath: A Nineteenth-Century Revolution in Bantu Africa* (Evanston, Ill.: Northwestern University Press, 1966), pp. 4, 174.

13. Omer-Cooper, *Zulu Aftermath*, pp. 115–155; Wilson and Thompson, *Oxford History of South Africa*, pp. 391–405. A detailed analysis of the impact of the Mfecane is also found in Thomas Tlou and Alec Campbell, *History of Botswana* (Gaborone: Macmillan Botswana, 1984), pp. 101–110.

14. Numerous variations in the spelling of the names of these tribes appear throughout the literature. Wherever possible, this text follows the examples found in the Constitution of Botswana, paragraph 78.

15. Omer-Cooper, *Zulu Aftermath*, p. 141.

16. Ibid., p. 171.

17. This has been singled out as a causal factor in the evolution of the Bamangwato Kingdom by Q. N. Parsons, "The Economic History of Khama's Country in Southern Africa," *African Social Research*, no. 18 (December 1974): 643–675 at 648, 649.

18. Kenneth Good, "Interpreting the Exceptionality of Botswana," *Journal of Modern African Studies* 30, no. 1 (1992): 69–95 at 80–84; Robert K. Hitchcock, "Water, Land and Livestock: The Evolution of Tenure and Administration Patterns in the Grazing Areas of Botswana," in Picard, *Evolution of Modern Botswana*, pp. 84–121 at 91; Adam Kuper, *Kalahari Village Politics: An African Democracy* (Cambridge: Cambridge University Press, 1970), pp. 104, 105; Edwin N. Wilmsen and Rainer Vossen, "Labour, Language and Power in the Construction of Ethnicity in Botswana," *Critique of Anthropology* 10, no. 1 (summer 1990): 7–37 at 17–21.

19. T. Tlou, "The Nature of Batswana States: Towards a Theory of Batswana Traditional Government—The Batawana Case," *Botswana Notes and Records* 6 (1974): 57–75 at 59, 67. See also the many works on this topic by Isaac Schapera, especially "The Political Organization of the Ngwato of Bechuanaland Protectorate," in M. Fortes and E. E. Evans-Pritchard, eds., *African Political Systems* (London: Oxford University Press, 1940), pp. 56–82; "Political Institutions," in I. Schapera, ed., *Bantu-Speaking Tribes of South Africa*, pp. 173–219; *A Handbook of Tswana Law and Custom* (London: Frank Cass, 1970); and "The Social Structure of the Tswana Ward," *African Studies* 31, no. 2 (1972): 91–109.

20. Louis A. Picard, *Politics of Development in Botswana*, pp. 25–31; P. Maylam, *Rhodes, the Tswana, and the British: Colonialism, Collaboration, and Conflict in the Bechuanaland Protectorate, 1885–1899* (London: Greenwood Press, 1980); A. J. G. M. Sanders, "Chieftainship and Western Democracy in Botswana," *Journal of Contemporary African Studies* 2, no. 2 (1983): 365–379 at 368, 369; Richard P. Stevens, *Lesotho, Botswana, and Swaziland: The Former High Commission Territories in Southern Africa* (London: Pall Mall Press, 1967), pp. 115–124.

21. Parsons, "Evolution of Modern Botswana," pp. 30, 31.

22. Ian Brownlie, *African Boundaries: A Legal and Diplomatic Encyclopaedia* (London: C. Hurst and Co., 1979), pp. 1073–1075, 1081–1084, 1091–1093, 1099–1107. These borders have not been hotly disputed and have been a source of differing interpretation almost only with reference to the Botswana/Zambia border on the Zambezi river. See ibid., pp. 1099–1107, and Christopher R. Hill, "The Botswana-Zambia Boundary Question: A Note of Warning," *The Round Table*, no. 252 (October 1973): 535–541.

23. Jack Parson, *Botswana: Liberal Democracy and the Labor Reserve in Southern Africa* (Boulder, Colo.: Westview Press, 1984), pp. 4, 6; Picard, *Politics of Development in Botswana*, pp. 7, 8.

24. Picard, *Politics of Development in Botswana*, pp. 39, 40; Parsons, "Evolution of Modern Botswana," pp. 34–36.

25. Sanders, "Chieftainship and Western Democracy in Botswana," p. 369.

26. Picard, *Politics of Development in Botswana*, p. 36.

27. Ibid., p. 38. In the terms of Rene Lemarchand, the chiefs moved away from a system of patrimonial clientelism and closer to a system of repressive clientelism. See Rene Lemarchand, "Comparative Political Clientelism: Structure and Optic," in Rene Lemarchand and S. N. Eisenstadt, eds., *Political Clientelism, Patronage and Development* (London: Sage, 1981), pp. 7–32.

28. Picard, *Politics of Development in Botswana*, pp. 64–66.

29. Ibid., p. 85.

30. Ibid., p. 91.

31. Gilfred Leroy Gunderson, "Nation-Building and the Administrative State: The Case of Botswana" (Ph.D. diss., University of California, 1970), pp. 96–120.

32. Mike Sill, "Sustaining a Success Story," *Geographical Magazine* (February 1993): 37–42 at 37.

33. Christopher Colclough and Stephen McCarthy, *The Political Economy of Botswana: A Study of Growth and Distribution* (Oxford: Oxford University Press, 1980), pp. 207–208.

34. Sill, "Sustaining a Success Story," p. 37.

35. Parson, *Liberal Democracy and the Labor Reserve in Southern Africa*, pp. 23–24; Picard, *Politics of Development in Botswana*, p. 110.

36. I. Schapera, *Migrant Labour and Tribal Life: A Study of Conditions in the Bechuanaland Protectorate* (Cape Town: Oxford University Press, 1947), p. 32.

37. Colclough and McCarthy, *Political Economy of Botswana*, p. 171.

38. Picard, *Politics of Development in Botswana*, p. 103.

39. World Bank, *World Development Report 1991* (New York: Oxford University Press, 1991), pp. 259, 261.

40. Picard, *Politics of Development in Botswana*, p. 85.

41. Simon Gillet, "The Survival of Chieftaincy in Botswana," *Botswana Notes and Records* 7 (1975): 103–108; David S. Jones, "Traditional Authority and State Administration in Botswana," *Journal of Modern African Studies* 21, no. 1 (1983): 133–139; Sanders, "Chieftainship and Western Democracy in Botswana," pp. 365–379; William Tordoff, "Local Administration in Botswana," part 1, *Journal of Administration Overseas* 12, no. 6 (October 1973): 172–183.

42. Marlies Bouman, "A Note on Chiefly and National Policing in Botswana," *Journal of Legal Pluralism*, nos. 25–26 (1987): 275–300 at 278, 279.

43. Holm, "Paternalistic Democracy," p. 214, footnote 89. James Polhemus also notes that tribal boundaries carried considerable weight in the first delimitation of electoral districts for the 1965 election. See James Polhemus, "Botswana Votes: Parties and Elections in an African Democracy," *Journal of Modern African Studies* 21, no. 3 (1983): 397–430 at 410.

44. Constitution of Botswana (Gaborone: Government Printer, n.d.), chapters IV, V, and VI; Holm, "Paternalistic Democracy," pp. 186, 187; Parson, *Liberal Democracy and the Labor Reserve*, pp. 38–41; Picard, *Politics of Development in Botswana*, pp. 146, 147.

45. Constitution of Botswana, chapter V, part III; J. H. Proctor, "The House of Chiefs and the Political Development of Botswana," *Journal of Modern African Studies* 6, no. 1 (May 1968): 59–79.

46. Motsamai Keyecwe Mpho, "Representation of Cultural Minorities in Policy Making," in John Holm and Patrick Molutsi, eds., *Democracy in Botswana: The Proceedings of a Symposium Held in Gaborone, 1–5 August 1988* (Athens, Ohio: Ohio University Press, 1989), pp. 133–138.

47. This aspect of the political system of Botswana has been densely researched over the more than 25 years since independence. Some of the more relevant publications are by John D. Holm, "Rural Development in Botswana: Three Basic Political Trends," *Rural Africana*, no. 18 (fall 1972): 80–92; James Leach, "Managing Rural Development in Botswana," *Public Administration and Development* 1 (1981): 265–270; Louis A. Picard, "Rural Development in Botswana: Administrative Structures and Public Policy," *Journal of Developing Areas* 13 (April 1979): 283–300; Louis A. Picard, "District Councils in Botswana: A Remnant of Local Autonomy," *Journal of Modern African Studies* 71, no. 2 (1979): 285–308; Louis A. Picard, "Independent Botswana: The District Administration and Political Control," *Journal of African Studies* 8, no. 3 (fall 1981): 98–110; Louis A. Picard, "Bureaucrats, Elections and Political Control: National Politics, the District Administration and the Multi-Party System in Botswana," in Picard, *Evolution of Modern Botswana*, pp. 176–205; Picard, *Politics of Development in Botswana*, pp. 177–201; William Tordoff, "Local Administration in Botswana," part 1, *Journal of Administration Overseas* 12, no. 6 (October 1973): 172–183; William Tordoff, "Local Administration in Botswana," part 2, *Journal of Administration Overseas* 13, no. 1 (1974): 293–304; Richard Vengroff, *Botswana: Rural Development in the Shadow of Apartheid* (London: Associated University Presses, 1977); Richard Vengroff, "Networks and Leadership in a Development Institution: The District Council in Botswana," *Political Anthropology* 1 (1975): 155–174.

48. Colclough and McCarthy, *Political Economy of Botswana*, p. 210.

49. Ibid.

50. Nimrod Raphaeli et al., *Public Sector Management in Botswana: Lessons in Pragmatism* (Washington, D.C.: World Bank, 1984), pp. 43, 44.

51. Colclough and McCarthy, *Political Economy of Botswana*, p. 210.

52. Raphaeli et al., *Public Sector Management in Botswana*, pp. 43, 44.

53. Frank, "Khama and Jonathan," pp. 173–198.

54. Picard, *Politics of Development in Botswana*, pp. 177–202; Holm, "Paternalistic Democracy," pp. 179–215; Holm, "Rural Development in Botswana," pp. 83–85; Louis A. Picard and Philip E. Morgan, "Policy Implementation and Local Institutions in Botswana," in Picard, *Evolution of Modern Botswana*, pp. 125–155.

55. For the full set of election returns for national parliamentary elections from 1965 to 1989, see Mpho G. Molomo, "The Political Process: Does Multi-Partyism Persist Due to the Lack of a Strong Opposition?" *Southern African Political and Economic Monthly* (May 1990): 5–9 at 6.

For a general analysis of parties and elections at both local and national levels through 1969, see Vengroff, *Botswana: Rural Development in the Shadow of Apartheid*, pp. 77–121; for 1979 at the national level, see Polhemus, "Botswana Votes," pp. 397–430; for 1984 at the national level, see Picard, *Politics of Development in Botswana*, pp. 151–174. For an analysis of the 1989 election, see Jack Parson, "Liberal Democracy, the Liberal State, and the 1989 General Elections in Botswana," in Stedman, *Political Economy of Democratic Development*, pp. 65–90.

56. A recent example of such a claim being made is by L. E. Serema, a lawyer and a member of the BDP. See L. E. Serema, "Elections and Democracy: How Democratic is the Process?" in Holm and Molutsi, *Democracy in Botswana*, pp. 177–181 at 177.

57. This has been remarked upon by John D. Holm, "Elections in Botswana: Institutionalization of a New System of Legitimacy," in Fred M. Hayward, ed., *Elections in Independent Africa* (Boulder, Colo.: Westview Press, 1987), pp. 121–147 at 132, 133; Holm, "Paternalistic Democracy," p. 190; R. Nengwekhulu, "Some Findings on the Origins of Political Parties in Botswana," *PULA* 1, no. 2 (1979): 47–75 at 74, 75; Polhemus, "Botswana Votes," pp. 402–406.

58. Polhemus, "Botswana Votes," pp. 402, 405.

59. Parson, "1989 General Elections," p. 77.

60. See (for example) Holm, "Elections in Botswana," p. 133.

61. This matter has been the subject of some debate. See John A. Wiseman, "Multi-Partyism in Africa: The Case of Botswana," *African Affairs* 76, no. 302 (January 1977): 70–79; Christopher Stevens and John Speed, "Multi-Partyism in Africa: The Case of Botswana Revisited," *African Affairs* 76, no. 304 (July 1977): 381–387; John A. Wiseman, "Multi-Partyism in Botswana: A Reply to a Rejoinder," *African Affairs* 77, no. 306 (January 1978): 149–150. Also relevant is John A. Wiseman, "Conflict and Conflict Alliances in the Kgatleng District of Botswana," *Journal of Modern African Studies* 16, no. 3 (September 1978): 487–494.

62. Picard, *Politics of Development in Botswana*, pp. 155–159; Wiseman, "Conflict and Conflict Alliances," pp. 487–494.

63. Holm, "Paternalistic Democracy," p. 191.

64. The absence of a class-based line of cleavage being represented in Botswana party politics through to the 1984 elections has been noted by, among others: Holm, "Elections in Botswana," pp. 138–140; and "Paternalistic Democracy," pp. 190–193. In the 1989 election the BNF again failed to consolidate such a constituency, according to Parson, "1989 General Elections in Botswana," pp. 77–79.

65. Frank, "Khama and Jonathan," pp. 187–198. Various authors have labeled the BDP's development priorities "technocratic." See Parson, "1989 General Elections," p. 77; John Stephen Morrison, "Botswana's Formative Late Colonial Experiences," in Stedman, *Political Economy of*

Democratic Development, pp. 27–49 at 45, 46; Picard, *Politics of Development in Botswana*, p. 264.

66. John Stephen Morrison, "Developmental Optimism and State Failure in Africa: How to Understand Botswana's Relative Success?" (Ph.D. diss., University of Wisconsin-Madison, 1987), pp. 567–573.

67. The figures for the 1971 census are taken from Europa Publications, *Africa South of the Sahara, 1993* (London: Europa Publications, 1993), p. 170; for the 1981 census from Brian Hunter, ed., *The Statesman's Yearbook: Statistical and Historical Annual of the States of the World for the year 1992–1993* (New York: St. Martin's Press, 1992), p. 224; and for 1991 from Parson, "1989 General Elections," p. 88, footnote 14.

68. Hunter, *Statesman's Yearbook*, p. 224.

69. Picard, *Politics of Development in Botswana*, p. 4.

70. Colclough and McCarthy, *Political Economy of Botswana*, p. 179.

71. Parson, "1989 General Elections," p. 70.

72. The figures for the size of Gaborone are taken from Graeme J. Hardie, "Informal Housing in Botswana: The Mobilization of Self-Help in the Provision of Housing," in D. J. Willers, ed., *Aspects of Black Housing in South Africa* (Johannesburg: South Africa Foundation, 1981), pp. 61–71 at 64; and from Parson, "1989 General Elections," p. 88, footnote 14. Assessments of the comparative growth rate of Gaborone are made by Morrison, "Developmental Optimism and State Failure in Africa," p. 482; and John van Nostrand, "Old Naledi and the Idea of Town: Strategies for Urban Upgrading from Botswana," *African Urban Quarterly* 2, no. 4 (November 1987): 444–451 at 445.

73. World Bank, *World Development Report 1991*, p. 207.

74. *Africa South of the Sahara, 1993*, p. 167.

75. Stephen John Stedman, "Introduction," in Stedman, *Political Economy of Democratic Development*, p. 1.

76. World Bank, *World Development Report 1991*, p. 207.

77. *Africa South of the Sahara, 1993*, pp. 166–167.

78. Ibid., p. 169; Colclough and McCarthy, *Political Economy of Botswana*, p. 177.

79. Figures about the annual increase in the labor market differ substantially. Colclough and McCarthy (*Political Economy of Botswana*, p. 17) report an increase of between 5,000 and 6,000 per year from 1968 to 1977. In *Africa South of the Sahara, 1993*, a figure of 20,000 is presented. However, both sources agree on the inability of formal sector growth to offer employment for all the new job seekers.

80. *Africa South of the Sahara, 1993*, p. 169; Picard, *Politics of Development in Botswana*, p. 234.

81. *Africa South of the Sahara, 1993*, p. 169.

82. Louis A. Picard, "Bureaucrats, Cattle, and Public Policy: Land Tenure Changes in Botswana," *Comparative Political Studies* 13, no. 3 (October 1980): 313–356 at 321, 322.

83. Rodger Yeager, "Democratic Pluralism and Ecological Crisis in Botswana," *Journal of Developing Areas* 23 (April 1989): 385–404 at 388.

84. Robert K. Hitchcock, "Water, Land and Livestock: The Evolution of Tenure and Administration Patterns in the Grazing Areas of Botswana," in Picard, *Evolution of Modern Botswana,* pp. 84–121.

85. Jack Parson, "Cattle, Class and the State in Rural Botswana," *Journal of Southern African Studies* 7, no. 2 (April 1981): 236–255; Isaac N. Mazonde, "The Inter-relationship between Cattle and Politics in Botswana's Economy," in Jeffrey C. Stone, ed., *The Exploitation of Animals in Africa* (Aberdeen: Aberdeen University African Studies Group, 1988), pp. 345–356.

86. Barbara Watanabe and Eva Mueller, "A Poverty Profile for Rural Botswana," *World Development* 12, no. 2 (1984): 115–127.

87. Colclough and McCarthy, *Political Economy of Botswana,* pp. 135, 137.

88. Ibid., pp. 112, 127–129, 191; Picard, "Rural Development in Botswana," p. 294; Parson, "Cattle, Class and the State," p. 236. Similar results from a different source are reported in Robert L. Curry, Jr., "Mineral-Based Growth and Development-Generated Socioeconomic Problems in Botswana: Rural Inequality, Water Scarcity, Food Insecurity, and Foreign Dependence Challenge New Governing Class," *American Journal of Economics and Sociology* 44, no. 3 (July 1985): 319–336; and Robert L. Curry, Jr., "Poverty and Mass Unemployment in Mineral-Rich Botswana," *American Journal of Economics and Sociology* 46, no. 1 (January 1987): 71–87.

89. The data from the agricultural survey are reported by H. A. Fosbrooke, "Land and Population," *Botswana Notes and Records* 3 (1971): 172–187 at 176. Claims of increasing inequalities of cattle ownership are made by Colclough and McCarthy, *Political Economy of Botswana,* p. 113.

90. Parson reports data from the official publication *The Household Income and Expenditure Survey: 1985/86,* which indicates a wide disparity in the incomes of rural and urban households. See Parson, "1989 General Elections," p. 71.

91. Parson, "1989 General Elections," p. 84.

92. World Bank, *World Development Report 1991,* p. 263.

93. Fred Pearce, "Enclosing for Beef," *The Ecologist* 23, no. 1 (January/February 1993): 25–29 at 26.

94. World Bank, *World Development Report 1991,* pp. 259, 261.

95. Morrison, "Botswana's Formative Late Colonial Experiences," p. 43.

96. Picard, *Politics of Development in Botswana,* p. 147.

2. Botswana: The Dynamics of State-Society Interaction

1. This brief checklist is taken from a number of sources. See Robert A. Dahl, *Polyarchy: Participation and Opposition* (New Haven, Conn.: Yale University Press, 1971); Samuel P. Huntington, "Will More Countries Become Democratic?" *Political Science Quarterly* 99, no. 2 (summer 1984); Huntington, *Third Wave*, especially chapter 2.

2. Huntington, "Will More Countries Become Democratic?" p. 209.

3. Picard, *Politics of Development in Botswana*; Morrison, "Developmental Optimism and State Failure in Africa."

4. Migdal, *Strong Societies and Weak States*, p. 4, footnote 3.

5. One authoritative source has in its section on Botswana but a single sentence under the heading of "Law Enforcement," which reads: "No information is available on the incidence or nature of crime in the country." See George Thomas Kurian, ed., *Encyclopedia of the Third World*, 4th ed., vol. 1 (New York: Facts on File, 1992), p. 215. Reluctance by official sources to make data available can therefore contribute to this state of affairs.

6. Holm, "Paternalistic Democracy," 179–216 at 213, footnote 64. Allegations of electoral fraud were made by the Botswana People's Party against the BDP in the 1974 as well as the 1979 elections. For a discussion and evaluation thereof, see Polhemus, "Botswana Votes," pp. 420, 421. In the 1989 election the BNF raised this objection again. See Parson, "1989 General Elections in Botswana," 80, 81, and 87 (footnote 3).

7. "Why the Vice President Resigned," *New African* (May 1992), p. 19.

8. An example of such interbureaucratic rivalry between three departments is discussed by Picard, *Politics of Development in Botswana*, chapter 8, pp. 177–201.

9. The only relevant data on potential urban-based strongmen I could find are reported by Graeme J. Hardie. In his analysis of the housing development in the Old Naledi shantytown in Gaborone in the 1970s, he briefly mentions the emergence of an informal power structure of senior men who in 1970 established some form of rule in the shantytown. They addressed the immediate problems of access to water and instituted an informal tribunal and court similar to the customary *kgotla*. When their upgrading scheme got under way in Old Naledi, they were quickly drawn into the ambit of the Gaborone Town Council in the form of a village planning committee. No evidence is presented of this group, especially their leader, being able to extract any concessions in return that exceeded the boundaries of legality. See Graeme J. Hardie, "Informal Housing in Botswana: The Mobilization of Self-Help in the Provision of Housing," in D. J. Willers, ed., *Aspects of Black Housing in South Africa* (Johannesburg: South Africa Foundation, 1981), pp. 61–71 at 65, 66.

10. Consider, for example, the rating Botswana has received in Raymond D. Gastil, *Freedom in the World: Political Rights and Civil Liberties*

1988–1989 (New York: Freedom House, 1989), pp. 355–356. On the political rights rating scale of 1 (high) to 7 (low), the country is rated at 2. On the identical 7-point rating scale for civil liberties it is rated at 3. This adds up to an overall freedom rating of 5 on a scale of 2 to 14 and places Botswana within the top bracket (1–5) of countries with a "high" overall rating.

11. Picard, *Politics of Development in Botswana*, p. 51.

12. Ibid., p. 63.

13. Ibid.

14. Ibid., pp. 155–157; Wiseman, "Conflict and Conflict Alliances." He later returned to Mochudi and, in his capacity as chief, continued to wield considerable influence within the district. See Sandy Grant, "'Reduced Almost to Nothing'? Chieftaincy and a Traditional Town. The Case of Linchwe II Kgafela and Mochudi," *Botswana Notes and Records* 12 (1980): 89–100.

15. Picard, *Politics of Development in Botswana*, p. 201, footnote 35.

16. Ibid., pp. 153, 154, 168, and 176 (footnote 53).

17. Gillet, "Survival of Chieftaincy in Botswana," p. 107; Morrison, "Developmental Optimism and State Failure in Africa," pp. 295, 296, 381.

18. Bouman, "Chiefly and National Policing," pp. 281, 284.

19. Morrison, "Developmental Optimism and State Failure in Africa," pp. 381–384.

20. Margo and Martin Russell, *Afrikaners of the Kalahari: White Minority in a Black State* (Cambridge: Cambridge University Press, 1979), p. 137.

21. R. Nengwekhulu, "Some Findings on the Origins of Political Parties in Botswana," *PULA*, 1, no. 2 (1979): 47–76 at 59. See also Polhemus, "Botswana Votes," for a discussion of the emergence of the BPP.

22. Colclough and McCarthy, *Political Economy of Botswana*, pp. 231–234.

23. Holm, "Elections in Botswana," p. 135.

24. Molomo, "Political Process," p. 242.

25. Colclough and McCarthy, *Political Economy of Botswana*, p. 234.

26. Europa Publications, *Africa South of the Sahara, 1971* (London: Europa Publications, 1971), p. 159; Hunter, *Statesman's Yearbook*, p. 227.

27. Andre Wilsenach, "The Provision of Urban Housing in Botswana, Lesotho and Swaziland: Policy and Strategy since Independence," *Africa Insight* 19, no. 2 (1989): 82–87; Colclough and McCarthy, *Political Economy of Botswana*, pp. 226–230.

28. Anita Larson, "Old Naledi: The Integration of an Upgraded Area into the Capital City of Botswana," *African Urban Quarterly* 2, no. 3 (August 1987): 311–319; John van Nostrand, "Old Naledi and the Idea of

Town; Strategies for Urban Upgrading from Botswana," *African Urban Quarterly* 2, no. 4 (November 1987): 444–452; Wilsenach, "Urban Housing in Botswana," pp. 85, 86.

29. Richard Morgan, "The Development and Application of a Drought Early Warning System in Botswana," *Disasters* 9, no. 1 (1985): 44–50 at 44, 45; Richard Morgan, "From Drought Relief to Post-Disaster Recovery: The Case of Botswana," *Disasters* 10, no. 1 (1986): 30–34 at 30, 31.

30. Roger W. Hay, "Famine Incomes and Employment: Has Botswana Anything to Teach Africa?" *World Development* 16, no. 9 (1988): 1113–1125 at 1115–1117. Similarly favorable assessments of the impact of the drought relief program are made by John Borton and Edward Clay, "The African Food Crisis of 1982–1986," *Disasters* 10, no. 4 (1986): 258–272 at 267; Curry, "Mineral-Based Growth and Development-Generated Socioeconomic Problems," p. 329; John D. Holm and Mark S. Cohen, "Enhancing Equity in the Midst of Drought: The Botswana Approach," *Ceres* 19, no. 6 (1986): 20–24; and John D. Holm and Richard G. Morgan, "Coping with Drought in Botswana: An African Success," *Journal of Modern African Studies* 23, no. 3 (September 1985): 463–482 at 466–469.

31. Morgan, "From Drought Relief to Post-Disaster Recovery," p. 33. This conclusion is shared by Ray Bush, "Drought and Famines," *Review of African Political Economy*, no. 33 (August 1985): 59–63; as well as by Hay, "Famine Incomes and Employment," pp. 1122–1125.

32. Holm and Morgan, "Coping with Drought in Botswana," p. 476; Morgan, "From Drought Relief to Post-Disaster Recovery," p. 33.

33. Morrison, "Developmental Optimism and State Failure in Africa," p. 360.

34. The overall aim of the BDP with the TGLP was to create more commercial cattle ranches. By the 1980s only about 150 of these ranches had been established after all interested parties had been consulted with great care. Even then the new ranches resembled the old cattle posts they were supposed to replace (Holm, "Elections in Botswana," p. 134).

35. Migdal, *Strong Societies and Weak States*, p. 274.

36. Quoted in Picard, *Politics of Development in Botswana*, p. 205.

37. Ibid., p. 209.

38. Picard, "Land Tenure Changes in Botswana."

39. The assessment of the technical contribution is made by Raphaeli et al., *Public Sector Management in Botswana*, p. 52. The presence as well as influence of the expatriate social justice movement (inside and outside the civil service) has been noted by John D. Holm, "The State, Social Class and Rural Development in Botswana," in Picard, *Evolution of Modern Botswana*, pp. 157–175 at 168–174.

40. The 1982 Citizenship Act, as amended in 1984, contains a number of provisions that strengthen the gelded condition of aliens such as expatriate employees. This act abolished the acquisition of citizenship by birth only and added that a person born in the country must also qualify by descent to become a citizen. Children of Batswana women who marry noncitizens are excluded from gaining citizenship in this way. Nor do these alien husbands of Batswana female citizens gain any special rights of residence or citizenship. Foreigners have to complete a 10-year term of residence and may still be deprived of citizenship on the basis of a number of grounds. See Athaliah Molokomme, "Political Rights in Botswana: Regression or Development?" in Holm and Molutsi, *Democracy in Botswana*, pp. 163–174 at 164, 165.

41. John D. Holm and Patrick P. Molutsi, "State-Society Relations in Botswana: Beginning Liberalization," in Goran Hyden and Michael Bratton, eds., *Governance and Politics in Africa* (Boulder, Colo.: Lynne Rienner, 1992), pp. 75–95 at 88.

42. This is of course not a perfect fit. If it were, then an immediate merger of the different legal systems without any modification of either would be possible. Nonetheless, they can and do coexist. It has also been noted that a tendency is developing for the customary law to adapt to the dominant legal system. Both these points are argued by A. J. G. M. Sanders, "The Internal Conflict of Laws in Botswana," *Botswana Notes and Records* 17 (1985): 77–88 at 84. Another analyst has gone so far as to depict the relationship as a "symbiotic" one in a process of "mutual adaptation." The practical effect of this closeness is that individuals can and do choose freely which legal system to use, depending on which one is the more "responsive" to their particular circumstances. These are the findings made by Anne Griffiths—see her "Legal Duality: Conflict or Concord in Botswana," *Journal of African Law* 27, no. 2 (1983): 150–161; and "Support for Women with Dependent Children under the Customary System of the Bakwena and the Roman-Dutch Common and Statutory Law of Botswana," *Journal of Legal Pluralism* 22 (1984): 1–15.

43. Indicative of the reach of these courts is the estimate from one source that there may be as many as 400 to 1,000 *lekgotla* operating as informal courts in Botswana. This is the calculation made by Malcolm J. Odell, Jr., "Local Government: Traditional and Modern Roles of the Village Kgotla," in Picard, *Evolution of Modern Botswana*, pp. 61–83 at 71. The institutional depth of these courts can be gauged by the fact that in the early 1960s the judicial population served per customary court in Botswana was stated to be as low as 3,400. See Richard L. Abel, "Western Courts in Non-Western Settings: Patterns of Court Use in Colonial and Neo-Colonial Africa," in Sandra B. Burman and Barbara E. Harrel-Bond, eds., *The Imposition of Law* (New York: Academic Press, 1979), pp. 167–200 at 179, table 10.3.

44. Hitchcock, "Water, Land and Livestock," p. 108.

45. This can probably explain in part, the extent of acquiescence among Batswana with the TGLP, despite the all-around condemnation it received in the academic literature. Had the populace shared these sentiments, outright revolt could have been expected.

46. Colclough and McCarthy, *Political Economy of Botswana*, p. 118. A similar bureaucratic process accompanies the establishment of so-called borehole syndicates. See Pauline E. Peters, "The Ideology and Practice of Tswana Borehole Syndicates: Co-Operative or Corporation?" in D. W. Attwood and B. S. Baviskar, eds., *Who Shares? Co-operatives and Rural Development* (Delhi: Oxford University Press, 1988), pp. 23–45.

47. Van Nostrand, "Old Naledi and the Idea of Town," p. 449.

48. Constitution of Botswana, p. 41, paragraph 62. In the early years of independence this exclusion created some substantial resentment among public servants and teachers. See John D. Holm, "Rural Development in Botswana: Three Basic Trends," *Rural Africana*, no. 18 (fall 1972): 88.

49. Holm, "Paternalistic Democracy," p. 193.

50. Patrick P. Molutsi and John D. Holm, "Developing Democracy When Civil Society Is Weak: The Case of Botswana," *African Affairs* 89, no. 356 (July 1990): 323–340 at 328. In an earlier article Holm claimed that "two-thirds of the wage earning population is employed by the government." See Holm, "Elections in Botswana," p. 126. My calculations tally with the lower estimate.

51. See note 14, this chapter.

52. Holm, "Paternalistic Democracy," p. 214, footnote 82.

53. Holm, "Elections in Botswana," p. 126.

54. John D. Holm, "Elections and Democracy in Botswana," in Holm and Molutsi, *Democracy in Botswana*, pp. 189–202; M. T. Motswagole, "Elections and Democracy in Botswana," in Holm and Molutsi, *Democracy in Botswana*, pp. 183–189; Polhemus, "Botswana Votes," pp. 409–414.

55. Bouman, "Chiefly and National Policing," pp. 285, 286; Holm, "Paternalistic Democracy," p. 194; Molokomme, "Political Rights in Botswana," pp. 165–167.

56. Morrison, "Developmental Optimism and State Failure in Africa," p. 164. A compact summary of Morrison's thesis is also presented in Morrison, "Botswana's Formative Late Colonial Experiences," in Stedman, *Political Economy of Democratic Development*, pp. 27–50.

57. Morrison, "Developmental Optimism and State Failure in Africa," pp. 342.

58. Ibid., p. 263.

59. Ibid., p. 309, original emphasis.

60. Ibid., p. 255.

61. Ibid., pp. 483–490. This rule change was initiated by the need to bail out the insolvent cooperatives, but it also became the rationale for the extensive drought aid programs the state launched in the mid-1980s.

62. Bouman, "Chiefly and National Policing in Botswana," p. 290.

63. Morag Bell, "Modern Sector Employment and Urban Social Change: A Case Study from Gaborone, Botswana," *Canadian Journal of African Studies* 15, no. 2 (1981): 259–276.

64. Larson, "Old Naledi," p. 314.

65. See note 9, this chapter.

66. These two propositions appear throughout his work but are fully and explicitly made in Parson, *Liberal Democracy and the Labor Reserve*, especially at pp. x, 13; as well as in Jack Parson, "The Peasantariat, Politics, and Democracy in Botswana," in Robin Cohen and Harry Goulbourne, eds., *Democracy and Socialism in Africa* (Boulder, Colo.: Westview Press, 1991), pp. 180–198 at 188, 189. The inability of redistributive policies to change this structure of society is noted in Parson, "1989 General Elections," p. 85.

67. Jack Parson, "The Peasantariat and Politics: Migration, Wage Labor, and Agriculture in Botswana," *Africa Today* 31 (4th quarter, 1984): 5–25 at 17.

68. Parson, "Cattle, Class and the State," p. 241.

69. Ibid., p. 254; Jack Parson, "The Trajectory of Class and State in Dependent Development: The Consequences of New Wealth for Botswana," *Journal of Commonwealth and Comparative Politics* 21, no. 3 (November 1983): 39–60 at 53; Parson, "Peasantariat and Politics," p. 23; Parson, "1989 General Elections," p. 76.

70. Parson, "Cattle, Class and the State," p. 255; Parson, *Liberal Democracy and the Labor Reserve*, p. 118; Parson, "1989 General Elections," pp. 78–79. This prediction is shared by Lionel Cliffe and Richard Moorsom, "Rural Class Formation and Ecological Collapse in Botswana," *Review of African Political Economy*, nos. 13–16 (May/December 1979): 35–52 at 51; and by Edwin N. Wilmsen and Rainer Vossen, "Labour, Language and Power in the Construction of Ethnicity in Botswana," *Critique of Anthropology* 10, no. 1 (summer 1990): 7–37 at 25.

71. Morrison, "Developmental Optimism and State Failure in Africa," p. 566.

72. Ibid., p. 160.

73. Parson, *Liberal Democracy and the Labor Reserve*, pp. 52–54.

74. "This mediation of class through the politics of tradition was important to peasantariat political life" (Parson, "1989 General Elections in Botswana," p. 76).

75. See chapter 1, note 64.

76. John D. Holm, "Political Culture and Democracy: A Study of Mass Participation in Botswana," in Stedman, *Political Economy of Democratic Development*, pp. 91–112 at 103, 104.

77. *Africa South of the Sahara, 1993*, pp. 175–178.

78. For an analysis of the precarious position of the press as a site of opposition to state and regime, for instance, see Sandy Grant and Brian Egner, "The Private Press and Democracy," in Holm and Molutsi, *Democracy in Botswana*, pp. 247–256; and James J. Zaffiro, "Regional Pressure and the Erosion of Media Freedom in an African Democracy: The Case of Botswana," *Journal of Communication* 38, no. 3 (summer 1988): 108–120.

79. This survey was conducted in the late 1980s. The then three organizations that had permanent offices were the Botswana Employers Federation (BEF), the Botswana Federation of Trade Unions (BFTU), and the Kalahari Conservation Society (KCS), as reported in John D. Holm, "How Effective Are Interest Groups in Representing Their Members?" in Holm and Molutsi, *Democracy in Botswana*, pp. 142–155 at 149. The KCS and the BEF were the only two effective lobbyists, according to Molutsi and Holm, "Developing Democracy When Civil Society Is Weak," p. 331.

80. Holm, "Political Culture and Democracy," p. 105; Molutsi and Holm, "Developing Democracy When Civil Society Is Weak," p. 330; Holm and Molutsi, "State-Society Relations in Botswana," pp. 85–86.

81. I. Schapera, *A Handbook of Tswana Law and Custom* (London: Frank Cass, 1970), p. 46.

82. I. Schapera, "The Work of Tribal Courts in the Bechuanaland Protectorate," *African Studies* 2 (1943): 27–40. The cases were drawn from written records for the Bangwaketse for 1910–16, 1928–30, 1932, 1934, and 1936–40; the Bakgatla for 1935–39; the Bakwena for 1935–38; the Bamangwato for 1937–38; and the Batawana for 1935–39.

83. Adam Kuper, *Kalahari Village Politics: An African Democracy* (Cambridge: Cambridge University Press, 1970), especially pp. 93–109 at 101. See also Adam Kuper, "The Work of Customary Courts: Some Facts and Speculations," *African Studies* 28, no. 1 (1969): 37–48.

84. Simon Roberts, "The Survival of the Traditional Tswana Courts in the National Legal System of Botswana," *Journal of African Law* 16, no. 2 (summer 1972): 103–129. Additional but not directly comparable data on the types of cases brought before *kgotla* courts in the Kweneng district are found in Richard Vengroff, "Traditional Political Structures in the Contemporary Context: The Chieftaincy in the Kweneng," *African Studies* 34, no. 1 (1975): 39–56 at 49–51.

85. The substance of what constitutes moral dignity and, hence, civil standards is culture bound. The traditional status of women in Tswana culture, for instance, would hardly be accepted within the prevailing Anglo-European conception of a civilized society. The further implication, not to be pursued here, is that to change the status of women in accordance with Anglo-European standards would risk a systemic change in the rules that define Tswana civil order. For an analysis of the problematic status of women in Botswana, read Athaliah Molokomme, "Marriage—What

Every Woman Wants or 'Civil Death'?: The Status of Married Women in Botswana," in Alice Armstrong, ed., *Women and Law in Southern Africa* (Harare: Zimbabwe Publishing House, 1987), pp. 181–218.

86. Tswana customary law has never been a static, rigid code. Its pliability has been thoroughly researched by Isaac Schapera, *Tribal Innovators: Tswana Chiefs and Social Change, 1795–1940* (New York: Humanities Press, 1970), especially chapter 2; and Isaac Schapera "The Sources of Law in Tswana Tribal Courts: Legislation and Precedent," *Journal of African Law* 1, no. 3 (1957): 150–162.

87. Migdal, *Strong Societies and Weak States*, pp. 32, 34.

3. RHODESIA: THE CONTEST FOR HEGEMONY IN A DIVIDED SOCIETY

1. Christine Sylvester, *Zimbabwe: The Terrain of Contradictory Development* (Boulder, Colo.: Westview Press, 1991), pp. 3–13.

2. Omer-Cooper, *Zulu Aftermath*, p. 151.

3. D. N. Beach, "Ndebele Raiders and Shona Power," *Journal of African History* 15, no. 4 (1974): 633–651 at 646.

4. Robert Blake, *A History of Rhodesia* (New York: Alfred A. Knopf, 1978), pp. 42–154.

5. Ian Brownlie, *African Boundaries: A Legal and Diplomatic Encyclopaedia* (London: C. Hurst and Company, 1979), pp. 1081–1090, 1219–1301.

6. With this classification the author is following the exposition by Masipula Sithole, "Ethnicity and Factionalism in Zimbabwe Nationalist Politics 1957–79," *Ethnic and Racial Studies* 3, no. 1 (January 1980): 17–39 at 21–24. It is noticeable that the Kalanga are classified as a Shona subgroup by M. Elaine Burgess, "Ethnic Scale and Intensity: The Zimbabwean Experience," Social Forces 59, no. 3 (March 1981): 601–626 at 607; by Morrison et al., *Black Africa*, p. 712; and by George Thomas Kurian, ed., *Encyclopedia of the Third World*, 4th ed., vol. 3 (New York: Facts on File, 1992), p. 2176. Sithole justifies his classification on the grounds that the Kalanga have, since the conquest by the Ndebele, been virtually completely incorporated into Ndebele society. Sithole uncritically accepts the linguistic diversity within the Shona language as indicative of intra-Shona ethnic divisions. Terence Ranger has argued that these linguistic differences emerged as "intellectual innovations," produced by teachers and evangelists when writing the early histories of these people. The presumed ethnic divisions are therefore, according to Ranger, nothing less than inventions, to be used later by the ethnic engineers of the Rhodesian state. See Terence Ranger, *The Invention of Tribalism*, Mambo Occasional Papers, Socioeconomic Series, no. 19 (Gweru: Mambo Press, 1985), pp. 3–20.

7. J. M. McEwan, "The European Population of Southern Rhodesia," *Civilisations* 13, no. 4 (1963): 429–441 at 429.

8. Jeffrey Herbst, *State Politics in Zimbabwe* (Berkeley, Calif.: University of California Press, 1990), p. 18.

9. Michael Bratton, "The Public Service in Zimbabwe," *Political Science Quarterly* 95, no. 3 (fall 1980): 441–464 at 442.

10. Herbst, *State Politics in Zimbabwe*, p. 24. Claire Palley, "Law and the Unequal Society: Discriminatory Legislation in Rhodesia under the Rhodesian Front from 1963 to 1969," parts 1 and 2, *Race* 12, no. 1 (July 1970): 15–47 at 20–22; no. 2 (October 1970): 139–167 at 140, 160–162; Blake, *History of Rhodesia*, p. 212.

11. Claire Palley, "A Note on the Development of Legal Inequality in Rhodesia: 1890–1962," *Race* 12, no. 1 (July 1970): 87–93 at 87.

12. Blake, *History of Rhodesia*, p. 150.

13. Palley, "Development of Legal Inequality," pp. 87, 88.

14. The white settlers' expectation of benefiting from application of the Durham Formula is described by Barry M. Schutz, "European Population Patterns, Cultural Persistence, and Political Change in Rhodesia," *Canadian Journal of African Studies* 7, no. 1 (1973): 3–25 at 10. On the establishment of the Dominions Office and its relationship with Rhodesia, see Blake, *History of Rhodesia*, p. 193.

15. Palley, "Development of Legal Inequality," pp. 88–90.

16. Blake, *History of Rhodesia*, p. 266.

17. Palley, "Development of Legal Inequality," pp. 90–92; Blake, *History of Rhodesia*, pp. 263–324.

18. Anthony Lemon, "Electoral Machinery and Voting Patterns in Rhodesia, 1962–1977," *African Affairs* 77, no. 309 (October 1978): 511–530 at 514, 515, and 529.

19. Palley, "Development of Legal Inequality," p. 93, footnote d.

20. James P. Barber, "Rhodesia: The Constitutional Conflict," *Journal of Modern African Studies* 4, no. 4 (1966): 457–469.

21. Blake, *History of Rhodesia*, pp. 402, 403; Lemon, "Electoral Machinery and Voting Patterns," pp. 516–518; Palley, "Law and the Unequal Society," part 1, pp. 30–34.

22. Palley, "Law and the Unequal Society," part 2, pp. 140–160, especially at 144,145.

23. Palley, "Law and the Unequal Society," part 1, pp. 38–44.

24. Palley, "Law and the Unequal Society," part 2, p. 160.

25. Robert B. Seidman and Martin Gagne, "The State, Law, and Development in Zimbabwe," *Journal of Southern African Affairs* 5, no. 2 (April 1980): 149–170 at 154; Palley, "Law and the Unequal Society," part 1, p. 18.

26. G. Kingsley Garbett, "The Rhodesian Chief's Dilemma: Government Officer or Tribal Leader?" *Race* 8, no. 2 (October 1966): 113–128 at 113–117.

27. Burgess, "Ethnic Scale and Intensity," p. 608; Garbett, "Rhodesian Chief's Dilemma," pp. 116, 117.

28. Garbett, "Rhodesian Chief's Dilemma," p. 118. Garbett records that of the 89, 41 were reduced in status to headmen and had to continue serving under other chiefs, to whom they were former equals; 11 were given pensions; and 37 lost their rank completely, becoming mere commoners in the eyes of the state.

29. Ibid., pp. 119, 120.

30. Claire Palley, *The Constitutional History and Law of Southern Rhodesia 1888–1965: With Special Reference to Imperial Control* (Oxford: Clarendon Press, 1966), pp. 659–667.

31. Garbett, "Rhodesian Chief's Dilemma," p. 121.

32. Ibid., p. 122. This conclusion is shared by J. F. Holleman, *Chief, Council and Commissioner: Some Problems of Government in Rhodesia* (London: Oxford University Press, 1968), pp. 366–370. It also applied to the chieftaincies of the Shiri and Guruuswa communities, according to the research done by A. K. H. Weinrich, *Chiefs and Councils in Rhodesia: Transition from Patriarchal to Bureaucratic Power* (London: Heineman, 1971), p. 190. A detailed analysis of these ineffectual efforts at state building, and the often tragic results for individual chiefs within the Makoni district in Mashonaland, is made by Terence Ranger, "Tradition and Travesty: Chiefs and the Administration in Makoni District, Zimbabwe, 1960–1980," *Africa* 52, no. 3 (1982): 20–41.

33. Michael Bratton, "Settler State, Guerrilla War, and Rural Underdevelopment in Rhodesia," *Rural Africana* 4–5 (spring–fall 1979): 115–129 at 120, 121.

34. Andrew Ladley, "Changing the Courts in Zimbabwe: The Customary Law and Primary Courts Act," *Journal of African Law* 26, no. 2 (1982): 95–114 at 96–99.

35. Ibid., p. 97. The importance of the Court of Appeals for African Civil Cases within this pillar of the legal system is explained by T. W. Bennet, "Practice and Procedure in District Commissioners' Courts," *Rhodesian Law Journal* 16 (1976): 109–151 at 137–149. The *obligation* of the incumbent district commissioners in interpreting and applying customary law has also been commented on by Bennet: "District commissioners [were] expected to be familiar with the traditional cultural values and attitudes of the African population" and might, on the basis of their own judgment, "either apply the common law, if the case warrants it, or apply African customary law or resort to judicial law-making, updating the rules of African customary law to meet modern needs." See T. W. Bennet, "The African Court System in Rhodesia: An Appraisal," *Rhodesian Law*

Journal 15 (1975): 133–151 at 147. An example of such changes in Shona customary law relating to marriage is found in G. L. Chavunduka, *A Shona Urban Court,* Mambo Occasional Papers, Socioeconomic Series, no. 14 (Gweru: Mambo Press, 1979) p. 11. Chavunduka concludes that "a distinction must be made between customary law and what the formal courts of Zimbabwe regard as customary law" (p. 11). (He was referring to the courts of what in this text is called Rhodesia.) Similar examples of the distortion of customary law relating to immovable property are cited by A. P. Cheater, "Fighting over Property: The Articulation of Dominant and Subordinate Legal Systems Governing the Inheritance of Immovable Property among Blacks in Zimbabwe," *Africa* 57, no. 2 (1987): 173–195. For a general treatment of the inconsistencies in the application of customary law, see Palley, *Constitutional History and Law of Southern Rhodesia,* pp. 504–512.

36. Ladley, "Changing the Courts in Zimbabwe," p. 99.

37. David Lan, *Guns and Rain: Guerrillas and Spirit Mediums in Zimbabwe* (London: James Currey, 1985), pp. 142, 143. See also Emmet V. Mittlebeeler, *African Custom and Western Law: The Development of the Rhodesian Criminal Law for Africans* (New York: Africana Publishing Co., 1976), pp. 135–162.

38. Herbst, *State Politics in Zimbabwe,* p. 22.

39. Palley, "Law and the Unequal Society," part 2, p. 145. The allocation and spatial distribution of land by race, and the changes in land policy in Rhodesia have been exhaustively documented. For the evolution of these policies at different stages, see Robin Palmer, *Land and Racial Domination in Rhodesia* (Berkeley, Calif.: University of California Press, 1977); Barry N. Floyd, "Land Apportionment in Southern Rhodesia," *Geographical Journal* 52 (1962): 566–582; and A. J. Christopher, "Recent Trends in Land Tenure in Rhodesia 1961–70," *Geography* 56 (1971): 140–144.

40. D. G. Clarke, "Land Inequality and Income Distribution in Rhodesia," *African Studies Review* 18, no. 1 (April 1975): 1–7 at 4.

41. Barry Munslow, "Prospects for the Socialist Transition of Agriculture in Zimbabwe," *World Development* 13, no. 1 (1985): 41–58 at 42. Even greater dependence of the agricultural economy on the core of white farmers is reported by Michael Bratton who gives a figure of 5,000 farmers producing 75 percent of the agricultural crops of the country. See Michael Bratton, "Development in Zimbabwe: Strategy and Tactics," *Journal of Modern African Studies* 19, no. 3 (1981): 447–475.

42. Bratton, "Settler State, Guerrilla War," p. 118.

43. This figure is reported by Munslow, "Prospects for the Socialist Transition," p. 42.

44. Michael Bratton, "Structural Transformation in Zimbabwe: Comparative Notes from the Neo-Colonisation of Kenya," *Journal of Modern African Studies* 15, no. 4 (December 1977): 591–611 at 601.

45. Bratton, "Settler State, Guerrilla War," p. 123. Educational discrimination in Rhodesia is analyzed at length by Tafirenyika Moyana, "Creating an African Middle Class: The Political Economy of Education and Exploitation in Zimbabwe," *Journal of Southern African Affairs* (July 1979): 324–346.

46. Palley, "Law and the Unequal Society," part 2, pp. 150–158.

47. Rukudzo Murapa, "Race and the Public Service in Zimbabwe: 1890–1983," in Michael G. Schatzberg, ed., *The Political Economy of Zimbabwe* (New York: Praeger, 1984), pp. 55–80 at 55–67.

48. Palley, "Law and the Unequal Society," part 1, p. 25.

49. Kenneth Good, "Settler Colonialism in Rhodesia," *African Affairs* 73, no. 290 (January 1979): 10–36 at 17. The numbers refer to Rhodesian dollars.

50. Seidman and Gagne, "State, Law, and Development," p. 151.

51. Palley, "Law and the Unequal Society," part 1, p. 30, footnote ee.

52. H. W. Smith, *Strategies of Social Research: The Methodological Imagination* (Englewood Cliffs, N.J. : Prentice-Hall, 1975), p. 319.

53. Richard L. Sklar, "Political Science and National Integration: A Radical Approach," *Journal of Modern African Studies* 5, no. 1 (May 1967): 1–11 at 6. An application of this kind of analysis at societal level to both Rhodesia and South Africa is made by Phyllis MacRae, "Race and Class in Southern Africa," *African Review* 4, no. 2 (1974): 37–57.

54. Peter L. Berger, *Pyramids of Sacrifice: Political Ethics and Social Change* (New York: Basic Books, 1974), pp. 123, 223, 224.

55. Donald L. Horowitz, *Ethnic Groups in Conflict* (Berkeley, Calif.: University of California Press, 1985), pp. 131–135, 236–243, 306–311.

56. Otwin Marenin, "Review Essay: Class Analysis in African Studies," *Journal of African Studies* 3, no. 1 (spring 1976): 133–138 at 135.

57. Ian Phimister, "White Miners in Historical Perspective: Southern Rhodesia, 1890–1953," *Journal of Southern African Studies* 3, no. 2 (April 1977): 187–206. Failed attempts at establishing multiracial unions during the early 1960s are reported by C. M. Brand, "Politics and African Trade Unionism in Rhodesia since Federation," *Rhodesian History* 2 (1971): 89–109 at 95.

58. O. B. Pollak, "Black Farmers and White Politics in Rhodesia," *African Affairs* 74, no. 296 (July 1975): 262–277 at 266.

59. M. C. Steele, "White Working-Class Disunity: The Southern Rhodesia Labor Party," *Rhodesian History* 1 (1970): 59–81 at 61–69.

60. M. W. Murphree, ed., *Education, Race and Employment in Rhodesia* (Salisbury: Association of Round Tables in Central Africa, 1975), pp. 199–201, 213–218, 221–234, 252–260, 297, and 298; Marshall W. Murphree, *Employment Opportunity and Race in Rhodesia*, vol. 4, monograph no. 4 (Denver: Studies in Race and Nations, 1973), pp. 1–39 at 7–15.

61. Phimister, "White Miners in Historical Perspective," p. 203.

62. Ibid., p. 204.

63. Ibid., p. 205.

64. Confirmation of this pattern in the early years of this century is found in the work of Charles van Onselen, "Worker Consciousness in Black Miners: Southern Rhodesia, 1900–1920," *Journal of African History* 14, no. 2 (1973): 237–255; and in later years by Brand, "Politics and African Trade Unionism in Rhodesia since Federation," pp. 89–109. An exception is recorded by Arthur Turner, "The Growth of Railway Unionism in the Rhodesia's, 1944–55," in Richard Sandbrook and Robin Cohen, eds., *The Development of an African Working Class* (London: Longman, 1975), pp. 73–96 at 85.

65. Pollak, "Black Farmers and White Politics in Rhodesia," pp. 263–277. The exception was the establishment of the Matabeleland Bantu Central Farmers' Association in 1942, which, according to Pollak, emerged "apparently out of dissatisfaction with the Mashonaland-based organization" (ibid., p. 268).

66. Burgess, "Ethnic Scale and Intensity," pp. 611–616; T. O. Ranger, *The African Voice in Southern Rhodesia, 1898–1930* (Evanston, Ill.: Northwestern University Press, 1970), pp. 148, 149; Charles van Onselen, *Chibaro: African Mine Labor in Southern Rhodesia, 1900–1933* (London: Pluto Press, 1976). pp. 198–204.

67. Ian Phimister and Charles van Onselen, "The Political Economy of Tribal Animosity: A Case Study of the 1929 Bulawayo Location 'Faction Fight,'" *Journal of Southern African Studies* 6, no. 1 (October 1979): 1–43 at 1, 40–43.

68. Horowitz, *Ethnic Groups in Conflict*, pp. 254–259.

69. Dane Kennedy, *Islands of White: Settler Society and Culture in Kenya and Southern Rhodesia, 1890–1939* (Durham, N.C.: Duke University Press, 1987), pp. 182, 187 respectively. This view is shared by Colin Leys, *European Politics in Southern Rhodesia* (Clarendon: Oxford University Press, 1960), p. 88. This sense of threat was one of the primary motivations for white support in the Marandellas district for UDI, according to Richard Hodder-Williams, "White Attitudes and the Unilateral Declaration of Independence: A Case Study," *Journal of Commonwealth Political Studies* 8, no. 3 (1970): 241–264 at 252.

70. Schutz, "European Population Patterns," pp. 5, 6.

71. Kennedy, *Islands of White*, pp. 148–166. The denigration of Africans that permeated white culture has been vividly captured in the expressions of white prejudice recorded by Julie Frederikse, *None But Ourselves: Masses versus Media in the Making of Zimbabwe* (Johannesburg: Ravan, 1982), pp. 20, 21.

72. Schutz, "European Population Patterns," p. 9.

73. Kennedy, *Islands of White*, p. 173; McEwan, "The European Population of Southern Rhodesia," pp. 437, 438; Schutz, "European Population Patterns," pp. 13, 18; J. C. Mitchell, "Race, Class and Status in South Central Africa," in Arthur Tuden and Leonard Plotnicov, eds., *Social Stratification in Africa* (New York: Free Press, 1970), pp. 303–344 at 321, 322; Leys, *European Politics in Southern Rhodesia*, pp. 93–97.

74. Kennedy, *Islands of White*, pp. 171–182; Hodder-Williams, "White Attitudes," pp. 255, 256.

75. Seidman and Gagne, "State, Law and Development," p. 168, footnote 11.

76. Larry W. Bowman, "Organisation, Power, and Decision-Making within the Rhodesian Front," *Journal of Commonwealth Political Studies* 7, no. 2 (July 1969): 145–165 at 164. See also Larry W. Bowman, *Politics in Rhodesia: White Power in an African State* (Cambridge, Mass.: Harvard University Press, 1973), pp. 91–109, 133–150. That support for UDI serves as an expression of a distinctive Rhodesian nationalism is also argued by Hodder-Williams, "White Attitudes," p. 256.

77. Kennedy, *Islands of White*, p. 152. Research done by Christopher Orpen in the early 1970s also supports the view that social distance between black and white Rhodesians was causally linked to feelings of superiority and inferiority. See Christopher Orpen, "The Reference Group Basis of Racial Attitudes: An Empirical Study with White and Black Rhodesians," *S. A. Journal of Sociology*, no. 6 (April 1973): 67–73.

78. Palley, "Law and the Unequal Society," part 1, p. 25.

79. Kennedy, *Islands of White*, p. 169. This view is endorsed by Richard Gray, *The Two Nations: Aspects of the Development of Race Relations in the Rhodesias and Nyassaland* (London: Oxford University Press, 1960), pp. 101, 102.

80. Schutz, "European Population Patterns," p. 16.

81. Horowitz, *Ethnic Groups in Conflict*, p. 337.

82. Marenin, "Class Analysis in African Studies," p. 135.

83. Masipula Sithole, *Zimbabwe Struggles within the Struggle* (Salisbury: Rujeko, 1979) and "Ethnicity and Factionalism," pp. 17–39 are the major presentations of this view. It is also summarized in Masipula Sithole, "Zimbabwe: In Search of a Stable Democracy," in Larry Diamond et al., *Democracy in Developing Countries*, vol. 2 (Boulder, Colo.: Lynne Rienner, 1988), pp. 217–257 at 221–225; and Masipula Sithole, "The Salience of Ethnicity in African Politics: The Case of Zimbabwe," pp. 49–60, in Anand C. Paranjpe, ed., *Ethnic Identities and Prejudices: Perspectives from the Third World* (London: E. J. Brill, 1986). Sithole's analysis is largely echoed by Solomon Mombeshora, "The Salience of Ethnicity in Political Development: The Case of Zimbabwe," *International Sociology* 5, no. 4 (December 1990): 427–444. Shorter analyses with a similar bearing have been made by W. J. Breytenbach, "Ethnic Factors in the Rhodesian Power Struggle," *Bulletin of the Africa Institute* 15, nos. 3 and 4 (1977): 70–75; by Clive Kileff and Leland W. Robinson, "From Rhodesia To Zimbabwe: Contemporary Black Nationalist Organizations," *International Reviews of History and Political Science* 15, no. 1 (February 1978): 39–57; and in "Rhodesia: Zimbabwe's Factional Farrago," *Africa Confidential* 18, no. 22 (November 4, 1977): 1–4.

84. Masipula Sithole, "Class and Factionalism in the Zimbabwe Nationalist Movement," *African Studies Review* 27, no. 1 (March 1984): 117–125, especially at 120–123.

85. The most comprehensive and authoritative accounts are David Lan, *Guns and Rain;* and Terence Ranger's *Peasant Consciousness and Guerrilla War in Zimbabwe: A Comparative Study* (London: James Currey, 1985). The role of spirit mediums in the earlier resistance is described in Allen Isaacman, "Social Banditry in Zimbabwe (Rhodesia) and Mozambique, 1894–1907: An Expression of Early Peasant Protest," *Journal of Southern African Studies* 4, no. 1 (October 1977): 1–30; and T. O. Ranger, *Revolt in Southern Rhodesia 1896–7: A Study in African Resistance* (London: Heinemann, 1967). The latter book emphasizes the continuity between these practices in the two different historical contexts. So does Ranger, "The Death of Chaminuka: Spirit Mediums, Nationalism and the Guerrilla War in Zimbabwe," *African Affairs* 81, no. 324 (July 1982): 349–369.

86. Lan, *Guns and Rain,* pp. 14, 31–49, 68–75, 100, 147, 149, 162–167, 171–172; Ranger, *Peasant Consciousness and Guerrilla War,* pp. 189, 197, 200, 208. The persuasive power of this technique rested on the prior acceptance of ancestral worship. In areas where Christianity had been securely established, accepting the status of the guerrillas entailed discarding the basic tenets of Christianity. This was not always a spontaneous process, as has been pointed out by M. Bourdillon and P. Gundani, "Rural Christians and the Zimbabwe War: A Case Study," in Carl F. Hallencreutz and Ambrose M. Moyo, eds., *Christianity South of the Zambezi,* vol. 3, *Church and State in Zimbabwe* (Gweru: Mambo Press, 1988), pp. 147–161.

87. Lan, *Guns and Rain,* pp. 166–170; Ranger, "Tradition and Travesty," pp. 35–37.

88. Lan, *Guns and Rain,* p. 129. To substantiate his findings, Lan cites the guerrillas' justification for killing prostitutes who used skin-lightening cream: "The prostitutes were killed because the comrades said: You are holding us back from winning our country. *The comrades were saying: the country is ours, we blacks*" (p. 129, emphasis added). What is perplexing is that such a statement is used to support the claims that ethnic identity was not intensely held, but that class identity was.

89. Ranger, *Peasant Consciousness and Guerrilla War,* p. 289.

90. Ibid., p. 26. See also pp. 31 and 40.

91. Ibid., p. 189. See also pp. 197, 200.

92. Lan, *Guns and Rain*, p. 98.

93. Ibid., p. 171.

94. Ibid., pp. 207, 222; Ranger, *Peasant Consciousness and Guerrilla War*, pp. 215, 216.

95. Terence Ranger, "The Changing of the Old Guard: Robert Mugabe and the revival of ZANU," *Journal of Southern African Studies* 7, no. 1 (October 1980): 71–90, especially at 83–86; Sithole, "Stable Democracy," p. 234.

96. Stephen John Stedman, *Peacemaking in Civil War: International Mediation in Zimbabwe, 1974–1980* (Boulder, Colo.: Lynne Rienner, 1991), pp. 109, 118.

97. Lan, *Guns and Rain*, p. 148.

98. Ranger, *Peasant Consciousness and Guerrilla War*, p. 177.

99. Lan, *Guns and Rain*, pp. 128, 201; Ranger, *Peasant Consciousness and Guerrilla War*, p. 179.

100. Official estimates placed the number of casualties at 30,000. The later revision was 40,000, according to Norma Kriger, *Zimbabwe's Guerrilla War: Peasant Voices* (Cambridge: Cambridge University Press, 1992), p. 4. Similar figures are reported by Stedman, *Peacemaking in Civil War,* p. vii.

101. Bratton, "Public Service in Zimbabwe," p. 447.

102. D. G. Clarke, "The Growth and Economic Impact of the Public Sector of Rhodesia," *Rhodesian Journal of Economics* 6, no. 3 (1972): 48–60 at 54–58; Herbst, *State Politics in Zimbabwe*, pp. 25–27.

103. Palley, "Law and the Unequal Society," part 1, p. 40.

104. Bratton, "Public Service in Zimbabwe," p. 453. In a later article Bratton puts the number of relocated people at 500,000. See Bratton, "Development in Zimbabwe," p. 458.

105. Palley, "Law and the Unequal Society," part 2, pp. 163, 164.

106. Bratton, "Settler State, Guerrilla War," p. 123; Tony Hodges, "Counterinsurgency and the Fate of Rural Blacks," *Africa Report* (September–October 1977): 15–20 at 17, 18; Robert E. Mazur, "Social Class Differential in the Impact of Repression and Guerrilla War on Rural Population and Development in Zimbabwe," *Journal of Developing Areas* 25, no. 4 (July 1991): 509–528 at 515–517; A. K. H. Weinrich, "Strategic Resettlement in Rhodesia," *Journal of Southern African Studies* 3, no. 2 (April 1977): 207–229.

107. The failure to actually establish such zones has been noted by Lan, *Guns and Rain*, p. 128; Ranger, *Peasant Consciousness and Guerrilla War*, p. 179; and Mazur, "Social Class Differential," p. 517.

108. The establishment of such courts was achieved with some measure of success, especially in Mashonaland, but less so in Matabeleland.

See Ladley, "Changing the Courts in Zimbabwe," p. 101, footnote 15; Robert B. Seidman, "How a Bill Became a Law in Zimbabwe: On the Problem of Transforming the Colonial State," *Africa* 52, no. 3 (1982): 56–76 at 59, 63, and 74, footnote 13.

109. Official figures released in 1982 show that 10 percent of all chiefs and headmen were killed during the course of the war. See Ladley, "Changing the Courts in Zimbabwe," p. 101, footnote 52.

110. Bratton, "Settler State, Guerrilla War," pp. 126, 127; Mazur, "Social Class Differential," pp. 513, 514; Michael Bratton, *Beyond Community Development: The Political Economy of Rural Administration in Zimbabwe* (London: Catholic Institute for International Relations, 1978), pp. 43–45.

111. Lan, *Guns and Rain,* pp. 113, 149, 165, 171; Ranger, *Peasant Consciousness and Guerrilla War,* pp. 18, 208.

112. Kriger, *Zimbabwe's Guerrilla War,* pp. 101–108, 116–169, 237–242. See also Norma Kriger, "The Zimbabwean War of Liberation: Struggles within the Struggle," *Journal of Southern African Studies* 14, no. 2 (January 1988): 304–322.

113. Kriger, *Zimbabwe's Guerrilla War,* pp. 170–211

114. Blake, *History of Rhodesia,* p. 387.

115. Robert O. Matthews, "Talking without Negotiating: The Case of Rhodesia," *International Journal* 35, no. 1 (winter 1979–80): 91–117 at 104.

116. Stedman, *Peacemaking in Civil War,* pp. 109, 118.

117. Jeffrey Davidow, *A Peace in Southern Africa: The Lancaster House Conference on Rhodesia, 1979* (Boulder, Colo.: Westview Press, 1984), p. 23.

118. Stedman, *Peacemaking in Civil War,* p. 138.

119. Davidow, *Peace in Southern Africa,* p. 22. Stedman also marks this as a crucial turning point in the overall process. See Stedman, *Peacemaking in Civil War,* p. 127.

120. Stedman, *Peacemaking in Southern Africa,* p. 127.

121. Davidow, *Peace in Southern Africa,* pp. 15, 42. For an analysis of the damaging impact of sanctions on the Rhodesian economy, see D. G. Clarke, "Zimbabwe's International Economic Position and Aspects of Sanctions Removal," in W. H. Morris-Jones, ed., *From Rhodesia to Zimbabwe: Behind and Beyond Lancaster House* (London: Frank Cass, 1980), pp. 28–54 at 29–42.

122. Davidow, *Peace in Southern Africa,* pp. 42, 44.

123. Ibid., p. 46; Stedman, *Peacemaking in Civil War,* pp. 173, 237; Sithole, "Stable Democracy," p. 235.

124. Stedman, *Peacemaking in Civil War,* p. 175.

125. Davidow, *Peace in Southern Africa,* p. 89.

126. Stedman, *Peacemaking in Civil War,* p. 203.

4. Zimbabwe: Reconstituting State and Society

1. Gastil, *Freedom in the World*, pp. 487–488 (see chapter 2, n. 10).

2. *Africa South of the Sahara, 1993*, p. 963; Hunter, *Statesman's Yearbook*, p. 1630; World Bank, *World Development Report 1992* (New York: Oxford University Press, 1992), pp. 218, 268, 278.

3. *Africa South of the Sahara, 1993*, p. 963.

4. The numbers are taken from W. J. Breytenbach, "Transition in 'Settler' Societies in Africa: Problems and Parallels Revisited," *Plural Societies* 22, nos. 1 and 2 (November 1992): 85–123 at 88. For a discussion of the factors influencing their exit, see Marshall W. Murphree, "Whites in Black Africa: Their Status and Role," *Ethnic and Racial Studies* 1, no. 2 (April 1978): 155–174; and A. R. Wilkinson, "The Impact of the War," in Morris-Jones, *From Rhodesia to Zimbabwe*, pp. 110–123.

5. Roger Riddell, "Zimbabwe's Land Problem: The Central Issue," in Morris-Jones, *From Rhodesia to Zimbabwe*, pp. 1–13 at 7.

6. The Economist Intelligence Unit, *Zimbabwe's First Five Years: Economic Prospects Following Independence*, EIU Special Report no. 111 (London: Economist Intelligence Unit Ltd., 1981), pp. 15, 16.

7. Colin Stoneman and Rob Davies, "The Economy: An Overview," in Colin Stoneman, ed., *Zimbabwe's Inheritance* (New York: St. Martin's Press, 1981), pp. 96 (table 6.1), 100 (table 6.2).

8. The Economist Intelligence Unit, *Zimbabwe's First Five Years*, pp. 31, 34.

9. Stoneman and Davies, "The Economy: An Overview," pp. 96 (table 6.1), 100 (table 6.2).

10. The Economist Intelligence Unit, *Zimbabwe's First Five Years*, p. 35.

11. Stoneman and Davies, "The Economy: An Overview," pp. 96 (table 6.1), 100 (table 6.2).

12. The Economist Intelligence Unit, *Zimbabwe's First Five Years*, pp. 39, 40; Thomas Lines, "Investment Sanctions and Zimbabwe: Breaking the Rod," *Third World Quarterly* 10, no. 3 (July 1988): 1182–1216 at 1187–1192.

13. Stoneman and Davies, "The Economy: An Overview," p. 100 (table 6.2).

14. Ibid., p. 95.

15. Wilkinson, "Impact of the War," p. 115.

16. Stoneman and Davies, "The Economy: An Overview," pp. 99, 104.

17. Colin Stoneman, "The Economy: Recognizing the Reality," in Colin Stoneman, ed., *Zimbabwe's Prospects: Issues of Race, Class and Capital in Southern Africa* (London: Macmillan, 1988), p. 51.

18. Stoneman and Davies, "The Economy: An Overview," p. 113.

19. *Africa South of the Sahara, 1993*, p. 969.

20. The Economist Intelligence Unit, *Zimbabwe's First Five Years*, p. 37.

21. Roger Riddell, "Prospects for Land Reform in Zimbabwe," *Rural Africana*, nos. 4–5 (spring/fall 1979): 17–31 at 23.

22. Riddell, "Zimbabwe's Land Problem," pp. 1–13 at 4.

23. Colin Stoneman, "Foreign Capital and the Prospects for Zimbabwe," *World Development* 4, no. 1 (1976): 25–28.

24. Colin Stoneman, "Foreign Capital and the Reconstruction of Zimbabwe," *Review of African Political Economy*, no. 11 (January/April 1978): 62–83, especially at 68–72.

25. The Economist Intelligence Unit, *Zimbabwe's First Five Years*, p. 63.

26. Ibid., pp. 34, 38, 41.

27. John Robertson, "The Economy: A Sectoral Overview," in Simon Baynham, ed., *Zimbabwe in Transition* (Stockholm: Almqvist & Wiksell International, 1992), pp. 64–100 at 89.

28. Lee Cokorinos, "The Political Economy of State and Party Formation in Zimbabwe," in Schatzberg, *Political Economy of Zimbabwe*, pp. 8–54 at 46.

29. William H. Shaw, "Towards the One-Party State in Zimbabwe: A Study in African Political Thought," *Journal of Modern African Studies* 24, no. 3 (1986): 373–394 at 374.

30. C. Gregory, "The Impact of Ruling Party Ideology on Zimbabwe's Post-Independence Domestic Development," *Journal of Social, Political and Economic Studies* 12, no. 2 (summer 1987): 115–156 at 115–117.

31. Jeffrey Herbst, "The Consequences of Ideology in Zimbabwe," in Baynham, *Zimbabwe in Transition*, pp. 45–63. See also Herbst, *State Politics in Zimbabwe*, pp. 31–33.

32. Colin Stoneman and Lionel Cliffe, *Zimbabwe: Politics, Economics and Society* (London: Pinter Publishers, 1989), p. 89. This view is shared by Herbst, *State Politics in Zimbabwe*, p. 9.

33. *Africa South of the Sahara, 1993*, p. 978; Kurian, *Encyclopedia of the Third World*, p. 2180; Welshman Ncube and Shepard Nzombe, "Continuity and Change in the Constitutional Development of Zimbabwe," in Preben Kaarsholm, ed., *Cultural Struggle and Development in Southern Africa* (London: James Currey, 1992), pp. 167–181 at 171–175.

34. Kurian, *Encyclopedia of the Third World*, p. 2180.

35. Sithole, "Stable Democracy," p. 229.

36. Herbst, *State Politics in Zimbabwe*, p. 30.

37. Bratton, "Development in Zimbabwe," p. 452.

38. Rukudzo Murapa, "Race and the Public Service in Zimbabwe: 1890–1983," in Schatzberg, *Political Economy of Zimbabwe*, pp. 55–80 at 71–72; Sithole, "Stable Democracy," pp. 228, 229.

39. Ronald Weitzer, "Continuities in the Politics of State Security in Zimbabwe," in Schatzberg, *Political Economy of Zimbabwe*, pp. 81–118 at 85.

40. Dominique Darbon, "*Fluctuat nec mergitur*: Keeping Afloat," in Baynham, *Zimbabwe in Transition*, pp. 1–23 at 3. A slightly lower percentage is cited by Murapa, "Race and the Public Service," p. 72.

41. Tony Hawkins, "Light at the End of Africa's Tunnel?" *Optima* 38, no. 1 (1991): 25–29 at 26.

42. Weitzer, "Politics of State Security," p. 85.

43. J. D. Jordan, *Local Government in Zimbabwe: An Overview*, Mambo Occasional Papers, Socioeconomic Series, no. 17 (Gweru: Mambo Press, 1984), pp. 7–19; N. D. Mutizwa-Mangiza, "Local Government and Planning in Zimbabwe: An Examination of Recent Changes, with Special Reference to the Provincial/Regional Level," *Third World Planning Review* 8, no. 2 (1986): 153–175; N. D. Mutizwa-Mangiza, "Decentralization and District Development Planning in Zimbabwe," *Public Administration and Development* 10 (October–December 1990): 423–435; Kamiel Wekwete, "The Local Government System in Zimbabwe: Some Perspectives on Change and Development," *Planning and Administration* 15, no. 1 (spring 1988): 18–27; K. H. Wekwete, "Decentralized Planning in Zimbabwe: A Review of Provincial, Urban and District Development Planning in Post-Dependence Zimbabwe (post 1980)," *Journal of International Development* 2, no. 1 (January 1990): 110–139.

44. J. A. Bennett, "The Legal System of Zimbabwe," *Zimbabwe Law Journal* 22, no. 2 (1982): 147–161 at 148–152; Ladley, "Changing the Courts in Zimbabwe," pp. 100–108.

45. Ladley, "Changing the Courts in Zimbabwe," p. 107.

46. M. Evans, "Gukurahundi: The Development of the Zimbabwe Defence Forces 1980–1987," *Strategic Review for Southern Africa* 10, no. 1 (1988): 1–37 at 10, 11.

47. Ronald Weitzer, "In Search of Regime Security: Zimbabwe since Independence," *Journal of Modern African Studies* 22, no. 4 (1984): 529–557 at 531–533; Weitzer, "Politics of State Security," p. 82.

48. P. S. Garlake, "Prehistory and Ideology in Zimbabwe," *Africa* 52, no. 3 (1982): 1–19 at 1; *Africa South of the Sahara, 1993*, p. 964.

49. These are a selection from more than 40 name changes to towns that were introduced by February 1984. Not all of these changes are overtly political, but even by merely "indigenizing" the spelling (such as renaming the Umniati River to the Munyati River) the same message is conveyed. See D. Hywel Davies, "Urban Change in Zimbabwe," *Africa Insight* 14, no. 3 (1984): 158–168 at 163.

50. A. P. Cheater, "Contradictions in Modelling 'Consciousness': Zimbabwean Proletarians in the Making?" *Journal of Southern African Studies* 14, no. 2 (January 1988): 291–303 at 299.

51. Lan, *Guns and Rain*, p. 222.

52. Albert P. Blaustein and Gisbert H. Flanz, eds., *Constitutions of the Countries of the World: Zimbabwe Supplement* (New York: Oceana), May 1991, p. 1, and May 1992, pp. 2, 3.

53. Herbst, *State Politics in Zimbabwe*, pp. 37–62.

54. Sylvester, *Terrain of Contradictory Development*, p. 73.

55. Herbst, *State Politics in Zimbabwe*, pp. 82–109. See also Jeffrey Herbst, "Societal Demands and Government Choices: Agricultural Producer Price Policy in Zimbabwe," *Comparative Politics* 20, no. 3 (April 1988): 265–288.

56. Herbst, *State Politics in Zimbabwe*, pp. 166–178.

57. Rene Loewenson and David Sanders, "The Political Economy of Health and Nutrition," in Stoneman, *Zimbabwe's Prospects*, pp. 133–152 at 140.

58. Tony Cavender, "The Professionalization of Traditional Medicine in Zimbabwe," *Human Organization* 47, no. 3 (fall 1988): 251–254; Samuel T. Agere, "Progress and Problems in the Health Care Delivery System," in Ibbo Mandaza, ed., *Zimbabwe: The Political Economy of Transition 1980–1986* (Dakar: Codesria, 1986), pp. 355–376 at 371.

59. Herbst, *State Politics in Zimbabwe*, pp. 193–220.

60. Fay Chung, "Education: Revolution or Reform?" in Stoneman, *Zimbabwe's Prospects*, pp. 118–132; Rungano Zvogbo, "Education and the Challenge of Independence," in Mandaza, *Political Economy of Transition*, pp. 319–354.

61. Joyce L. Kazembe, "The Women Issue," in Mandaza, *Political Economy of Transition*, pp. 377–404; Sylvester, *Terrain of Contradictory Development*, pp. 143–152; A. K. H. Weinrich, "Changes in the Political and Economic Roles of Women in Zimbabwe since Independence," *Cultures* 8, no. 2 (1982): 43–62.

62. *Africa South of the Sahara, 1993*, pp. 967, 968; L. M. Sachikonye, "The Debate on Democracy in Contemporary Zimbabwe," *Review of African Political Economy*, no. 45/46 (1989): 117–125 at 120; Sylvester, *Terrain of Contradictory Development*, pp. 85–87.

63. Darbon, "Keeping Afloat," pp. 11–15; Jeffrey Herbst, "Political Impediments to Economic Rationality: Explaining Zimbabwe's Failure to Reform Its Public Sector," *Journal of Modern African Studies* 27, no. 1 (1989): 67–84 at 81.

64. Herbst, *State Politics in Zimbabwe*, p. 173.

65. Mutizwa-Mangiza, "Decentralization and District Development Planning," p. 430.

66. Ladley, "Changing the Courts in Zimbabwe," pp. 101–103.

67. K. Makamure, "A Comparative Study of Comrades' Courts under Socialist Legal Systems and Zimbabwe's Village Courts," *Zimbabwe Law Review* 3, no. 1/2 (1985): 34–61 at 57.

68. Doris Peterson Galen, "Internal Conflicts between Customary Law and General Law in Zimbabwe: Family Law as a Case Study," *Zimbabwe Law Review* 1 and 2 (1983–84): 3–42.

69. Cheater, "Contradictions in Modelling 'Consciousness,'" p. 301. This possibility was foreseen by T. W. Bennett, "Conflict of Laws: The Application of Customary Law and the Common Law in Zimbabwe," *International and Comparative Law Quarterly* 30 (January 1981): 59–103 at 88–90.

70. Makamure, "Comparative Study of Comrades' Courts," pp. 59, 60.

71. Lan, *Guns and Rain*, p. 221.

72. Ibid., p. 220.

73. Terence Ranger, "Religion and Witchcraft in Everyday Life in Contemporary Zimbabwe," in Kaarsholm, *Cultural Struggle and Development in Southern Africa*, pp. 149–165 at 158.

74. Sylvester, *Terrain of Contradictory Development*, p. 75. This conclusion is endorsed by M. F. C. Bourdillon, "Religious Symbols and Political Change," *Zambezia* 12 (1984/5): 39–54 at 48.

75. Sylvester, *Terrain of Contradictory Development*, p. 76; *Africa South of the Sahara, 1993*, p. 966.

76. *Africa South of the Sahara, 1993*, p. 966; Virginia Curtin Knight, "Political Consolidation in Zimbabwe," *Current History* 83, no. 491 (March 1984):109–112 (at 111), 135; Lawyers Committee for Human Rights, *Zimbabwe: Wages of War. A Report on Human Rights* (New York: Lawyers Committee for Human Rights, 1986), p. 33; Weitzer, "Regime Security," p. 546.

77. Lawyers Committee, *Wages of War*, pp. 1–13.

78. Richard Hodder-Williams, "Conflict in Zimbabwe: The Matabeleland Problem," *Conflict Studies*, no. 151 (1983): 1–20 at 6.

79. Sithole, "Stable Democracy," p. 239.

80. Ibid., p. 249.

81. Weitzer, "Regime Security," p. 543.

82. Samuel. E. Finer, "State- and Nation-Building in Europe: The Role of the Military," in Charles Tilly, ed., *The Formation of National States in Western Europe* (Princeton, N.J.: Princeton University Press, 1975), pp. 84–163.

83. Loewenson and Sanders, "Political Economy of Health and Nutrition," p. 146; Erich Leistner, "Zimbabwe's Economy: Problems and Prospects," *Africa Insight* 19, no. 3 (1989): 147–152 at 152.

84. Leistner, "Zimbabwe's Economy," p. 151.

85. World Bank, *World Development Report 1992*, pp. 176, 177, 220, 221.

86. John Robertson, "Public Finance," in Baynham, *Zimbabwe in Transition*, pp. 101–128 at 116.

87. Leistner, "Zimbabwe's Economy: Problems and Prospects," p. 151.

88. *Africa South of the Sahara, 1993*, p. 973; Leistner, "Zimbabwe's Economy: Problems and Prospects," p. 151. See also Clayton G. Mackenzie, "Zimbabwe's Educational Miracle and the Problems It Has Created," *International Review of Education* 34, no. 3 (1988): 337–353 at 346.

89. Tony Hawkins, "Zimbabwe's Socialist Transformation," *Optima* 35, no. 4 (December 1987): 186–195 at 193; *Africa South of the Sahara, 1993*, p. 973.

90. Robertson, "Public Finance," p. 119.

91. Ibbo Mandaza, "The State and Politics in the Post-White Settler Colonial Situation," in Mandaza, *Political Economy of Transition*, pp. 21–74 at 61–69; Obert I. Nyawata, "Macroeconomic Management, Adjustment and Stabilization," in Stoneman, *Zimbabwe's Prospects*, pp. 90–117, especially at 97, 115; Christine Sylvester, "Continuity and Discontinuity in Zimbabwe's Development History," *African Studies Review* 28, no. 1 (March 1985): 19–44 at 39.

92. Hawkins, "Zimbabwe's Socialist Transformation," pp. 186–195; Hawkins, "Light at the End of Africa's Tunnel?"; Robertson, "Public Finance," pp. 101–128.

93. *Africa South of the Sahara, 1993*, p. 969.

94. Herbst, *State Politics in Zimbabwe*, especially chapters 5, 6, and 7; Robertson, "Public Finance," pp. 101–128.

95. The national debt increased fourfold from 1979/80 to June 1988. Foreign debt increased sevenfold in the same period, and interest repayments grew 446 percent in the seven years from 1981/82 to 1988/89. See Leistner, "Zimbabwe's Economy: Problems and Prospects," p. 148. By 1990 the balance of payments deficit stood at 6 percent of GDP and the budget deficit at 10 percent of GDP, and the debt servicing costs stood at more than 22 percent of export earnings. See *Africa South of the Sahara, 1993*, p. 972; Hawkins, "Light at the End of Africa's Tunnel?" p. 26.

96. Jeffrey Herbst, "Racial Reconciliation in Southern Africa," *International Affairs* 65, no. 1 (winter 1988/89): 43–54 at 46. See also Herbst, *State Politics in Zimbabwe*, pp. 221–227.

97. Murapa, "Race and the Public Service," p. 77.

98. Michael Bratton, "Corporatism or Neopatrimonialism? The Merger of Farmer Unions in Zimbabwe" (paper presented at the 35th annual meeting of the African Studies Association, Seattle, Wash., November 20–23, 1992), p. 28 (footnote 30). See also the discussion of the IBDC by Jonathan Moyo, "State Politics and Social Domination in Zimbabwe," *Journal of Modern African Studies* 30, no. 2 (1992): 305–330 at 323, 324.

99. Herbst, *State Politics in Zimbabwe*, p. 223.

100. Marshall W. Murphree, "The Salience of Ethnicity in African States: A Zimbabwean Case Study," *Ethnic and Racial Studies* 11, no. 2 (April 1988): 119–138.

101. Anthony Lemon, "The Zimbabwe General Election of 1985," *Journal of Commonwealth and Comparative Politics* 26, no. 1 (March 1988): 3–21 at 19. This interpretation is supported by Lionel Cliffe, Joshua Mpofu, and Barry Munslow, "Nationalist Politics in Zimbabwe: The 1980 Elections and Beyond," *Review of African Political Economy*, no. 18 (May–August 1980): 44–67; Herbst, *State Politics in Zimbabwe*, pp. 170, 171; Hodder-Williams, "Matabeleland Problem," p. 13; Tony Rich, "Legacies of the Past? The Results of the 1980 Election in Midlands Province, Zimbabwe," *Africa* 52, no. 3 (1982): 42–55; Sithole, "Stable Democracy," p. 237; and D. S. Tevera, "Voting Patterns in Zimbabwe's Elections of 1980 and 1985," *Geography* 74, no. 2 (1989): 162–165. The articles by Cliffe et al., Rich, and Hodder-Williams refer to the 1980 elections only.

102. Sithole, "Salience of Ethnicity in African Politics," p. 57; Christine Sylvester, "Zimbabwe's 1985 Elections: A Search for National Mythology," *Journal of Modern African Studies* 24, no. 1 (1986): 229–255.

103. *Africa South of the Sahara, 1993*, pp. 967, 968; Sam Kongwa, "Zimbabwe's 1990 General Election and the Search for Direction," *Africa Institute Bulletin* 30, no. 3 (1990): 6–8; Lloyd Sachikonye, "The 1990 Zimbabwe Elections: A Post-Mortem," *Review of African Political Economy*, no. 48 (autumn 1990): 92–99; Christine Sylvester, "Unities and Disunities in Zimbabwe's 1990 Election," *Journal of Modern African Studies* 28, no. 3 (1990): 375–400.

104. Gregory, "Impact of Ruling Party Ideology," pp. 115–156.

105. Evans, "Development of the Zimbabwe Defence Forces," pp. 1–37 at 12, 13, 30–32.

106. Andrew Ladley and David Lan, "The Law of the Land: Party and State in Rural Zimbabwe," *Journal of Southern African Studies* 12, no. 1 (October 1985): 88–101 at 92.

107. Wekwete, "Decentralized Planning in Zimbabwe," p. 128.

108. Sylvester, *Terrain of Contradictory Development*, pp. 137–164.

109. Ibid., p. 81.

110. Bratton, "Corporatism or Neopatrimonialism?" p. 24.

111. Sithole, "Stable Democracy," p. 229.

112. Lemon, "General Election of 1985," pp. 13, 14; Kongwa, "Zimbabwe's 1990 General Election," p. 6.

113. Sachikonye, "1990 Zimbabwe Elections: A Post-Mortem," p. 95.

114. Herbst, *State Politics in Zimbabwe,* pp. 120, 222; Hawkins, "Light at the End of Africa's Tunnel?" p. 26; Robertson, "Public Finance," p. 108.

115. Weitzer, "Regime Security," pp. 538–539, 547–557; Weitzer, "Politics of State Security," pp. 88, 89, 116, 117.

116. Cokorinos, "State and Party Formation in Zimbabwe," pp. 31–35.

117. Herbst, *State Politics in Zimbabwe,* p. 32; Lan, *Guns and Rain,* pp. 128, 201.

118. Herbst, *State Politics in Zimbabwe,* pp. 9, 120, 227–230.

119. Ibid., p. 156.

120. For a detailed analysis of the content of this document, see John Robertson, "Zimbabwe: A Framework for Economic Reform 1991–1995," *Africa Institute Bulletin* 31, no. 4 (1991): 1–4.

121. Early signals of wavering resolve in implementing this policy shift are discussed by John Robertson in "Zimbabwe: Setbacks for Economic Reform," *Africa Institute Bulletin* 32, no. 1 (1992): 3–4.

122. Patrick Quantin, "The General Elections in Zimbabwe: Step towards a One-Party State?" in Baynham, *Zimbabwe in Transition,* pp. 24–44 at 32.

123. Ladley and Lan, "Law of the Land," pp. 99, 100.

124. Ibid., p. 100.

5. South Africa: The Apartheid State and the Divided Society

1. Hermann Giliomee and Lawrence Schlemmer, *From Apartheid to Nation-Building* (Cape Town: Oxford University Press, 1989), p. 64.

2. Merle Lipton, *Capitalism and Apartheid: South Africa, 1910–1986* (Cape Town: David Philip, 1986), p. 36.

3. T. R. H. Davenport, *South Africa: A Modern History,* 3rd ed. (Johannesburg: Macmillan, 1987), pp. 7–12, 32, 33.

4. Omer-Cooper, *Zulu Aftermath* (see chap. 1, n. 12).

5. This politically inspired migration came to be known as the Great Trek, an event central to the political mythology of Afrikaner nationalism. See Davenport, *South Africa,* pp. 49–53.

6. Hermann Giliomee and Richard Elphick, "The Structure of European Domination at the Cape, 1652–1820," in Richard Elphick and Hermann Giliomee, eds., *The Shaping of South African Society* (Cape Town: Longman, 1979), pp. 359–390.

7. Leonard Thompson, "The Subjection of the African Chiefdoms, 1870–1898," in Monica Wilson and Leonard Thompson, eds., *The Oxford History of South Africa,* vol. 2, *South Africa 1870–1966* (Oxford: Oxford University Press, 1975), pp. 245–284.

8. W. D. Hammond-Tooke, *Command or Consensus: The Development of Transkeian Local Government* (Cape Town: David Philip, 1975), p. 23; J. B. Peires, *The Dead Will Arise: Nongqawuse and the Great Xhosa Cattle-Killing Movement of 1856–7* (Johannesburg: Ravan, 1989).

9. Davenport, *South Africa,* pp. 214–217. Leonard Thompson cites a slightly lower casualty figure of 25,000, but both agree on the casualty rate of 344 per 1,000 per annum at the height of the epidemics. See Leonard Thompson, "The Compromise of Union," in Wilson and Thompson, *Oxford History of South Africa,* vol. 2, pp. 325–364 at 328; and also S. B. Spies, *Methods of Barbarism?* (Cape Town: Human and Rousseau, 1977).

10. Davenport, *South Africa,* pp. 243–252; Thompson, "Compromise of Union."

11. Ben Roux, "Parliament and the Executive," in Denis Worrall, ed., *South Africa: Government and Politics* (Pretoria: J. L. van Schaik, 1975), pp. 29–74 at 36–40; Thompson, "Compromise of Union," pp. 362, 363.

12. Davenport, *South Africa,* pp. 228–229; Giliomee and Schlemmer, *From Apartheid to Nation-Building,* pp. 11–12; David Welsh, "The Cultural Dimension of Apartheid," *African Affairs* 71, no. 282 (1972): 35–53 at 40.

13. Giliomee and Schlemmer, *From Apartheid to Nation-Building,* pp. 14–21.

14. A note on terminology needs to be made at this point. The titles of the laws bearing on people who were not considered white changed continually throughout the period of white rule. The official terminology for Bantu-speaking people changed from "Native" to "Bantu" to "African" and then eventually to "Black." In this text the laws will be named as the authors from the works cited used them, and no standardization will be attempted.

15. The legislation and policies of the era of segregation are described and assessed in among others, Davenport, *South Africa,* pp. 242–252, 258–260, 292–296, 309–313; Giliomee and Schlemmer, *From Apartheid to Nation-Building,* pp. 14–36; Muriel Horrell, *Legislation and Race Relations* (Johannesburg: South African Institute of Race Relations, 1971), pp. 1–8; Muriel Horrell, *Laws Affecting Race Relations in South Africa: 1948–1976* (Johannesburg: South African Institute of Race Relations, 1978), pp. 1–8; David Welsh, "The Growth of Towns," in Wilson and Thompson, *Oxford History of South Africa,* vol. 2, pp. 172–243.

16. The cultural complexity of the African population is described by van Warmelo, "Grouping and Ethnic History" (see chap. 1, n. 9). The linguistic diversity of the country can be read from the tables in *South Africa 1992* (Johannesburg: South Africa Foundation, 1991), p. 11; and from Carole Cooper et al., *Race Relations Survey 1992/93* (Johannesburg: South African Institute of Race Relations, 1993), p. 256.

17. The operative principles of apartheid and the major legislative instruments created to achieve it are well summarized in Giliomee and

Schlemmer, *From Apartheid to Nation-Building*, pp. 44–60; and Lipton, *Capitalism and Apartheid*, pp. 14, 15, 22–37; and extensively described in Horrell, *Laws Affecting Race Relations in South Africa*, which the following account draws on.

18. A further note on terminology is required here. These four categories of people assumed extreme social significance after decades of apartheid, as they were the units for the differential and highly unequal distribution of public goods by the state. These population categories thus became indispensable for the description of such inequities in the South African state and society. In this text these categories are therefore used as essential descriptive instruments and not as an implicit endorsement of the ideology these categories are intended to serve. In addition, when the African, Colored, and Indian population categories are referred to collectively, the term "black" is used.

19. For general analyses of the state-building process in the homelands, see Horrell, *Legislation and Race Relations*, pp. 9–110; Muriel Horrell, *The African Homelands of South Africa* (Johannesburg: South African Institute of Race Relations, 1973); Horrell, *Laws Affecting Race Relations in South Africa*, pp. 37–56, 203–231; Robert Schrire, "The Homelands: Political Perspectives," in Robert Schrire, ed., *South Africa: Public Policy Perspectives* (Cape Town: Juta, 1982), pp. 113–140; Newell M. Stultz, "Some Implications of African 'Homelands' in South Africa," in Robert M. Price and Carl G. Rosberg, eds., *The Apartheid Regime: Political Power and Racial Domination* (Cape Town: David Philip, 1980), pp. 194–216.

20. Davenport, *South Africa*, pp. 363–366, 378–379, 419–421; Horrell, *Laws Affecting Race Relations in South Africa*, pp. 29–36; Wolfgang Thomas, "The Coloured People and the Limits to Segregation," in Schrire, *Public Policy Perspectives*, pp. 141–164; W. B. Vosloo and R. A. Schrire, "Subordinate Political Institutions," in Anthony de Crespigny and Robert Schrire, eds., *The Government and Politics of South Africa* (Cape Town: Juta, 1978), pp. 77–93.

21. W. H. B. Dean "The Judiciary," in de Crespigny and Schrire, *Government and Politics of South Africa*, pp. 32–53; G. C. Olivier, "The Executive," in de Crespigny and Schrire, *Government and Politics of South Africa*, pp. 17–31; N. J. J. Olivier, and D. H. van Wyk, "Parliament," in de Crespigny and Schrire, *Government and Politics of South Africa*, pp. 1–17; Roux, "Parliament and the Executive," in Worrall, *South Africa: Government and Politics*, pp. 29–74; F. van Zyl Slabbert and David Welsh, *South Africa's Options: Strategies for Sharing Power* (Cape Town: David Philip, 1979), pp. 77–89; Jerold Taitz, "The Administration of Justice and Due Process," in Schrire, *Public Policy Perspectives*, pp. 1–53.

22. Horrell, *Laws Affecting Race Relations in South Africa*, pp. 412–479.

23. Deon Geldenhuys and Hennie Kotzé, "Aspects of Decision-making in South Africa," *Politikon* 10, no. 1 (June 1983): 33–45; Annette Seegers,

"Extending the Security Network to the Local Level," in Chris Heymans and Gerhard Totemeyer, eds., *Government by the People?* (Cape Town: Juta, 1988), pp. 119–139; Annette Seegers, "Extending the Security Network to the Local Level: A Clarification and Some Further Comments," *Politeia* 7, no. 2 (1988): 50–70.

24. Short descriptions of the 1983 constitution can be found in D. Marais, *Constitutional Development of South Africa*, 2nd ed. (Johannesburg: Macmillan, 1985); and Johan David van der Vyver, *Die Grondwet van die Republiek van Suid-Afrika* (Johannesburg; Lex Patria, 1984). The most thorough analyses of this constitution are by L. J. Boulle, *South Africa and the Consociational Option: A Constitutional Analysis* (Cape Town: Juta, 1984); and David Welsh, "Constitutional Changes in South Africa," *African Affairs* 83, no. 331 (1984): 147–162.

25. T. W. Bennet, *Application of Customary Law in Southern Africa: The Conflict of Personal Laws* (Cape Town: Juta, 1985); A. J. G. M. Sanders, ed., *The Internal Conflict of Laws in South Africa* (Cape Town: Butterworths, 1990); Taitz, "Justice and Due Process," pp. 5–9.

26. Giliomee and Schlemmer, *From Apartheid to Nation-Building*, p. 79.

27. Lipton, *Capitalism and Apartheid*, pp. 24, 25.

28. Analyses of the various control measures aimed at controlling the black urbanization process can be found in T. R. H. Davenport, "African Townsmen? South African Natives (Urban Areas) Legislation through the Years," *African Affairs* 68, no. 271 (1969): 95–109; T. R. H. Davenport, "The Triumph of Colonel Stallard: The Transformation of the Natives (Urban Areas) Act between 1923 and 1937," *South African Historical Journal* 2 (1970): 77–96; Davenport, *South Africa*, pp. 373, 374, 407, 555, 556; Lipton, *Capitalism and Apartheid*, pp. 34–37; David Welsh, "The Policies of Control: Blacks in the Common Areas," in Schrire, *Public Policy Perspectives*, pp. 87–112; Martin E. West, "The 'Apex of Subordination': The Urban African Population of South Africa," in Price and Rosberg, *The Apartheid Regime*, pp. 127–151.

29. Horrell, *Laws Affecting Race Relations in South Africa;* Hermann Giliomee, "Afrikaner Politics: How the System Works," in Heribert Adam and Hermann Giliomee, *The Rise and Crisis of Afrikaner Power* (Cape Town: David Philip, 1979), pp. 196–257 at 222.

30. Roger Southall, "African Capitalism in Contemporary South Africa," *Journal of Southern African Studies* 7, no. 1 (1980): 38–70 at 44.

31. Horrell, *Laws Affecting Race Relations in South Africa*, pp. 115–117, 131, 132.

32. J. V. O. Reid, "Health," in Sheila T. van der Horst and Jane Reid, eds., *Race Discrimination in South Africa: A Review* (Cape Town: David Philip, 1981), pp. 127–151 at 129.

33. Francis Wilson and Mamphela Ramphele, *Uprooting Poverty: The South African Challenge* (Cape Town: David Philip, 1989), pp. 216, 217.

34. Loraine Gordon, ed., *Survey of Race Relations in South Africa 1979* (Johannesburg: South African Institute of Race Relations, 1980), p. 465.

35. Anthony Lemon, "The Apartheid City," in Anthony Lemon, ed., *Homes Apart: South Africa's Segregated Cities* (Cape Town: David Philip, 1991), pp. 1–25 at 11.

36. This calculation has been made by the Surplus Peoples Project and is widely quoted. See Laurine Platzky and Cheryl Walker, *The Surplus People: Forced Removals in South Africa* (Johannesburg: Ravan, 1985). See also Davenport, *South Africa*, pp. 445–449; Wilson and Ramphele, *Uprooting Poverty*, pp. 216, 217. For analyses of the legal and logistic mechanics of the removal of Africans, read Alan Baldwin, "Mass Removals and Separate Development," *Journal of Southern African Studies* 1, no. 2 (1975): 215–227; and Martin West, "From Pass Courts to Deportation: Changing Patterns of Influx Control in Cape Town," *African Affairs* 81, no. 325 (1982): 463–477.

37. Giliomee and Schlemmer, *From Apartheid to Nation-Building*, p. 101; Wilson and Ramphele, *Uprooting Poverty*, p. 223. See also Gerry Mare, *African Population Relocation in South Africa* (Johannesburg: South African Institute of Race Relations, 1980); Schrire, "Homelands: Political Perspectives," p. 134.

38. Lipton, *Capitalism and Apartheid*, pp. 38–43.

39. Davenport, *South Africa*, p. 408.

40. M. D. McGrath, "Income and Material Inequality in South Africa," in Lawrence Schlemmer and Eddie Webster, eds., *Change, Reform and Economic Growth in South Africa* (Johannesburg: Ravan, 1978), pp. 149–172 at 160 (table 11). Additional data on income inequality can be found in Norman Bromberger, "Government Policies Affecting the Distribution of Income," in Schrire, *Public Policy Perspectives*, pp. 165–203.

41. Mike McGrath, "Economic Growth and the Distribution of Racial Incomes in the South African Economy," *South Africa International* 15, no. 2 (April 1985): 223–232.

42. The official data were reported in *Die Burger*, November 15, 1993.

43. Lipton, *Capitalism and Apartheid*, p. 43.

44. Hermann Giliomee, "The Afrikaner Economic Advance," in Adam and Giliomee, *Rise and Crisis of Afrikaner Power*, pp. 145–176 at 173, 174.

45. *Africa South of the Sahara, 1993*, p. 777.

46. Norman Bromberger and Kenneth Hughes, "Capitalism and Underdevelopment in South Africa," in Jeffrey Butler et al., eds., *Democratic Liberalism in South Africa: Its History and Prospect* (Cape Town: David Philip, 1987), pp. 203–223 at 215.

47. Servaas van der Berg, "Long-Term Economic Trends and Development Prospects in South Africa," *African Affairs* 88, no. 351 (1989): 187–203 at 195 (figure 9).

48. Lipton, *Capitalism and Apartheid*, p. 45. Data on rural poverty can be found in Jill Nattrass, "The Dynamics of Black Poverty in South Africa," in Hermann Giliomee and Lawrence Schlemmer, eds., *Up Against the Fences: Poverty, Passes and Privilege in South Africa* (Cape Town: David Philip, 1985), pp. 16–27.

49. Bromberger and Hughes, "Capitalism and Underdevelopment in South Africa," p. 219.

50. Wilson and Ramphele, *Uprooting Poverty*, p. 142.

51. G. Trotter, "Education and the Economy," in N. Nattrass and E. Ardington, eds., *The Political Economy of South Africa* (Cape Town: Oxford University Press, 1990), pp. 241–259 at 248.

52. Gordon, *Survey of Race Relations*, p. 487.

53. Wilson and Ramphele, *Uprooting Poverty*, pp. 138, 139.

54. Ibid., p. 145.

55. Cooper et al., *Race Relations Survey*, p. 575.

56. Hansi Pollak, "State Social Pensions, Grants and Social Welfare," in van der Horst and Reid, *Race Discrimination in South Africa*, pp. 152–185.

57. Wilson and Ramphele, *Uprooting Poverty*, pp. 125–134.

58. Reid, "Health."

59. Van den Berg, "Long-Term Economic Trends," p. 197.

60. Giliomee, "The Afrikaner Economic Advance," in Adam and Giliomee, *Rise and Crisis of Afrikaner Power*, p. 146.

61. Jill Nattrass, *The South African Economy: Its Growth and Change*, 2nd ed. (Cape Town: Oxford University Press, 1988), p. 234 (table 10.1). See also P. S. Botes, "Public Service Reform," *Politikon* 7, no. 2 (December 1980): 167–174, for a description of the growth in government departments and expenditure.

62. Giliomee, "Afrikaner Economic Advance," p. 165.

63. Nattrass, *South African Economy*, p. 248 (table 10.7).

64. Wilson and Ramphele, *Uprooting Poverty*, p. 212; West, "Influx Control in Cape Town," pp. 474–477.

65. Michael Savage, "Imposition of Pass Laws," *African Affairs* 85, no. 339 (1986): 181–205

66. Donald Rothchild, "Hegemonial Exchange: An Alternative Model for Managing Conflict in Middle Africa," in Dennis L. Thompson and Dov Ronen, eds., *Ethnicity, Politics and Development* (Boulder, Colo.: Lynne Rienner, 1986), pp. 65–104 at p. 99 (footnote 28). Rothchild, as noted in the appendix, uses the "hard state/soft state" distinction, drawing on the work of Myrdal.

67. Lipton, *Capitalism and Apartheid*, p. 45.

68. Savage, "Imposition of Pass Laws," p. 190.

69. For compact surveys of this aspect of state-society interaction, see Leo Kuper, "African Nationalism in South Africa, 1910–1964," in Wilson and Thompson, *Oxford History of South Africa*, vol. 2, pp. 424–476; and Tom Lodge, *Black Politics in South Africa since 1945* (Johannesburg: Ravan, 1983).

70. Davenport, *South Africa*, pp. 249–252, 301, 312; Kuper, "African Nationalism in South Africa," pp. 432, 439, 440, 444, 450; Lodge, *Black Politics in South Africa*, p. 3.

71. For an analysis of events leading up to and following the Sharpeville confrontation, read Gail M. Gerhart, *Black Power in South Africa: The Evolution of an Ideology* (Berkeley, Calif.: University of California Press, 1978).

72. A detailed account of this confrontation is found in John Kane-Berman, *Soweto: Black Revolt, White Reaction* (Johannesburg: Ravan, 1978).

73. Hammond-Tooke, *Command or Consensus*, p. 207.

74. Ibid., p. 212. See also David Hammond-Tooke, "Chieftainship in Transkeian Political Development," *Journal of Modern African Studies* 2, no. 4 (1964): 513–529 at 523, 524.

75. J. Graaff, "Towards an Understanding of Bantustan Politics," in Nattrass and Ardington, *Political Economy of South Africa*, pp. 55–72 at 65, 66; Lodge, *Black Politics in South Africa*, pp. 261–294; Welsh, "Cultural Dimension of Apartheid," p. 47.

76. John Hund and Malebo Kotu-Rammopo, "Justice in a South African Township: The Sociology of *Makgotla*," *Comparative and International Law Journal of South Africa* 16 (1983): 179–208 at 182, 183.

77. West, "Influx Control in Cape Town," pp. 468–473.

78. Tensions within the bureaucracy at different times are analyzed in Giliomee, "Afrikaner Politics," pp. 221–232; Lawrence Schlemmer, "South Africa's National Party government," in Peter L. Berger and Bobby Godsell, eds., *A Future South Africa: Visions, Strategies and Realities* (Cape Town: Human and Rousseau and Tafelberg, 1988), pp. 7–54 at 28–36.

79. F. van Zyl Slabbert, "Afrikaner Nationalism, White Politics, and Political Change in South Africa," in Leonard Thompson and Jeffrey Butler, eds., *Change in Contemporary South Africa* (Berkeley, Calif.: University of California Press, 1975), pp. 3–18.

80. Vosloo and Schrire, "Subordinate Political Institutions," p. 91.

81. D. A. Kotzé, "African Politics," in Crespigny and Schrire, *Government and Politics of South Africa*, pp. 116–135 at 130, 131.

82. Urban Foundation, "An Analysis of the First 29 Elections Held under the 1982 Black Local Authorities Act" (Urban Foundation, unpublished report, March 1984), p. 4.

83. Anthony Lemon, "The Indian and Coloured Elections: Co-optation Rejected," *South Africa International* 18, no. 2 (1984): 84–107 at 97.

84. Alexander Johnston, "Weak States and National Security: The Case of South Africa in the Era of Total Strategy," *Review of International Studies* 17 (1991): 149–166 at 161. Johnston relies on the definition of state strength used by Barry Buzan.

85. Dan O'Meara, *Volkskapitalisme: Class, Capital and Ideology in the Development of Afrikaner Nationalism, 1934–1948* (Johannesburg: Ravan Press, 1983). A close second in a strong presentation of class analysis of South Africa is Stanley Greenberg, *Race and State in Capitalist Development* (New Haven, Conn.: Yale University Press, 1980). See also his later work, *Legitimating the Illegitimate: State, Markets, and Resistance in South Africa* (Berkeley, Calif.: University of California Press, 1987). Giliomee's views on Afrikaner nationalism are found in all the works by him cited in this chapter thus far, as well as in "Constructing Afrikaner Nationalism," *Journal of Asian and African Studies* 18, nos. 1–2 (1983): 83–98. The status of O'Meara's work can be gauged from the assessment by David Welsh, a scholar strongly opposed to the class perspective, who wrote in 1987, "Dan O'Meara's *Volkskapitalisme* is probably the most sophisticated structuralist class analysis on a South African theme yet to appear" ("Democratic Liberalism and Theories of Racial Stratification," in Butler et al., *Democratic Liberalism in South Africa*, pp. 185–202 at 199). The importance of Giliomee's writing is reflected in the prominence accorded to him in the survey of the field by Simon Bekker, *Ethnicity in Focus: The South African Case* (University of Natal: Indicator South Africa Issue Focus, 1993), pp. 39–41, 68, 73–75.

86. O'Meara, *Volkskapitalisme*, p. 247. See also p. 175.

87. Giliomee, "Growth of Afrikaner Identity," in Adam and Giliomee, *Rise and Crisis of Afrikaner Power*, pp. 83–127 at 117.

88. O'Meara, *Volkskapitalisme*, pp. 6–8.

89. Giliomee, "Constructing Afrikaner Nationalism," pp. 91, 92.

90. A detailed critique of O'Meara's application of the concept of class to this assemblage of Afrikaners (those who supported the National Party and the policies of apartheid) is made by Welsh, "Democratic Liberalism and Theories of Racial Stratification," pp. 199–201.

91. O'Meara, *Volkskapitalisme*, p. 244.

92. Giliomee, "Constructing Afrikaner Nationalism," p. 88.

93. Giliomee, "Growth of Afrikaner Identity," pp. 83, 84, 110, 111.

94. Giliomee and Schlemmer, *From Apartheid to Nation-Building*, pp. 82–86.

95. Taitz, "Justice and Due Process," p. 11.

96. J. M. du Preez, *Africana Afrikaner: Master Symbols in South African School Textbooks*, (Alberton, South Africa: Librarius, 1983).

97. Davenport, *South Africa*, p. 379; Lodge, *Black Politics in South Africa*, pp. 91–113.

98. David Yudelman, *The Emergence of Modern South Africa: State, Capital, and the Incorporation of Organized Labor on the South African Gold Fields, 1902–1939* (Cape Town: David Philip, 1983).

99. These data, produced by Jan Lange, were reported in the *Financial Mail* (Johannesburg) of October 12, 1979, pp. 138, 140.

100. Giliomee, "Constructing Afrikaner Nationalism," pp. 85, 86.

101. L. Pretorius and W. B. Vosloo, "Interest Groups in the Republic of South Africa," *Annals of the American Academy of Political and Social Science* 413 (May 1974): 72–85 at 75–77; Peter Harris, "Interest Groups in the South African Political Process," in Worrall, *South Africa: Government and Politics*, pp. 253–284 at 260–264.

102. Horrell, *Laws Affecting Race Relations in South Africa*, pp. 144–149.

103. Judy Cornell and Oscar Wolheim, "Recreational Facilities, Sport and Voluntary Organizations," in van der Horst and Reid, *Race Discrimination in South Africa*, pp. 211–236 at 233.

104. The research findings on racial and ethnic animosity and social distance are well summarized in Horowitz, *Democratic South Africa?* pp. 42–86.

105. Pretorius and Vosloo, "Interest Groups," pp. 76–77.

106. Slabbert, "Political Change in South Africa," p. 9.

107. Lawrence Schlemmer, "Theories of the Plural Society and Change in South Africa," *Social Dynamics* 3, no. 1 (1977): 3–16 at 7.

108. Horrell, *Laws Affecting Race Relations in South Africa*, pp. 377–397; Cornell and Wolheim, "Recreational Facilities, Sport and Voluntary Organizations," pp. 221–236; Gordon, *Survey of Race Relations*, pp. 592–603.

109. The dynamics of this process among white youth has been confirmed through a number of detailed studies by Booysen, Gagiano, and Kotzé. See S. J. Booysen, "Die Politieke Sosialisering van Universiteitstudente: 'n Teoretiese en Paneelstudie" (Litt.D and Ph.D. diss., Rand Afrikaans University, 1987); Susan Booysen, "The Legacy of Ideological Control: The Afrikaner Youth's Manipulated Political Consciousness," *Politikon* 16, no. 1 (June 1989): 7–25; Susan Booysen and Hennie Kotzé, "The Political Socialization of Isolation: A Case-Study of the Afrikaner Student Youth," *Politikon* 12, no. 2 (December 1985): 23–46; Jannie Gagiano, "Meanwhile back on the 'Boereplaas,'" *Politikon* 13, no. 2 (December 1986): 3–23; Jannie Gagiano, "The Scope of Regime Support: A Case

Study," in Hermann Giliomee and Lawrence Schlemmer, eds., *Negotiating South Africa's Future* (Bergvlei: Southern, 1989), pp. 52–62; H. Kotzé, "Political Education and Socialization: A Comparative Perspective at Two Afrikaans Universities," *South African Journal of Sociology* 21, no. 3 (1990): 133–144; Idasa, *Worlds of Difference: The Political Attitudes of White Students in South Africa*, Idasa Research Report (Cape Town: Idasa, 1990). Two studies that compare and contrast socialization patterns among white and black youth are by H. J. Kotzé, "Mass media and the Matriculant Mind: A Case Study of Political Socialization in South Africa," *Communicare* 4, no. 2 (1985): 26–37; H. J. Kotzé and A. J. Norval, "'n Kruis-kulturele studie in politieke sosialisering," *Suid-Afrikaanse Tydskrif vir Sosiologie* 14, no. 1 (1983): 15–25. The "socialization of isolation" among black youth is detailed in Philip Frankel, "Political Culture and Revolution in Soweto," *Journal of Politics* 43, no. 3 (August 1981): 831–849; and Paulus Zulu, "Youth in the Extra-Parliamentary Opposition," in Giliomee and Schlemmer, *Negotiating South Africa's Future*, pp. 69–74.

110. Glen Mills, "Space and Power in South Africa: The Townships as a Mechanism of Control," *Ekistics* 334/335 (1989): 65–74; John Western, *Outcast Cape Town* (Cape Town: Human and Rousseau, 1981).

111. Giliomee and Schlemmer, *From Apartheid to Nation-Building*, p. 89.

112. Lipton, *Capitalism and Apartheid*, pp. 37, 38.

113. Wilson and Ramphele, *Uprooting Poverty*, pp. 152–160.

6. South Africa: The Contest for Hegemony

1. For the sources of this checklist see chapter 2, note 1.

2. Thomas Pakenham, *The Boer War* (Johannesburg: Jonathan Ball, 1979), p. xv.

3. Gerhart, *Black Power in South Africa*, p. 32–39.

4. Kuper, "African Nationalism in South Africa," pp. 424–476 at 439, 440, 444, 450, 451.

5. Gerhart, *Black Power in South Africa*, pp. 67, 68.

6. Lodge, *Black Politics in South Africa*, pp. 33–66.

7. Sheridan Johns, "Obstacles to Guerrilla Warfare: A South African Case Study," *Journal of Modern African Studies* 11, no. 2 (1973): 267–303 at 287–290; Dirk Kotze, "Morogoro: Out of the Whirlwind," *Politikon* 16, no. 1 (1989): 58–68; Andrew Prior, "South African Exile Politics: A Case Study of the African National Congress and the South African Communist Party," *Journal of Contemporary African Studies* 3, no. 1/2 (1983/84): 181–196 at 189–193.

8. Hennie Kotzé and Anneke Greyling, *Political Organizations in South Africa, A–Z* (Cape Town: Tafelberg, 1991), p. 37.

9. South African Communist Party, "The Path to Power: Programme of the South African Communist Party Adopted at the 7th Congress, 1989," *African Communist* 118 (1989): 72–127, especially 102, 107, 108.

10. Tom Lodge, "The African National Congress in the 1990s," in Glen Moss and Ingrid Obery, eds., *South African Review 6* (Johannesburg: Ravan, 1992), pp. 44–78 at 45.

11. Tom Lodge et al., eds., *All, Here, and Now: Black Politics in South Africa in the 1980s* (Cape Town: David Philip, 1991), pp. 58–140.

12. An early assessment to this effect, with an accurate prediction of its failure, was made by F. van Zyl Slabbert, "Sham Reform and Conflict Regulation in a Divided Society," *Journal of Asian and African Studies* 18, no. 1–2 (1983): 34–47. This view is endorsed by Lawrence Schlemmer, writing five years later, in describing the reform initiatives as amounting to attempts at "sharing power without sacrificing domination." See Schlemmer, "South Africa's National Party Government," p. 51

13. Giliomee and Schlemmer, *From Apartheid to Nation-Building*, pp. 123–126.

14. Lipton, *Capitalism and Apartheid*, pp. 65, 66.

15. Trotter, "Education and the Economy," p. 248.

16. Desiree Hansson, "Changes in Counter-Revolutionary State Strategy in the Decade 1979 to 1989," in Desiree Hansson and Dirk van Zyl Smit, eds., *Towards Justice? Crime and State Control in South Africa* (Cape Town: Oxford University Press, 1990), pp. 28–62.

17. Carole Cooper et al., *Race Relations Survey 1989/90* (Johannesburg: South African Institute of Race Relations, 1990), p. 172.

18. Carole Cooper et al., *Race Relations Survey 1988/89* (Johannesburg: South African Institute of Race Relations, 1989), p. 552.

19. This synthesis is drawn from the basic documents of the ANC, PAC, and SACP: the Freedom Charter, the Manifesto of the Azanian People, and the Path to Power. The first two documents can be found in Lodge et al., *All, Here, and Now*, while the latter is reprinted in the *African Communist* (see note 9). Complementing these are the interpretive policy statements by then UDF activists Murphy Morobe, "Towards a People's Democracy," *South Africa International* 18, no. 1 (July 1987): 30–38; and Zwelakhe Sisulu, "Forward to People's Power," in Lodge et al., *All, Here, and Now*, pp. 336–343. The final interpretive sources are academic analyses by Tom Lodge in the chapter "Ideology and People's Power" from the same book (pp. 127–140), and by Jannie Gagiano, "The Contenders," in Pierre du Toit and Willie Esterhuyse, eds., *The Myth Makers: The Elusive Bargain for South Africa's Future* (Halfway House: Southern, 1990), pp. 10–35.

20. The concept of "liberatory intolerance" was used by Pallo Jordan in "Why Won't Afrikaners Rely on Democracy," *Die Suid-Afrikaan*, February 1988, p. 29.

21. Tom Lodge, "The Launch of the United Democratic Front," in Lodge et al., *All, Here, and Now,* pp. 47–62 at 51 (table 1). For confirmation, read also Jeremy Seekings, "Civic Organisations in South African Townships," in Moss and Obery, *South African Review 6,* pp. 216–238 at 218–223.

22. Hennie Kotzé and Pierre du Toit, "The State, Civil Society and Democratic Transition in South Africa: A Survey of Elite Attitudes," *Journal of Conflict Resolution* 39, no. 1 (1995): 27–48 at 40, 41. The data are from a 1992 sample of 2,282 positional elites. The following question was put to the respondents: "Please indicate how sympathetic or unsympathetic you feel towards the following institutions." The choices were presented as a Likert-type scale measuring "very sympathetic," "sympathetic," "neutral," "unsympathetic," and "very unsympathetic." Forty-six variables were included in the factor analysis, which is a statistical technique for determining the degree to which a given set of variables is part of a common underlying phenomenon. The closer the numerical value of each reading to 1.00, the stronger the underlying commonality. In this case the common phenomenon is the extent to which civic institutions are perceived to coalesce with political institutions into a cluster of bodies to which individuals either are or are not attracted. Six such clusters (factors) were identified with principle component extraction with orthogonal rotation, the first three of which together explained 53.2 percent of the variation. The first factor explained 28.9 percent of the variation. The cutoff point of 0.5 was used in the analysis. Institutions that would normally be found in civil society are marked with an asterisk in the table.

23. Davenport, *South Africa,* pp. 435–437; Gordon, *Survey of Race Relations,* pp. 7–9.

24. Cooper et al., *Race Relations Survey 1988/89,* pp. 74–84, 125, 130; *Cooper et al., Race Relations Survey 1989/90,* pp. 484, 503, 512, 518; Carole Cooper et al., *Race Relations Survey 1992/93* (Johannesburg: South African Institute of Race Relations, 1993), p. 26, 33.

25. Cooper et al., *Race Relations Survey 1988/89,* p. 554.

26. Carole Cooper et al., *Race Relations Survey 1991/92* (Johannesburg: South African Institute of Race Relations, 1992), pp. 492–494; Cooper et al., *Race Relations Survey 1992/93,* pp. 27, 28.

27. Deneys Coombe, "'Of Murder and Deceit': The Trust Feed Killings," in Anthony Minnaar, ed., *Patterns of Violence: Case Studies of Conflict in Natal* (Pretoria: Human Sciences Research Council, 1992), pp. 227–242.

28. Cooper et al., *Race Relations Survey 1991/92,* pp. 483, 484.

29. Cooper et al., *Race Relations Survey 1989/90,* pp. 222–227.

30. John Kane-Berman, *South Africa's Silent Revolution,* 2d ed. (Johannesburg: South African Institute of Race Relations and Southern, 1991), pp. 25–58.

31. Cooper et al., *Race Relations Survey 1992/93,* p. 110. For an indepth analysis of this sector of the economy, see Eleanor Preston-Whyte and Christian Rogerson, eds., *South Africa's Informal Economy* (Cape Town: Oxford University Press, 1991).

32. Anthea Jeffrey, ed., *Forum on Mass Mobilization* (Johannesburg: South African Institute of Race Relations, 1991), p. 11. A detailed analysis of this strategy within the context of the wider state-society contest is found in Matthew Chaskalson, Karen Jochelson, and Jeremy Seekings, "Rent Boycotts, the State, and the Transformation of the Urban Political Economy in South Africa," *Review of African Political Economy* 40 (1988), pp. 47–64.

33. Cooper et al., *Race Relations Survey 1992/93*, pp. 355, 433.

34. Cooper et al., *Race Relations Survey 1991/92*, p. 484.

35. Jeremy Seekings, "People's Courts and Popular Politics," in Glenn Moss and Ingrid Obery, eds., *South African Review 5* (Johannesburg: Ravan, 1989), pp. 119–135 at 132.

36. Lodge, "Ideology and People's Power," pp. 127–140 at 135.

37. Seekings, "People's Courts and Popular Politics," p. 123. For general analyses of these structures, see Sandra Burman, "The Role of Street Committees: Continuing South Africa's Practice of Alternative Justice," in Hugh Corder, ed., *Democracy and the Judiciary* (Cape Town: Institute for a Democratic Alternative for South Africa, 1988), pp. 141–166; Sandra Burman and Wilfried Scharf, "Creating People's Justice: Street Committees and People's Courts in a South African City," *Law and Society Review* 24, no. 3 (1990): 693–744; Wilfried Scharf, "The Role of People's Courts in Transitions," in Corder, *Democracy and the Judiciary*, pp. 167–184.

38. Republic of South Africa, *Annual Report of the Commissioner of the South African Police 1990* (1991), p. 2; Cooper et al., *Race Relations Survey 1992/93*, p. 455.

39. Cooper et al., *Race Relations Survey 1988/89*, p. 512.

40. Cooper et al., *Race Relations Survey 1991/92*, p. 490.

41. Jeffrey, *Forum on Mass Mobilization*, p. 18.

42. Republic of South Africa, *Annual Report of the Commissioner of the South African Police 1990*, pp. 33–35; Republic of South Africa, *Annual Report of the Commissioner of the South African Police 1991* (1992), pp. 2, 99–102.

43. Tom Lodge, "The African National Congress in South Africa, 1976–1983: Guerrilla War and Armed Propaganda," *Journal of Contemporary African Studies* 3, no. 1/2 (1983/84): 153–180; Lodge, "African National Congress in the 1990s," p. 45.

44. Paul Maylam, "The Rise and Decline of Urban Apartheid in South Africa," *African Affairs* 89, no. 354 (1990): 57–84 at 81.

45. Ivor Sarakinsky, "State, Strategy and Extra-Parliamentary Opposition in South Africa, 1983–1988," *Politikon* 16, no. 1 (June 1989): 69–82.

46. Hansson, "Changes in Counter-Revolutionary State Strategy," p. 55.

47. There is a sound body of literature arguing this line. Foremost is certainly the early analysis by Heribert Adam, *Modernizing Racial Modernization: The Dynamics of South African Politics* (Berkeley, Calif.: University of California Press, 1971).

48. These two sets of factors are highlighted by Merle Lipton and Charles Simkins, "Introduction," in Merle Lipton and Charles Simkins, eds., *State and Market in Post-Apartheid South Africa* (Johannesburg: Witwatersrand University Press, 1993), pp. 1–34 at 9–13.

49. The weakening resolve can be traced back to the decline of intellectual support for apartheid from within Afrikaner ranks, as noted by Giliomee and Schlemmer, *From Apartheid to Nation-Building*, pp. 59, 120.

50. *Annual Report of the Commissioner of the South African Police 1990*, pp. 34, 35; *Annual Report of the Commissioner of the South African Police 1991*, pp. 100, 101.

51. Steven Collins, "'Things Fall Apart': The Culture of Violence Becomes Entrenched," in Minnaar, *Patterns of Violence*, pp. 95–106; Mike Morris and Doug Hindson, "The Disintegration of Apartheid: From Violence to Reconstruction," in Moss and Obery, *South African Review 6*, pp. 152–170 at 166, 167; Jeremy Seekings, *Heroes or Villains? Youth Politics in the 1980s* (Johannesburg: Ravan, 1993), pp. 45, 65–67, 68–85, 90–95; Gill Straker, *Faces in the Revolution: The Psychological Effects of Violence on Township Youth in South Africa* (Cape Town: David Philip, 1992).

52. Charles Simkins, "Household Composition and Structure in South Africa," in Sandra Burman and Pamela Reynolds, eds., *Growing Up in a Divided Society: The Contexts of Childhood in South Africa* (Evanston, Ill.: Northwestern University Press, 1986), pp. 16–42 at 32.

53. Sandra Burman and Rebecca Fuchs, "When Families Split: Custody and Divorce in South Africa," in Burman and Reynolds, *Growing Up in a Divided Society*, pp. 115–138 at 115–117.

54. Catherine Campbell, "Learning to Kill? Masculinity, the Family and Violence in Natal," *Journal of Southern African Studies* 18, no. 3 (September 1992): 614–627 at 618–622.

55. Colin Bundy, "Street Sociology and Pavement Politics: Aspects of Youth and Student Resistance in Cape Town, 1985," *Journal of Southern African Studies* 13, no. 3 (1987): 303–330; Seekings, *Heroes or Villains?*; Ari Sitas, "The Making of the 'Comrades' Movement in Natal, 1985–91," *Journal of Southern African Studies* 18, no. 3 (September 1992): 629–641.

56. Wilfried Scharf and Baba Ngcokoto, "Images of Punishment in the People's Courts of Cape Town 1985–7: From Prefigurative Justice to Populist Violence," in N. Chabani Manganyi and Andre du Toit, eds., *Political Violence and the Struggle in South Africa* (London: Macmillan, 1990), pp. 341–371 at 358, 359.

57. Hund and Kotu-Rammopo, "Justice in a South African Township."

58. Leslie Swartz and Ann Levett, "Political Oppression and Children in South Africa: The Social Construction of Damaging Effects," in Manganyi and du Toit, *Political Violence and the Struggle in South Africa*, pp. 265–286 at 265.

59. Frank Chikane, "Children in Turmoil: The Effects of Unrest on Township Children," in Burman and Reynolds, *Growing Up in a Divided Society*, pp. 333–344; Fiona McLachlan, "Children in Prison," in Burman and Reynolds, *Growing Up in a Divided Society*, pp. 345–359; Straker, *Faces in the Revolution*, pp. 82–86.

60. McLachlan, "Children in Prison," p. 358.

61. Charles Carter, "'We Are the Progressives': Alexandra Youth Congress Activists and the Freedom Charter, 1983–85," *Journal of Southern African Studies* 17, no. 2 (June 1991): 197–220; Sitas, "Making of the 'Comrades' Movement." Also of interest is the informative but highly partisan account by Nkosinathi Gwala, "Political Violence and the Struggle for Control in Pietermaritzburg," *Journal of Southern African Studies* 15, no. 3 (April 1989): 506–524.

62. A. W. Stadler, "Birds in the Cornfield: Squatter Movements in Johannesburg, 1944–1947," *Journal of Southern African Studies* 6, no. 1 (October 1979): 93–123 at 104–109.

63. Josette Cole, *Crossroads: The Politics of Reform and Repression 1976–1986* (Johannesburg: Ravan, 1987).

64. Hilary Sapire, "Politics and Protest in Shack Settlements of the Pretoria-Witwatersrand-Vereeniging Region, South Africa, 1980–1990," *Journal of Southern African Studies* 18, no. 3 (September 1992): 670–697 at 681–688.

65. Hund and Kotu-Rammopo, "Justice in a South African Township," p. 180.

66. Anthony Minnaar, "Hostels and Violent Conflict on the Reef," in Anthony Minnaar, ed., *Communities in Isolation: Perspectives on Hostels in South Africa* (Pretoria: Human Sciences Research Council, 1993), pp. 10–47 at 10.

67. Monica Wilson and Archie Mafeje, *Langa: A Study of Social Groups in an African Township* (Cape Town: Oxford University Press, 1963).

68. Mamphela Ramphele, *A Bed Called Home: Life in the Migrant Labor Hostels of Cape Town* (Cape Town: David Philip, 1993), pp. 60–62, 89–106, 115–125, 128–132. See also Julia Segar, "Hostels in the Western Cape," in Minnaar, *Communities in Isolation*, pp. 97–113 at 110. Both these analyses describe the structures in the predominantly Xhosa-speaking hostels of Cape Town. The closely analogous structures in Zulu-speaking hostels are briefly described by Minnaar, "Hostels and Violent Conflict on the Reef," p. 30.

69. The urban practice of traditional medicine in the 1950s is described in L. Longmore, "Medicine, Magic and Witchcraft among Urban

Africans on the Witwatersrand," *Central African Journal of Medicine* 4, no. 6 (June 1958): 242–249. The more contemporary status of this practice is explored in R. W. S. Cheetham and J. A. Griffiths, "The Traditional Healer/Diviner as Psychotherapist," *SA Medical Journal* 62 (December 11, 1982): 957–958; Rolf P. A. Dauskardt, "The Changing Geography of Traditional Medicine: Urban Herbalism on the Witwatersrand, South Africa," *GeoJournal* 22, no. 3 (1990): 275–283; Rolf Dauskardt, "Urban Herbalism: The Restructuring of Informal Survival in Johannesburg," in Preston-Whyte and Rogerson, *South Africa's Informal Economy*, pp. 87–100.

70. Sitas, "Making of the 'Comrades' Movement in Natal," pp. 636, 637.

71. Jeremy Evans, "Muti Murders: Ritual Responses to Stress," *Indicator South Africa* 8, no. 4 (1991): 46–48; Jeremy Evans, "'Scapegoat Intended': Aspects of Violence in Southern KwaZulu," in Minnaar, *Patterns of Violence*, pp. 215–226; Anthony Minnaar, Dirkie Offringa, and Catherine Payze, "The Witches of Venda: Politics in Magic Potions," *Indicator South Africa* 9, no. 1 (1991): 53–56; A. de V. Minnaar, D. Offringa, and C. Payze, *To Live in Fear: Witchburning and Medicine Murder in Venda* (Pretoria: Human Sciences Research Council, 1992); Edwin Ritchken, "Burning the Herbs," *Work in Progress* (July 1987): 17–22.

72. *The Argus*, December 2, 1992.

73. Morris and Hindson, "Disintegration of Apartheid," pp. 163, 164

74. Pierre du Toit and Jannie Gagiano, "Strongmen on the Cape Flats," *Africa Insight* 23, no. 2 (1993): 102–111.

75. Anthony Minnaar, "'Undisputed Kings': Warlordism in Natal," in Minnaar, *Patterns of Violence*, pp. 61–94.

76. This figure is compiled from data in Cooper et al., *Race Relations Survey 1991/92*, pp. 485, 486; and Cooper et al., *Race Relations Survey 1992/93*, pp. 417, 449.

77. Lauren Segal, "The Human Face of Violence: Hostel Dwellers Speak," *Journal of Southern African Studies* 18, no. 1 (March 1991): 190–231 at 213. This interpretation is also advanced by Campbell, "Learning to Kill?" p. 627; Morris and Hindson, "Disintegration of Apartheid," pp. 155–157; and Sapire, "Politics and Protest in Shack Settlements," pp. 672, 696.

78. The most comprehensive critical survey of the field is Bekker, *Ethnicity in Focus*.

79. Len Bloom, "Collective Obsessions: Self and Society," *Indicator South Africa* 10, no. 3 (winter 1993): 40–42 at 42. This line of analysis is also followed by Rupert Taylor, "The Myth of Ethnic Division: Township Conflict on the Reef," *Race and Class* 33, no. 2 (1991): 1–14; and by Gerhard Mare, *Brothers Born of Warrior Blood: Politics and Ethnicity in South Africa* (Johannesburg: Ravan, 1992), especially pp. 104, 108.

80. Examples are the findings of Sapire, "Politics and Protest in Shack Settlements," p. 687; Segal, "Human Face of Violence," pp. 218–226;

Gavin Woods, "Hostel Dwellers: A Socio-Psychological and Humanistic Perspective; Empirical Findings on a National Scale," in Minnaar, *Communities in Isolation,* pp. 64–79 at 74, 75.

81. The leading example of this interpretation is by Heribert Adam and Kogila Moodley, *The Opening of the Apartheid Mind: Options for the New South Africa* (Berkeley, Calif.: University of California Press, 1993), especially pp. 14, 29, 140, 150.

82. Seventeen of the more prominent right-wing organizations are described in Kotzé and Greyling, *Political Organizations in South Africa A–Z.* For general treatments of the right wing, see Janis Grobbelaar, "'Bittereinders': Dilemmas and Dynamics on the Far Right," in Moss and Obery, *South African Review 6,* pp. 102–111; Janis Grobbelaar et al., *Vir Volk en Vaderland: A Guide to the Right Wing* (University of Natal: Indicator South Africa Issue Focus, 1989); and Helen Zillie, "The Right Wing in South African Politics," in Berger and Godsell, *A Future South Africa,* pp. 55–94.

83. Adam and Moodley, *Opening of the Apartheid Mind,* p. 150.

84. This has been done by Johann van Rooyen, "The White Right Wing in South African Politics: A Descriptive Study of Its Roots, an Assessment of Its Strength, and an Elucidation of Its Territorial Policies and Political Strategies: 1969–1991" (Ph.D. diss., University of Cape Town, 1992).

85. Timothy D. Sisk, *Democratization in South Africa: The Elusive Social Contract* (Princeton, N.J.: Princeton University Press, 1995), pp. 88–126.

86. Stoffel van der Merwe, "The Government's Framework for Constitutional Change and Negotiation," in Giliomee and Schlemmer, *Negotiating South Africa's Future,* pp. 41–44.

87. For a penetrating description and analysis of CODESA, see Steven Friedman, ed., *The Long Journey: South Africa's Quest for a Negotiated Settlement* (Johannesburg: Ravan, 1993). See also Marina Ottaway, *South Africa: The Struggle for a New Order* (Washington, D.C.: Brookings Institution, 1993), pp. 157–178.

88. *Africa Confidential* 33, no. 25 (1993).

89. Cooper et al., *Race Relations Survey 1991/92,* p. 231.

90. Cooper et al., *Race Relations Survey 1992/93,* p. 315.

91. Brian Huntley et al., *South African Environments into the 21st Century* (Cape Town: Human and Rousseau and Tafelberg, 1989), p. 57.

92. Cooper et al., *Race Relations Survey 1991/92,* pp. xliii, 231.

93. *Sunday Times* (Johannesburg), February 10, 1991.

94. Cooper et al., *Race Relations Survey 1992/93,* p. 525.

95. Carole Cooper et al., *Race Relations Survey 1993/94* (Johannesburg: South Africa Institute of Race Relations, 1994), p. 371.

96. Cooper et al., *Race Relations Survey 1992/93,* p. 525.

97. Susan Booysen, "Changing Relations of Political Power in South Africa's Transition: The Politics of Conquering in Conditions of Stalemate," *Politikon* 19, no. 3 (December 1992): 64–80.

98. Cooper et al., *Race Relations Survey 1989/90*, pp. xxxv–lxxxix; Cooper et al., *Race Relations Survey 1991/92*, pp. xxix–cxi.

99. Hermann Giliomee, "*Broedertwis*: Intra-Afrikaner Conflicts in the Transition from Apartheid," *African Affairs* 91, no. 364 (1992): 339–364 at 360; Kotzé and Greyling, *Political Organizations in South Africa, A–Z*, pp. 55–56.

100. Hermann Giliomee, "The Last Trek? Afrikaners in the Transition to Democracy," *South Africa International* 22, no. 3 (January 1992): 111–120 at 113.

101. Ibid.

102. Ottaway, *Struggle for a New Order*, pp. 175, 176.

103. Friedman, *Long Journey*, p. 174.

104. South African Communist Party, "Path to Power," p. 124.

105. African National Congress, Department of Political Education, *The Road to Peace* (1990), pp. 17, 20.

106. Friedman, *Long Journey*, pp.177, 178.

107. The case for power-sharing was made by Joe Slovo, "Negotiations: What Room for Compromise?" *African Communist* (3rd quarter 1992): 36–39.

108. Indicator Project South Africa, *An Overview of 'Political Conflict in South Africa Data Trends 1984–1988'* (Durban: University of Natal, 1989); Simon Bekker, *Capturing the Event: Conflict Trends in the Natal Region 1986–1992* (Durban: University of Natal, 1992).

109. Timothy D. Sisk, "The Violence-Negotiation Nexus: South Africa in Transition and the Politics of Uncertainty," *Negotiation Journal* (January 1993): 77–94 at 88.

110. Friedman, *Long Journey*, p. 22.

111. T. W. Bennett, *A Sourcebook of African Customary Law for Southern Africa* (Cape Town: Juta, 1991), pp. viii–x.

112. *Cape Times*, January 18, 1994.

7. The Incentives for Sustaining Democracy

1. This definition is offered by the World Commission on Environment and Development and is quoted in World Resources Institute, *World Resources 1992–93* (Oxford: Oxford University Press, 1992), p. 2.

2. Picard, "Land Tenure Changes in Botswana," p. 324.

3. Hitchcock, "Water, Land and Livestock," pp. 84, 108.

4. Colclough and McCarthy, *Political Economy of Botswana*, p. 236.

5. Ibid., p. 114; Fosbrooke, "Land and Population," pp. 172–187.

6. Rodger Yeager, "Governance and Environment in Botswana: The Ecological Price of Stability," in Stedman, *Political Economy of Democratic Development*, pp. 123–138 at 129, 130.

7. Ibid., p. 128. For general treatments of the environmental impact of public policies in Botswana, see also Cliffe and Moorsom, "Rural Class Formation and Ecological Collapse in Botswana," pp. 35–52; Patrick P. Molutsi, "The State, Environment and Peasant Consciousness in Botswana," *Review of African Political Economy*, no. 42 (1988): 40–47; Rodger Yeager, "Democratic Pluralism and Ecological Crisis in Botswana," *Journal of Developing Areas* 23 (April 1989): 385–404.

8. Colclough and McCarthy, *Political Economy of Botswana*, p. 116. The logic behind this process is spelled out in the classic article by Garrett Hardin, "The Tragedy of the Commons," *Science* 162 (December 1968): 1243–1248.

9. As Hardin puts it, "Individuals locked into the logic of the commons are free only to bring on universal ruin: once they see the necessity of mutual coercion, they become free to pursue other goals." Ibid., p. 1248.

10. Yeager, "Governance and Environment in Botswana," pp. 128–134.

11. The specific slice of the commons at stake here is the Okavango Delta, a unique wetland refuge for wildlife. For the details of this controversy, see Colclough and McCarthy, *Political Economy of Botswana*, pp. 137, 238; Jenny Macgregor, "Botswana: Is This Sustainable Development?" *Africa Institute Bulletin* 31, no. 6 (1991): 1–3; and Fred Pearce, "Botswana: Enclosing for Beef," *Ecologist* 23, no. 1 (January/February 1993): 25–29 at 28, 29.

12. Yeager, "Governance and Environment in Botswana," p. 133.

13. Morrison, "Developmental Optimism and State Failure in Africa," p. 535.

14. Ibid., p. 536.

15. In 1991 and 1992 the diamond market experienced some uncharacteristic volatility, due in part to international factors. The stability of the market was reputedly upset by large-scale illegal sales from Angola and regions of the former USSR. The Central Selling Organization, with a near monopoly on global marketing of diamonds, was unable to assert control over this flow, which forced a drop in prices and had a negative impact on Botswana's revenue from diamond sales. See "Diamond Revenue Falls as Soda-Ash Exports Begin," *African Business* (September 1991): 36–38; "Is the Diamond Sparkle Flawed?" *Weekend Argus*, September 26, 1992, p. 5; "Namibia's CDM Slices Diamond Production," *Cape Times*, November 10, 1992, p. 11.

16. The general systemic position of Africa in terms of this perspective is presented by Samir Amin, "Underdevelopment and Dependence in

Black Africa: Origins and Contemporary Forms," *Journal of Modern African Studies* 10, no. 4 (1972): 503–524. The specific position of Botswana in this world system is explained by Frank Baffoe, "Some Aspects of the Political Economy of Economic Cooperation and Integration in Southern Africa: The Case of South Africa and the Countries of Botswana, Lesotho and Swaziland (BLS)," *Journal of Southern African Affairs* 3, no. 3 (July 1978): 327–342; Jack Parson, "Botswana in the Southern African Periphery: The Limits of Capitalist Transformation in a 'Labor Reserve,'" *Bulletin* 11, no. 4 (1980): 45–52; Parson, "The Consequences of New Wealth for Botswana" (see chap. 2, n. 69); Parson, "Peasantariat and Politics" (see chap. 2, n. 67).

17. Baffoe, "Some Aspects of the Political Economy of Economic Cooperation," p. 339.

18. Thomas M. Callaghy, "Africa and the World Economy: Caught between a Rock and a Hard Place," in John W. Harbeson and Donald Rothchild, eds., *Africa in World Politics* (Boulder, Colo.: Westview Press, 1991), pp. 39–68 at 43, 44.

19. Parson, "Consequences of New Wealth for Botswana," p. 58.

20. Morrison, "Developmental Optimism and State Failure in Africa," p. 563.

21. The scope of international donor support for Botswana is analyzed by Patrick P. Molutsi, "International Influences on Botswana's Democracy," in Stedman, *Political Economy of Democratic Development*, pp. 51–61.

22. Colclough and McCarthy, *Political Economy of Botswana*, p. 246.

23. *Africa South of the Sahara, 1993*, p. 964; Davies, "Urban Change in Zimbabwe," pp. 160–164 (see chap. 4, n. 49); George Kay, "Zimbabwe's Independence: Geographical Problems and Prospects," *Geographical Journal* 147, no. 2 (July 1981): 179–187 at 185; Riddell, "Prospects for Land Reform in Zimbabwe," p. 21 (see chap. 4, n. 21).

24. Jeffrey Herbst, "The Dilemmas of Land Policy in Zimbabwe," *Africa Insight* 21, no. 4 (1991): 269–276 at 275; Herbst, *State Politics in Zimbabwe*, p. 49; Erich Leistner, "Zimbabwe's Land Resettlement Programme," *Africa Institute Bulletin* 31, no. 3 (1991): 2–4 at 4. See also D. Hywel Davies, "Zimbabwe: Resettlement and Rural Change," *Africa Insight* 14, no. 4 (1984): 249–257.

25. Herbst, *State Politics in Zimbabwe*, p. 206; Tony Hawkins, "Zimbabwe's Socialist Transformation," pp. 186, 187 (see chap. 4, n. 89).

26. James Barber, "Zimbabwe's Regional Role: Prospects for a Land-Locked Power," *Conflict Studies*, no. 243 (July/August 1991): 1–29 at 7.

27. John Robertson, "Public Finance," in Simon Baynham, ed., *Zimbabwe in Transition* (Stockholm: Almqvist and Wiksell International, 1992), pp. 101–128 at 104.

28. John Robertson, "The Economy: A Sectoral Overview," in Baynham, *Zimbabwe in Transition*, pp. 64–100 at 70, 71.

29. Hawkins, "Zimbabwe's Socialist Transformation," p. 186.

30. Barber, "Zimbabwe's Regional Role," pp. 6, 23–25.

31. Urban Foundation, *Informal Housing. Part 1, The Current Situation* (Johannesburg: Urban Foundation, 1991), p. 4.

32. Van den Berg, "Long-Term Economic Trends," p.199.

33. Ibid., p. 200.

34. Huntley et al., *South African Environments,* pp. 61–71.

35. Cooper et al, *Race Relations Survey 1992/93,* p. 146.

36. Wilson and Ramphele, *Uprooting Poverty,* p. 45.

37. Cooper et al., *Race Relations Survey 1992/93,* pp. 144, 145.

38. This view is repeatedly expressed in a number of contributions to the special edition of *DSA in Depth* titled "Reconstructing the State" (August/September 1993).

39. Hennie Kotzé, *Transitional Politics in South Africa: An Attitude Survey of Opinion-Leaders* (University of Stellenbosch: Center for International and Comparative Politics, 1992), pp. 34, 35, 47, 55, 70, 71, 74, 75, 88.

40. Greg Mills and Geoffrey Wood, "Ethnicity, Integration and the South African Armed Forces," *South African Defence Review,* no. 12 (1993): 22–36.

41. Timothy D. Sisk, "South Africa's National Peace Accord," *Peace and Change* 19, no. 1 (January 1994): 50–70 at 58.

42. Ibid., p. 63. This view is endorsed by Mark Shaw, "Crying Peace Where There Is None? The Functioning and Future of Local Peace Committees of the National Peace Accord," research report no. 31 (Johannesburg: Center for Policy Studies, August 1993), pp. 1–31 at 8; and also Mark Shaw, "War and Peace: Resolving Local Conflict," *Indicator South Africa* 10, no. 3 (winter 1993): 63–68 at 64.

43. Suzanne Nossel and Marion Shaer, "Groundswell at the Grassroots: The Challenge Posed by Peace Accord Dispute Resolution Committees" (paper read at the Fifth Annual Conference on Negotiation and Mediation in Community and Political Conflict in South Africa, under the auspices of the South African Association for Conflict Intervention, University of Port Elizabeth, November 25–28, 1992).

44. *The Economist,* December 26, 1992–January 8, 1993, p. 20.

45. Welsh, "Growth of Towns," in Wilson and Thompson, *Oxford History of South Africa,* vol. 2, pp. 213–221.

46. Andrew Khehla Lukhele, *Stokvels in South Africa: Informal Savings Schemes by Blacks for the Black Community* (Johannesburg: Amagi Books, 1990), p. 1.

47. Cooper et al., *Race Relations Survey 1992/93,* pp. 112, 113.

48. Ibid., p. 113.

49. Horowitz, *Democratic South Africa?* p. 154.

50. Ibid., p. 224.

51. District council election returns for the 1965, 1969, and 1974 elections show that opposition parties were able to elect members to all nine district councils as well as to the four town councils of Gaborone, Francistown, Lobatse, and Selebi-Pikwe. See Picard, *Politics of Development in Botswana,* pp. 189–199, especially table 8.3, p. 191.

52. Kenneth Kirkwood, "Review Article: Zimbabwe: The Politics of Ethnicity," *Ethnic and Racial Studies* 7, no. 3 (July 1984): 435–438 at 435.

53. Horowitz, *Democratic South Africa?* p. 274.

54. Ibid., pp. 277, 278.

55. Adam and Moodley, *Opening of the Apartheid Mind,* especially chapters 2 and 3.

56. Kotzé, *Transitional Politics in South Africa,* pp. 81, 82.

57. Herbst, *State Politics in Zimbabwe,* p. 131.

EPILOGUE

1. Republic of South Africa, Constitution of the Republic of South Africa Second Amendment Bill, section 160, 1(b).

2. *Cape Times,* May 11, 1994.

3. *Weekly Mail and Guardian,* May 6–12, 1994.

APPENDIX: STATE BUILDING AND CONFLICT IN DIVIDED SOCIETIES

1. Rothchild examines state-society relations in contemporary "Middle African" states and finds a pattern of conflict management in which the state and a wide range of ethnic groups engage in a process of *hegemonial exchange*: "As an ideal type, hegemonial exchange is a form of state-facilitated coordination in which a somewhat autonomous central-state actor and a number of considerably less autonomous ethno-regional interests engage, on the basis of commonly accepted procedural norms, rules, or understandings, in a process of mutual understandings." Rothchild, "Hegemonial Exchange," p. 72 (see chap. 5, n. 66). See also D. Rothchild, "State-Ethnic Relations in Middle Africa," in G. M. Carter and P. O'Meara, eds., *African Independence: The First Twenty-Five Years* (Bloomington, Ind.: Indiana University Press, 1985), pp. 71–96.

2. Arguably the leading exponent of this view is Charles Tilly. See his chapters "Reflections on the History of European State-Making," in Tilly, *Formation of National States in Western Europe,* pp. 3–83 (see chap. 4, n. 82); and "War Making and State Making as Organized Crime," in Peter B. Evans, Dietrich Rueschemeyer, and Theda Skocpol, eds., *Bringing the*

State Back In (Cambridge: Cambridge University Press, 1985), pp. 169–191.

3. Migdal, *Strong Societies and Weak States*, pp. 20–24 (see Introduction, n. 9).

4. Timothy Mitchell, "The Limits of the State: Beyond Statist Approaches and Their Critics," *American Political Science Review* 85 (March 1991): 77–96 at pp. 92, 93.

5. Michael Mann, "The Autonomous Power of the State: Its Origins, Mechanisms and Results," *European Journal of Sociology* 25, no. 2 (1984): 185–213. This dimension of state power is also identified by Lewis W. Snider "Identifying the Elements of State Power: Where Do We Begin?" *Comparative Political Studies* 20, no. 3 (October 1987): 314–356.

6. Migdal, *Strong Societies and Weak States*, pp. 4, 5, 30–33.

7. Ibid., pp. 41, 208. The link between the institutional depth of state sovereignty and the value accorded to citizenship by individual members of a state is also argued forcefully by Stephen D. Krasner, "Sovereignty: An Institutional Perspective" *Comparative Political Studies* 21, no. 1 (1988): 66–94 at 74.

8. Robert H. Jackson and Carl G. Rosberg, "Why Africa's Weak States Persist: The Empirical and Juridical in Statehood," *World Politics* 35 (October 1982): 1–24.

9. Elements of Migdal's depiction of the weak state are contained in Gunmar Myrdal's earlier description of "soft" states, in which "policies [that are] decided on are often not enforced, if they are enacted at all, and in that the authorities, even when framing policies, are reluctant to place obligations on people." G. Myrdal, *Asian Drama: An Inquiry into the Poverty of Nations*, vol. 1 (London: Twentieth Century Fund, 1968), p. 66. Rothchild relies on Myrdal's definition of the soft state in his theory of hegemonial exchange.

10. Migdal, *Strong Societies and Weak States*, p. 39.

11. Ibid., pp. 91–93.

12. Ibid., pp. 247–255.

13. Ibid., pp. 35, 37.

14. Robert A. Fishman, "Rethinking State and Regime: Southern Europe's Transition to Democracy," *World Politics* 42 (April 1990): 422–440.

15. Fishman, "Rethinking State and Regime," p. 428.

16. Migdal, *Strong Societies and Weak States*, pp. 217–226.

17. Victor Azarya and Naomi Chazan, "Disengagement from the State in Africa: Reflections on the Experience of Ghana and Guinea," *Comparative Studies in Society and History* 29 (January 1987): 106–131; Naomi Chazan, "The New Politics of Participation in Tropical Africa," *Comparative Politics* 14, no. 2 (January 1982): 169–189; as well as the essays assembled in D. Rothchild and N. Chazan, eds., *The Precarious Balance: State and Society in Africa* (Boulder, Colo.: Westview Press, 1988). An outstanding review of the literature on the role of the state in development on the African continent can be found in Morrison, "Developmental Optimism and State Failure in Africa," chapters 1 and 2.

18. Azarya and Chazan, "Disengagement from the State in Africa," p. 121.

19. Ibid., p. 126.

20. Naomi Chazan, "Africa's Democratic Challenge," *World Policy Journal* 9, no. 2 (spring 1992): 279–307 at 283.

21. Ibid., p. 289.

22. Robert D. Putnam with Robert Leonardi and Rafaella Y. Nanetti, *Making Democracy Work: Civic Traditions in Modern Italy* (Princeton, N.J.: Princeton University Press, 1993), pp. 86–91.

23. Michael Bratton, "Beyond the State: Civil Society and Associational Life in Africa," *World Politics* 41, no. 3 (April 1989): 407–430 at 148; Arnaud Sales, "The Private, the Public and Civil Society: Social Realms and Power Structures," *International Political Science Review* 12, no. 4 (October 1992): 295–312 at 296.

24. Larry Diamond, "Introduction: Civil Society and the Struggle for Democracy," in Larry Diamond, ed., *The Democratic Revolution: Struggles for Freedom and Pluralism in the Developing World* (New York: Freedom House, 1992), pp. 7, 10.

25. Chazan, "Africa's Democratic Challenge," p. 292.

26. Edward Shils "The Virtue of Civil Society," *Government and Opposition* 26 (winter 1991): 3–20 at 4.

27. Ibid., p. 4.

28. Krasner, "Sovereignty," p. 74.

29. Tilly, "Reflections on the History of European State-Making," p. 38.

30. Horowitz, *Ethnic Groups in Conflict*, p. 52 (see chap. 3, n. 55).

31. Ibid., pp. 22–36.

32. Shils, "Virtue of Civil Society," p. 13.

33. Horowitz, *Ethnic Groups in Conflict*, pp. 142–147, 185–228 at 224.

34. Alvin Rabushka and Kenneth A. Shepsle, *Politics in Plural Societies: A Theory of Democratic Instability* (Columbus, Ohio: Charles E. Merrill, 1972), pp. 84, 85.

35. This point is well argued by Ernst Gellner, "Democracy and Industrialization," in S. N. Eisenstadt, ed., *Readings in Social Evolution and Development* (Oxford: Pergamon Press, 1970), pp. 247–275. The quotation from Sir Ivor Jennings is taken from Benjamin Neuberger, *National Self-Determination in Post-Colonial Africa* (Boulder, Colo.: Lynne Rienner, 1971), p. 19.

36. Robert A. Dahl, *Democracy and Its Critics* (New Haven, Conn.: Yale University Press, 1989), p. 207.

37. Authors who have drawn this analogy include Horowitz, *Ethnic Groups in Conflict*, pp. 31, 95, 581, 584; and Vernon van Dyke, "The Individual, the State and Ethnic Communities in Political Theory," *World Politics* 29, no. 3 (April 1977): 343–369 at 353.

38. Dahl, *Polyarchy: Participation and Opposition*, pp. 1–16 (see chap. 2, n. 1).

39. Claude Ake, "The Case for Democracy," in *African Governance in the 1990's: Objectives, Resources and Constraints* (Working Papers from the second annual seminar of the African Governance Program, Carter Center of Emory University, Atlanta, Georgia, March 23–25, 1990), p. 5.

40. Francois Misser, "Zaire after the Cyclone," *New African* (November 1991): 11–12.

41. Claude Ake, "Rethinking African Democracy," *Journal of Democracy* 2, no. 1 (winter 1991): 32–44 at 38.

42. Migdal, *Strong Societies and Weak States*, pp. 274, 275.

43. Ibid., p. 6 (footnote 5).

44. Ernst Gellner, *Nations and Nationalism* (London: Cornell University Press, 1983), p. 15.

45. Ibid.

46. Ake, "Case for Democracy," p. 5.

47. Pierre du Toit, "Bargaining about Bargaining: Inducing the Self-Negating Prediction in Deeply Divided Societies—The Case of South Africa," *Journal of Conflict Resolution* 33, no. 2 (June 1989) 210–230 at 215.

48. J. Z. Rubin and B. R. Brown, *The Social Psychology of Bargaining and Negotiation* (New York: Academic Press, 1975), pp. 43–48; Bert R. Brown, "Face-Saving and Face-Restoration in Negotiation," in Daniel Druckman, ed., *Negotiations, Social-Psychological Perspectives* (Beverly Hills, Calif.: Sage Publications, 1977), pp. 275–299.

49. S. B. Bacharach and E. J. Lawler, *Bargaining: Power, Tactics and Outcomes* (San Francisco: Jossey Bass, 1981), pp. 41–79; E. J. Lawler and S. B. Bacharach "Power Dependence in Collective Bargaining," *Advances in Industrial and Labor Relations* 3 (1986): 193–201.

50. P. H. Gulliver, *Disputes and Negotiations* (New York: Academic Press, 1979), pp. 122–124.

51. The early work in this field is led by Daniel Druckman, "Dogmatism, Prenegotiation Experience, and Simulated Group Representation as Determinants of Dyadic Behavior in a Bargaining Situation," *Journal of Personality and Social Psychology* 6, no. 3 (1967): 279–290; as well as Druckman, "Prenegotiation Experience and Dyadic Conflict Resolution in a Bargaining Situation," *Journal of Experimental Social Psychology* 4 (1968): 367–383. The need to develop this body of theory further has been argued by Harold Saunders, "We Need a Larger Theory of Negotiation: The Importance of Pre-Negotiation Phases," *Negotiation Journal* 1 (July 1985): 249–262; and I. William Zartman and Maureen Berman, *The Practical Negotiator* (New Haven, Conn.: Yale University Press, 1982). More recent contributions are found in Janice Gross Stein, ed., *Getting to the Table: The Process of Inter-national Prenegotiation* (Baltimore: Johns Hopkins University Press, 1989); du Toit "Bargaining about Bargaining"; and the contributions to the special edition of the *Jerusalem Journal of International Relations* 13, no. 1 (1991).

52. Cecilia Albin, "Negotiating Indivisible Goods: The Case of Jerusalem," *Jerusalem Journal of International Relations* 13, no. 1 (1991): 45–76; Jacob Bercovitch, "International Negotiations and Conflict Management: The Importance of Prenegotiation," *Jeru-salem Journal of International Relations* 13, no. 1 (1991): 7–21; Jay Rothman, "Negotiation as Consolidation: Prenegotiation in the Israeli-Palestinian Conflict," *Jerusalem Journal of International Relations* 13, no. 1 (1991): 22–44; Janice Gross Stein, "Getting to the Table: The Triggers, Stages, Functions, and Consequences of Prenegotiation," in Stein, *Getting to the Table,* pp. 239–268; I. William Zartman, "Prenegotiation: Phases and Functions," in Stein, *Getting to the Table,* pp. 1–17.

53. Zartman, "Prenegotiation," pp. 6, 7.

54. Arend Lijphart, *Democracy in Plural Societies: A Comparative Exploration* (New Haven, Conn.: Yale University Press, 1977), p. 100; as well as *Power-Sharing in South Africa,* Policy Papers in International Affairs, no. 24 (Berkeley, Calif.: University of California, Institute of International Studies, 1985), pp. 130.

55. Albin, "Negotiating Indivisible Goods," p. 47.

56. Ibid., p. 59.

57. Ibid., p. 64.

58. This option of recolonization has in fact been recognized by Rabushka and Shepsle as a potential but unpractical method for containing ethnic conflict. See Rabushka and Shepsle, *Politics in Plural Societies,* pp. 213, 214.

59. Peter Gourevitch, "The Second Image Reversed: The International Sources of Domestic Politics," *International Organization* 32, no. 4 (autumn 1978): 881–912.

60. Ibid., pp. 884–896.

61. Ibid., pp. 896–900.

62. Migdal, *Strong Societies and Weak States,* p. 21.

63. Gourevitch, "The Second Image Reversed," p. 911.

✻ INDEX ✻

United States Institute of Peace

The United States Institute of Peace is an independent, nonpartisan federal institution established by Congress to promote research, education, and training on the peaceful resolution of international conflicts. Established in 1984, the Institute meets its congressional mandate through an array of programs, including research grants, fellowships, professional training programs, conferences and workshops, library services, publications, and other educational activities. The Institute's Board of Directors is appointed by the President of the United States and confirmed by the Senate.

Chairman of the Board: Chester A. Crocker
Vice Chairman: Max M. Kampelman
President: Richard H. Solomon
Executive Vice President: Harriet Hentges

Board of Directors

Chester A. Crocker (Chairman), Distinguished Research Professor of Diplomacy, School of Foreign Service, Georgetown University

Max M. Kampelman, Esq. (Vice Chairman), Fried, Frank, Harris, Shriver and Jacobson, Washington, D.C.

Dennis L. Bark, Senior Fellow, Hoover Institution on War, Revolution and Peace, Stanford University

Theodore M. Hesburgh, President Emeritus, University of Notre Dame

Christopher H. Phillips, former U.S. ambassador to Brunei

Elspeth Davies Rostow, Stiles Professor of American Studies Emerita, Lyndon B. Johnson School of Public Affairs, University of Texas

Mary Louise Smith, civic activist; former chairman, Republican National Committee

W. Scott Thompson, Professor of International Politics, Fletcher School of Law and Diplomacy, Tufts University

Allen Weinstein, President, Center for Democracy, Washington, D.C.

Harriet Zimmerman, Vice President, American-Israel Public Affairs Committee

Members ex officio

Ralph Earle II, Deputy Director, U.S. Arms Control and Disarmament Agency

Toby Trister Gati, Assistant Secretary of State for Intelligence and Research

Ervin J. Rokke, Lieutenant General, U.S. Air Force; President, National Defense University

Walter B. Slocombe, Under Secretary of Defense for Policy

Richard H. Solomon, President, United States Institute of Peace (nonvoting)

Jennings Randolph Program for International Peace

As part of the statute establishing the United States Institute of Peace, Congress envisioned a fellowship program that would appoint "scholars and leaders of peace from the United States and abroad to pursue scholarly inquiry and other appropriate forms of communication on international peace and conflict resolution." The program was named after Senator Jennings Randolph of West Virginia, whose efforts over four decades helped to establish the Institute.

Since it began in 1987, the Jennings Randolph Program has played a key role in the Institute's effort to build a national center of research, dialogue, and education on critical problems of conflict and peace. Through a rigorous annual competition, outstanding men and women from diverse nations and fields are selected to carry out projects designed to expand and disseminate knowledge on violent international conflict and the wide range of ways it can be peacefully managed or resolved.

The Institute's Distinguished Fellows and Peace Fellows are individuals from a wide variety of academic and other professional backgrounds who work at the Institute on research and education projects they have proposed and participate in the Institute's collegial and public outreach activities. The Institute's Peace Scholars are doctoral candidates at American universities who are working on their dissertations.

Institute fellows and scholars have worked on such varied subjects as international negotiation, regional security arrangements, conflict resolution techniques, international legal systems, ethnic and religious conflict, arms control, and the protection of human rights, and these issues have been examined in settings throughout the world.

As part of its effort to disseminate original and useful analyses of peace and conflict to policymakers and the public, the Institute publishes book manuscripts and other written products that result from the fellowship work and meet the Institute's high standards of quality.

Joseph Klaits
Director

STATE BUILDING AND
DEMOCRACY IN
SOUTHERN AFRICA

This book is set in Bookman; the display type is Avenir.
Cover design by Marie Marr-Williams; interior design by
Joan Engelhardt and Day W. Dosch. Page makeup by
Helene Y. Redmond of HYR Graphics. Editing by Nigel
Quinney; copyediting by Mia Cunningham of EEI.